WHERE'S B**KSY?

Published in the United States of America, May 2022.

Gingko Press, Inc.
2332 Fourth Street, Suite E
Berkeley, CA 94710, USA
www.gingkopress.com

Published under license from Graffito Books

ISBN: 978-1-58423773-0

Printed in China

Art Direction: Karen Wilks
Managing Editor: Serena Pethick
Research Editor: Lucy Radford-Earle

This is not an official publication. This is also an unauthorised work examining the political and social background to the foremost street art polemicist of our dystopian age; however the mysterious, enigmatic, untraceable and hidden artist who creates under the moniker BANKSY had no part in its inception or creation.

The contents, analysis and interpretations within express the views and opinions **of Graffito Books Ltd only**. This publication has been prepared solely by Graffito Books Ltd. We recognize that some words, model names and designations mentioned herein are the property of the trademark holder. We use them for identification purposes only.

The information in this book is true and complete to the best of our knowledge. All recommendations are made without any guarantee on the part of the author or Publisher, who also disclaim any liability incurred in connection with the use of this data or specific details.

All images in this book have been reproduced with the knowledge and prior consent of the photographers concerned. The copyright in each image remains with the photographers. Every effort has been made to ensure that credits accurately comply with information supplied.

British Library cataloguing-in-publication data:
A catalogue record of this book is available at The British Library.

Printed in China.

WHERE'S B***KSY?

XAVIER TAPIES

GINGKO PRESS

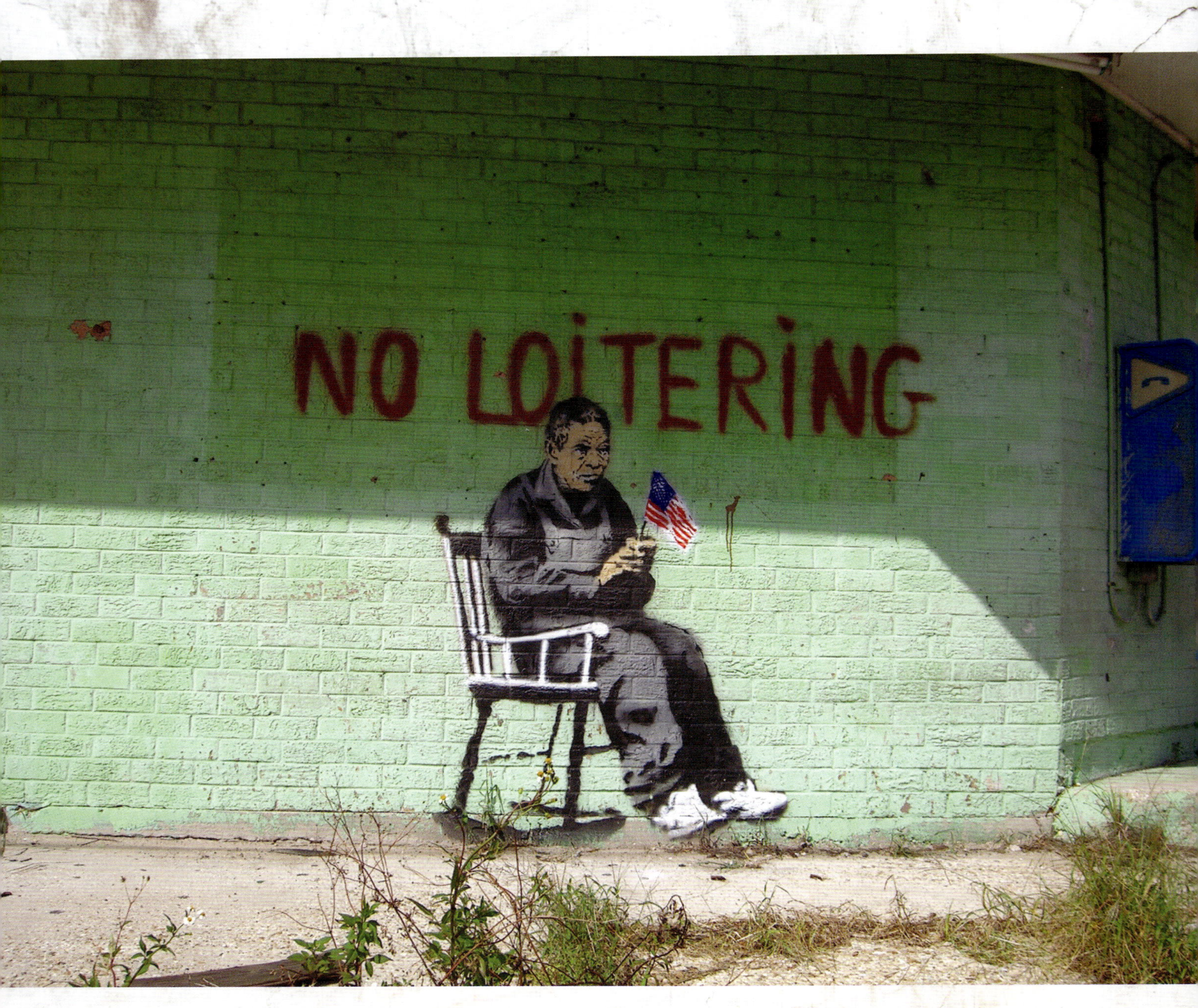

2008 | NEW ORLEANS | USA

CONTENTS

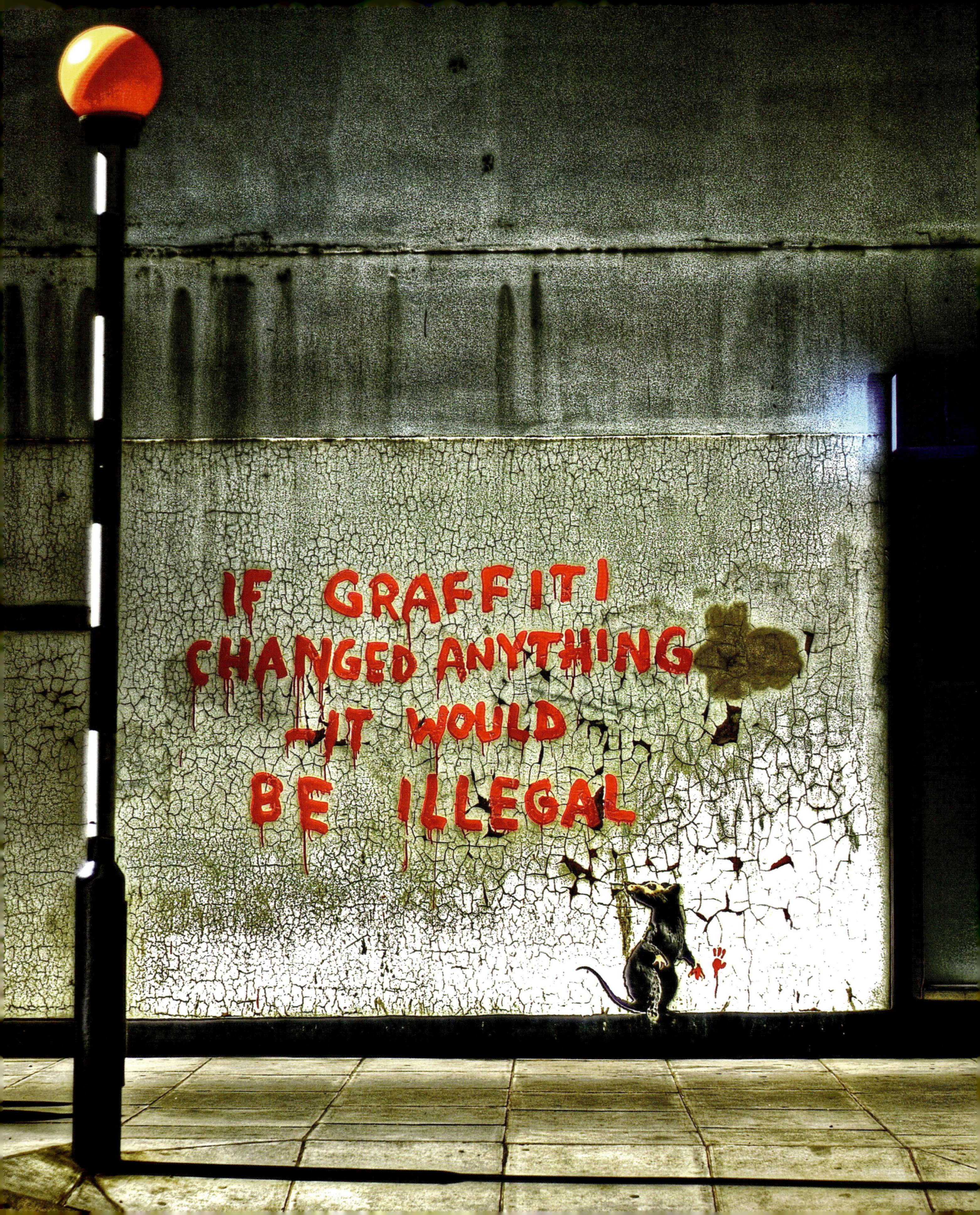

IF GRAFFITI
CHANGED ANYTHING
-IT WOULD
BE ILLEGAL

INTRODUCTION

"Art should comfort the disturbed and disturb the comfortable." Banksy.

Banksy is an enigma's enigma. We suspect he might exist, but we can't be sure. We don't know whether the 'works' here are by him, or by a group, or a mixture of both. He doesn't want us to know. We're happy with that and find attempts to unmask him (or is it her? hunch tells us not) trite and tedious and against the very nature of the phenomenon that goes under the signifier of 'Banksy'. This isn't 'art'. It's something new and infinitely more interesting that we are implicitly a part of.

We don't like the word 'art' and we like the term 'street art' even less. Both suggest galleries, vested interests, rules of taste, the market. We're way beyond all that. What we are dealing with here is a new phenomenon, for which the term 'street art' acts as a kind of short-hand. The characteristics of the phenomenon are first of all the street, a public space, a place of freedom, which defines so much of our identities: New Yorker, Los Angeleno, Londoner, Parisian, Muscovite, Sao Pauloite. It is a place without barriers or boundaries. It is, or should be, classless. Yet the street has been a political battleground, where the forces of capitalism have tried to own the aesthetic, the influence, with hoardings to make us buy, buy, slowly wrecking our globalised, digitised and shrinking planet. As we creep insidiously towards the privatisation of the street – signs banning and directing, CCTV of higher and higher definition, private security guards, nauseating luxury malls, gated communities – we are mirroring the growing seepage of inequality, to levels now last seen in 1928. It's a new dystopia, and we are swimming in it.

Street art is the reaction. Politics is pointless, particularly in democracies, where the electorate is simply bribed come each election with their own money. The power of vested interests neuters any opposition before it gets going. The press is in the pockets of the state or a few individuals, all part of the same controlling network. Banksy makes the point more eloquently in the image opposite, a take on anarchist Emma Goldman's comment that "if voting changed anything, it would be illegal."

I first became aware of this in 2006 when I was writing *Street Art and the War on Terror*. The bare-faced lying of Western leaders in the face of UN analyst Hans Blix's evidence, as to whether Saddam had weapons of mass destruction or not, still stuns me. Not even 3,000 protests around the globe, involving 36 million demonstrators, influenced the decision to invade, against that evidence, taken by the Bush administration, supported by Blair.

A primary purpose of this book is to show how Banksy the phenomenon is so much bigger than the bourgeois concerns which characterise art. Banksy is political. He is above all a provocateur, a polemicist, a man using public walls to send searing messages opposing the hypocrisy, corruption and ghastliness which the political establishment has created. Looking at his equivalents they are not Blek, Eine, D*Face or JR – all interesting street artists. His work is more akin to the Mexican engraver José Posada, or the young Hans Holbein (and his scabrous *Dance of Death* series which got him into serious trouble in the 16th century), or James Gillray, all, in their day, anti-establishment satirists.

When we analyse the development of Banksy's work chronologically in the pages that follow, we are not just looking at the political evolution of perhaps the world's most effective popular critic of established power, we are also, in tandem, seeing how the whole notion of street art was born and has shifted over the past fifteen years. Banksy starts with an illegal medium, hugely important in giving him authenticity as a rebel. He then sets up a dialogue between his work, the street and the public who propagate it through social media. Context is everything with a Banksy, the location an intrinsic part of the whole work. Because it starts as an illegal act and yet is so clever and full of wit, and deeply educated and perceptive, all our notions about graffiti are turned upside down and the notion of street art is born – permissable illegality for the middle classes. Having presented this, Banksy then begins the process of puncturing middle class sacred cows, such as the hermetically sealed world of art, as exclusive an establishment as the world of political control. The world of art then tries to appropriate him, but he's a bit too clever for that. Banksy, far from rowing towards the establishment, becomes more political, more provocative and his own brilliant impresario. He refuses to reveal his identity, he risks Israeli army gunfire to highlight the plight of the Palestinians on the West Bank Wall, he slags off the bankers, he slags off the art establishment and its buyers. In 2014 he auctions a print entitled *I Can't Believe Any of You Morons Actually Buy This Shit* at Sotheby's. It sells for thousands. Everyone loves it.

Our contention is that the reason that everyone loves it is that, deep down, we know that Banksy means it. When he gives the street one of his works and we react in the context of those surroundings, it is a mirror with the distinct ring of truth. And the reason we think this is that, as we can see from the pages that follow, the vast majority of Banksy's work (and for us it's only the street work that is relevant) is deeply felt and deeply political. We know we need to be reminded about the plight of the Palestinians. We know that Guantanamo is against every founding principle of the USA. We know we got shafted by the bankers and we let them get away with it. We know that Western policy in Iraq and Syria has loads of collateral civilian damage. We know that we, like cowards, put up with constant surveillance. We know that thousands have drowned in the waters of the Mediterranean trying to escape their impossible lives. We know we are vapid consumers, in denial about the way it is destroying the planet. And yet we do nothing.

Whether by accident or design, Banksy has become our guilty conscience. Like the cleverest satirists, he gets that, if he is going to get through to us, he has to engage, cajole, tease, amuse, intrigue. Sure, along the way he has some fun himself (*Exit Through the Gift Shop*, his street art documentary, perhaps the prime example). Sure he knocks around notions about the perception and meaning of art, representation, and street art, and laughs at our stupid search for it and at our attempts to attach value, so we can commoditise it. But what is really striking about Banksy is that he has not let up over time on his political concerns one iota. Take the Palestinians. In 2005 he was in the West Bank showing up the hell of the Wall. In 2015, after all his success and fame and ability to sell out, he was back, again under cover, reminding us of the continuing nightmare the incarcerated Palestinians still live under. In 2016 he highlighted the plight of the desperate migrants escaping their war-torn lands, stencilling his *Cosette* image (inspired by *Les Misérables)* right under the nose of the French embassy in London – two establishments with one stone, as it were. Sure these pieces were done in a clever, sardonic fashion, but they were calls to action. 'Street artist' is too bland and incorrect a term. In our opinion he is, rather, the master polemicist-provocateur of our times and we hope this volume serves to illustrate his mould-breaking methodology and techniques. It's time the people in Washington, London, Paris and Berlin who have the power to act actually listened to him. Then we could all feel, and become, a lot less guilty.

Xavier Tapies

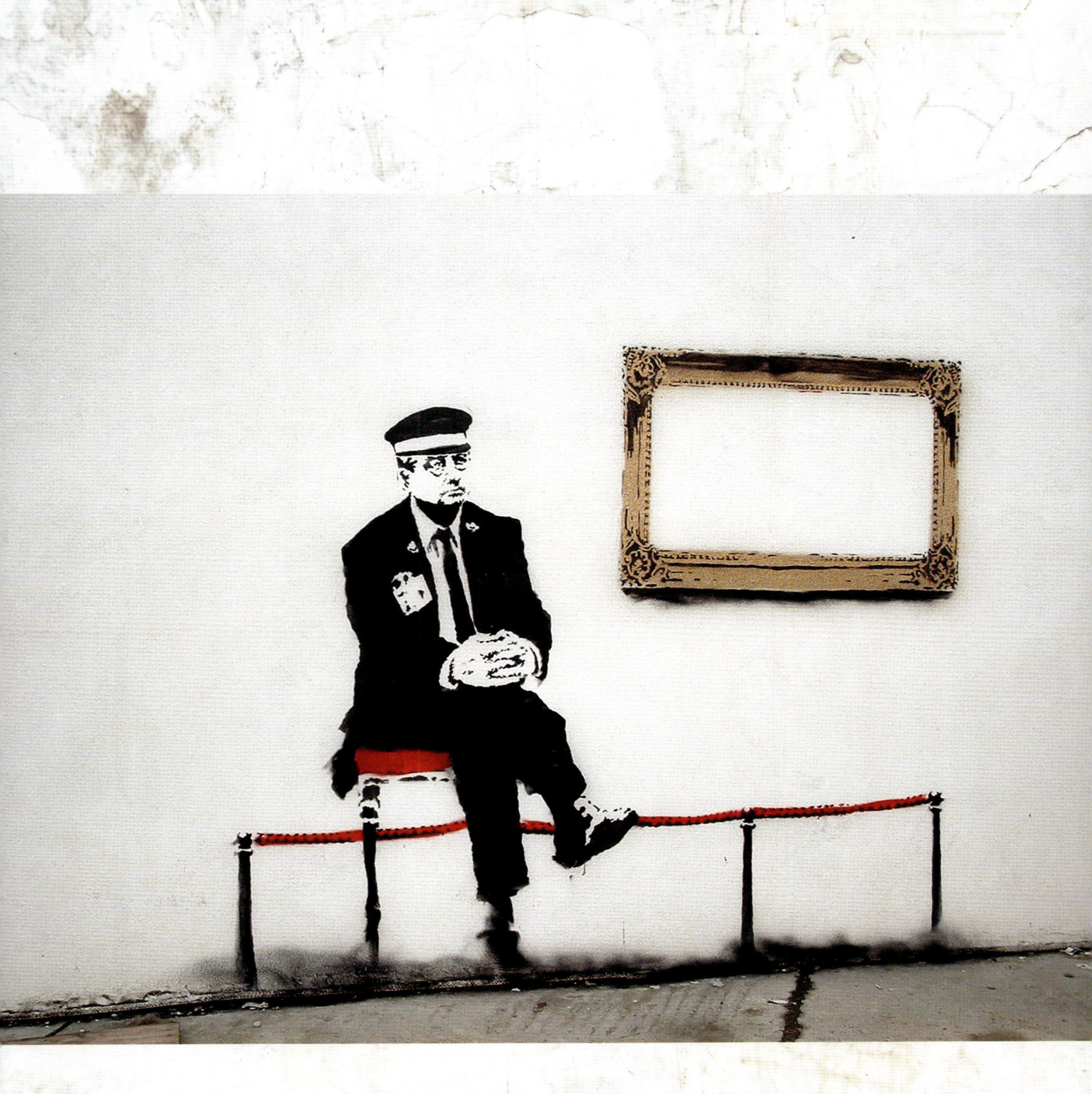

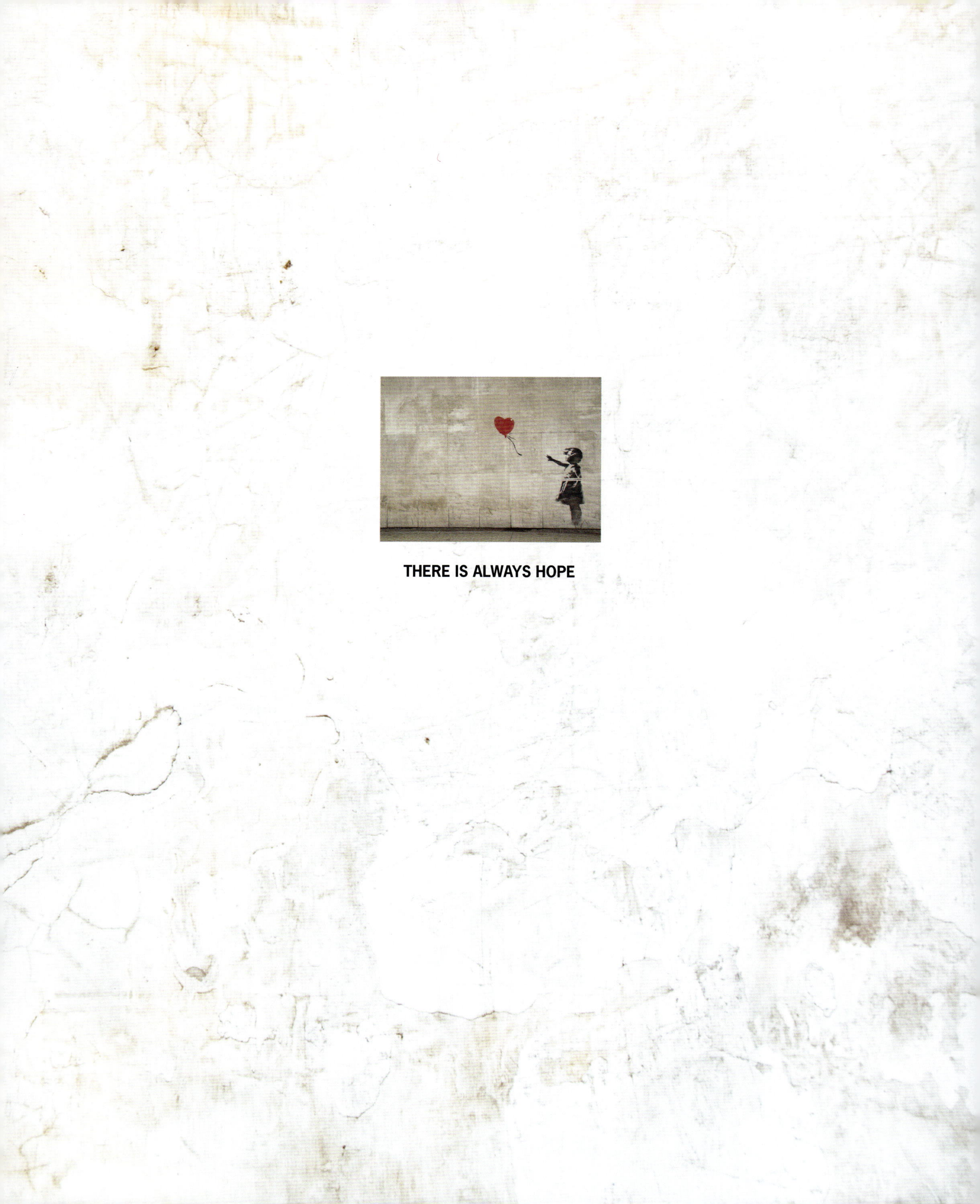

THERE IS ALWAYS HOPE

THE EARLY YEARS

We know that Banksy got going with the graffiti gang in the Barton Hill area of Bristol, but he was never really a graffiti artist. From the get-go he was someone who had stumbled and developed a bigger vision of how the street could be commandeered to amazing effect. These early works – from 2002 – laid down themes that would live through his work to the present day. From the punning language, to the sencing-up of authority figures and, most significantly, some highly politicised anti-war messages. Banksy was launched on several fronts very early on.

THE MILD MILD WEST
GORILLA IN A PINK MASK
THERE IS ALWAYS HOPE
PULP FICTION
ANARCHIST GUARD
HAPPY CHOPPERS

BANKSY EARLY YEARS

We know very little about the early years. Banksy is mixing it with various graffiti artists in Bristol, Inkie and Robert Del Naja included. At first only the signature is stencilled. Then we have the switch to using the stencil for the main image and the use of satire and humour emerges and Bristol begins to love *The Mild, Mild West*. And then Banksy moves to London and things begin to snowball. It is in London that we first see Banksy using street art to convey his political messages.

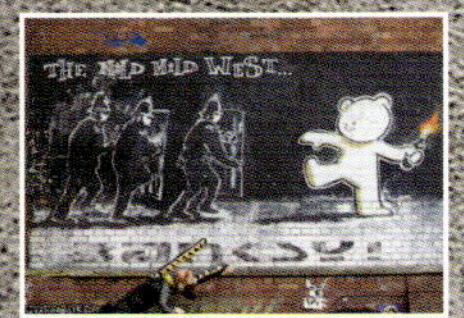

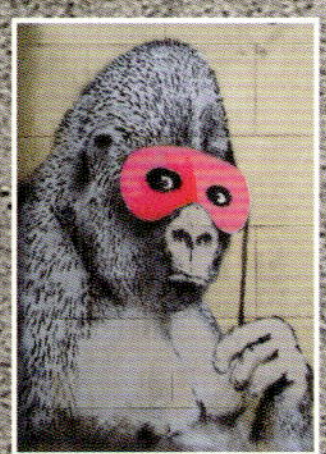

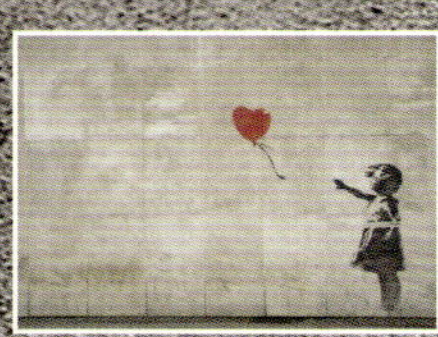

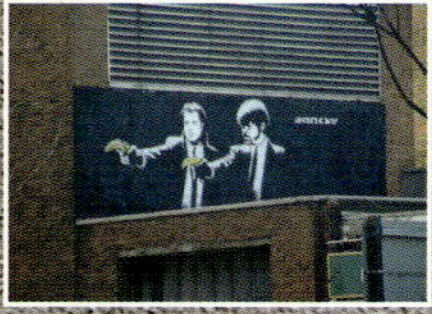

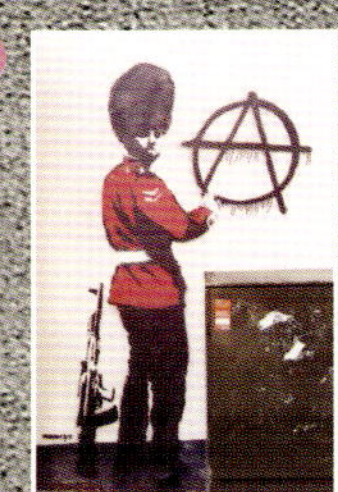

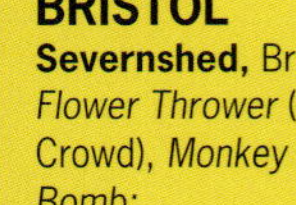

BRISTOL
Severnshed, Bristol, *Flower Thrower* (in a Crowd), *Monkey Riding Bomb;* March 2000.

LOS ANGELES
Existencilism, 33.33 Gallery, Silver Lake; 2002.

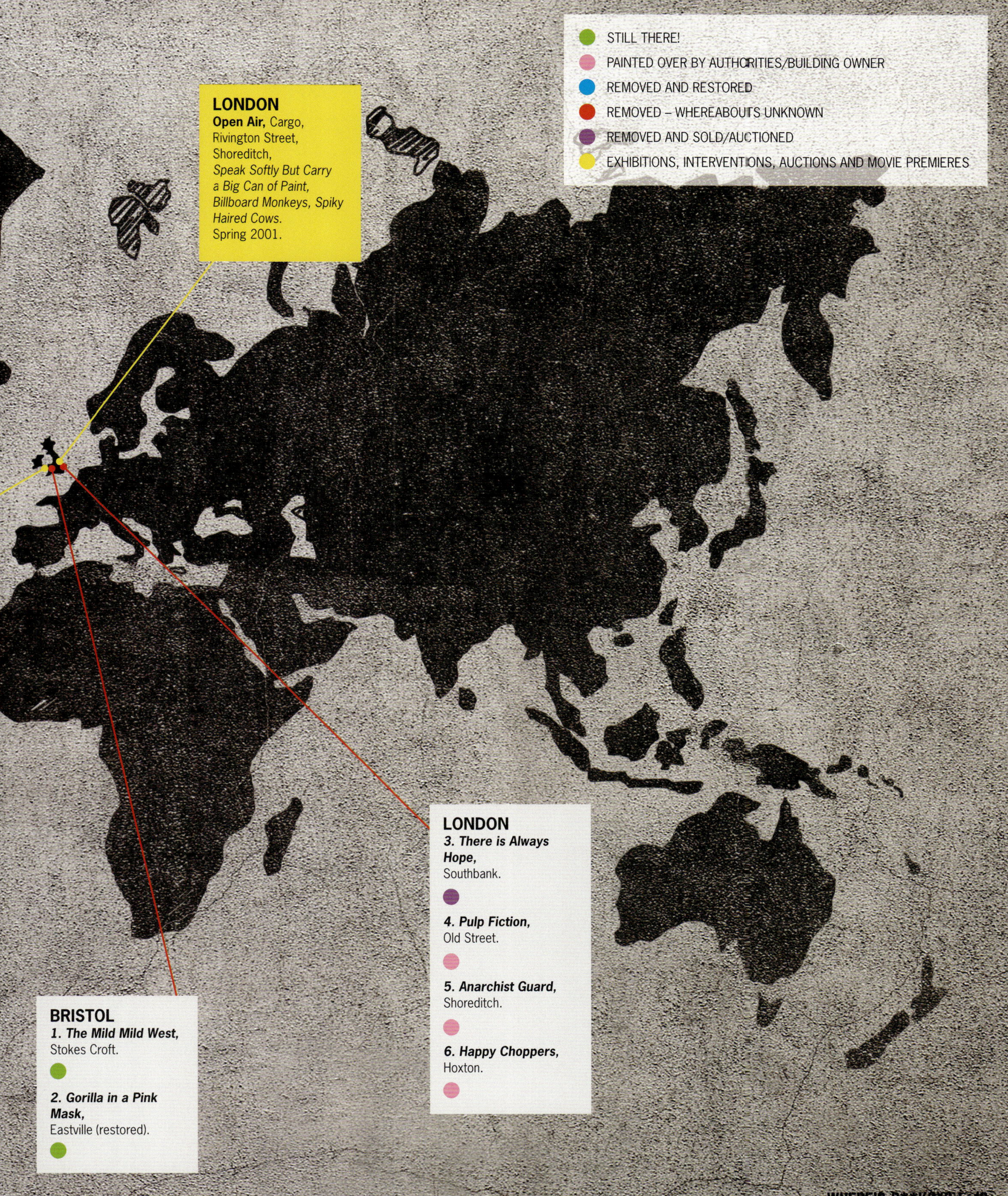

STILL THERE!
PAINTED OVER BY AUTHORITIES/BUILDING OWNER
REMOVED AND RESTORED
REMOVED – WHEREABOUTS UNKNOWN
REMOVED AND SOLD/AUCTIONED
EXHIBITIONS, INTERVENTIONS, AUCTIONS AND MOVIE PREMIERES

LONDON
Open Air, Cargo, Rivington Street, Shoreditch, Speak Softly But Carry a Big Can of Paint, Billboard Monkeys, Spiky Haired Cows. Spring 2001.

LONDON
3. There is Always Hope, Southbank.

4. Pulp Fiction, Old Street.

5. Anarchist Guard, Shoreditch.

6. Happy Choppers, Hoxton.

BRISTOL
1. The Mild Mild West, Stokes Croft.

2. Gorilla in a Pink Mask, Eastville (restored).

THE MILD MILD WEST

"I didn't become a graffiti artist so I could have someone else tell me what to do." **Banksy, quoted in** *Time Out*.

One of the earliest works by Banksy which still survives. It was painted shortly before Banksy left Bristol for London. It might look a bit like a stencil, but this is in fact one of Banksy's last freehand works. It does show, however, that at the core of every Banksy is a brilliantly witty, visual idea which can operate on many levels.

Here we have an early example of future themes in Banksy's work – the sending up of both corporate humbug and authority figures. *The Mild, Mild West* (obviously a play on *The Wild, Wild, West*) sounds like one of those tourist authority campaigns, the sort of groan-inspiring play on words which corny copywriters for low budget promotions seem to go for. Bristol lies in the West of England, but in 2002 it wasn't in fact the scene of any inner-city riots. There had been some serious race riots in the St Paul's area of Bristol in the 1980s (in which this piece lies), but nothing in recent memory.

So it seems, rather, that this piece is just a fun comment on heavy-handed policing, but also on how silly the police can be. The policemen still have their PC Plod outfits on, but are carrying riot shields, to deal with a teddy bear. The teddy is about to throw a molotov cocktail, but really he looks quite cuddly and as though he is just having fun. This could be a reference to the fun of the graffiti scene, or of Bristol's big party scene. Maybe Banksy identifies with the teddy bear, cuddly, but he can also get quite angry.

Unsually the piece has a huge signature. That stencilled design was to be retained with a few variations in later Banksys (and eventually dropped altogether as his fame grew), but in much smaller form. In 2010, the piece was voted online as the best alternative landmark for Bristol in a BBC poll. It was briefly vandalised before being restored and is today, irony of ironies, protected by a CCTV camera.

WHERE IS IT ?
STOKES CROFT,
BRISTOL,
UK.

Latitude: 51.4628ºN
Longitude: 2.5896ºW

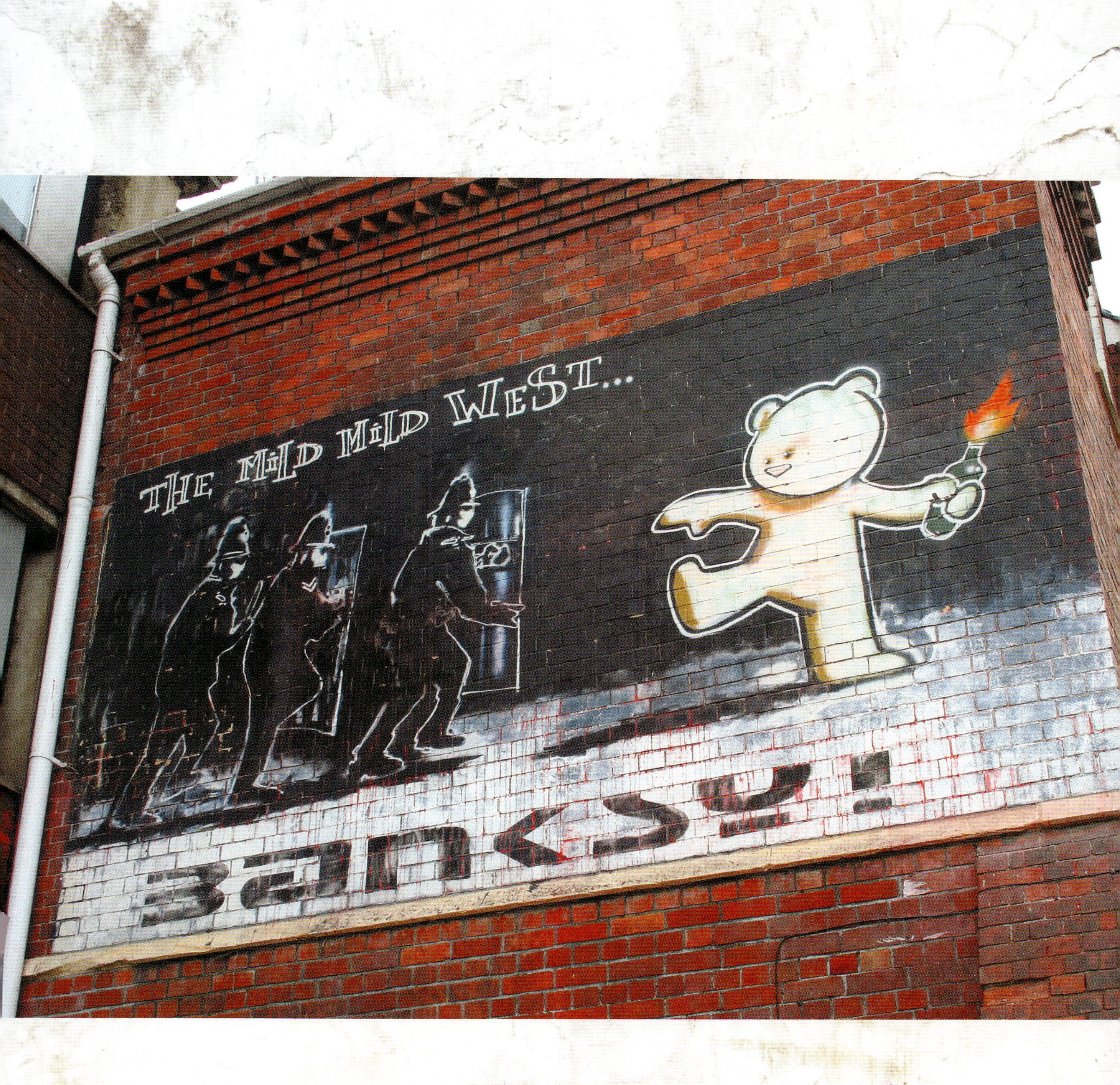

THE MiLD MiLD WeST...
BanKSY!

GORILLA IN A PINK MASK

"I thought it was worthless. I didn't know it was valuable. That's why I painted over it." Representative from the Muslim Cultural Centre, Bristol.

You really couldn't make it up. A man working for a cultural centre paints over a Banksy two years after a Banksy sold for $1.9 million at a charity auction in New York. Really, who wouldn't have heard of Banksy in 2011, in Bristol of all places?

Of course there is a long history of Banksys being vandalised, particularly by jealous rivals. But this was an honest, innocent mistake (he did apologise and it was later restored). Looking at the image again it's almost as though the gorilla knows what's coming: that mask is really rather poignant, almost saying "I'm pretending you don't know who I am, but I know you do."

At the time that it was painted, this was just a bit of fun by Banksy. This time he is sending up the idea of masculinity: our mega-strong, brutal gorilla is really a big softy, and rather shy, hiding behind a very feminine electric pink mask. Banksy was to repeat this idea of juxtaposing pink against a monochromatic stencil many times, each time the colour performing the same ironic, de-masculating role (see, for instance, *Security Guard with Balloon Dog* of 2010). When the piece was painted, the location was a social centre. Maybe there is a further layer of irony there: shy gorilla makes his presence very obvious, although too scared to go in and mingle.

WHERE IS IT ?
EASTVILLE,
BRISTOL,
UK.
WAS PAINTED OVER IN 2011 AND
HAD TO BE RESTORED. NOW A
SHADOW OF ITS FORMER SELF.

Latitude: 51.5478ºN
Longitude: 0.0547ºW

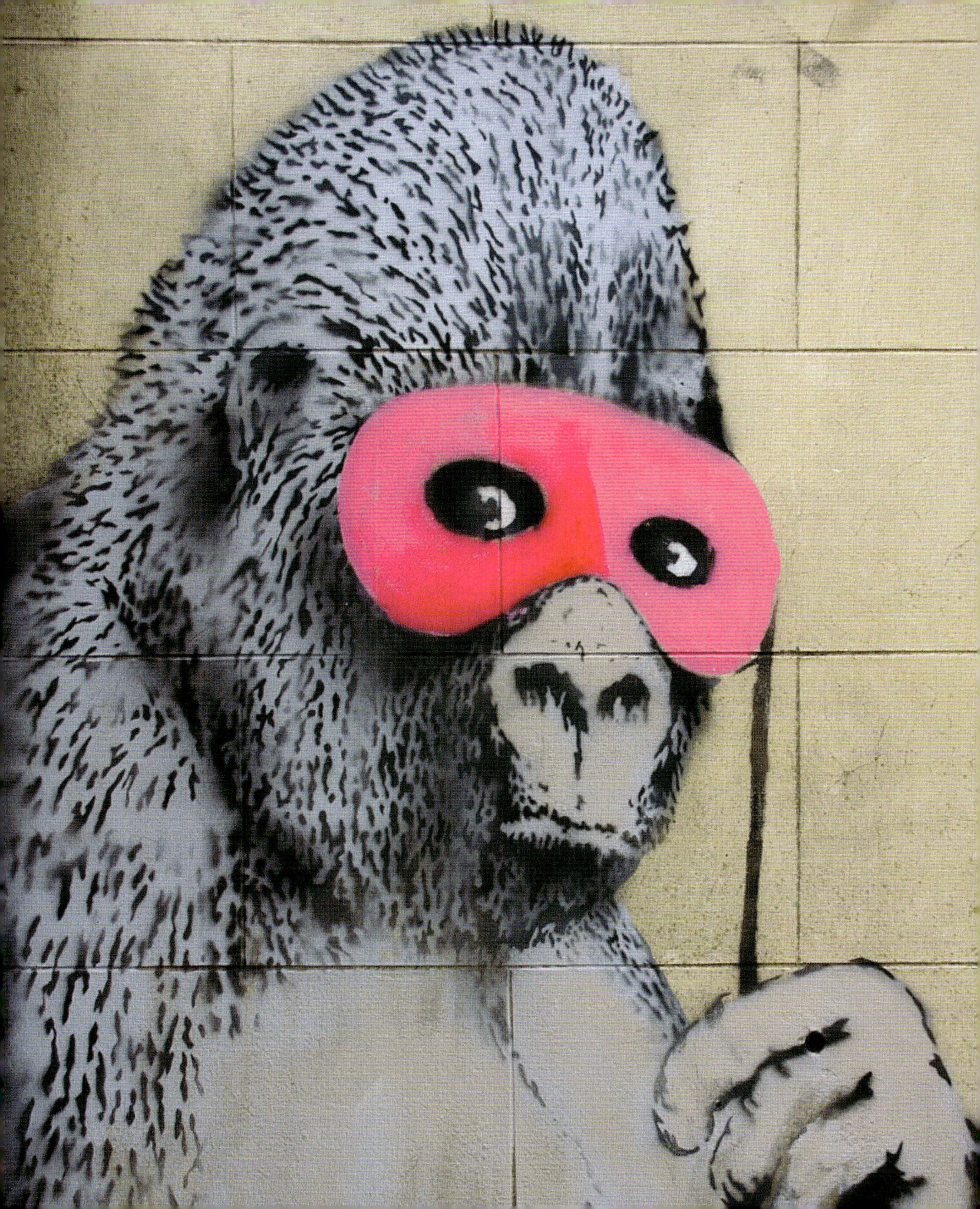

THERE IS ALWAYS HOPE

"Banksy paints over the line between aesthetics and language."
Shepard Fairey

It is tempting to see 2002 as the formative year for Banksy, a year in which we see him developing such a broad range in his art, with many themes set, to which he would return in subsequent years. This piece, still one of his most popular images (if sales of canvases and t-shirts are a measure) reveals a hugely sensitive side to Banksy and also sees him using the image of a child to devastating effect. Images of children were to prove a rich vein for him, carrying with them, as they do, big emotional punch.

The piece is brilliantly conceived. It is clearly windy, telling from the girl's hair, and this is what has blown her balloon away. At that moment of release the girl looks at the balloon with incredulity – Banksy perfectly captures that moment of innocence when a child, without the weight of experience, will rely on hope that the balloon will come back. We rather know that it won't. Or is she casting it off wishing it well?

The shape of the balloon – the heart – is harder to fathom. It makes the piece even more poignant. This is Banksy not saying anything too specific, not making a point, but perfectly capturing an emotion. It is up to the viewer to add an interpretation. For us it is perhaps the loveliness of childhood that time will blow away. But it will somehow always be there, a memory to be loved.

In many of his pieces, Banksy shows a remarkable ability to capture the idyll of a very English sense of childhood, rooted in 1950s imagery of girls in pinafore dresses and boys in ragamuffin clothes. It is Banksy in a retro mode, with echoes of Ladybird books, Start-rite shoes and *Janet and John* stories. It illustrates what an original talent, unbridled by fashion, Banksy really is.

WHERE IS IT ?
SOUTHBANK,
LONDON,
UK.
EAST STAIRCASE LEADING UP
TO WATERLOO BRIDGE.

Latitude: 51.4921ºN
Longitude: 0.1197ºW

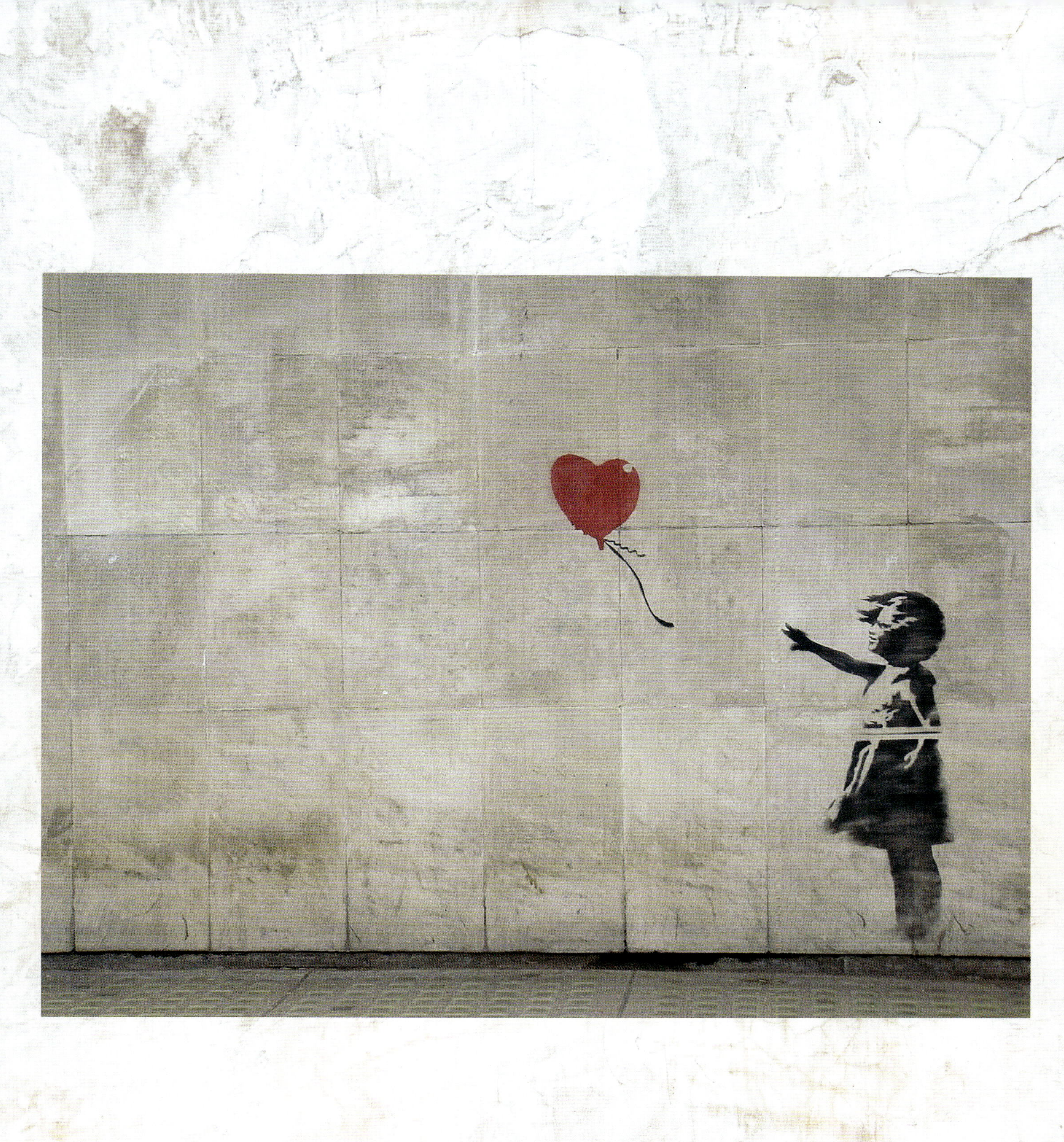

PULP FICTION

"We take a tough line on removing graffiti. There are those who view Banksy's work as art, but we have no intention of changing our policy." London Transport.

This homage to the 1994 cult movie is very much in the spirit of Quentin Tarantino's original. With its stylised satirical take on extreme gang violence, it is amusing to see John Travolta's Auto-Ordnance 1911A1 and Samuel L. Jackson's Star Model B 9mm guns replaced by bananas.

Bananas have been used satirically by a number of street artists, notably by Norwegian artist Dolk, who placed a banana in a psychiatrist's chair. Unusually for a Banksy however, the piece does not have many layers of meaning or ambiguity. One suspects this is more of an homage to Tarantino. It is, after all, hard to satirise one of the cleverest Hollywood satires ever.

Just when we might have been thinking that, although we like the image, it is not one of Banksy's most effective, London Transport comes to the rescue. In 2007 they painted over the piece, which was stencilled on Old Street Station, because it was considered violent and created, a spokesman stated, "an atmosphere of neglect and social decay, which in turn encourages crime." One wonders whether they were referring to the many art lovers who would turn up every day to photograph the image, which at the time of its removal was estimated to be worth £300,000.

As if that wasn't enough humourlessness and institutional idiocy, the spokesman added that London Transport's graffiti removal teams were "staffed by professional cleaners not professional art critics." How that must have delighted Banksy – the suggestion was either that you had to be a professional art critic before you could judge something to be art, or that cleaners are not equipped to appreciate Banksy. Banksy responded by showing Travolta and Jackson wearing full-length banana suits, but this time carrying the real pistols. This was the piece subsequently vandalised by Ozone, leaving a note: "If it's better next time I'll leave it."

Banksy, rather movingly, returned to this spot to create his *Memoriam* piece to Ozone, after the latter was killed by an underground train (see page 84).

WHERE IS IT ?
OLD STREET,
LONDON,
UK.

BUFFED BY LONDON TRANSPORT.
REPLACED BY BANKSY'S *MEMORIAM* PIECE.

Latitude: 51.5259ºN
Longitude: 0.0876ºW

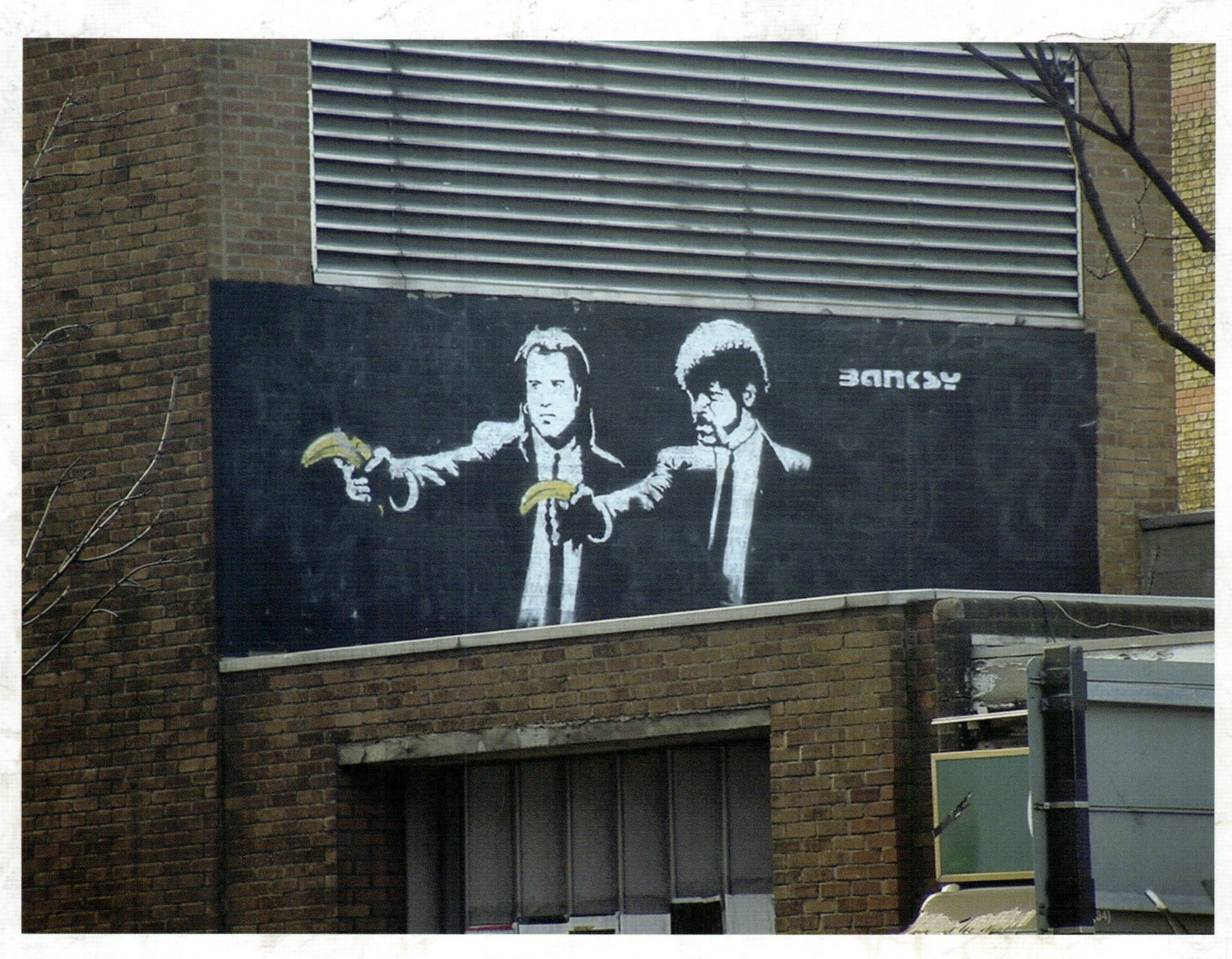

BANKSY

ANARCHIST GUARD

"The greatest crimes in the world are not committed by people breaking the rules, but by people following the rules."
Banksy, *Wall and Piece*.

The Guards are the ultimate symbol of the British Establishment. Formed of seven regiments that were raised to protect the exiled King Charles II in 1656, they have directly protected the monarch ever since. They are also an indelible part of Britain's branding, as they parade from St James's Palace to the front of Buckingham Palace, at 11am every morning, to the delight of hundreds of thousands of tourists every year.

This is what makes this Banksy so wonderfully effective. Having the ultimate symbol of establishment power spray-paint the A in a circle – the Anarchists' symbol – is absurdly unlikely and therefore hilarious. This is Banksy showing the unique effect street art can have – a stomach-tickling rebelliousness.

Banksy imbues the picture with total good humour. The guard is slightly passive and the symbol he has drawn is really quite neat. His expression is at once not embarrassed and seems also to be saying "ooops", in schoolboy fashion. He has put his gun down, he is a bit square and not at all scary.

As ever with Banksy there are more layers of irony than at first meet the eye. The A inside the O stands in fact for "Anarchy is the mother of Order", from a quotation by French politician Pierre-Joseph Proudhon, the first major political figure to declare himself an anarchist. (Proudhon was good at quotes; he also came up with "Property is theft!"). One can imagine the order bit appealing to a guard. The symbol was occasionally used in the Spanish Civil War and then was used by several punk bands in the 1970s. Banksy is just laughing, both at rebels inside establishment uniforms, but also at the sillyness of placing symbols on walls.....even guards are doing it, he suggests, that's how mainstream it has become.

WHERE IS IT ?
SHOREDITCH,
LONDON,
UK.

Latitude: 51.5285ºN
Longitude: 0.0847ºW

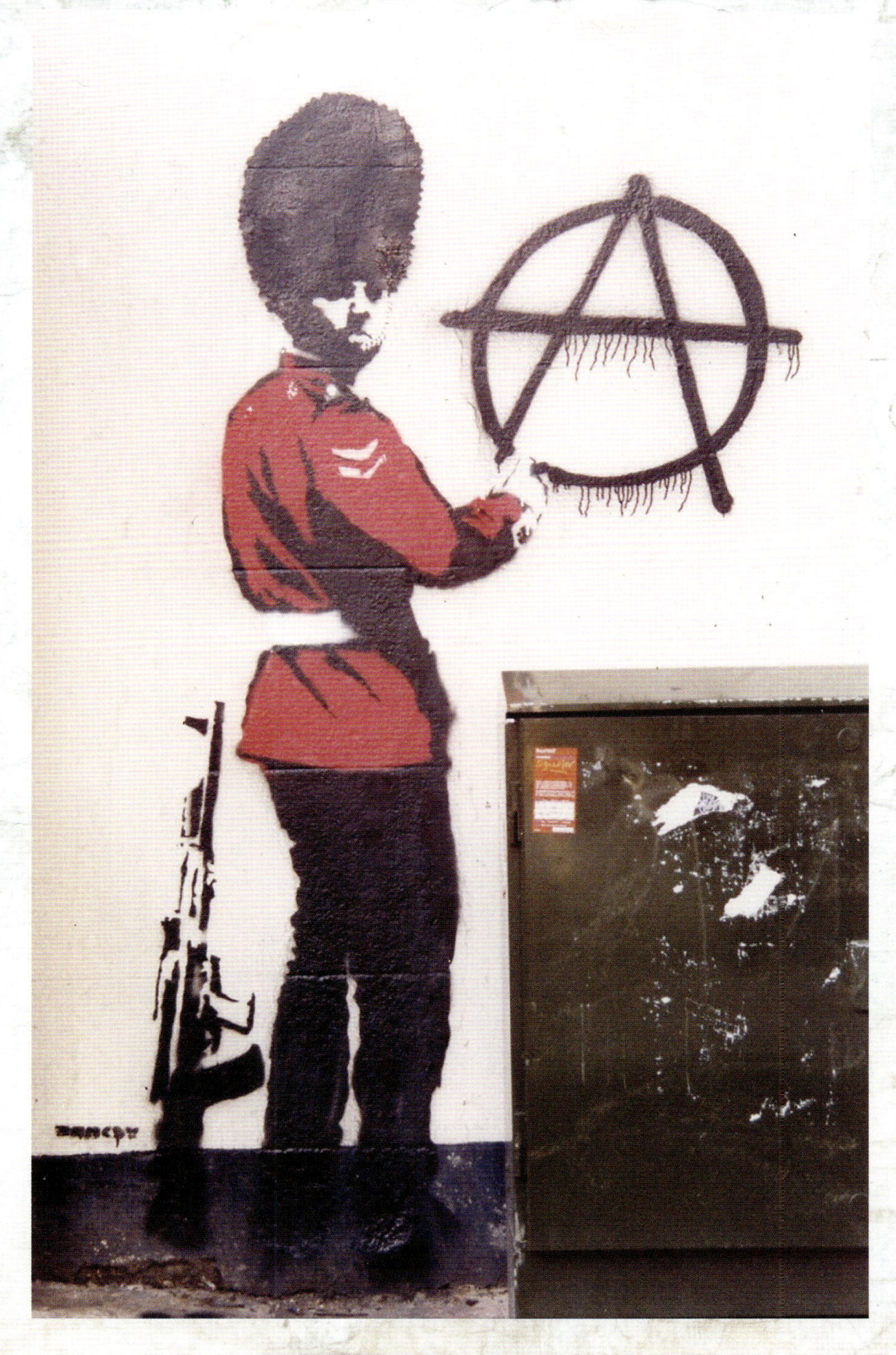

HAPPY CHOPPERS

"We will do what we can to minimise the suffering of the Afghan people as a result of the conflict." UK Prime Minister, Tony Blair.

Banksy has often highlighted the way the West likes to present an anodyne, 'precision bombing' view of its wars in the media, as if war is surgical without the hell of extreme violence, innocent children killed, families destroyed, homes razed to the ground, and hundreds still alive but with life-changing deformities and injuries. This was a view of war which many Western commentators took from the CNN broadcasts of the first Gulf War. The West has continued to push that PR line ever since.

Banksy's heavily ironic – to the point of surrealistic – image opposite, first created on a wooden scaffolding hoarding in London's Whitecross Street Market in 2002, gives the lie to the West's image merchants. It shows a squadron of Apache Attack helicopers going into battle, with the pretence that this will be a friendly, childish affair, as suggested by the pink bows. We are here to deliver a lovely present, they seem to say. No mention of course of the Hellfire missiles and 70mm unguided rockets, or of the video-game-ish helmet-mounted display, which can track the additional automatic 30mm chain gun to wherever the pilot happens to be looking.

The Apache was extensively used in Afghanistan by US and UK forces – during the absurdly named Operation Enduring Freedom – at the time this piece was painted.

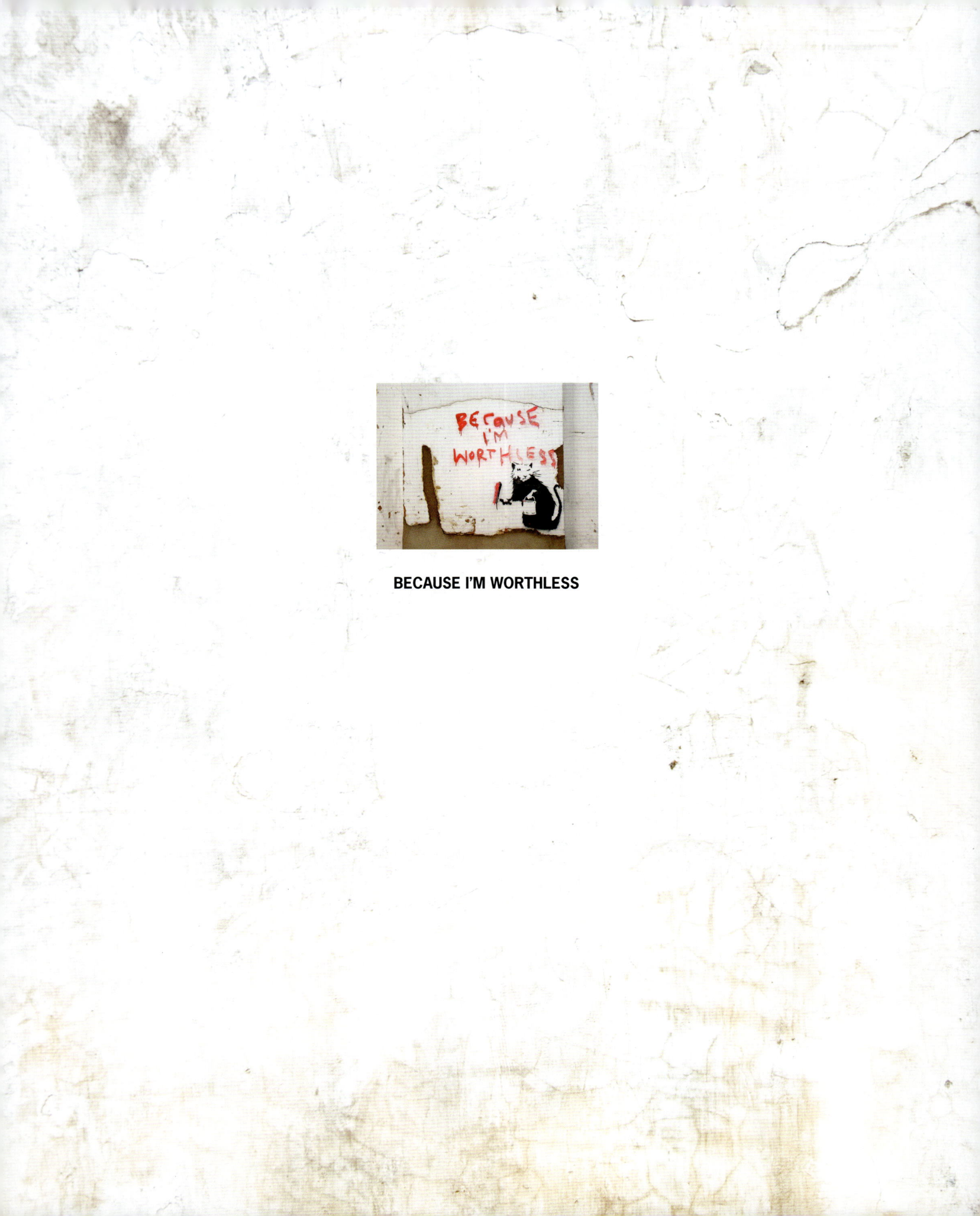

BECAUSE I'M WORTHLESS

2003-2004

One of Banksy's most powerful works – Flower Thrower – emerged in 2003, and highlighted his preoccupation with the plight of the Palestinians on the West Bank and Gaza Strip. At this point Banksy was still creating in Bristol, the west country and London, in addition to the Middle East. During this period we see the first eloquent use of the rat, a nod to French street art maestro Blek. We also see the emergence of a second major political strand to his work: surveillance and the overweening power of the state over the individual.

THE GRIM REAPER
RAGE: THE FLOWER THROWER
DYNAMITE ICE CREAM
BECAUSE I'M WORTHLESS
DRUNKEN ANGEL
KISSING COPPERS
THUG FOR LIFE BUNNY
TOURIST INFORMATION
THIS IS NOT A PHOTO OPPORTUNITY
WHAT ARE YOU LOOKING AT?

BANKSY 2003-2004

Banksy is still mostly working in the UK, with works appearing in his home town of Bristol, in London and a couple of works in Brighton, on the English south coast. 2003 however marks a significant development – Banksy's first work in Israel – *Rage: The Flower Thrower*, his most political work to date, and a theme he would return to in future years.

2003 also marks Banksy's first gallery intervention – at Tate Britain in October that year.

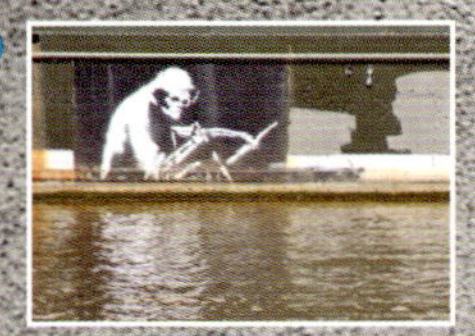

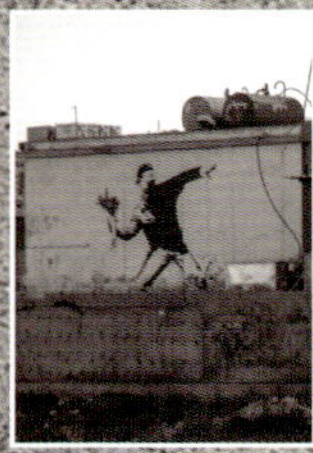

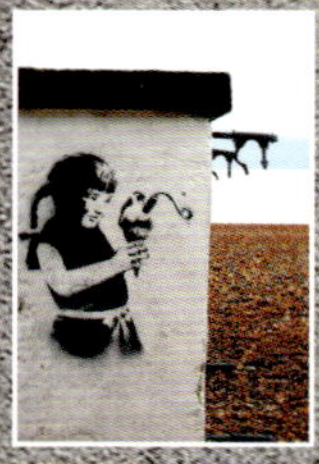

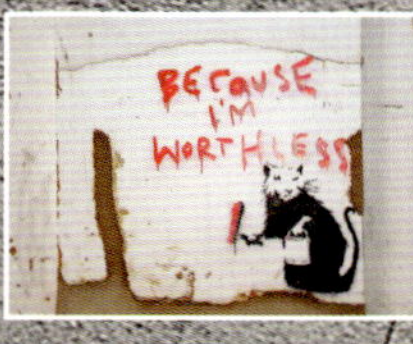

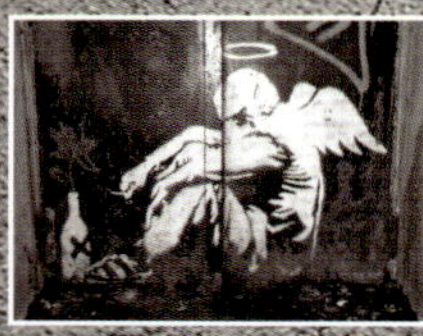

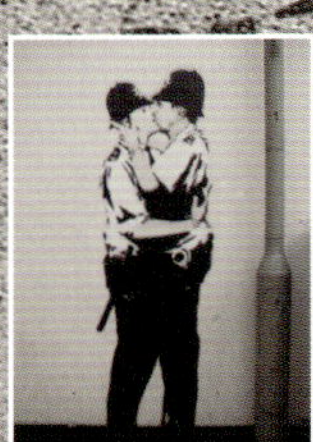

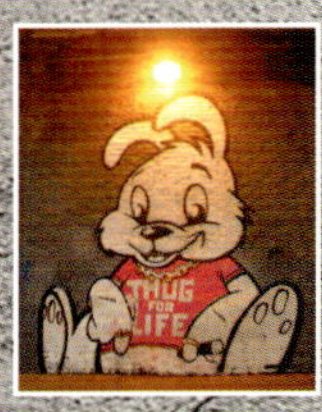

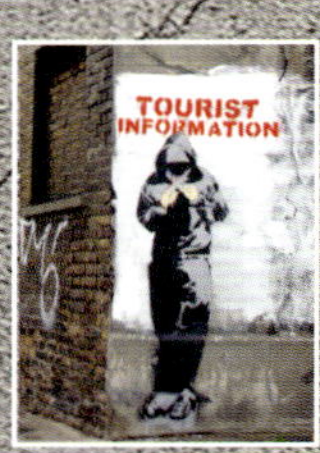

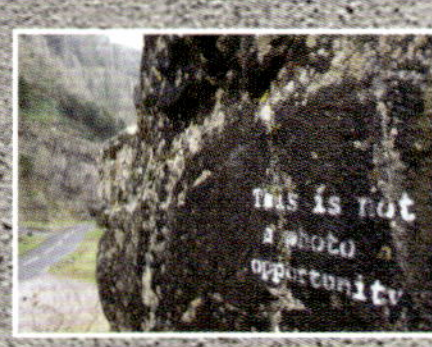

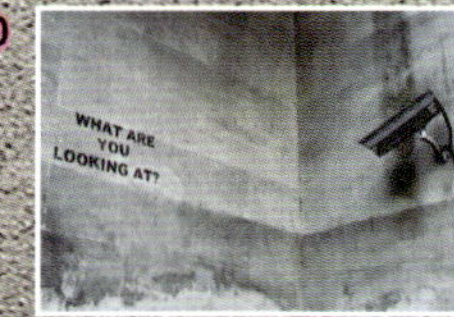

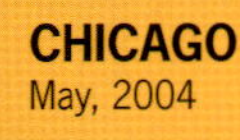

CHICAGO
May, 2004

SOMERSET
9. This is Not a Photo Opportunity,
Cheddar Gorge.

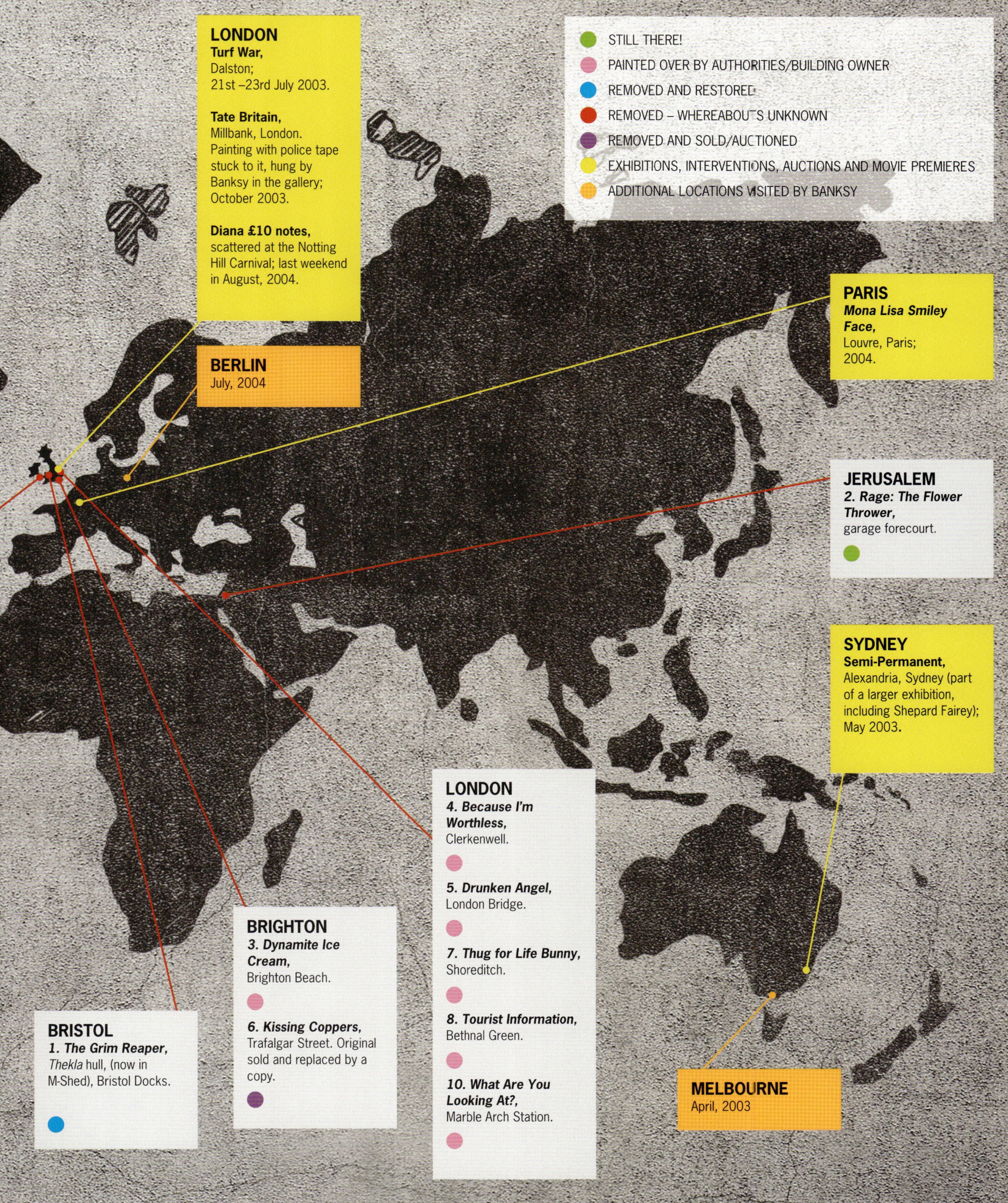

LONDON
Turf War,
Dalston;
21st –23rd July 2003.

Tate Britain,
Millbank, London.
Painting with police tape
stuck to it, hung by
Banksy in the gallery;
October 2003.

Diana £10 notes,
scattered at the Notting
Hill Carnival; last weekend
in August, 2004.

STILL THERE!
PAINTED OVER BY AUTHORITIES/BUILDING OWNER
REMOVED AND RESTORED
REMOVED – WHEREABOUTS UNKNOWN
REMOVED AND SOLD/AUCTIONED
EXHIBITIONS, INTERVENTIONS, AUCTIONS AND MOVIE PREMIERES
ADDITIONAL LOCATIONS VISITED BY BANKSY

BERLIN
July, 2004

PARIS
Mona Lisa Smiley
Face,
Louvre, Paris;
2004.

JERUSALEM
2. Rage: The Flower
Thrower,
garage forecourt.

SYDNEY
Semi-Permanent,
Alexandria, Sydney (part
of a larger exhibition,
including Shepard Fairey);
May 2003.

LONDON
4. Because I'm
Worthless,
Clerkenwell.

5. Drunken Angel,
London Bridge.

7. Thug for Life Bunny,
Shoreditch.

8. Tourist Information,
Bethnal Green.

10. What Are You
Looking At?,
Marble Arch Station.

BRIGHTON
3. Dynamite Ice
Cream,
Brighton Beach.

6. Kissing Coppers,
Trafalgar Street. Original
sold and replaced by a
copy.

BRISTOL
1. The Grim Reaper,
Thekla hull, (now in
M-Shed), Bristol Docks.

MELBOURNE
April, 2003

THE GRIM REAPER

"We have no intention of selling the Banksy." Owners of the *Thekla*, Bristol.

Painted directly onto the hull of *Thekla*, a party boat anchored in Bristol harbour, this haunting image is at first hard to decipher. Given its context, and what we know of Banksy's sardonic sense of humour, it's quite funny to show the reaper in a location where everyone is getting loved-up, dancing, thinking they will live forever. The reaper is also wearing a hoodie, typical standard wear for Banksy and other graffiti artists not wishing to be recognised.

There is a more disturbing interpretation from its location in Bristol Dock, however. Bristol was a major centre of the slave trade in the eighteenth century and the city owes much of its subsequent wealth to this trade, first with Africa and then the Americas and Caribbean. It is estimated that around half of each cargo of slaves did not survive the trip to the Americas. Between 1697, when the trade really started booming, and 1807, when slavery was abolished in Britain, Bristol was responsible for transporting over 500,000 slaves. Many Bristolians were active investors in the 20 or more slave voyages that sailed from the dock each year.

By 2016 the piece, a fêted feature of Bristol and a draw for tourists, was deteriorating. The decision was taken, when the *Thekla* was in dry dock, to cut out the *Reaper* and to preserve it away from the elements. It is now housed in the M Shed, a museum in the harbour. It's a bit of a grim reaper result for this particular Banksy.

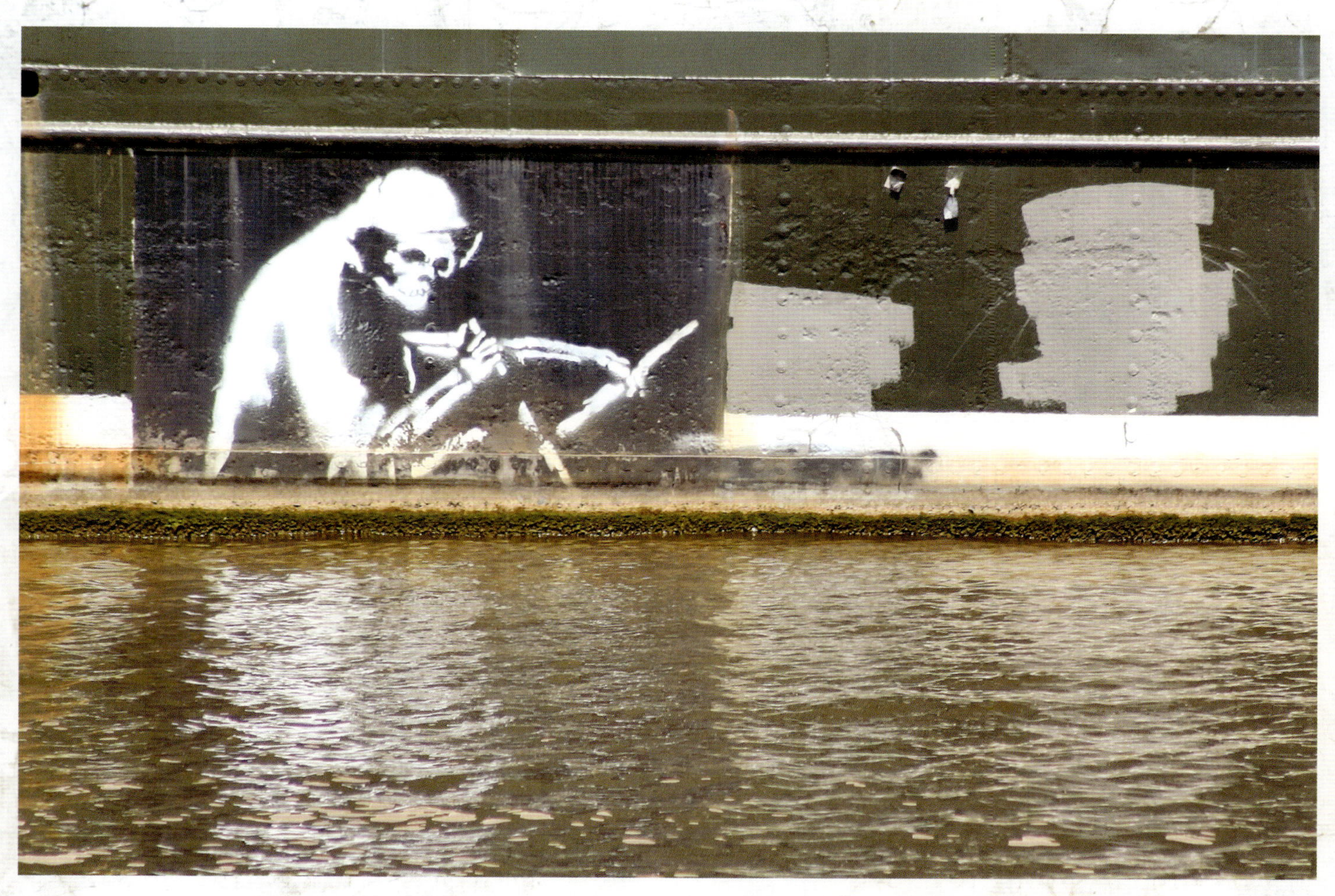

RAGE: THE FLOWER THROWER

"The innocent imprisoned. Movement restricted. Trade suffocated. Homes demolished. Human rights abuses are rife in Israel and the Occupied Palestinian Territories." Amnesty International, 2016.

The Israeli-Palestinian conflict is one which has pre-occupied Banksy, and where he has taken considerable risks, to both highlight it to the wider world and to use his artistic powers to try and express a way of ending the deadlock. *Flower Thrower* might well be his best-known and evocative single work, not least because it formed the cover of Banksy's seminal *Banksy Wall and Piece* book. If we assume that Banksy had a close say on the cover, it's probably safe to surmise that this image means much to him personally.

The image first appeared in Jerusalem in 2003. It was painted on a wall in a garage forecourt. The absolute immediacy of the composition – a young guy in a reversed baseball cap, his body full of energy as if about to throw a molotov cocktail, instead of which he holds a bunch of flowers – is Banksy at his most viscerally successful. Look more carefully and you see that the figure in this stance, usually one associated with Palestinian youth chucking stuff at Israeli soldiers, exasperated at the hideous conditions on the West Bank, is not necessarily an Arab. Instead he looks Western, well-off, possibly American. Given the guy's appearance and that this was painted in an Israeli sector of Jerusalem, this is very clearly Banksy's call to action addressed to Israeli and Western youth: how about throwing the Palestinians some peace? How about loving them a little instead of all the hatred? How about using all the energy of war in search for a solution?

Many Israelis share Banksy's sentiment; figures like conductor Daniel Barenboim, using music to try and do his bit for understanding. Alas, at the time of writing, the moderate Israeli political parties had still not managed, thirteen years after this work was created, to get any nearer to power. The most recent elections returned the hawkish Binyamin Netanyahu as prime minister, heading a right-wing coalition. One day there may be flowers, but not any time soon.

WHERE IS IT ?
GARAGE FORECOURT,
JERUSALEM,
ISRAEL.
PRESERVED
UNDER PERSPEX.

Latitude: 31.7008ºN
Longitude: 35.2241ºE

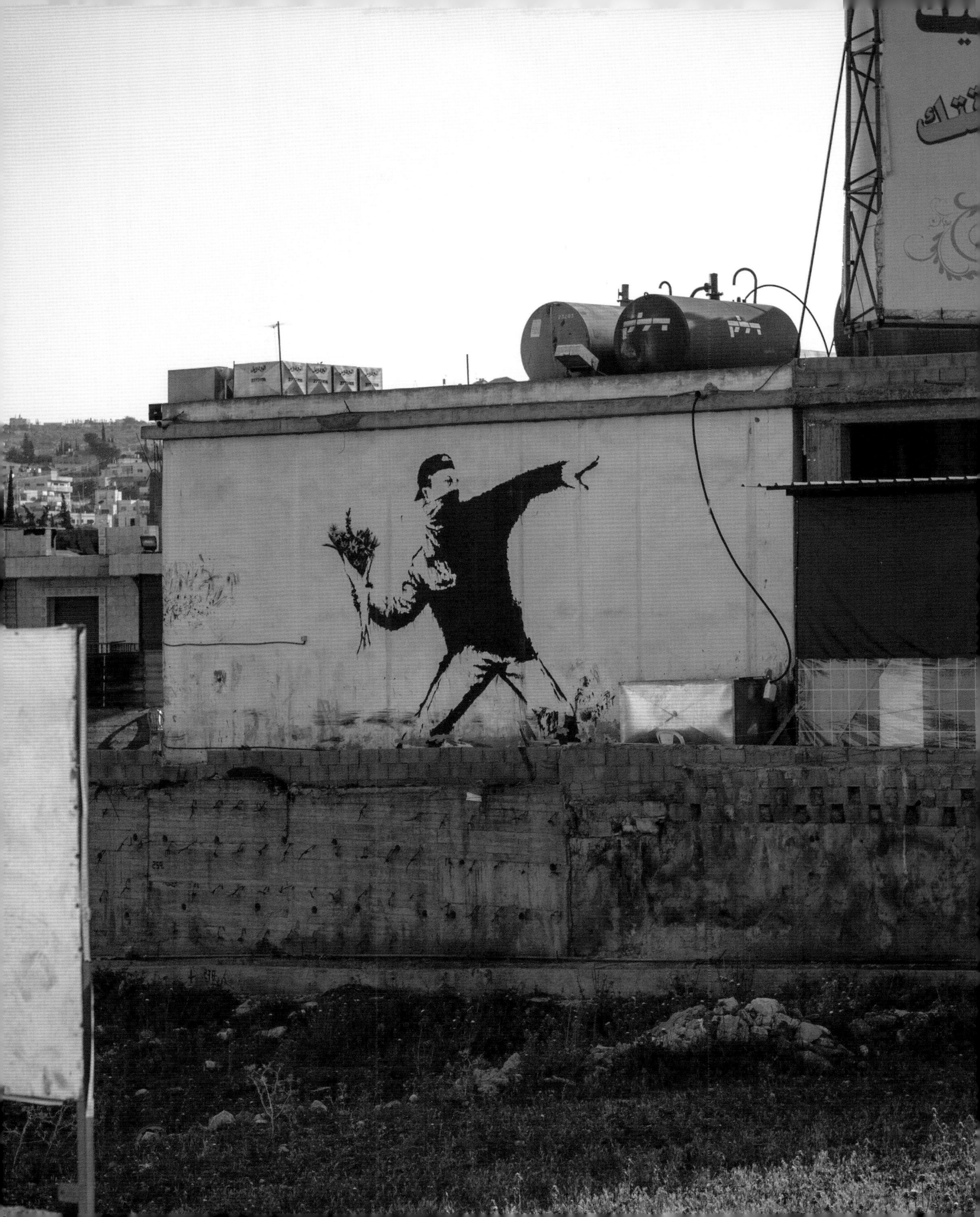

DYNAMITE ICE CREAM

"A lot of mothers will do anything for their children, except let them be themselves." Banksy, *Wall and Piece.*

A witty piece, appearing on Brighton Beach in southern England. It's hard to see any obvious message here; rather this is Banksy just having fun. A little girl in a traditional dress, with a pony tail, having an ice cream at the beach.

Except that this ice-cream has a stick of dynamite in place of a traditional chocolate flake, and there is a fuse which has been lit and which will, before too long, explode. Is this a poignant comment on how short an innocent childhood is, how time is ticking, how all the childish pleasures of the beach will come to an end? Perhaps. Or is it a comment on the WOW! taste which is to come, that delicious hit of the first lick? Some suggestions that it is a warning that too many ice creams are a diabetes bomb waiting to happen are a bit of a stretch.

Sometimes, Banksy just wants to have fun. He was at the beach: let the man relax!

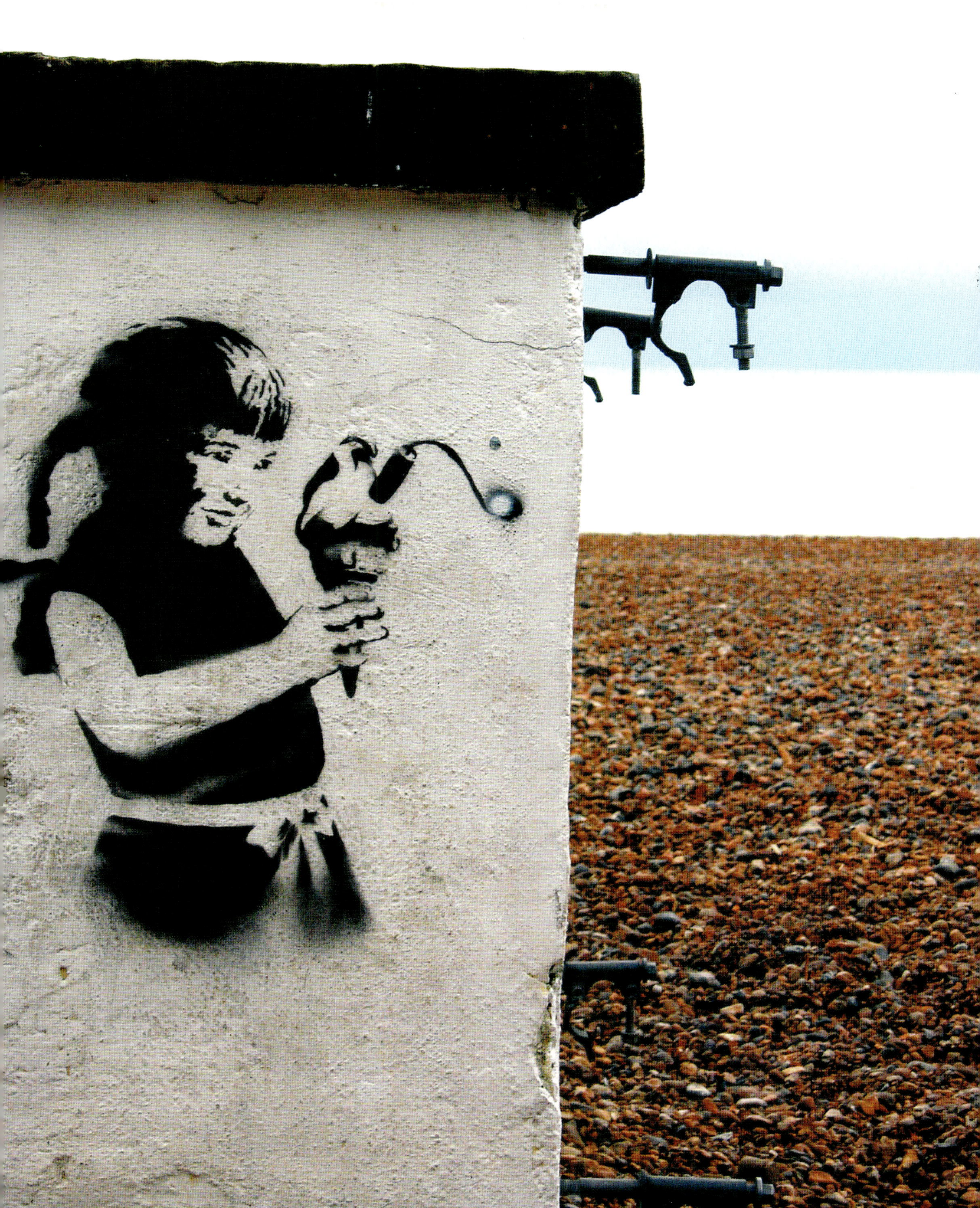

BECAUSE I'M WORTHLESS

"There's no way round it – commercial success is a mark of failure for a graffiti artist." Banksy, interviewed in *Village Voice.*

A delicious send-up of the nauseating, ubiquitous, vapid L'Oreal campaign strap-line. That stream of tedium which saw various models repeat the moronic line "Because I'm worth it" over and over and over again, is here transformed into a brilliant piece of wit.

This is an early manifestation of a Banksy rat, looking quite intent, with his can of paint and roller. OK, one can quibble – it's hard to see how those letters could have been painted with a roller. But the comment on the generalised view of street artists as law-breaking miscreants is great: street artists are vermin, no better than rats. It could also be taken as a side-point about the inaccessibility of the gallery world for so many artists, but on balance that interpretation feels a bit serious.

The irony, with the benefit of hindsight, is delicious, an effect that many Banksy works seem to acquire, viewed over time. Banksy, one of the most successful artists on the planet worthless? Yeah, right.... A version of this, featuring a rat holding a placard with the same legend, sold at Bonhams auctioneers for £8,125 in 2012. It was a signed screenprint on paper, number 55 in an edition of 75. If we extrapolate, that edition of the print would be worth a total of £609,375, assuming the price hasn't gone up. We don't suppose L'Oreal asked Banksy to do a commercial for them, although he clearly is so worth it.

WHERE IS IT ?
CLERKENWELL,
LONDON,
UK.

Latitude: 51.5228ºN
Longitude: 0.1038ºW

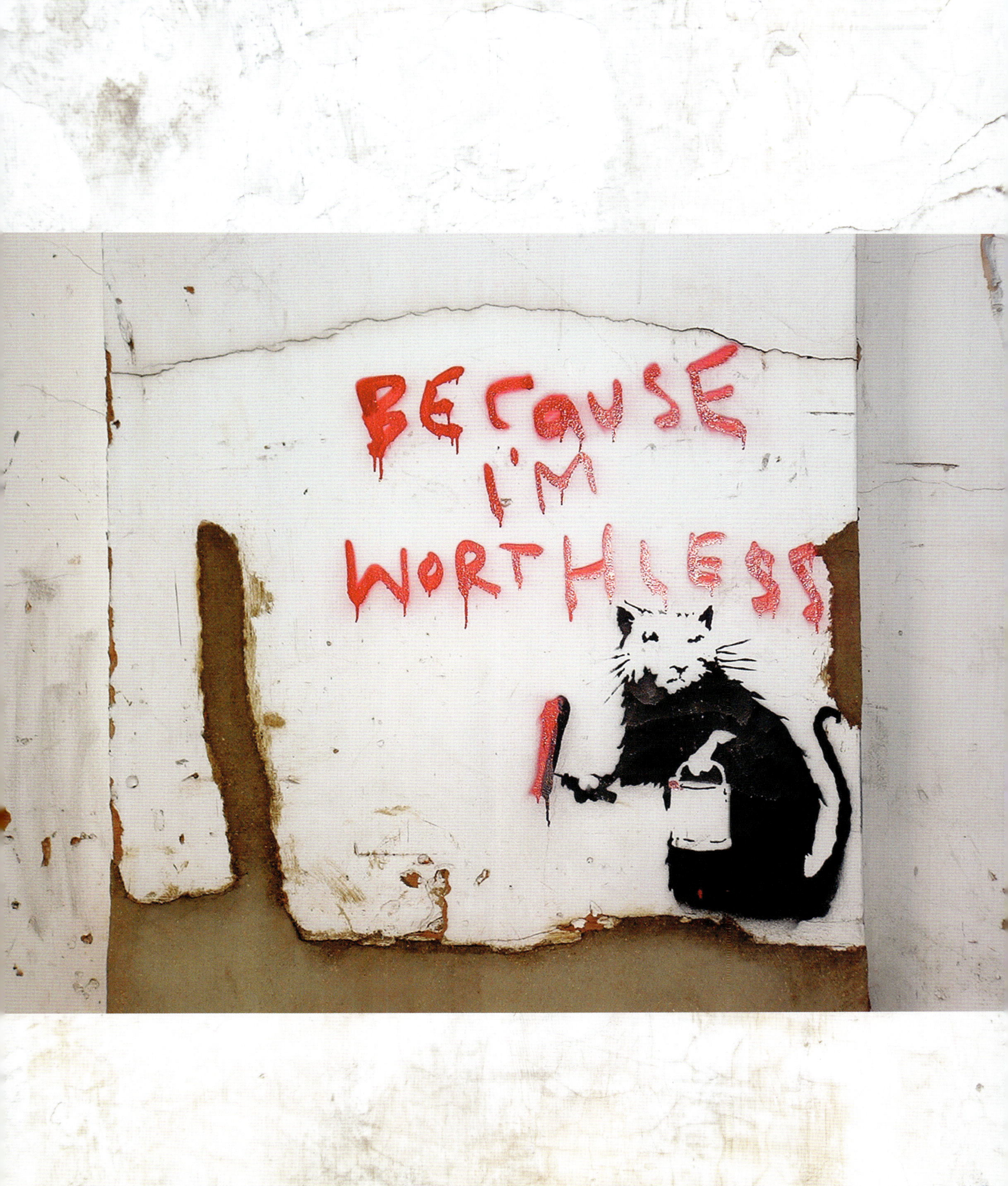
BECAUSE
I'M
WORTHLESS

DRUNKEN ANGEL

"People are drinking less – but deaths from excessive drinking are rising steadily." The Guardian.

A rather heartfelt piece by Banksy, painted in a well on the south side of London Bridge. It's an image of despair, of hitting bottom. The bottle, marked 'X' as traditionally used for poisons, a cigarette in hand. This doesn't look like a guy who is going to get up.

So, he may be a tramp, an alcoholic, but he's also an angel. The halo is still there and the wings haven't been drawn in. Is this one of those Banksy's which retain hope in the face of adversity?

This isn't Banksy's most arresting image. Unlike his images of children, an adult like this just doesn't illicit the usual sparkling reaction to Banksy's cleverness and wit. We suspect it's because he didn't want it to: it has a more personal quality than much of his work. Banksy has done a number of pieces as homages to friends. This may be in that category.

WHERE IS IT ?
LONDON BRIDGE, SOUTH SIDE,
LONDON,
UK.
WAS BUFFED SHORTLY AFTER APPEARING.

Latitude: 51.5068ºN
Longitude: 0.0879ºW

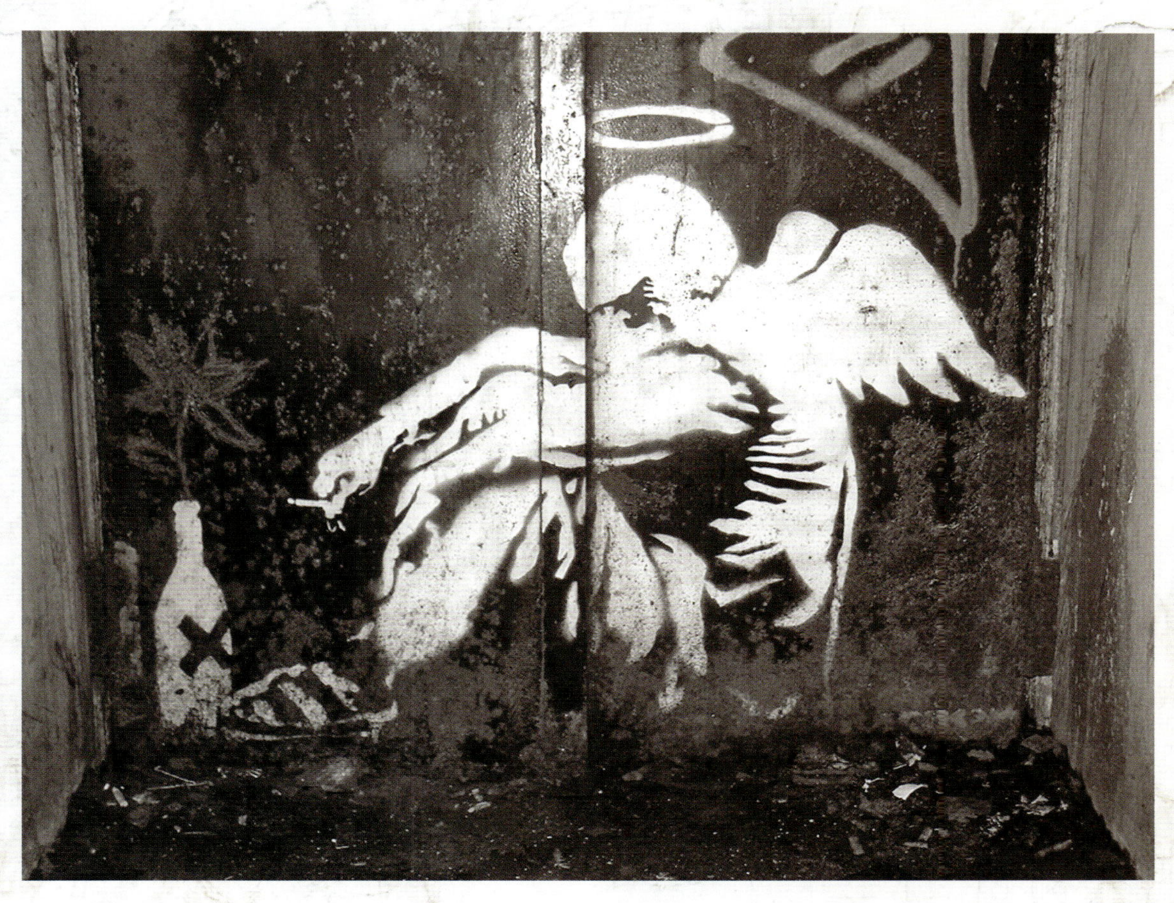

KISSING COPPERS

"When he put it on the pub it belonged to the pub and, if it is sold, all the money will go back to the pub." **Chris Seward, owner of the Prince Albert.**

One of Banksy's iconic works, painted on the side of the Prince Albert pub in central Brighton, the gay capital of the UK.

Banksy has form in cocking a snook at establishment figures and the police are in good company with the Queen and Royal Guards, to name a few. This piece is perfect as a celebration of tolerance in a city noted for its gay-friendly vibe since the 1960s. If there is anything illicit about this, it's that the police might be having a naughty snog whilst on the job, debunking the hard-working image they like to project. Or perhaps these are a couple of coppers at Brighton's gay pride event? The officer on the right is older and, telling from his epaulettes, of higher rank, than the newer recruit on the left. It's one of those Banksy pieces that just makes you smile.

Things weren't always so tolerant. Until 2000, homosexuals were still barred from serving in the British armed forces. Section 28, an act introduced by Margaret Thatcher to ban councils and schools from promoting homosexuality in 1987, was not repealed until 2003. It was only in the same year that gay policemen were allowed to march in uniform at gay pride events. The Civil Partnership Act, giving same-sex couples the same rights as heterosexual couples, was not introduced until 2004. In other words, when Banksy stencilled this piece, gay rights were still a big issue.

In 2011, the piece was cut out and shipped to New York in search of a buyer. It ended up in the capable hands of renowned art dealer Stephan Keszler, who eventually sold the piece at auction in Miami in 2014, where it fetched $575,000.

WHERE IS IT ?
ORIGINALLY TRAFALGAR STREET,
BRIGHTON,
UK.
REMOVED FROM PUB WALL AND SOLD TO PRIVATE BUYER AT AUCTION IN MIAMI IN 2014.
A REPLICA HAS NOW REPLACED THE ORIGINAL.

Latitude: 50.8283ºN
Longitude: 0.1387ºW

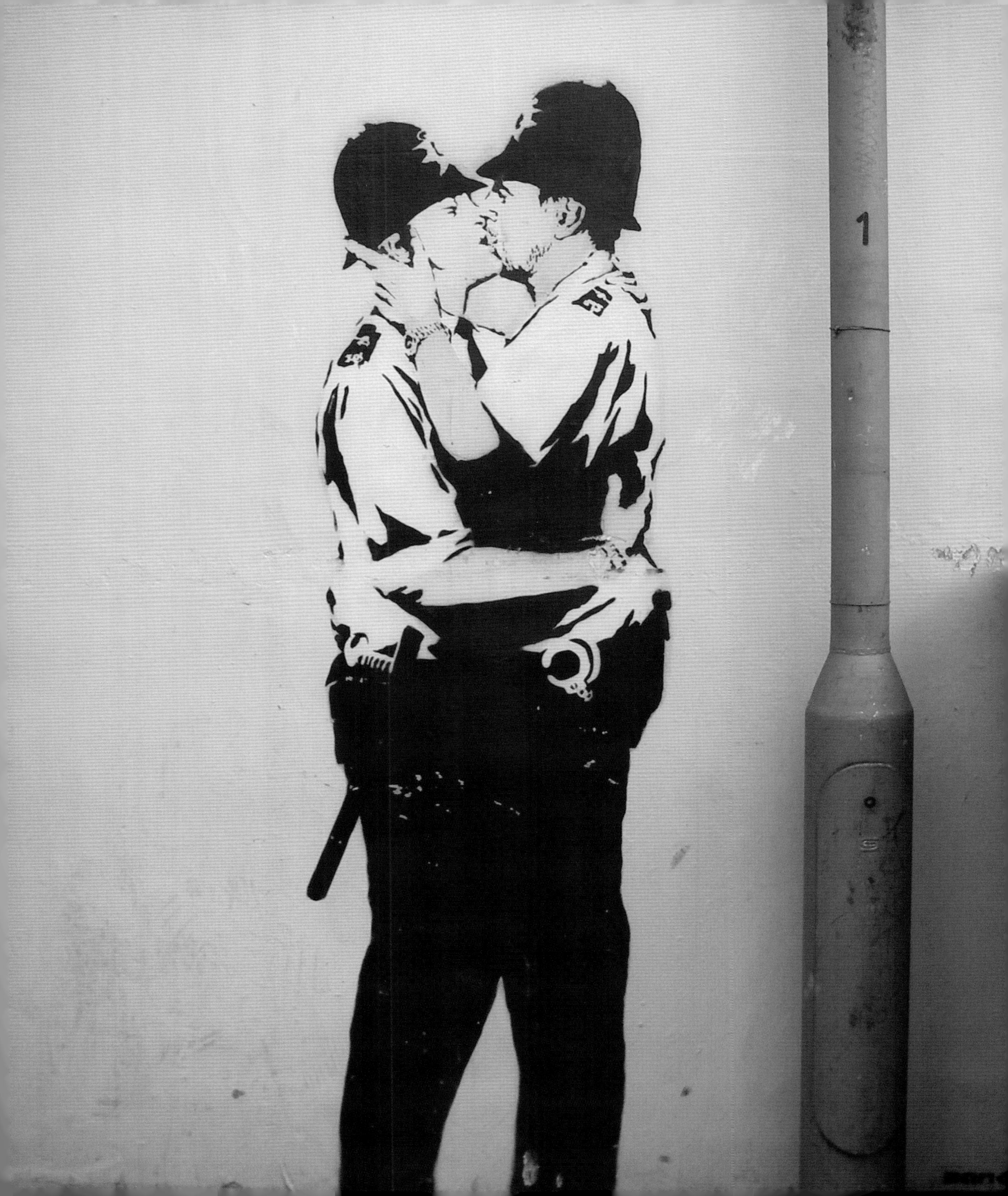

1

THUG FOR LIFE BUNNY

"You could stick all my shit in Tate Modern and have an opening with Kate Moss on rollerblades handing out vol-au-vents and it wouldn't be as exciting as when you go out and paint something big where you shouldn't."
Banksy, interviewed in *The Guardian*.

There aren't that many cartoon characters in Banksy's work. This, painted under a railway bridge in east London, seems to depict a blingy hip-hop musician, really smug and pleased with himself. Somehow the positioning under the light, suggesting that a thought has just come into the bunny's head, adds to the sense that this bunny is slightly stupid.

Another reading is that east London will always have its share of gangsters. With his gold chain, rings on his forefingers and cigar, there's more than an echo of the infamous Kray twins. Around the corner where this was painted is The Carpenter's Arms, once owned by Reggie and Ronnie Kray, where legend has it that the bar was made from coffin lids.

It isn't Banksy's best and the piece has now been painted over, perhaps because no property developer in this rapidly yuppifying part of London could make use of it – given its position under a bridge – to sell hipster flats to bankers.

WHERE IS IT ?
CLERKENWELL,
LONDON,
UK.
HAS BEEN PAINTED OVER.

Latitude: 51.5261ºN
Longitude: 0.0807ºW

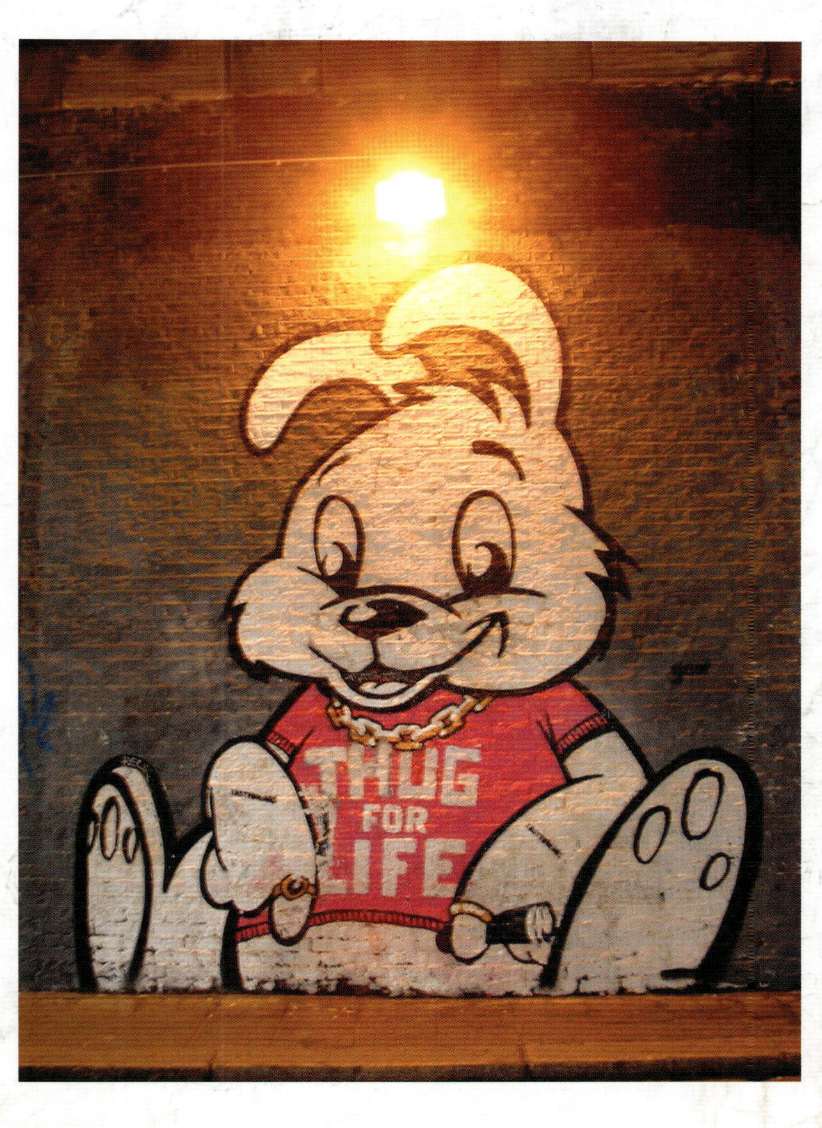

TOURIST INFORMATION

"Banksy feels an affinity with people who provide content for free on street corners." Village Voice.

This relatively early Banksy piece either shows remarkable prescience (that is, in the future power street art developed to draw visitors), Banksy's own potential to attract attention, or London's nascent reputation for seeing great works on the street, or of course all three. It's a great example of a work which has acquired more meaning over time: the sheer power of Banksy to draw visitors was proved again by *Dismaland* in 2015 (see page 208), which, with only a six week run, was completely sold out and drew over 150,000 Banksy 'tourists' and, in local tourist authority jargon, contributed over £20 million to the local economy of Weston-super-Mare.

At the time of creation of course, the piece would have been heavily ironic. Street artists in hoodies were figures of fear, chased by the police. The last thing this figure wants to tell you about is where they will commit their next street art 'crime'. He's got his headphones plugged in. He's anti-establishment. He's completely uninterested in you, and as far from the banality of city authority marketing as you can get.

Wind forwards a decade, and banality, you could argue, has won. That is if the text on www.visitlondon.com is anything to go by: "London is full of interesting urban art, from Banksy pieces to works by undiscovered artists." Undiscovered? As if. Bristol is even worse: "Bristol is also where Banksy hails from; the elusive graffiti artist extraordinaire has an enormous collection of artistic works featured on the streets......for the largest and most diverse selection...join a street walking tour...for an insider's guide." This is the world turned inside-out: tourists can become insiders, street art 'crimes' are sanctified by walking tours, and you might well ask the figure on the right for some visiting tips. Anyone want to analyse the authenticity in all this?

WHERE IS IT ?
TOWER HAMLETS,
LONDON,
UK.

Latitude: 51.5296ºN
Longitude: 0.0709ºW

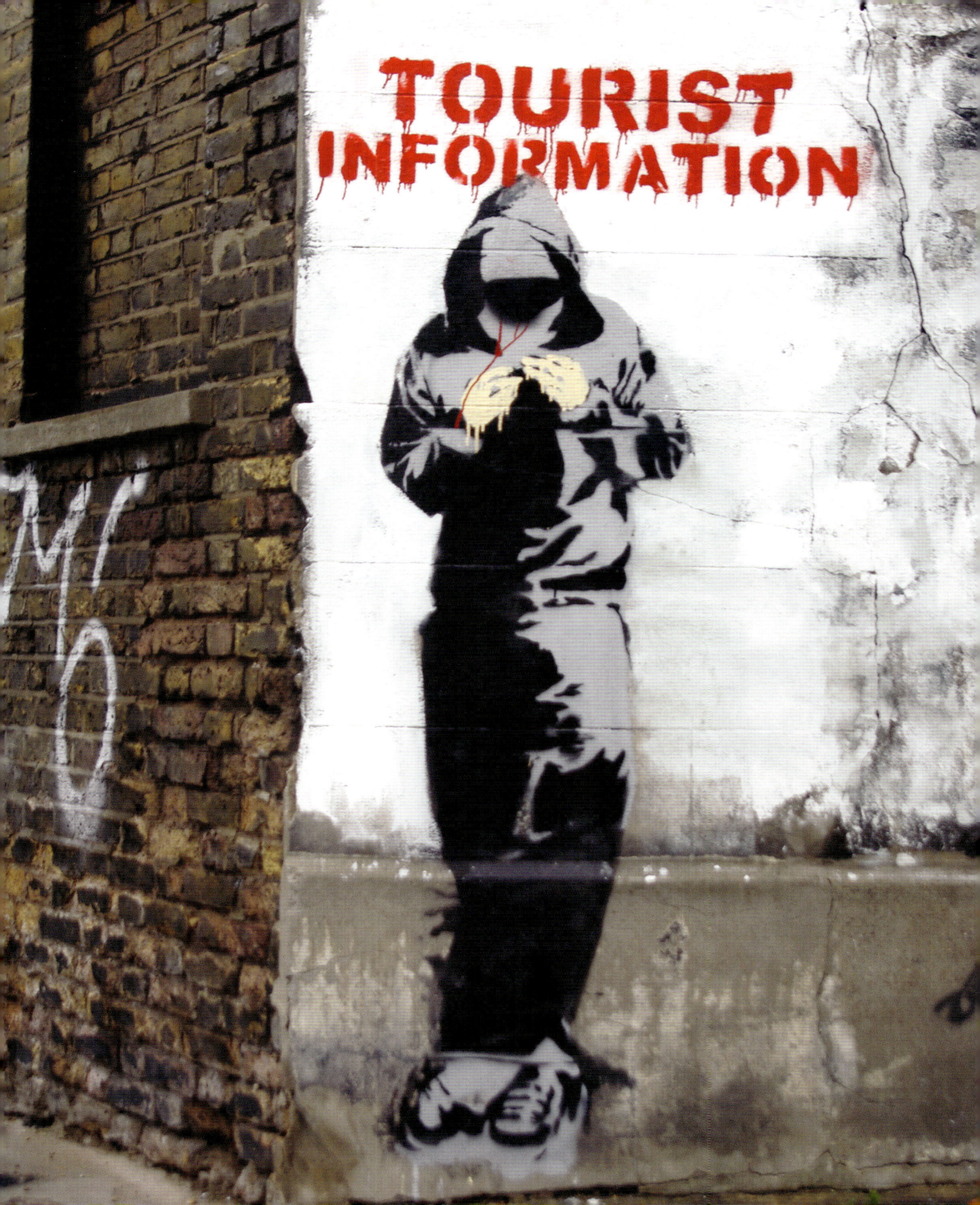

TOURIST
INFORMATION

THIS IS NOT A PHOTO OPPORTUNITY

"Tourism is not a spectator sport." Banksy, *Wall and Piece.*

The Cheddar Gorge is in an area of Outstanding Natural Beauty and a Site of Special Scientifc Interest in Somerset, a county on the doorstep of Banksy's home town of Bristol. Half a million tourists flock there every year and stop to take pictures. It's a West Country holiday cliché.

The 'defacing' of the rock, was the first outing for what has become one of Banksy's most famous catch phrases. Banksy uses the tone of officialese to instruct the viewer that what they are looking at is *not* interesting. The effectiveness of the stencil is to place it at the point of maximum photo op. And it has become a challenge. Where a smart phone or camera would in the past be pointed, in this case, at the view, it is now much more likely to capture the Banksy. What is not a photo opportunity now is, because it tells us it is not. Banksy is the photo op.

So Banksy emerges not just as a master of the stencil, but a master of the turn of phrase, pricker of human cliché, maestro of the situation. The mind-play is brilliant and, over time, it has also succeeded in becoming its own cliché.

Easy to replicate, many stencils of the phrase have appeared, some by Banksy, many not. One stencilled across the river from the Houses of Parliament is authentic, a perfect comment on the quality, or not, of the members within.

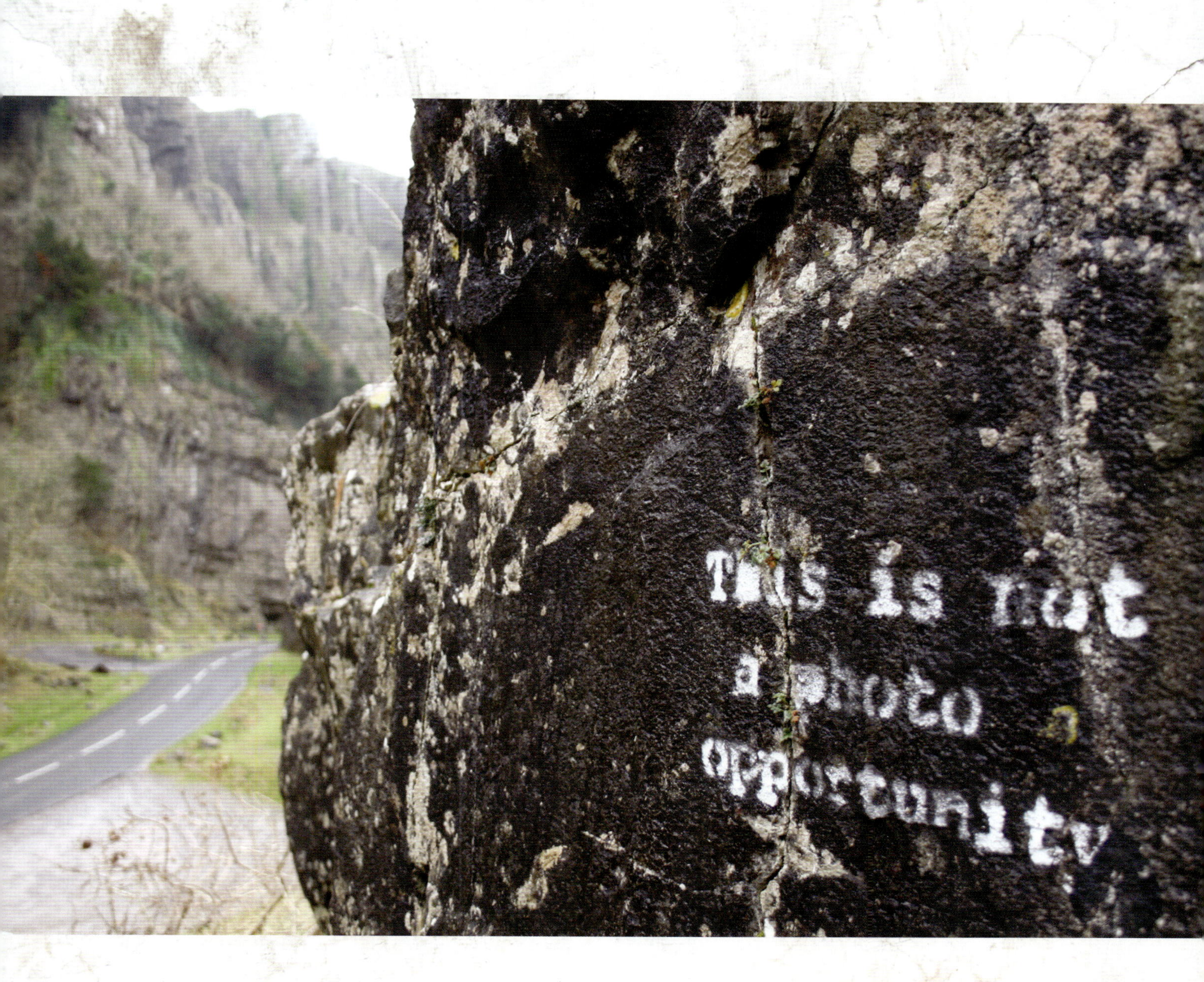
This is not
a photo
opportunity

WHAT ARE YOU LOOKING AT?

"My anxiety is that we don't sleepwalk into a surveillance society."
Richard Thomas, UK Information Commissioner, interview in _The Times_.

Without any public discussion or democratic debate, the UK became the most surveilled nation on Earth at the turn of the 21st century. Retail outlets, streets, private addresses, railway stations, underground stations, buses, taxis... pretty much everywhere. There was no need to seek permission to set up a security camera and the police in particular decided this was where they were going to spend money.

Banksy has always had a good nose for authoritarian power-grabs. The oppressive nature of constant surveillance which crept up on the British people by stealth was always going to be a ripe subject for him. The piece works on a number of counts. Firstly this is a ridiculous camera, staring at a blank wall; the guy who was monitoring it on screen must have been so bored. It could be read as an indignant, aggressive question, as in "What the hell do _you_ think _you're_ looking at?!" But instead Banksy makes it a flat question, which does show up the surveillors for the idiots they are. It could almost be taken as a philosophical question – the surveillance met by a question, rather than any answers.

The piece was created before the Islamist extremist terrorist attacks on London of 7/7, before the appalling attacks on Paris and Brussels in 2015 and 2016. The mood was different then, more ballsy, more anti-establishment. The amount of surveillance of everyone's communications permitted by law in 2016, makes this seem like surveillance from a less tense time. That all this surveillance did nothing to stop these terrorist attacks is an irony that hasn't gone unnoticed.

The tedious authorities of course painted this piece over, despite its wit and elegance. They also quietly removed the very stupidly placed camera. Game, set and match: Banksy.

WHERE IS IT ?
MARBLE ARCH STATION,
LONDON,
UK.
HAS BEEN PAINTED OVER AND THE SECURITY
CAMERA HAS ALSO BEEN REMOVED.

Latitude: 51.5134ºN
Longitude: 0.1589ºW

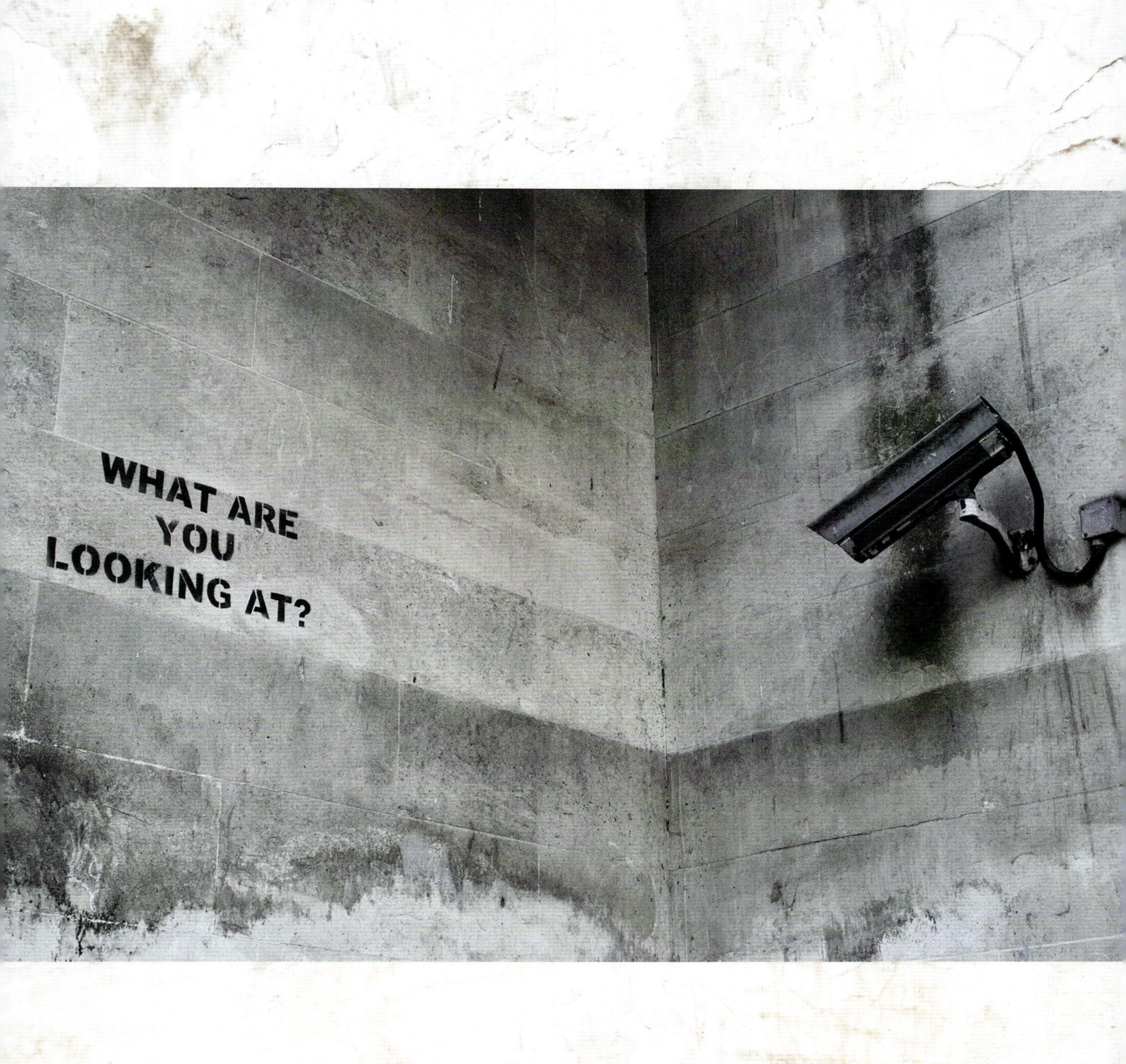
WHAT ARE
YOU
LOOKING AT?

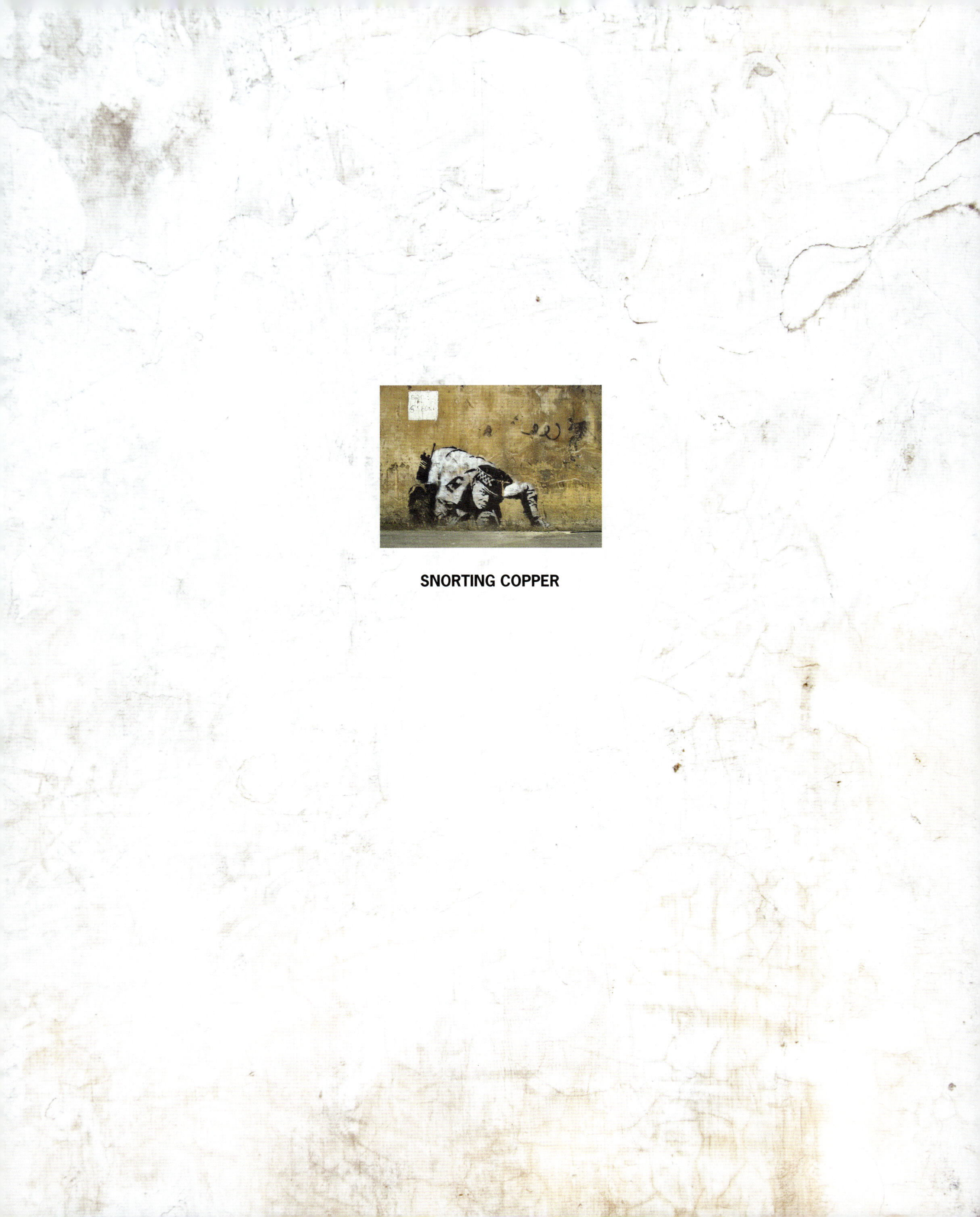

SNORTING COPPER

2005-2006

Banksy is starting to become a significant figure in the UK. *The Guardian* in particular latched onto him. His works are sought out by London hipsters. The themes of surveillance and druggy cops are continued in his work. The biggest shift in 2005 is his Guantanamo stint at Disneyland in California, which hugely raises his profile in the US. Now Hollywood A-listers start collecting him. Back in London he creates the image that was later to achieve his then all-time highest sale price, *Keeping it Spotless*, with Damien Hirst. It would remain his most expensive work until *Devolved Parliament* in 2019.

UP PERISCOPE

GUANTANAMO

PHOTOGRAPHER RAT

THUG FOR LIFE

SNORTING COPPER

BALLOON DEBATE

BOY AT THE BEACH

WELL HUNG LOVER

SWEEPING IT UNDER THE CARPET

GRAFFITI REMOVAL HOTLINE

NO MORE HEROES

I'M OUT OF BED AND DRESSED

BANKSY 2005-2006

This is the period when Banksy's work steps up several gears and becomes truly international. Banksy creates significant works in London, his very influential series along the West Bank Wall and in Los Angeles.

More museum interventions take place in 2005 – at the Louvre in Paris and at the Metropolitan, Brooklyn, MOMA and Natural History museums in New York.

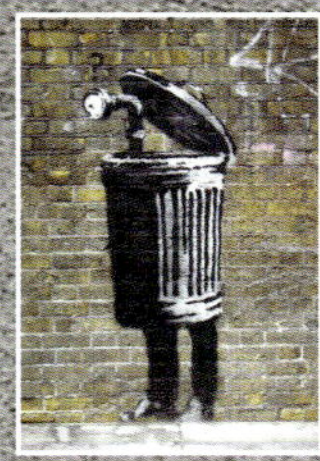

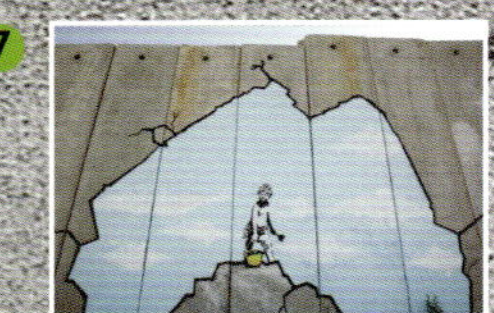

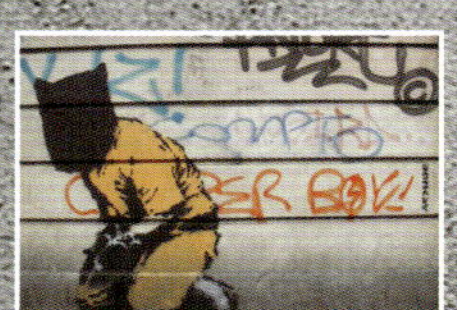

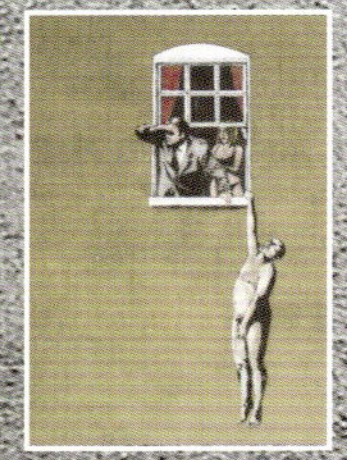

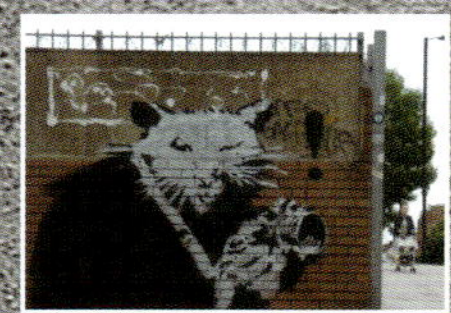

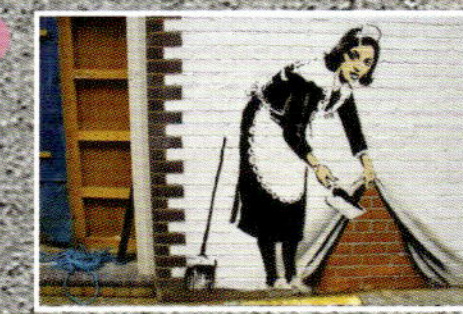

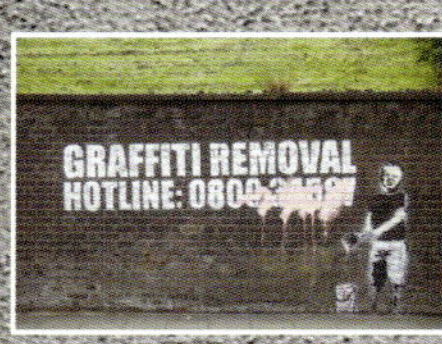

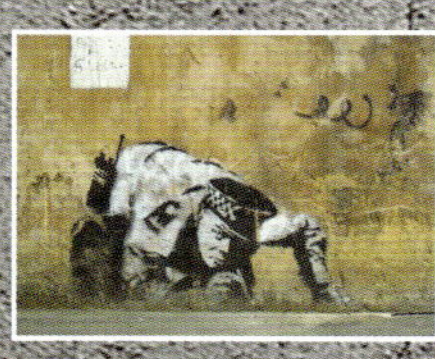

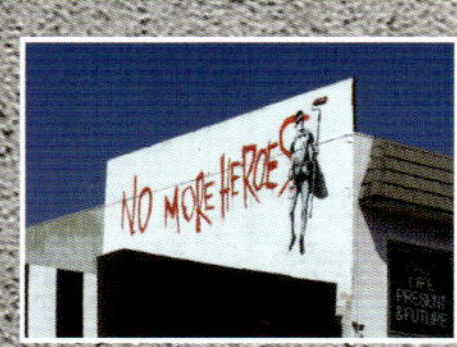

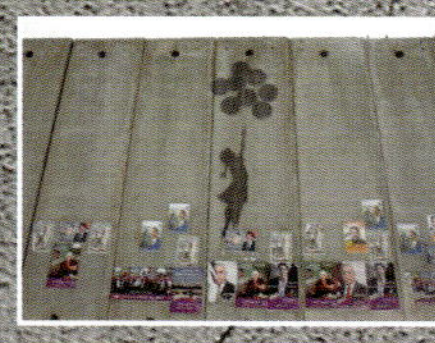

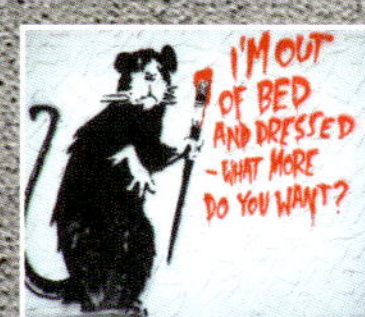

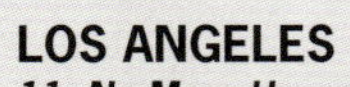

LOS ANGELES

11. No More Heroes, Melrose Avenue.

12. I'm Out of Bed and Dressed, Melrose Avenue.

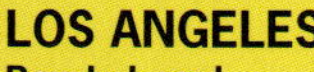

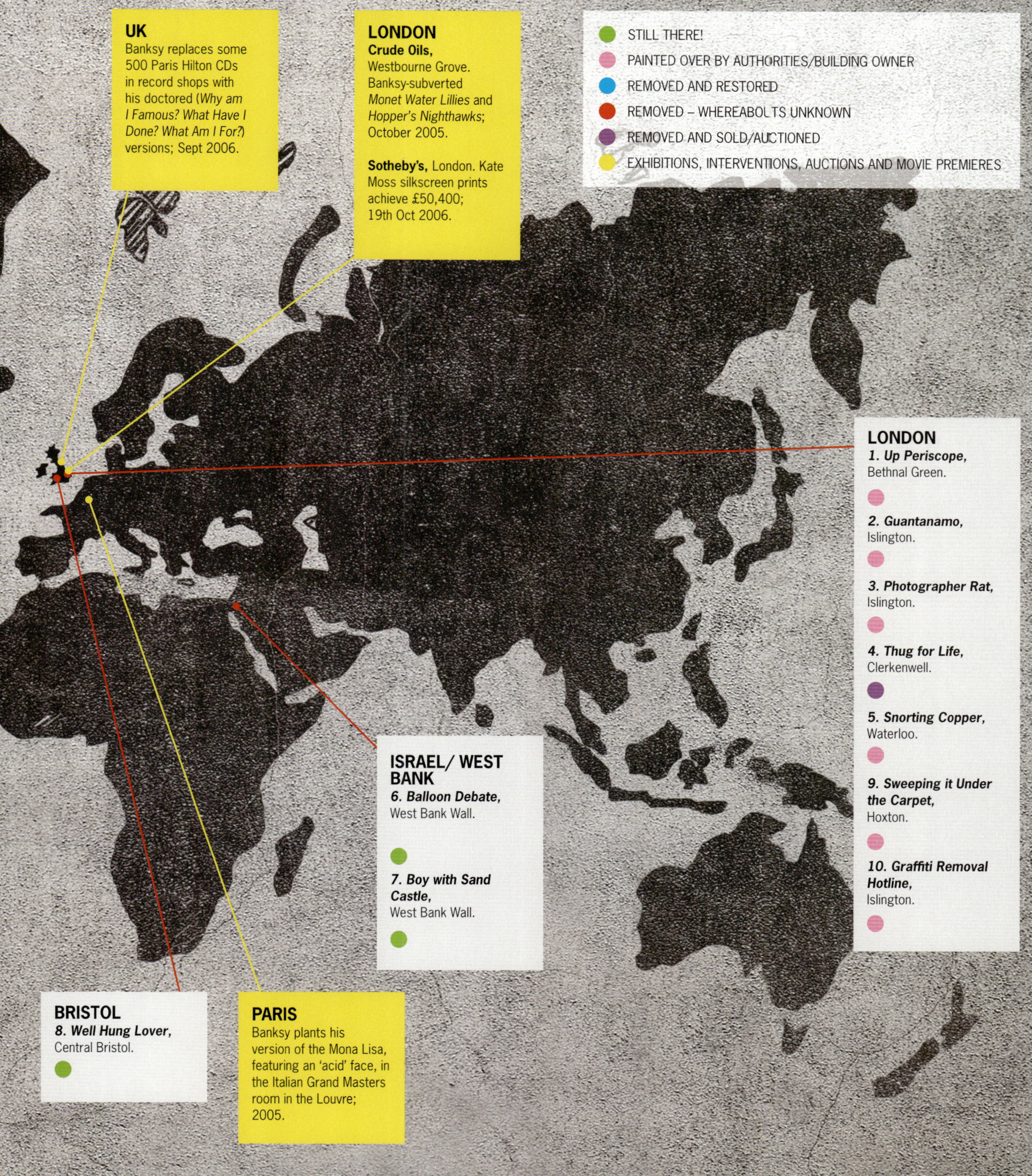

UK
Banksy replaces some 500 Paris Hilton CDs in record shops with his doctored (Why am I Famous? What Have I Done? What Am I For?) versions; Sept 2006.

LONDON
Crude Oils, Westbourne Grove. Banksy-subverted Monet Water Lillies and Hopper's Nighthawks; October 2005.

Sotheby's, London. Kate Moss silkscreen prints achieve £50,400; 19th Oct 2006.

STILL THERE!
PAINTED OVER BY AUTHORITIES/BUILDING OWNER
REMOVED AND RESTORED
REMOVED – WHEREABOLTS UNKNOWN
REMOVED AND SOLD/AUCTIONED
EXHIBITIONS, INTERVENTIONS, AUCTIONS AND MOVIE PREMIERES

LONDON
1. Up Periscope, Bethnal Green.

2. Guantanamo, Islington.

3. Photographer Rat, Islington.

4. Thug for Life, Clerkenwell.

5. Snorting Copper, Waterloo.

9. Sweeping it Under the Carpet, Hoxton.

10. Graffiti Removal Hotline, Islington.

ISRAEL/ WEST BANK
6. Balloon Debate, West Bank Wall.

7. Boy with Sand Castle, West Bank Wall.

BRISTOL
8. Well Hung Lover, Central Bristol.

PARIS
Banksy plants his version of the Mona Lisa, featuring an 'acid' face, in the Italian Grand Masters room in the Louvre; 2005.

UP PERISCOPE

"If you have nothing to hide, you have nothing to fear."
Richard Graham, Tory MP for Gloucester, UK.
The phrase was also used by Joseph Goebbels, Nazi minister of propaganda.

Increasing surveillance in the UK has been a consistent concern of Banksy's and has inspired some of his most memorable work. This piece is in that vein. The idea of ubiquity, that you might be filmed from something as everyday and mundane as a dustbin, is the message. The dustbin is a standard galvanised steel British one, now slightly retro as the march of plastic advances. Coming out of it is something akin to a periscope, with an eye-ball seemingly in place of a lens. Hidden inside is a spy who can check you out, follow you, and then, just before you turn, can squat, the lid can come down and you would be none the wiser. It's all got a touch of *Chitty Chitty Bang Bang* or of a 1940s Ealing comedy.

This piece has particular resonance in a British context, where local councils were caught using anti-terrorism legislation to spy on residents and their bin habits. Those who did not put out the right sort of recycling on the right day were filmed and then received letters in the post, with heavy fines.

Surveillance really is rubbish.

WHERE IS IT ?
BETHNAL GREEN,
LONDON,
UK.

Latitude: 51.5319ºN
Longitude: 0.1075ºW

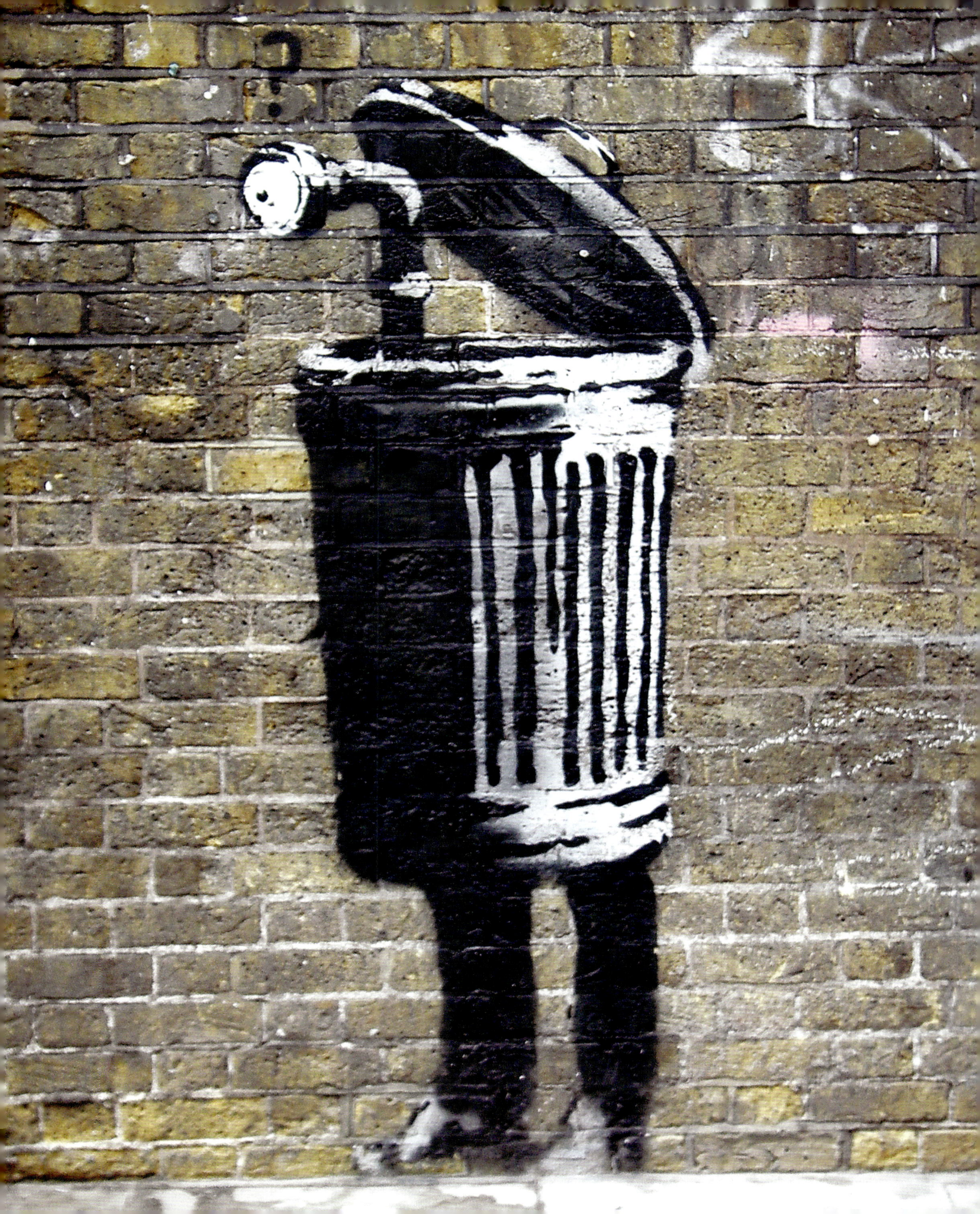

GUANTANAMO

"It gives us a very, very bad name, not just internationally."
James A. Baker III, former US Secretary of State, *LA Times*.

The Guantanamo Bay Detention Camp was set up by Secretary of Defense Donald Rumsfeld in 2002 in US Guantanamo Bay Naval Base in Cuba. Bizarre that it's on Cuban soil, but it is the oldest US overseas naval base, and has been 'leased' since 1903, notwithstanding that, since the Cuban revolution in 1959, the Cuban government has deemed it illegal under international law.

The base has been used to detain 'unlawful combatants' – suspected Islamist terrorists and militants – captured in Afghanistan and Iraq during the US's post-9/11 War on Terror. Inmates, of whom there were eventually 779, were held without charge and without the legal means to challenge their detentions. US President George W. Bush maintained that, as the base was not on US territory, the US government was not required to observe the Geneva Conventions regarding POWs. The US government was condemned for its stance by Amnesty International, Human Rights Watch, the EU and the Organization of American States. In 2006 the US Supreme Court ruled that the military commissions used to try detainees was a violation of their rights. In 2008 the Court also declared that detainees did have the right to challenge their detentions in US federal courts.

Banksy created this piece before the Supreme Court ruling and at the height of revulsion at the injustice of US actions from millions around the world, a revulsion he clearly shared. The daily parade of prisoners, who were filmed handcuffed in orange boiler suits, with black hoods over their heads, for all the world to see, provided a potent image of the plight of the prisoners. Banksy used the same stance, which also has the suggestion of supplication, for the viewer to do something. Placed on a busy shopping street in north London, the image had huge power to shock, was a call to act and a searing shaming of the US.

In September 2006 Banksy targeted Disneyland, California, where he managed to sneak a life-sized inflatable doll, dressed in Guantanamo garb, complete with handcuffs, into the Thunder Mountain Railroad ride. Given Disney's tight security, this was risky (prospect of arrest under terrorist legislation) and a real achievement. The doll stayed there for over an hour before Disney officials realised, and shut the ride in order to remove it. The stunt got huge global attention. Mission Accomplished.

WHERE IS IT ?
ISLINGTON,
LONDON,
UK.
THE IMAGE HAS SINCE BEEN BUFFED.

Latitude: 51.5326ºN
Longitude: 0.1059ºW

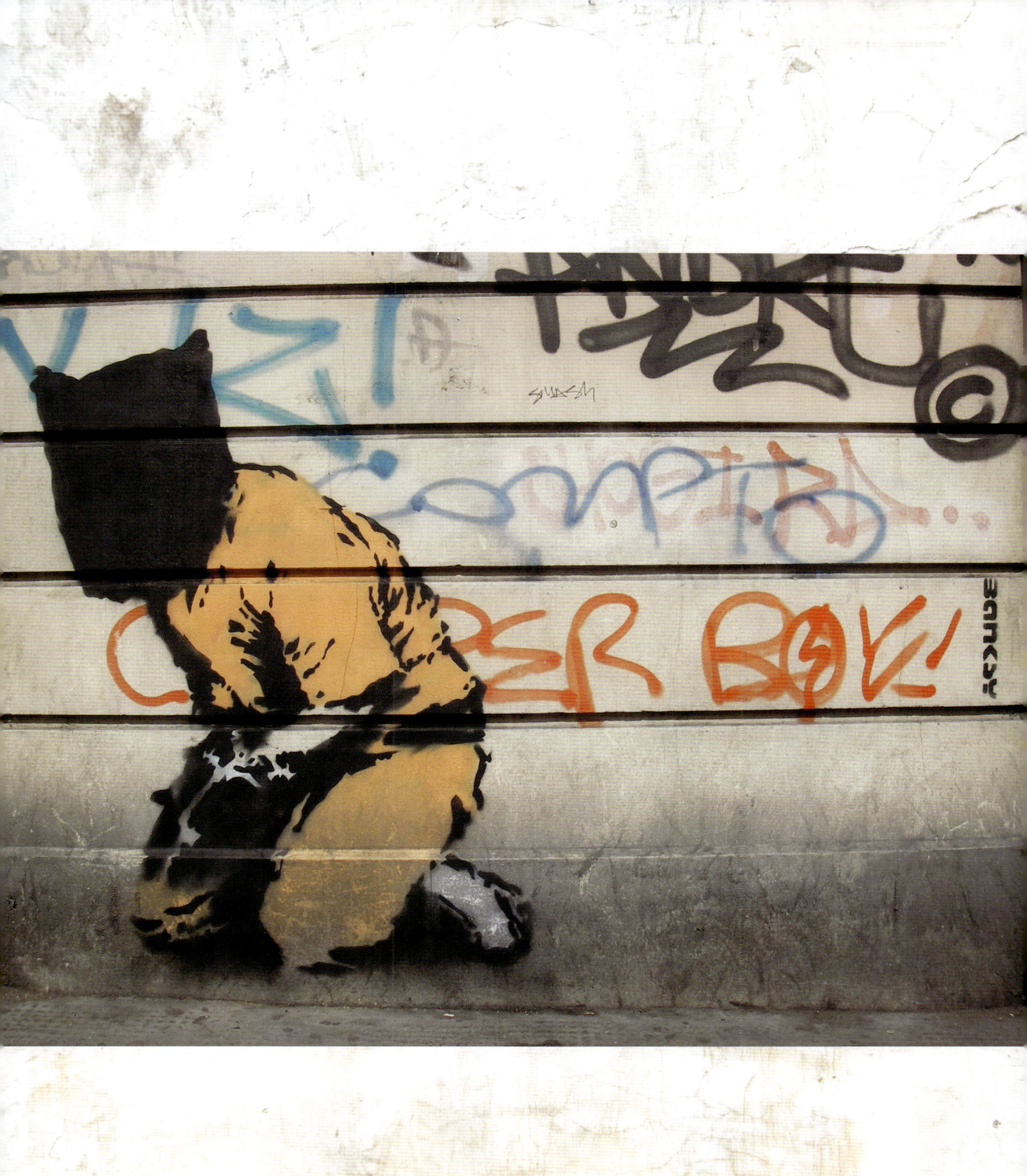
SMASH
BANKSY

PHOTOGRAPHER RAT

"Rats are a good role model...they have no respect for the hierarchy of society and they have sex 50 times a day." Banksy.

A larger than usual rat from Banksy, holding what looks like a Nikon SLR, with shoulder strap, one eye shut, as though he has just taken an image of the viewer. Banksy has declared his debt to veteran French street artist Xavier Prou, a.k.a. Blek Le Rat, who stencilled rats coming in from the outer suburbs to inhabit the bijou centre of the city, "because rats are the only wild animals living in cities, and only rats will survive when the human race dies out and disappears."

With Banksy, the rat almost becomes synonymous with the street artist, considered vermin, yet there under the surface (they say you're only ever a few yards from a rat), ready to come out at night, and cleverer, more resilient and more devious than the average human.

Here the rat is reversing roles. He looks at the viewer with a "gotcha" expression, as though the human is the unexpected pestilence. This one is rather more human than Banksy's other rats, not least his large, bulky silhouette and hunched shoulders. This is a sinister, evidence-collecting rat, the sort of rat who delights in skewering his errant victims.

WHERE IS IT ?
ISLINGTON,
LONDON,
UK.

Latitude: 51.5306ºN
Longitude: 0.1010ºW

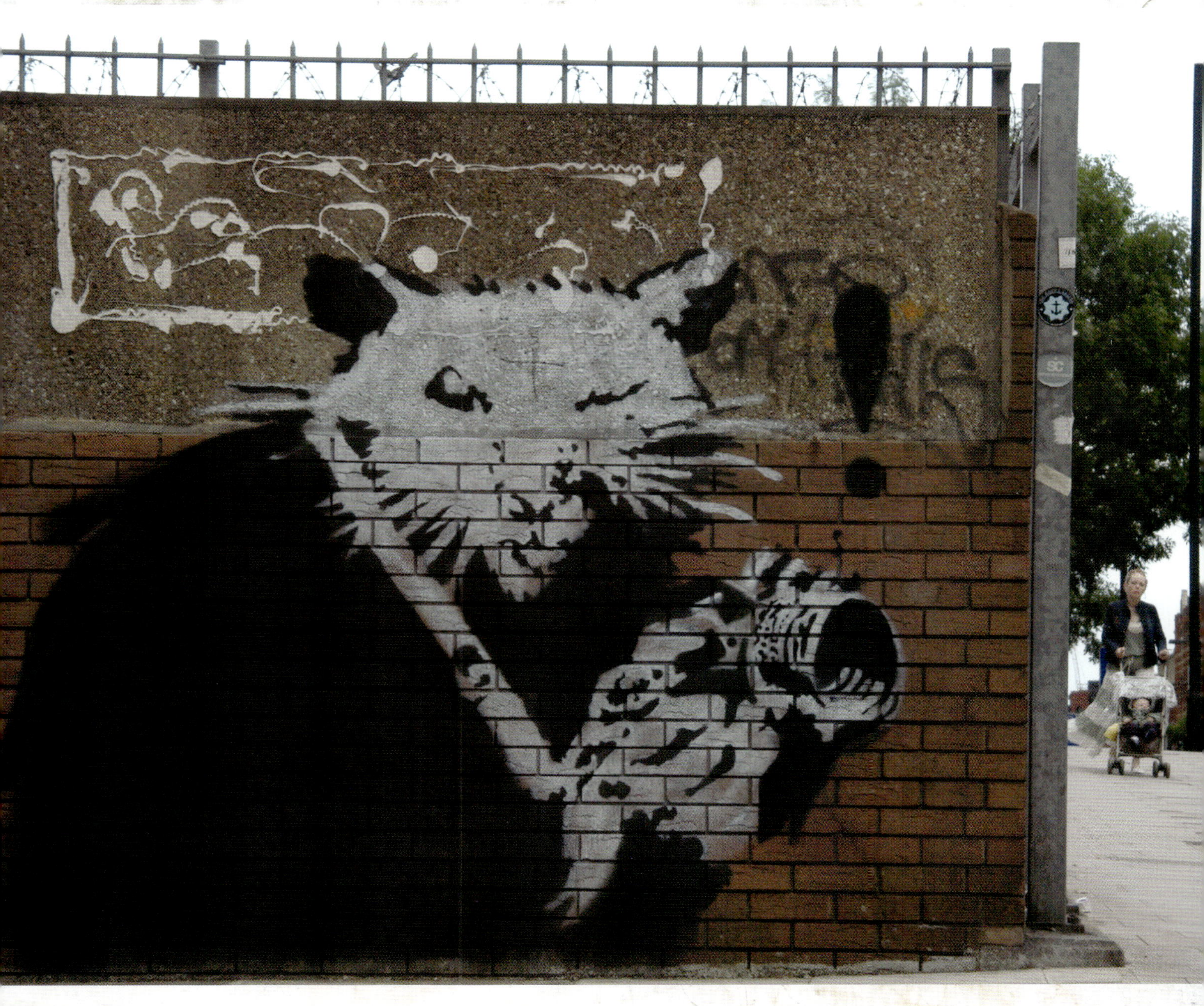

THUG FOR LIFE

"*I plead not guilty to selling out. But I plead it from a bigger house than I used to live in.*" Banksy, interviewed by *Time Out.*

Four pensioners still behaving disgracefully, living up to the title of this piece. Banksy seems to be celebrating their spirit and perhaps this is a declaration of intent, Banksy and three of his friends declaring that fifty years hence they will still be adding stencils to walls?

There's a bit of a hip-hop theme going on here. The figure on the left has a $ belt; the one middle left a bit of bling around his neck and a ghetto blaster; the one middle right perhaps smoking what might be a spliff; the far right figure a reversed baseball cap.

Extra interest is added by the fact that these are clearly guys in old women's drag. We've got old ladies' glasses with the wheely bag, curlers in hair and old ladies' raincoat in the middle and the zimmer frame on the right. OK, so that last one isn't in drag: perhaps this is a Banksy self-portrait?

When the building which featured this was repainted, the owners thoughtfully painted around it. The original slogan was subsequently painted out and replaced with 'Old Skool'. We don't know whether this was Banksy or another street artist. If Banksy, it's hard to escape the idea that this is a group portrait of Banksy with some Bristol school chums, as well as a comment on their advancing years.

WHERE IS IT ?
CLERKENWELL,
LONDON.
HAS BEEN BUFFED.

Latitude: 51.5228ºN
Longitude: 0.1038ºW

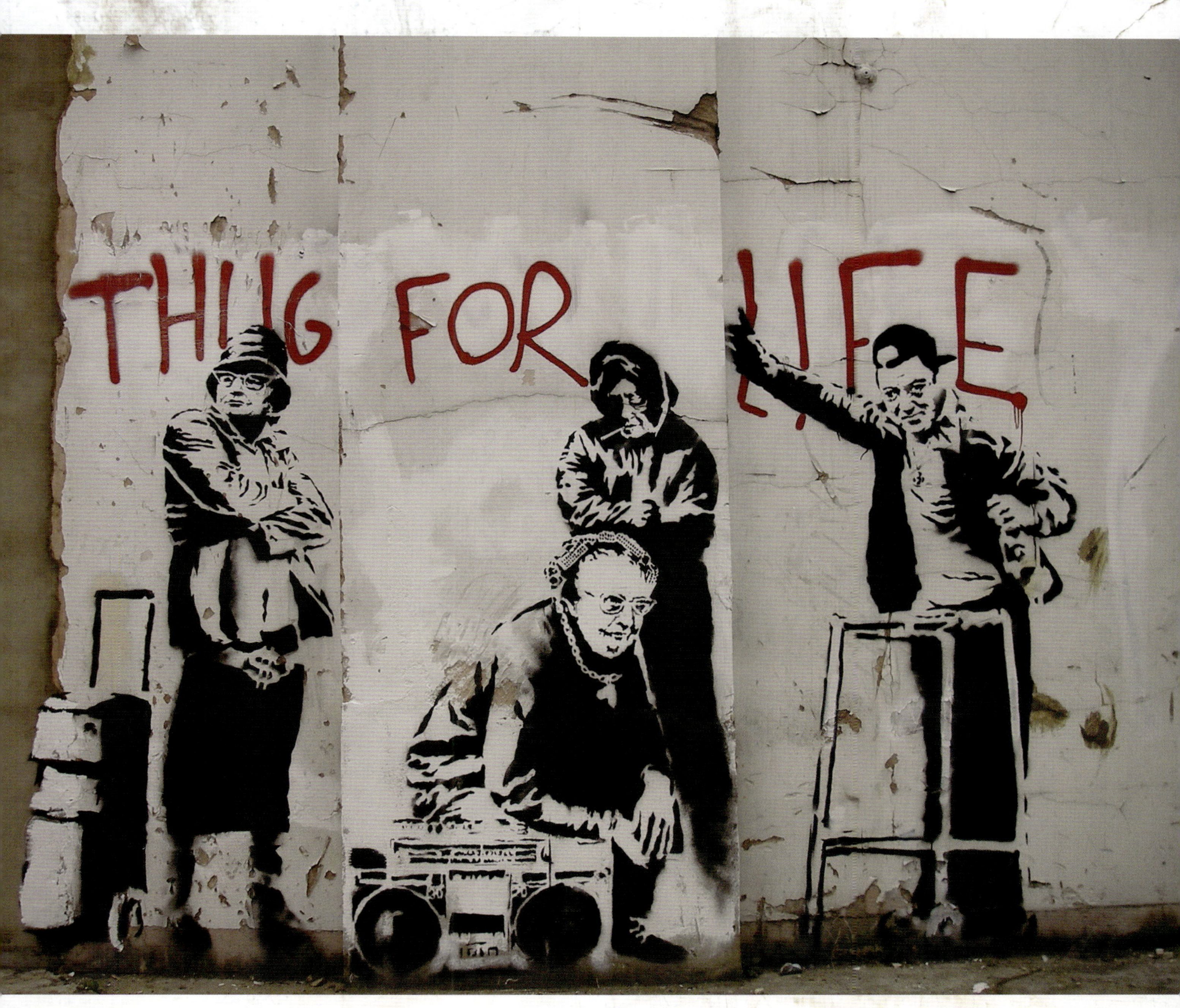
THUG FOR LIFE

SNORTING COPPER

"My main problem with cops is that they do what they're told. They say 'sorry mate, I'm just doing my job' all the fucking time."
Banksy, *Banging Your Head Against a Brick Wall*.

A brilliant situationist piece, mining Banksy's rich vein of policemen caught in compromised situations. The police are really some of the prime butts of Banksy's jokes, payback for all those times they hassled and nearly busted him as he stencilled his work. Here the officer is snorting a line of coke, represented by the dust on the pavement. He has the same puzzling expression of other Banksy cops – not too surprised, not too embarrassed, almost a "what are you going to do about it" look. It's the normality of it that makes it so funny, with a touch of the surreal.

This image appeared in various locations around London, including Leake Street in Waterloo and Curtain Road in Shoreditch, in 2005. One manifestation of it saw a long line of white paint, meandering through various streets, which led eventually to the cop's rolled bank note. The old-fashioned (and supposedly slighty useless) chunky radio of the era, now gives the piece a rather retro quality.

WHERE IS IT ?
WATERLOO,
LONDON,
UK.

Latitude: 51.5024ºN
Longitude: 0.1158ºW

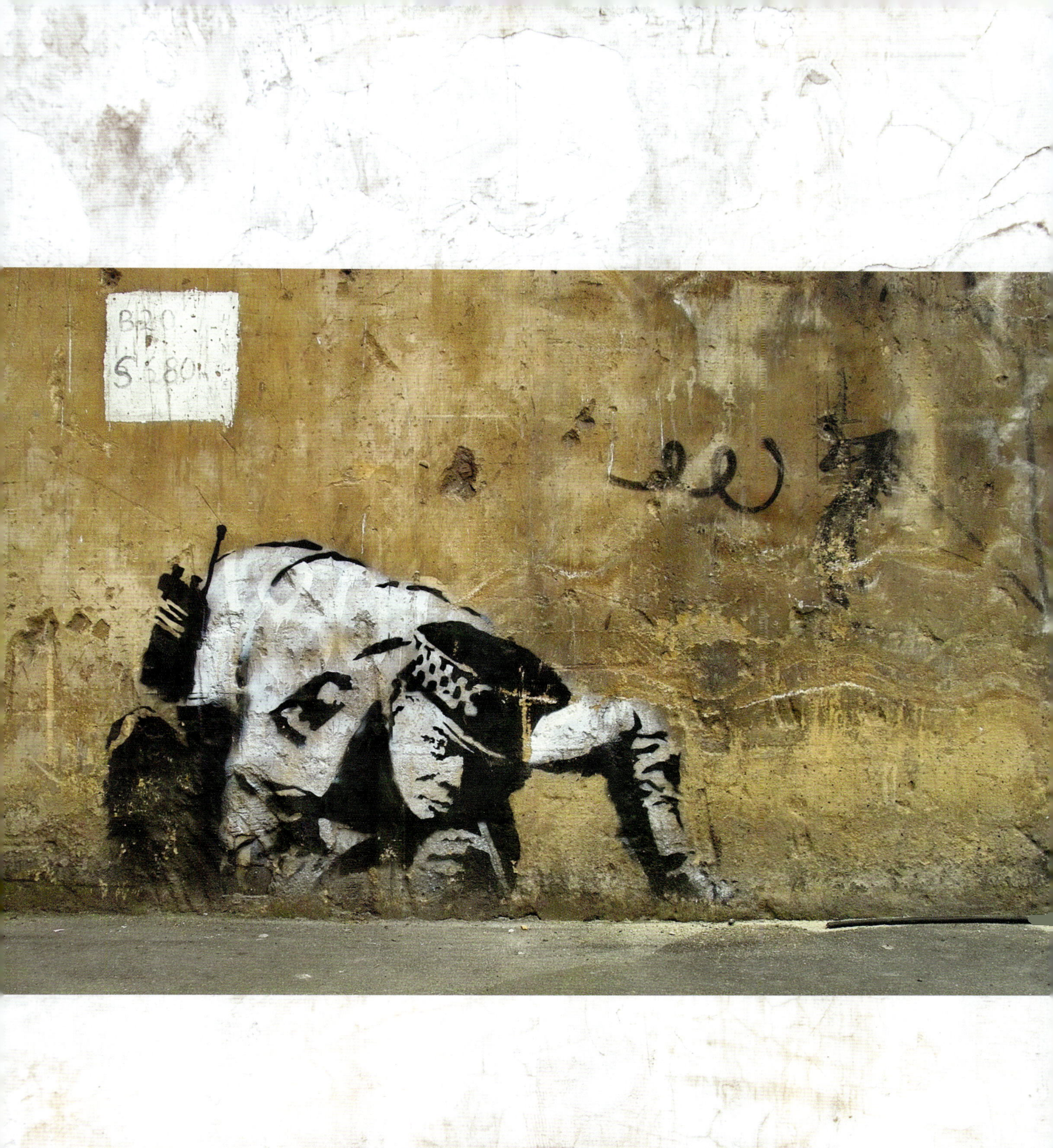

BALLOON DEBATE

"The construction of the wall, and its associated regime, are contrary to international law." International Court of Justice, 2004.

Euphemistically described as a 'separation fence' by the Israeli government, the West Bank Wall is, for much of its length, a 25-foot high brutalist concrete barrier, effectively a cage, running for 430 miles (700 km), very roughly along the Jordanian-Israeli 1949 ceasefire line (the 'Green Line'), built between 2000 and 2014. The wall was built to reduce the incidence of suicide bombings, but had the effect of making life very difficult for around 30,000 Palestinians, isolated on the Israeli side of the wall, and trapping 124,000 on the Palestinian side. The wall has had a devastating impact on ordinary Palestinians, separating families, cutting them off from all-important wells (now on the Israeli side), and destroying farmers' livelihoods (the wall is built on some of the most fertile Palestinian land and in many instances actually splits farms in two). In many places, where the Green Line for 'logistical reasons' could not be followed, the authorities simply appropriated Palestinian land. Where existing Palestinian shops or buildings were in the way of the wall, they were demolished. Most of all the wall is a daily, oppressive humiliation, with military checkpoints which can take many hours to get through, armed watchtowers and patrols. The net effect is to make the Palestinians feel like a caged people.

Instead of getting mired in political debate, Banksy created a series of nine searing images on the Wall, of which this is one. The stencil of a little girl dreaming of being carried up to freedom is all that needs to be said about the oppressiveness of this construction. The sense of weightlessness of the image emphasises the contrasting reality – the heavy weight of imprisonment. That this is being done to children is utterly hideous, the piece implies.

It took enormous bravery on the part of Banksy to get his images onto the Wall. As he did so, Israeli security forces shot live rounds threateningly into the air, and pointed guns at him to scare him off. As a symbol of solidarity with the Palestinian cause, Banksy's work has proved so much more enduring than any number of statements from the International Court or the UN (whose resolutions with regards to Israel are in any case usually automatically vetoed by the US in the Security Council).

WHERE IS IT ?
WEST BANK WALL,
PALESTINIAN SIDE,
WEST BANK.

Latitude: 31.8624ºN
Longitude: 35.2273ºE

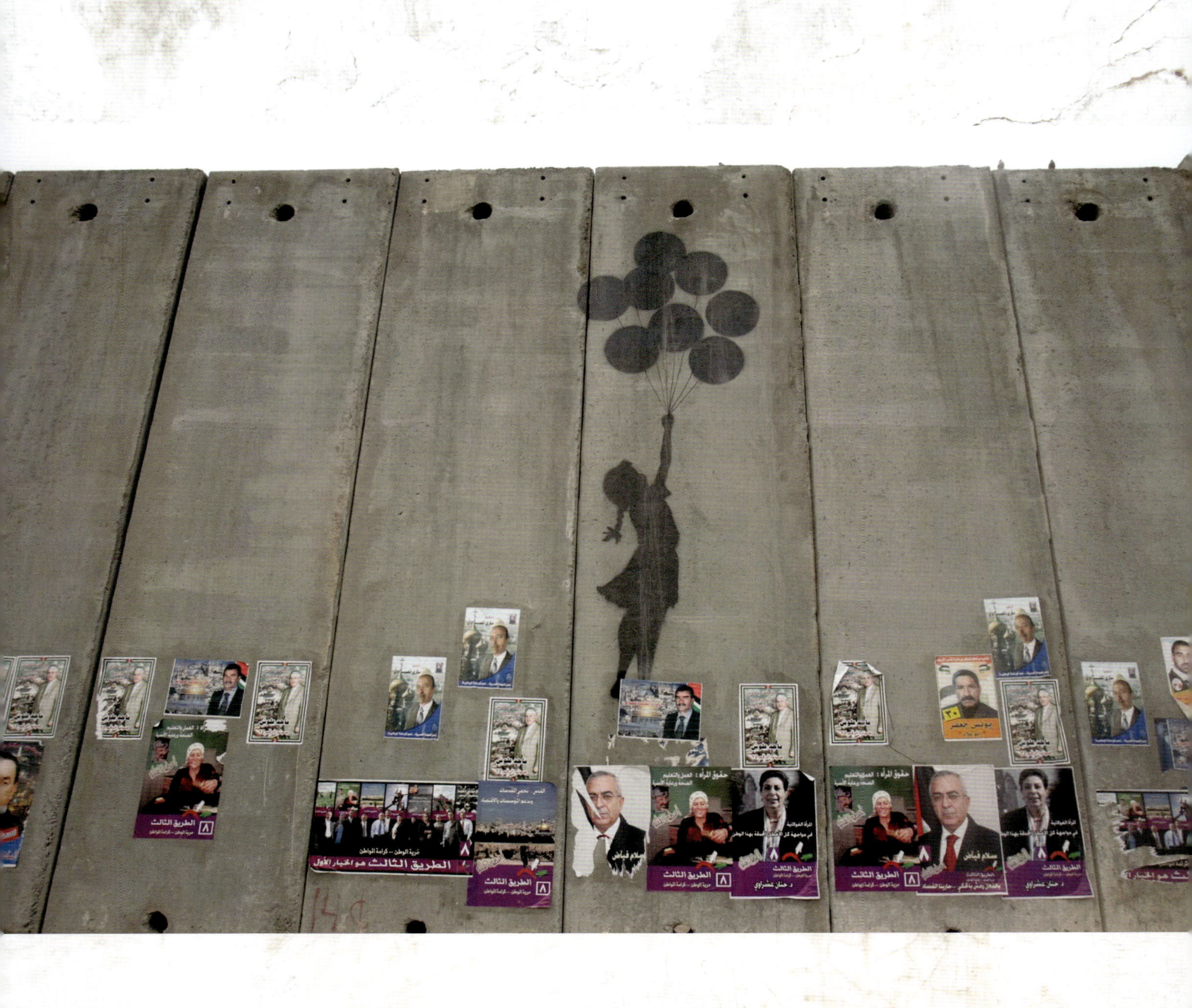

BOY AT THE BEACH

"A wall is a very big weapon. It's one of the nastiest things you can hit someone with." Banksy, *Banging Your Head Against a Brick Wall.*

All of Banksy's nine images from his 2005 visit to the West Bank, where he highlighted the inhuman nature of the West Bank Wall, have an extraordinary visual punch and live long in the memory.

This was one of four where Banksy created an idealised vision of a world where the Wall has been punched in. Against the brutalist concrete we have a scene of sheer optimism and charm. A perfect summer's day, with light fluffy clouds set against a sunny blue sky. Pictured atop a visual hillock, is a lad who could be eight or nine, enjoying the simplest of pleasures – building sand castles by the sea. He is stencilled in black and white, has a happy, determined face and is set off by his yellow sand bucket. This is a boy straight out of a perfect 1950s English childhood.

Nothing could be further from the reality of a Palestinian lad his own age. Encased and brutalised by the Wall, under effective military occupation, having to suffer the viciousness of an internecine conflict, he will have none of these freedoms. Banksy again makes his point by the force of the contrast, a contrast so stark it verges on the surreal, with sardonic overtones. What is brilliant about the image, however, is that it is aimed at Western eyes, using the brutal concrete wall as his canvas. It is saying, how can you allow your children this idyll and yet do nothing about what is happening here, an ostensibly civilized country? How can you put up with the contrast? How can some children be so blessed, whilst others are so abused? How can some children simply have no childhood?

Perhaps the fact that the image shows cracks appearing in the Wall, that it is beginning to collapse, is a sign of hope. Or is it saying, take the Wall down, break down barriers, and all this could be ours? Of course the politics of the Middle East don't make for such simple solutions, but by appealing to our better nature, Banksy is speaking very directly to Western political leaders – and specifically those in the US – effectively declaring: you've got to do something about the hideous injustice of the Israeli-Palestinian conflict.

WHERE IS IT ?
PALESTINIAN SIDE,
WEST BANK WALL,
WEST BANK.

Latitude: 31.9485ºN
Longitude: 35.3033ºE

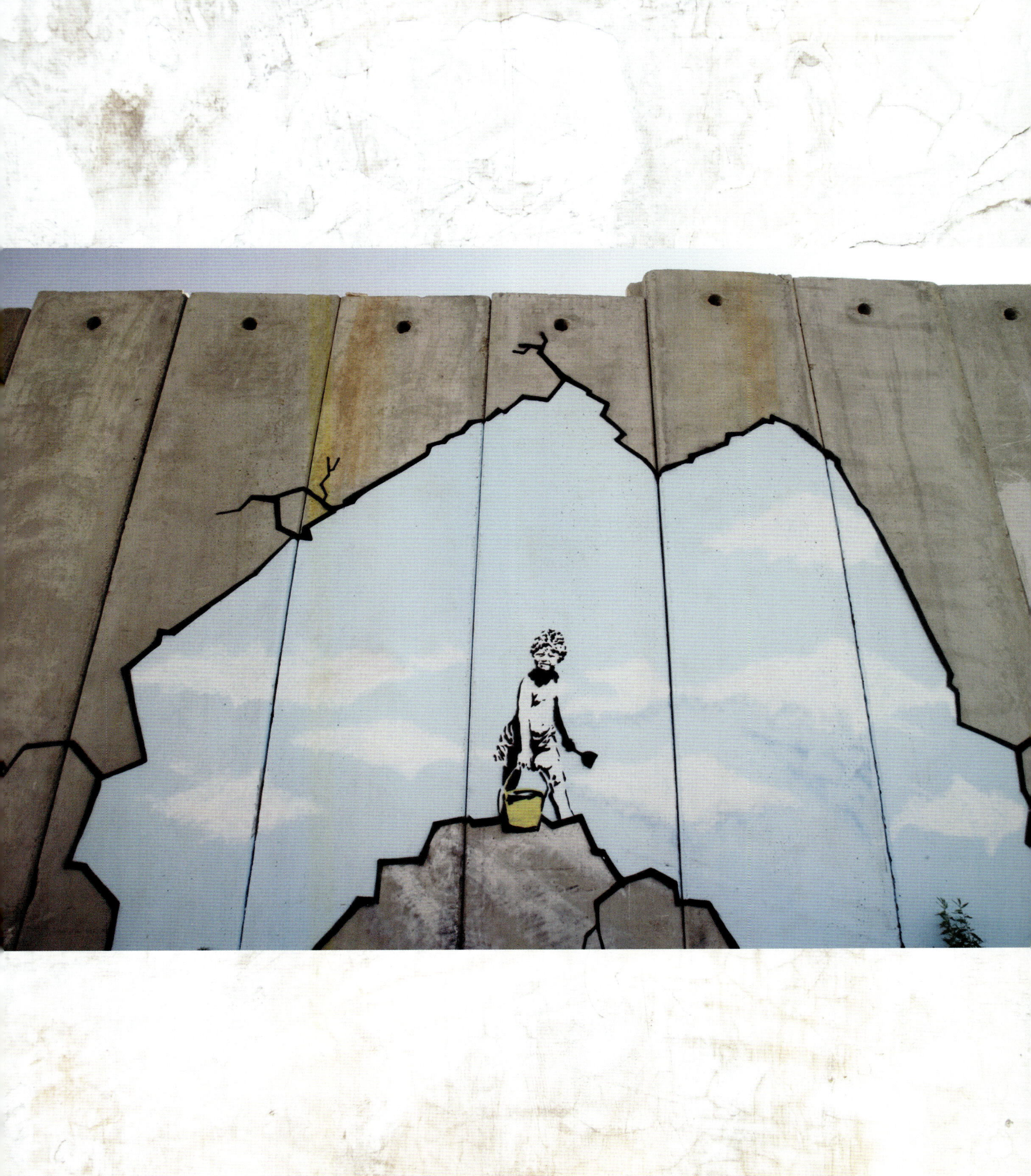

WELL HUNG LOVER

"Banksy didn't realise the building contained a sexually transmitted disease clinic." Manager, STD clinic, Bristol.

A brilliant Banksy in Bristol, with his signature tightly-packed image and word play. The piece appeared on the side of a building housing a clinic for treating sexually transmitted diseases. Banksy makes full use of the wall; his painted window, where there might well be one, lends the piece an added sense of realism.

We can't quite see whether the lover is well-hung, but he is hanging out, with all his middle-aged spread on show. The figure that's been hung-out to dry, metaphorically, is the suited corporate husband, seemingly taking action – "Where is he? Where is he?" – but in his self-important pompous way missing the blindingly obvious. His wife, in bra and knickers, is playing the faux innocent, with her hand on her husband's shoulder, a wonderfully 'supportive' gesture.

Just as Banksy loves tweaking the tail of authority figures, so here he is laughing at middle-class, middle-aged respectability. It makes this quite a rare piece in his oeuvre, but in its satirical humour, very typical.

Given the fact that Banksy didn't realise the building housed an STD clinic, the piece has acquired a hilarious, inadvertent faux-moral tone: "let this be a warning that STDs are as much a risk for respectable middle-aged couples as for any one else!" By chance, a report realised at around the same time revealed that many STDs were being contracted by this age group rather than randy youngsters.

Bristol City Council debated whether to have the piece buffed. They ran a referendum in 2010 asking local residents their opinion. 93% of those who responded elected to have it preserved.

WHERE IS IT ?
FROGMORE STREET, BRISTOL, UK.
HAS BEEN PRESERVED.

Latitude: 51.4545ºN
Longitude: 2.5854ºW

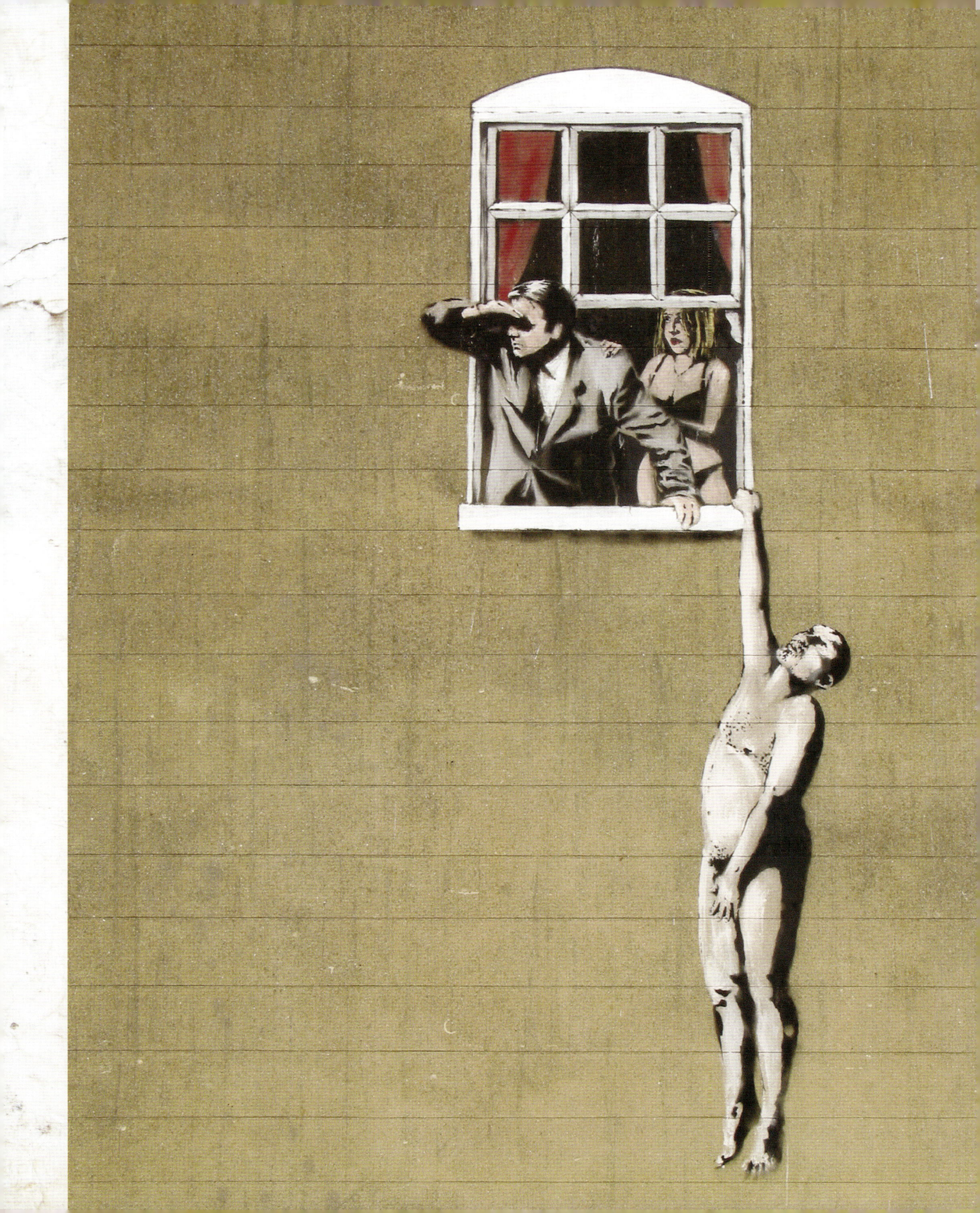

SWEEPING IT UNDER THE CARPET

"In the bad old days, it was only popes and princes who had the money for their portraits to be painted." Banksy on banksy.co.uk

When Banksy is assessed in a century's time as one of the defining artists of our age, this piece will come to be seen as perhaps the most iconic, encapsulating everything that defines the artist, street art in general, and the move of street art into the world's major galleries and auction houses.

Painted on the side of White Cube Gallery in Hoxton Square, east London, the image ostensibly depicts a maid, Leanne – "a quite feisty lady" – who once cleaned Banksy's room in an L.A. motel. Perhaps it's a likeness, but it looks to us as though Leanne is dressed in the uniform of an English Edwardian country house maid. In a brilliant conceit she is lifting the curtain of White Cube's white walls, showing that it's all red brick beneath (the red was in fact painted by Banksy). Is this a comment on the degree of 'front' in the modern art gallery business? That the minimalist cool is only skin deep? Is it the rubbish from the streets being placed within? Is it a more general comment on cover-ups? Hard to say, but wonderfully thought-provoking.

White Cube, coincidentally owned by Damien Hirst's London dealer, Jay Jopling, allowed the piece to stay for a while before buffing it. But that wasn't the end of Leanne. She reappeared in a piece wittily entitled *Keeping it Spotless.* Hirst had invited Banksy to 'deface' one of his spot paintings for a charity auction held in New York on February 14th, 2008, and Banksy reused this image to brilliant effect. The world's most expensive living artist meeting the world's most renowned street artist: *spray paint and household gloss on canvas.* The result was electric. Estimated at $350,000, the piece achieved an eye-watering $1,700,000, before commission. It remained the highest price achieved by a Banksy until 2019, when *Devolved Parliament* was auctioned at Sotheby's in London and achieved £9,800,000.00.

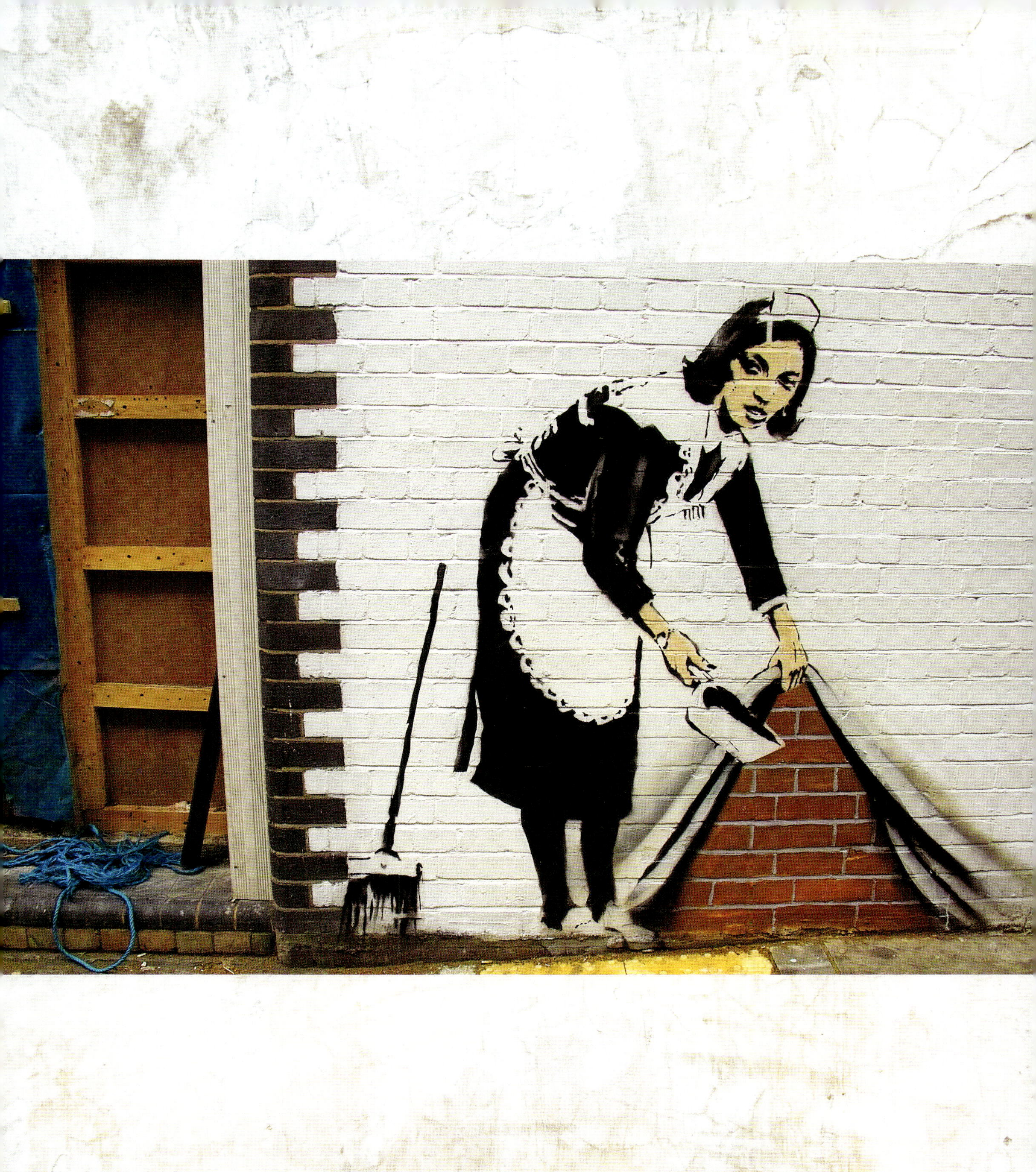

GRAFFITI REMOVAL HOTLINE

"There's nothing more dangerous than someone who wants to make the world a better place." Banksy.

Councils in England started running hotlines for traffic offences, litter problems and, of course, graffiti from around 2000. It became a sort of institutional cliché, encouraging a streak of vigilantism, with their 0800 numbers allowing free calls. There was nothing hot about the hotlines, however: it usually took ages to get through.

This piece appeared on a major road in Islington, north London. The irony of the message is direct, typically clever-dick Banksy. What is less obvious is the figure of the boy. He is wearing what looks like a football shirt, but then his trousers are almost like plus-twos, with shoes reminiscent of the 1930s.

His grimace is at once thuggish, but also upset. It is odd that he is painting in pink, and his graffito is really a bit of a mess: he could easily have painted over the numbers to obscure them all, but that is clearly not his intent.

This looks like a comment on how there is a distinction between graffiti and street art. The graffito is baby pink, childish, inept. Banksy's piece is witty, accomplished and really makes one think. Just when one thought this is a simple direct work, it's clear that there are rather more layers of meaning.

WHERE IS IT ?
ISLINGTON,
LONDON,
UK.
BUFFED SHORTLY AFTER APPEARING.

Latitude: 51.5318ºN
Longitude: 0.1089ºW

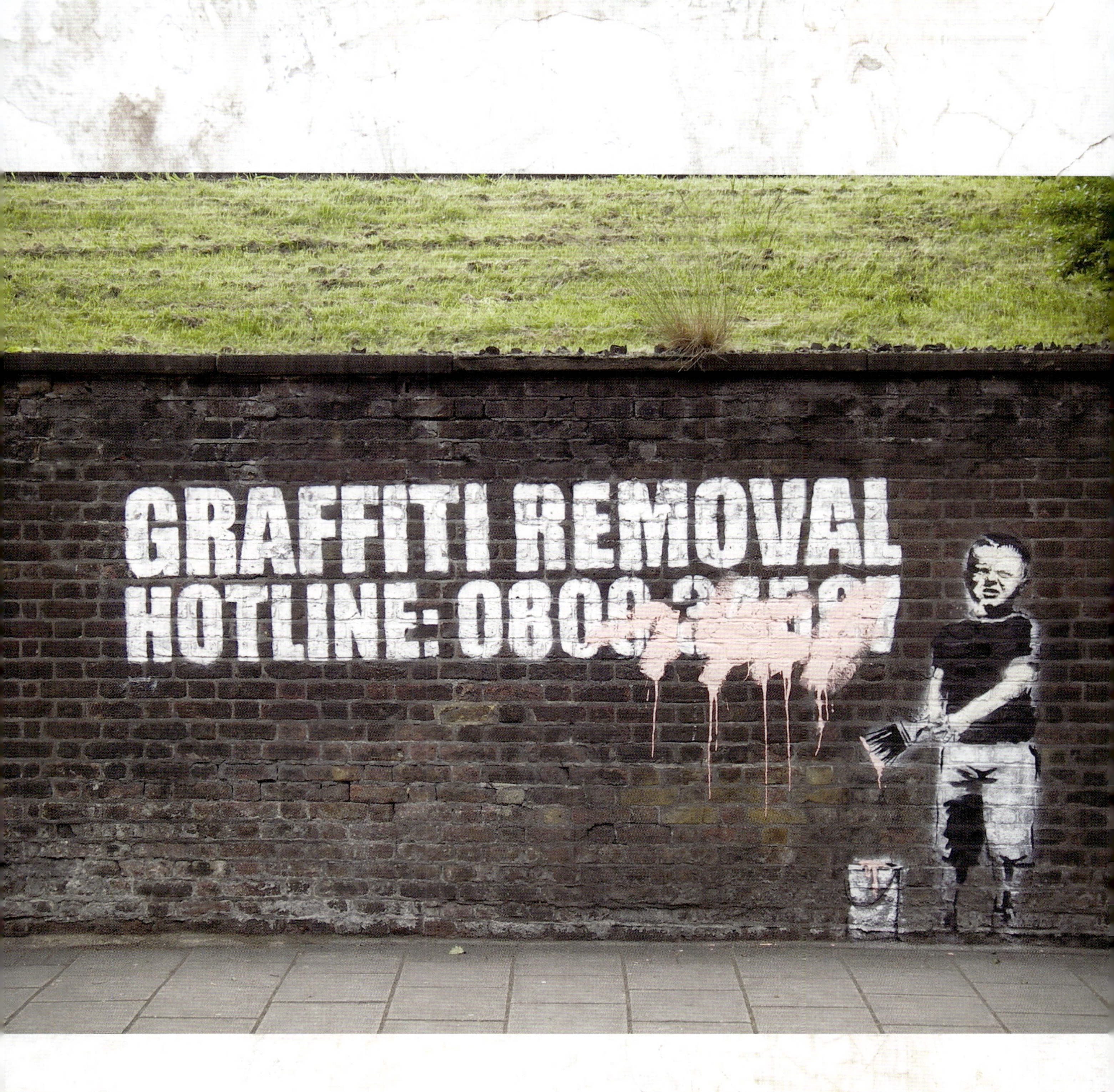

GRAFFITI REMOVAL
HOTLINE: 0800

NO MORE HEROES

"We don't need any more heroes. We just need someone to take out the recycling." Banksy, *Wall and Piece.*

L.A.'s mix of one and two storey buildings along avenues like Melrose, where this piece appeared, make for fantastic canvases for street art. A simple ladder is all you need. You can approach them from the back along the service passage and, in the morning, the crisp sunlight can really make your art stand out, especially if you use red and black.

A wonderfully camp Robin holds one of Banksy's ubiquitous rollers and a little pot of red paint as he minces on his feet. The roller would not fit in the paint pot and is too wide for the letters. It's absurd. The words remind one of the Strangler's song of the same name, but also seems to be a reference to a quote in Banksy's *Wall and Piece* book from 2005, when he says "We don't need any more heroes; we just need someone to take out the recycling."

This is a great piece of fun, and very much in keeping with Banksy's other pieces on this trip to L.A.. There's no political message here, not really. Sure, maybe one could read it as the US should stop fighting wars and should get in touch with its caring – Robin – side. If it stopped being so wasteful of resources, that would be a start. Or is it saying that there are only villains left in L.A.?

Or is this perhaps a reference to the derivation of Banksy's moniker? If it started as Robin Banks (get it?), is this an in-joke to say this is a work by Robin, Banksy as we now know him?

We don't know. We don't really need to know. This is just Banksy at his most fun.

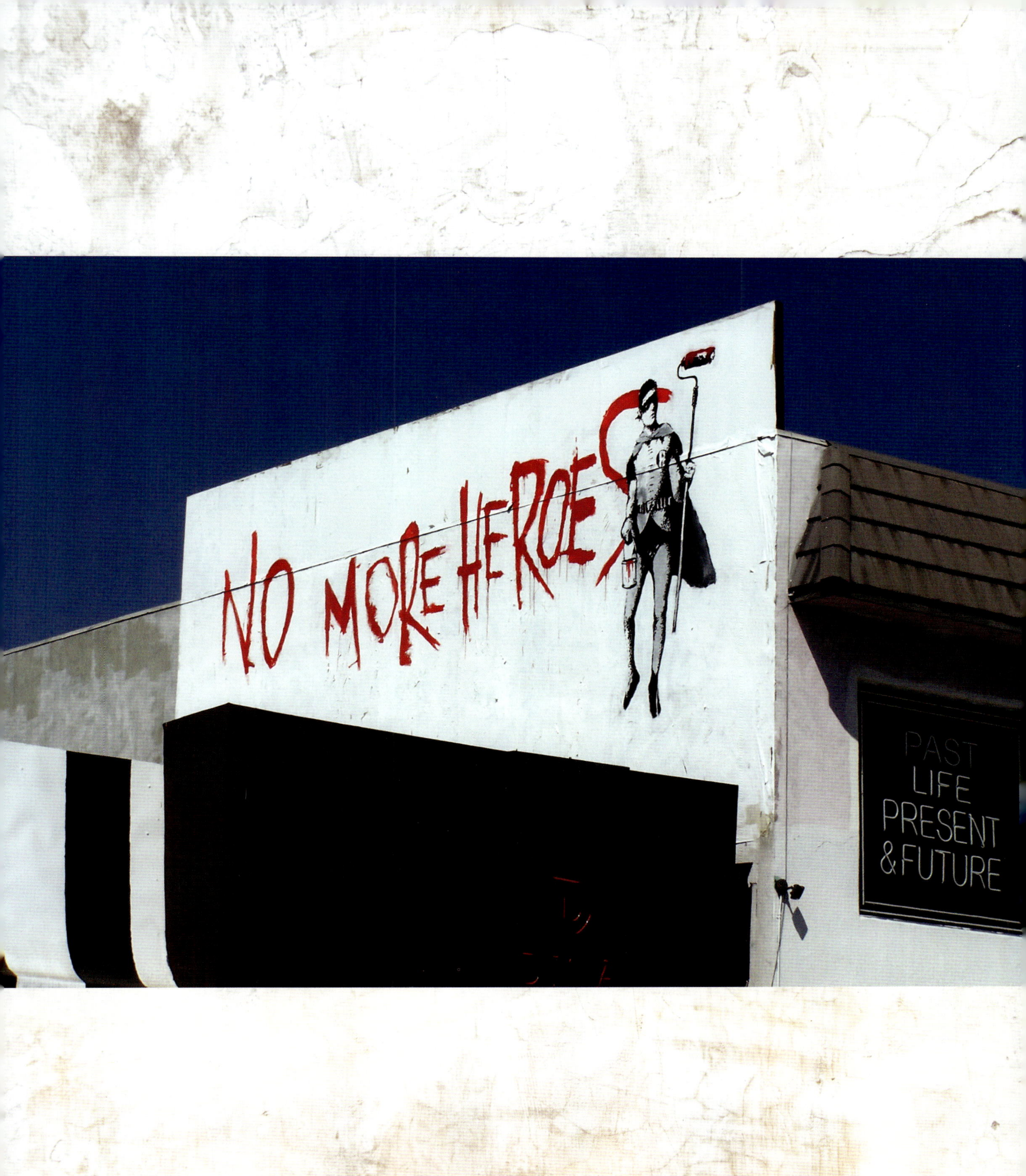

NO MORE HEROES
PAST
LIFE
PRESENT
& FUTURE

I'M OUT OF BED AND DRESSED

"He was cool, he was human, he is like what he represents. I really like him."
Thierry Guetta on Banksy in *Exit Through the Gift Shop*.

The creation of this piece was famously featured in *Exit Through the Gift Shop*, from the details of the fine stencils (amazing how many separate bits are involved), to the stencilling of the piece late at night, high up on a building, a spot chosen by the hilarious commentator in *Exit*, Thierry Guetta.

This stencil, a particular favourite apparently with teenagers, is Banksy in pure fun mode. The rat looks half dressed, half naked. He is at least wearing gloves. Like all Banksy's rats he's wonderfully anthropomorphic, yet still all rat. The expression is perfect, a bit grumpy, full of attitude. We probably need to say more when commenting on Banksy's work about the incredible skill he shows in stencilling looks on faces and poses: no other street artist gets close.

For the rat, you can read Banksy, and the joke is that actually putting this stencil up is really all we want – a big new Banksy to wake up to in the morning, with a clever, snide comment to make us smile.

Placing this in LaLaLand feels right. Rat as actor, rat as model, rat as wannabe. In L.A.'s vapid culture you can't be seen to be making an effort, to be working at it. It's smoke and mirrors, working hard at being so chilled that you become that character. You can just hear the agents saying that this Banksy rat would be just *perfect* for that role.

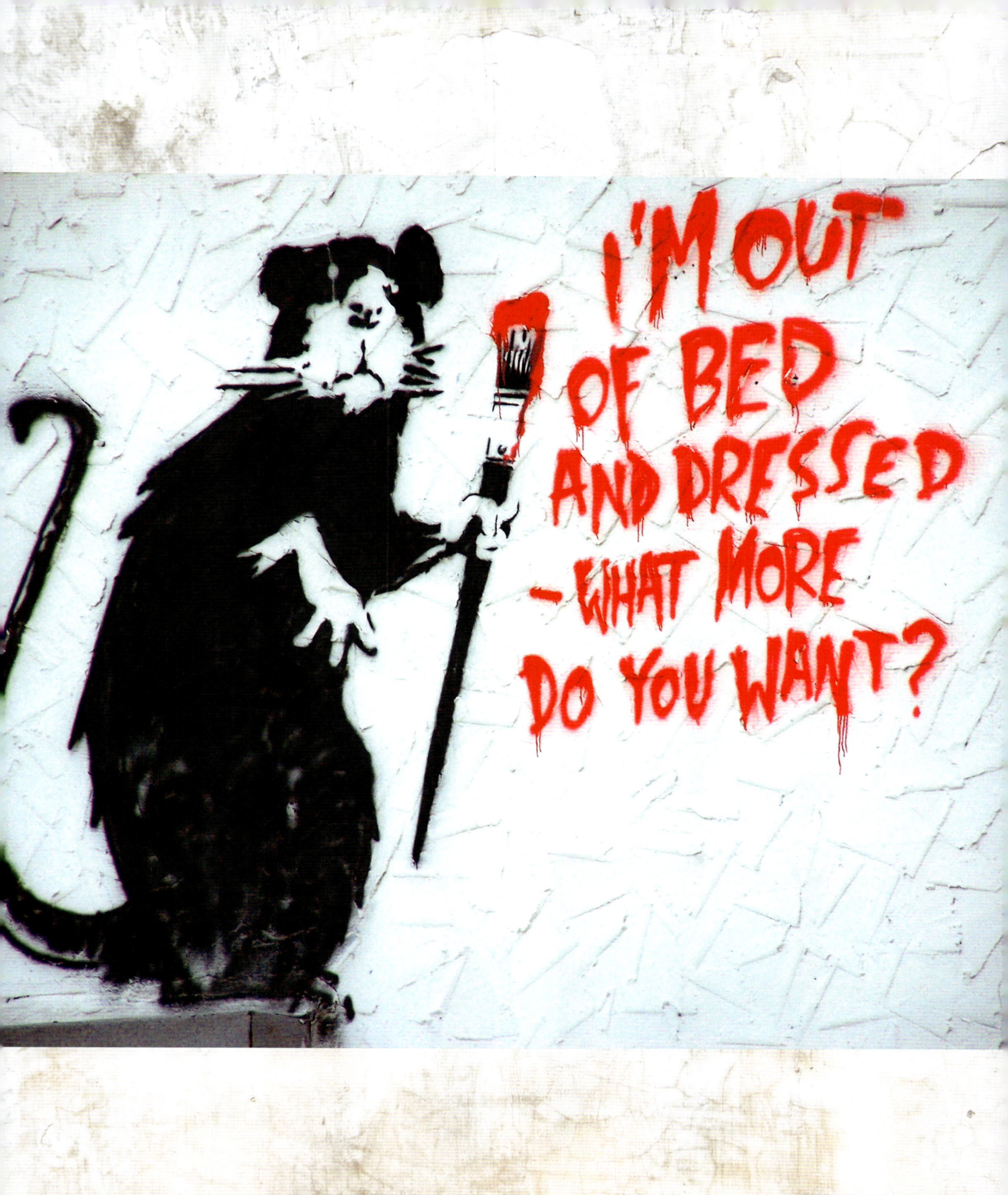
I'M OUT
OF BED
AND DRESSED
- WHAT MORE
DO YOU WANT?

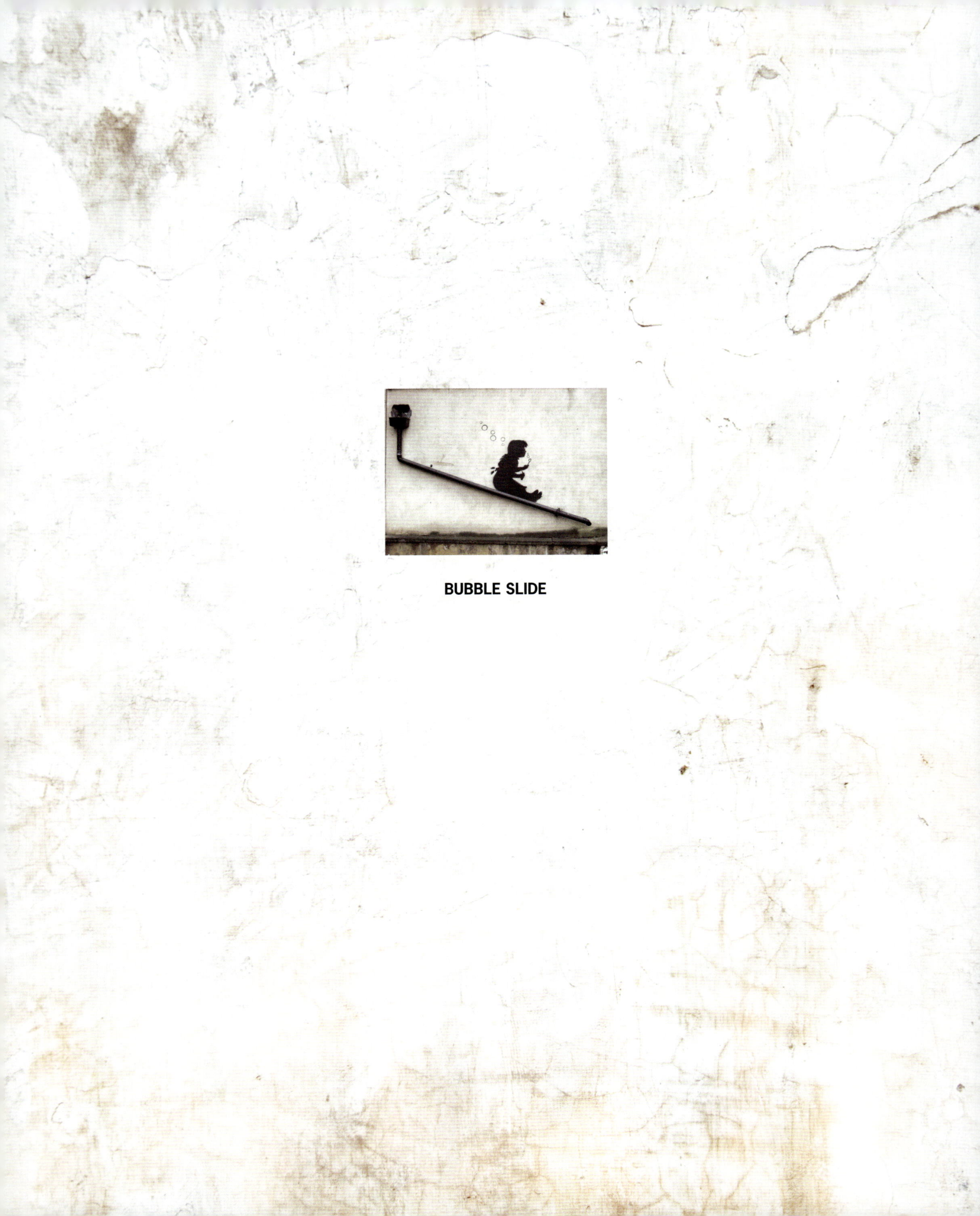

BUBBLE SLIDE

2007-2008

A period of brilliant invention and of hugely successfu
interventions, particularly the Cans Festival in London. Most
striking is his work in London in reaction to the global financial
crash, which Banksy is almost prophetic about with his ATM
piece. And then there is the very moving and angry work in
New Orleans – a searing reaction to Bush's failures in the
wake of Hurricane Katrina.

POLICE SNIPER WITH BOY
ANGEL IN A BULLET PROOF VEST
VANDALISM IS ART
ATM GIRL
YELLOW LINES FLOWER PAINTER
YOU LOOKED BETTER ON MYSPACE
GIRL SEARCHING SOLDIER
DOVE OF PEACE
VERY LITTLE HELPS
BUBBLE SLIDE GIRL
CAVEMAN
AERIAL FLOWER GIRL
ONE NATION UNDER CCTV
LET THEM EAT CRACK
FLOWER GIRL
WHITEWASHING LASCAUX
NOLA GIRL WITH UMBRELLA
ABE LINCOLN
LOOTING NATIONAL GUARDS

BANKSY 2007-2008

Banksy's international travels continue. He's back in Israel, New York and Los Angeles. He creates a new work in Bristol and launches the hugely successful Cans Festival in London. One new location in this period – New Orleans, to investigate and comment on the aftermath of Hurricane Katrina. At a charity auction in Sotheby's, New York, *Keeping it Spotless* achieves a world record (for a Banksy) of $1.9 million dollars.

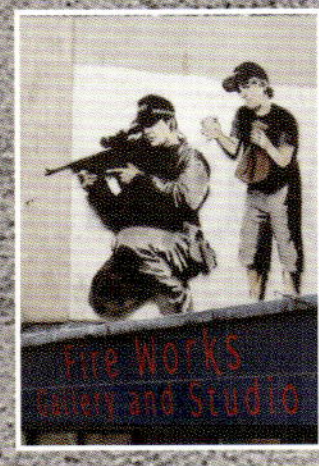

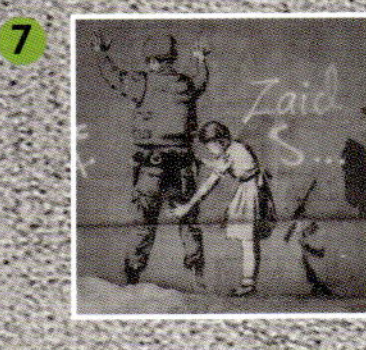

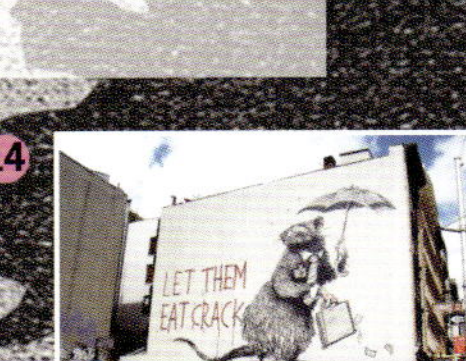

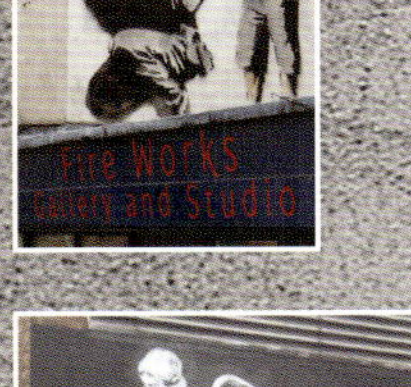

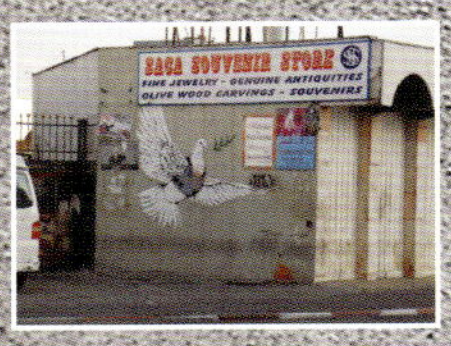

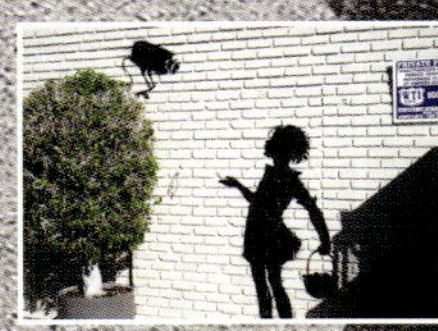

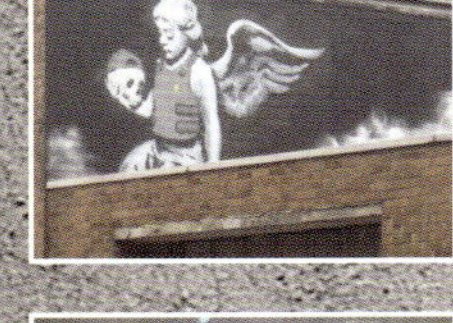

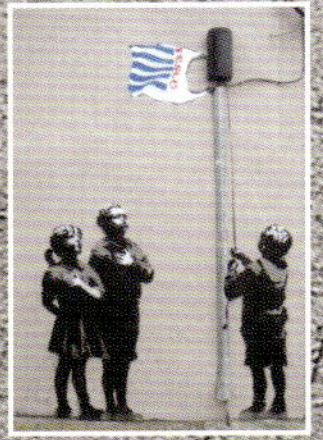

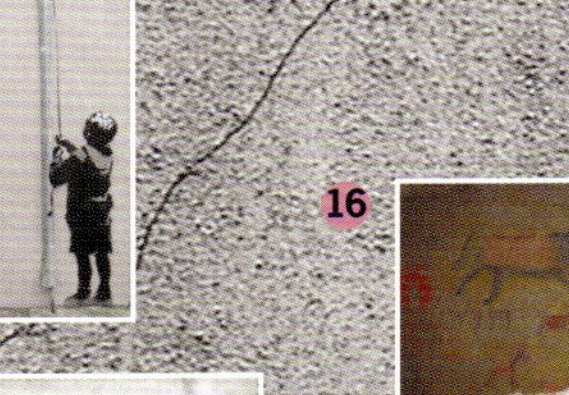

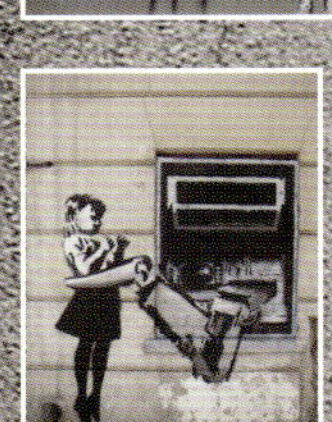

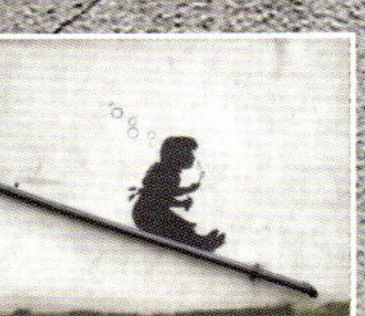

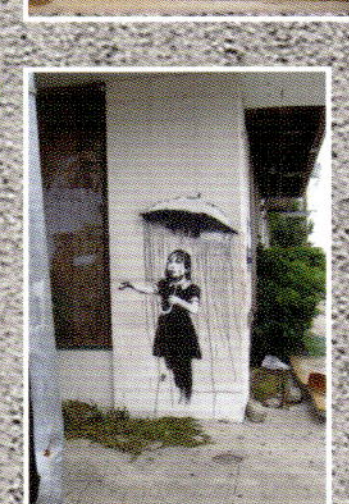

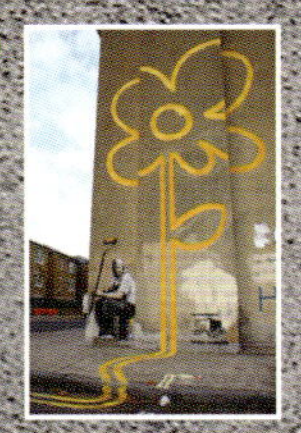

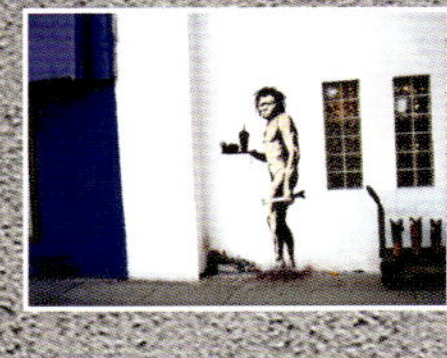

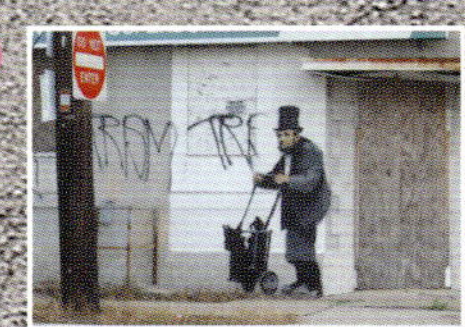

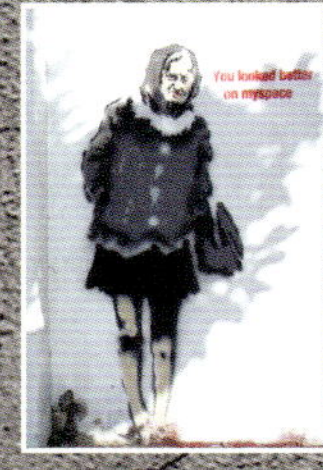

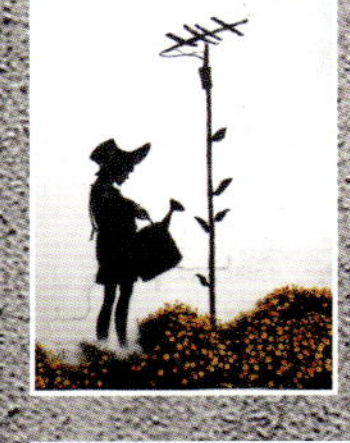

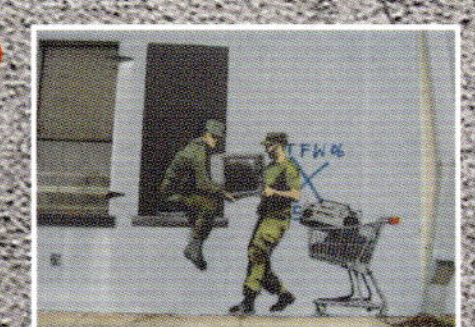

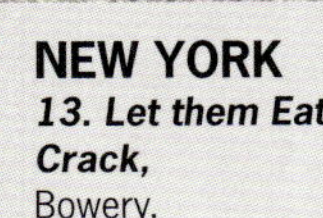

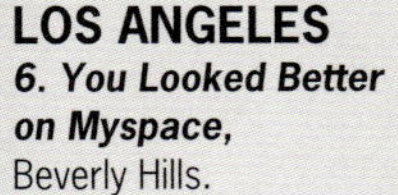

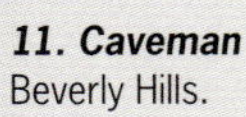

NEW YORK
13. *Let them Eat Crack,* Bowery.

LOS ANGELES
6. *You Looked Better on Myspace,* Beverly Hills.

11. *Caveman* Beverly Hills.

12. *Flower Aerial Girl,* Hollywood.

15. *Flower Girl* Hollywood.

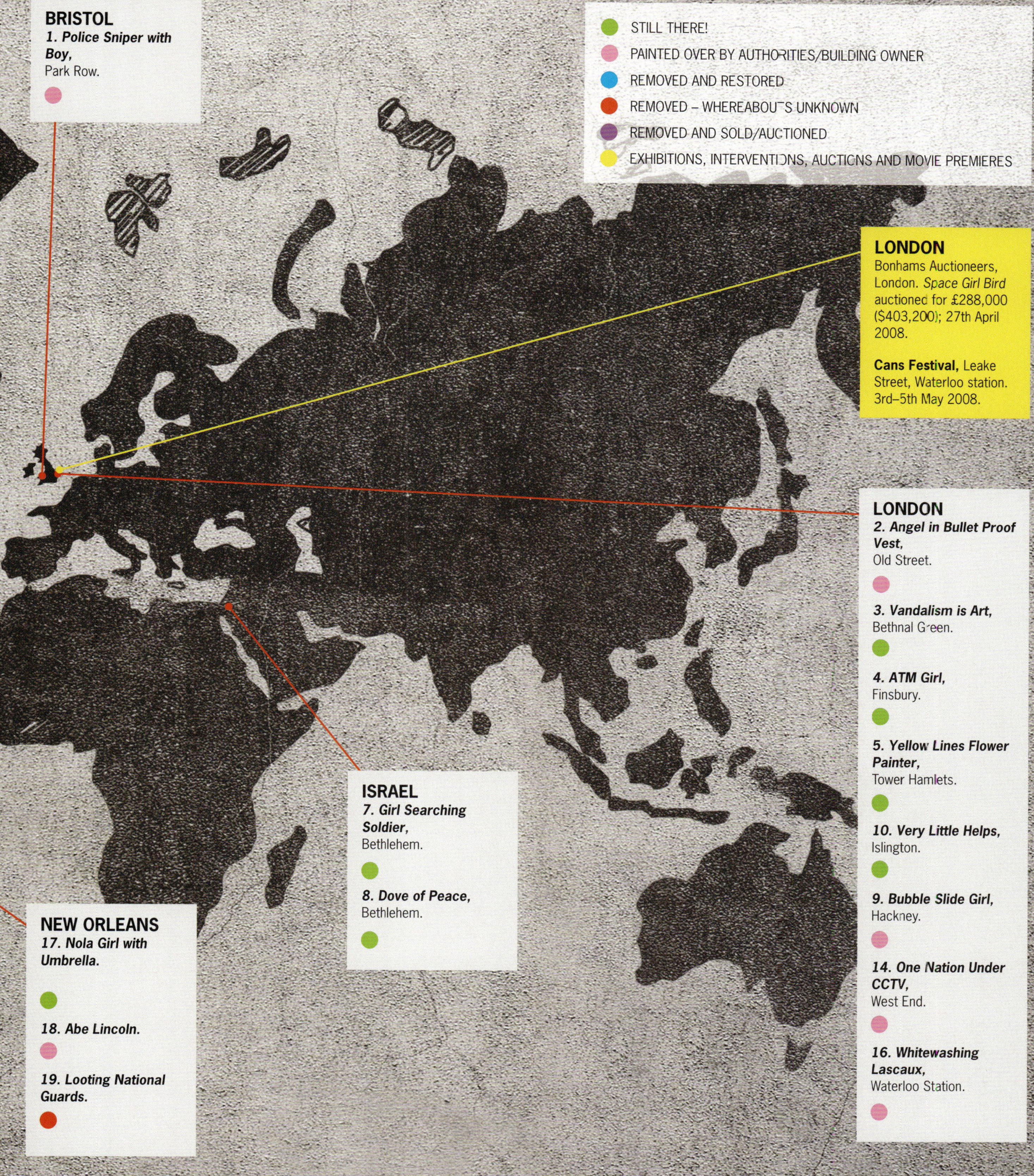

STILL THERE!
PAINTED OVER BY AUTHORITIES/BUILDING OWNER
REMOVED AND RESTORED
REMOVED – WHEREABOUTS UNKNOWN
REMOVED AND SOLD/AUCTIONED
EXHIBITIONS, INTERVENTIONS, AUCTIONS AND MOVIE PREMIERES
BRISTOL
1. Police Sniper with Boy,
Park Row.
LONDON
Bonhams Auctioneers, London. Space Girl Bird auctioned for £288,000 ($403,200); 27th April 2008.
Cans Festival, Leake Street, Waterloo station. 3rd–5th May 2008.
LONDON
2. Angel in Bullet Proof Vest,
Old Street.
3. Vandalism is Art,
Bethnal Green.
4. ATM Girl,
Finsbury.
5. Yellow Lines Flower Painter,
Tower Hamlets.
10. Very Little Helps,
Islington.
9. Bubble Slide Girl,
Hackney.
14. One Nation Under CCTV,
West End.
16. Whitewashing Lascaux,
Waterloo Station.
ISRAEL
7. Girl Searching Soldier,
Bethlehem.
8. Dove of Peace,
Bethlehem.
NEW ORLEANS
17. Nola Girl with Umbrella.
18. Abe Lincoln.
19. Looting National Guards.

POLICE SNIPER WITH BOY

"The decision to shoot is the officer's alone."
House of Commons briefing paper.

This piece was created by Banksy on the side of a building which faced Bristol Children's Hospital buildings. The rather surreal, sardonic idea that an elite police marksman would take aim at some mischievous kid opposite is slightly at odds with Banksy's usual desire, when featuring images of the police, to make a specific political or social point, over and above the wit of the piece.

It is hysterical that the kid behind is about to create a big 'bang' with his paper bag. One can imagine the cop thinking that someone has been shot and going into action, or perhaps falling off his perch in surprise. Maybe Banksy is trying to say that these serious police marksmen are just playing, that they are just really silly boys with guns.

Of course, part of the joke is the name of the shop.

The piece was defaced in 2012, for no apparent reason, with black paint. Another piece of street art (not by Banksy), of the Queen masquerading as David Bowie, took its place.

The Banksy was better.

WHERE IS IT ?
BRISTOL,
UK.
PAINTED OVER WITH BLACK PAINT.

Latitude: 51.4569ºN
Longitude: 2.5973ºW

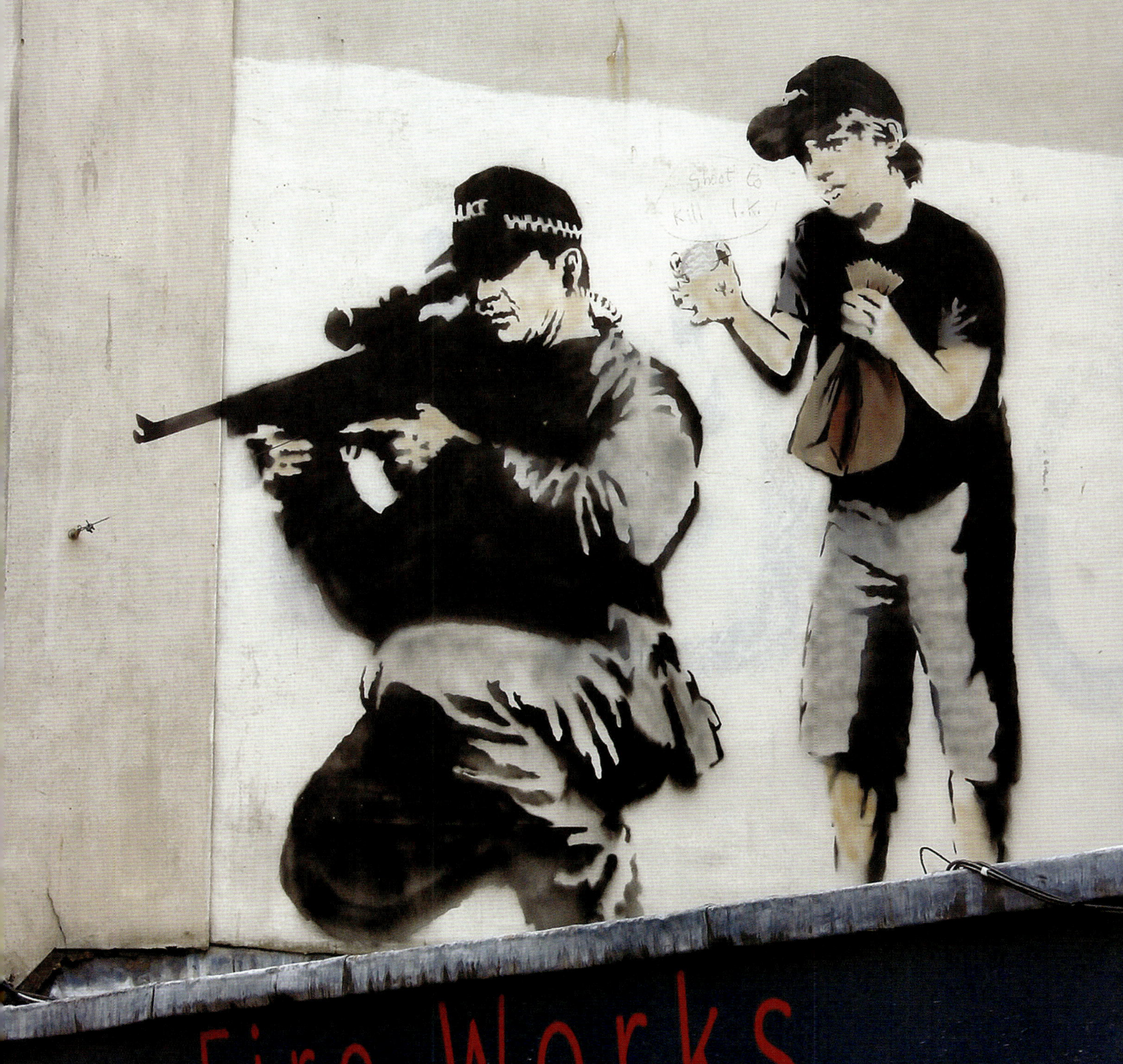
Shoot to
Kill I.K
Fire Works
Gallery and Studio

ANGEL IN A BULLET PROOF VEST

In Memoriam

A rare occasion where Banksy has painted over one of his own works with a new work. This piece, a tribute to well-known graffiti writer Ozone, was painted over Banksy's famous *Pulp Fiction* piece (see page 20).

Ozone had in fact not thought much of Banksy's original. Banksy explained on his website: "The last time I hit this spot I painted a crap picture of two men in banana costumes waving hand guns. A few weeks later a writer called Ozone completely dogged it and wrote "If it's better next time, I'll leave it" in the bottom corner.

Ozone was hit by an underground train, together with fellow graffiti writer WANTS, in Barking, east London, on 12th January 2007. Both were killed. They were spotted spraying graffiti at a London Underground train depot by security guards. When they heard the guards, they dashed across the tracks and were struck by a westbound District line train.

Banksy's rather moving image shows an angel in a bullet-proof vest, holding Ozone's skull, with signature reversed baseball cap. It is a contemporary take on a classical *memento mori.* The vest suggests that Ozone's spirit and memory is bullet-proof. It is apposite that the piece is on the side of a London tube station.

WHERE IS IT ?
OLD STREET
TUBE STATION,
LONDON,
UK.

Latitude: 51.5259ºN
Longitude: 0.0876ºW

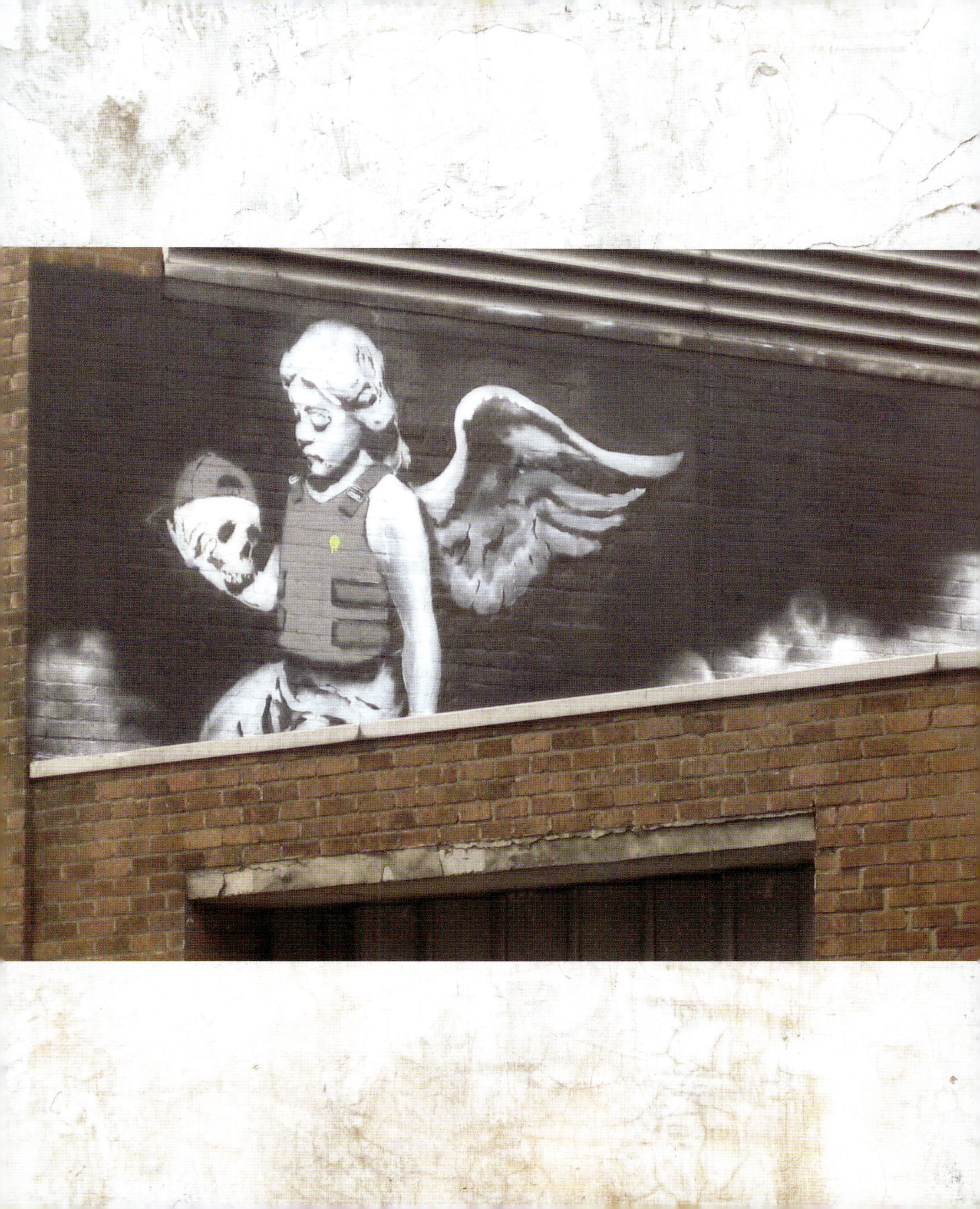

VANDALISM IS ART

"All artists are willing to suffer for their work. But why are so few prepared to learn to draw?" Banksy.

One of Banksy's most amusing pieces, for its wit and sheer childishness. Pictured is the artist as Old Master – the rather arrogant, almost baroque pose, the important, inspired moment where oils come alive on the canvas, all that artistic energy flowing in one direction. And in this case he is drawing the sort of spunking cock that is most likely the work of an 11-year old boy. We've all drawn them: those scrotal hairs look remarkably, in terms of early teens art, familiar.

This is Banksy once more operating on a number of levels. The simple fact is that street art *is* vandalism, except when it's art, and then again sometimes it's both. This just-pubescent cock is the simplest, most stupid, form of graffiti. By placing his witty artist daubing his inspired oils, Banksy transforms it into art, and it lives up to its title. If we had just the artist, it would have no point... so art, in this instance, needs its vandalism.

The figure of the artist is brilliantly drawn, and evokes that of Velazquez's self-portraits. On closer inspection, however, he is a strange mash-up of various periods. The pose is late sixteenth century, the tray on its stand is nineteenth century, but yet he is wearing plus fours and what look like argyle socks – a touch of golfing kit from the 1910s, in other words.

We're unsure whether Banksy saw the graffito of the cock first, then added the stencil. It's likely that he painted the whole composition, as the paint-match on the artist's palette is exact.

WHERE IS IT ?
BETHNAL GREEN,
LONDON.
UK.

Latitude: 51.5275ºN
Longitude: 0.0556ºW

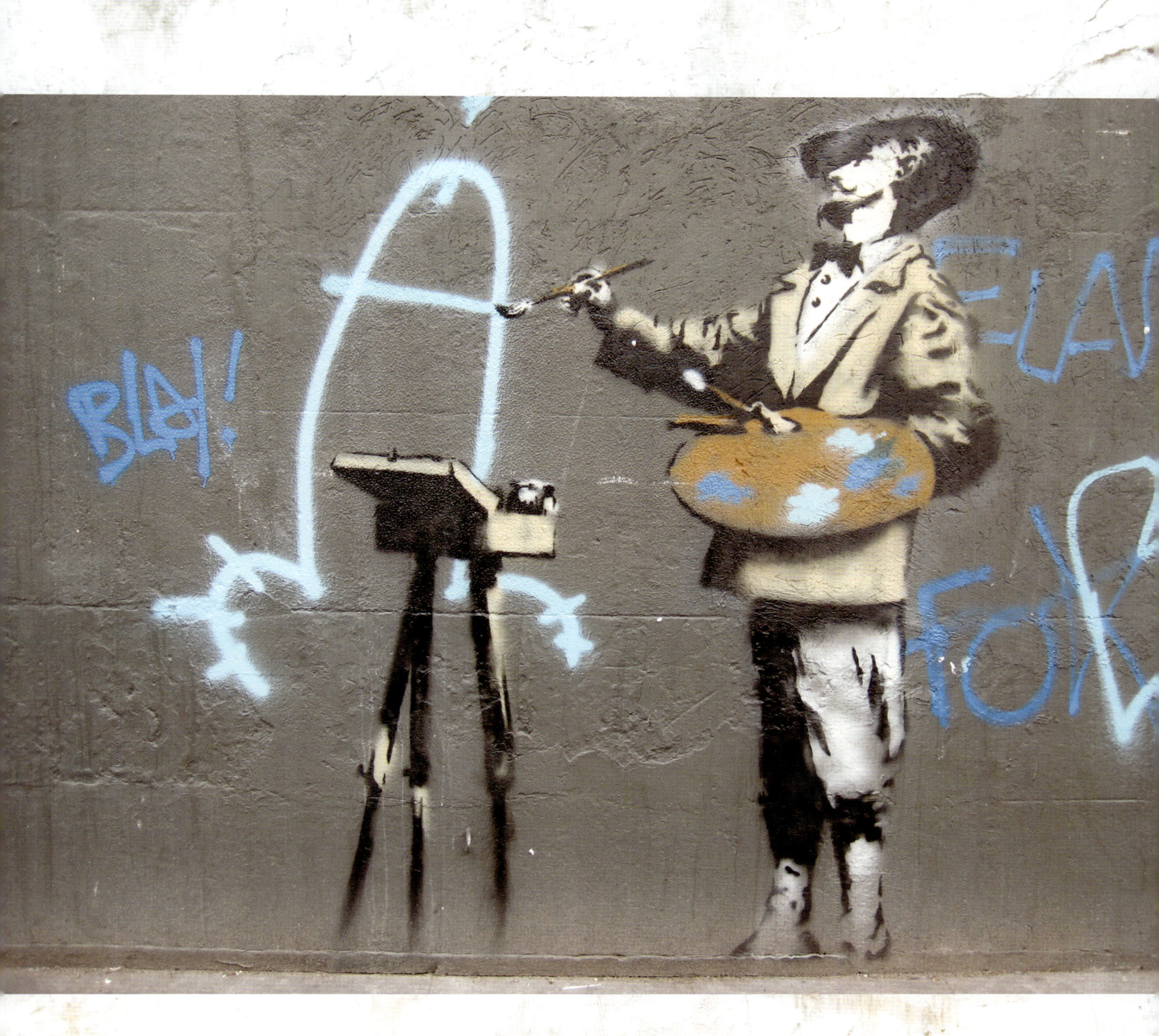

BLAH!

ATM GIRL

"Cost of the global financial crash of 2007-08: $2,800,000,000,000 (2.8 trillion dollars)." *The Guardian*, **quoting a Bank of England report in 2008.**

One amazing thing about Banksy is how astute he is politically, how ahead of the curve he is in identifying critical issues, sometimes it's almost as though he has stumbled on an issue just before it has become of massive public concern.

ATM Girl is a classic case in point. This was created in 2007, a few months before the biggest financial crash since the 1930s, when the world's most 'respectable' banks were shown to be the most corrupt, from selling sub-prime mortgage securities (even when they knew they were worthless) as AAA stock, to mis-selling payment protection insurance (which has to date cost the banks $55 billion in fines).

At the time, though, the press just thought this piece was a comment on UK banks' tendency to treat their customers like cashcows to be milked for exaggerated penalty charges, particularly from its younger customers: it was almost a case of the more vulnerable you were, the more they would fleece you. The banks were also making obscene profits. In 2006, the biggest UK banks' *profits* were as follows: Lloyds £3.47 billion; HBOS £4.8 billion; Barclays £5.2 billion; Royal Bank of Scotland £7.94 billion; HSBC £11.9 billion. What is still so mind-boggling is that by 2008 they were ALL effectively bust from sheer greed – it was only because the tax-payer stepped in that any of them survived. And this pattern was repeated throughout most of the Western world.

As ever, Banksy uses the figure of a child to great effect. The robotised arm grabbing the girl reflects the automated indifference of financial institutions. There is a sense that the machine – the bank – will stick the girl in its maw (we love the idea of a cashpoint as a mouth), treat her as fodder and destroy her childhood, with as much emotion as a wall-eyed shark would expend in the same process.

Since 2008 and the crash, this image has acquired even more resonance. It remains perhaps the most powerful image of financial capitalism's psychopathic nature created since the 1930s.

WHERE IS IT ?
EXMOUTH MARKET,
FINSBURY,
LONDON,
UK.

Latitude: 51.5259ºN
Longitude: 0.1092ºW

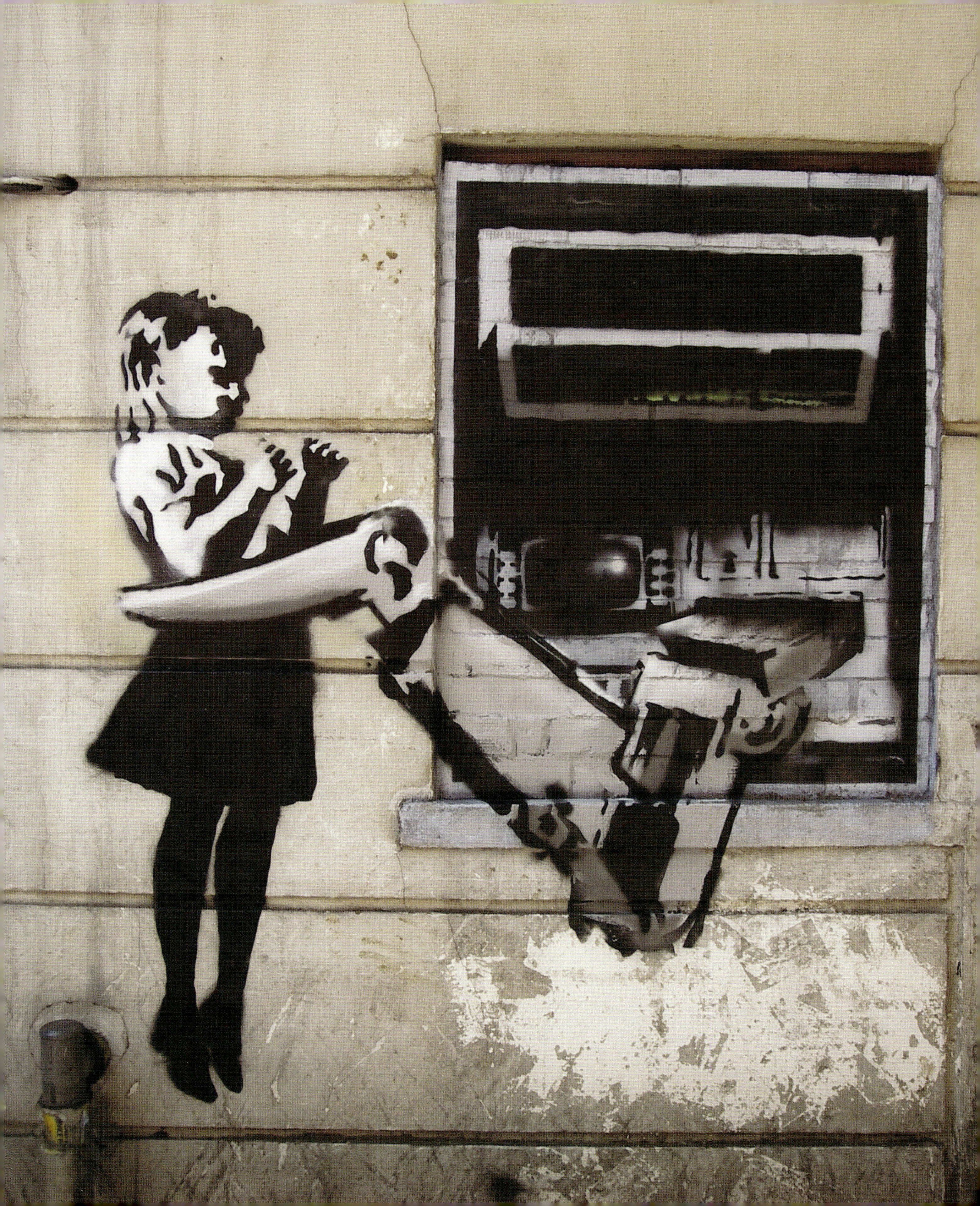

YELLOW LINES FLOWER PAINTER

"A lot of people never use their initiative because no one told them to."
Banksy.

Double yellow parking lines indicate no parking at any time on UK streets. Since the 1990s, local authorities have become almost fascistic in their interpretations of the rules as a way of touching motorists for money. There's barely a motorist in London who hasn't seen their car towed away for a minor infringement, to then be met with a £400 fine. It is the sort of petty local oppression that makes any contact with government so tedious.

So, hardly a burning issue of international importance (unlike, say, the migrant crisis in Europe which Banksy has also addressed), but one which Banksy turns into an opportunity for wry humour. The hapless line painter has transformed himself into an artist. He sits on his paint pot, with his roller, posing with pride in his work. The banality of the yellow line is transformed into a simple sign of optimism, adding the image of a flower to a bleak urban cityscape. The painter also seems to be having a well-earned rest; it is no accident that Banksy painted this on the side of a working men's social club. Always awake to bureaucratic cliché, Banksy usurps the over-use of self-congratulatory logos by local authorities, in this case a stencil of east London's Tower Hamlets borough council supposedly 'claiming' authorship.

Banksy seems to have a fondness for rollers, probably not the best tool for these particular lines, but graphically it makes for a better image.

WHERE IS IT ?
BETHNAL GREEN,
LONDON,
UK.
LINES ON PAVEMENT BUFFED BY LOCAL COUNCIL.
ONLY THE FLOWER ON THE WALL REMAINS.

Latitude: 51.5278ºN
Longitude: 0.0630ºW

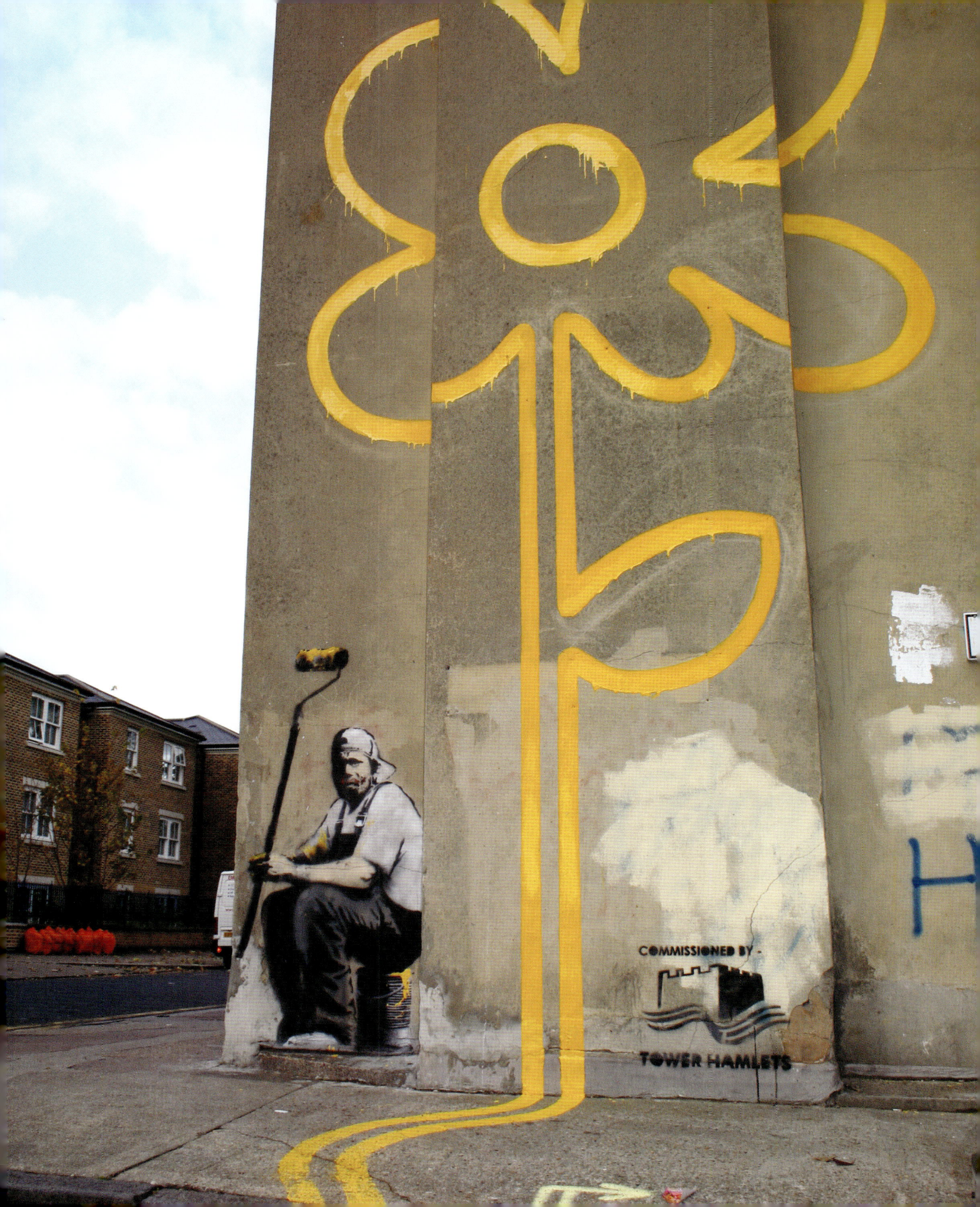

COMMISSIONED BY
TOWER HAMLETS

YOU LOOKED BETTER ON MYSPACE

"If you want to say something...then you have to wear a mask." Banksy.

It is strange to think that in 2007, when this piece was created, MySpace was the largest social networking site in the world and more visited in the US even than Google. A year later Facebook had overtaken MySpace. The latter went from being worth around $700 million in 2007, to being bought for around $35 milllion in 2011.

Banksy has commented, in various pieces, on social media, our addiction to it, and what it says about human interaction. MySpace had launched a dating side to the site in 2006 and this is a hilarious comment (even if a little mean to old ladies) on the tendency of people to lie about their age, to post photos of when they were younger, to narcissistically detach themselves from their own reality.

As usual Banksy creates a mish-mash of clothing. This old lady is wearing a sexy mini skirt, what looks like a santa outfit with a white fur collar and a hoody. She has applied a botched splurge of red lipstick. The hunched shoulders and slighty knock-knees convey her embarrassment.

The effectiveness of this piece has diminished over time, paradoxically because Banksy was too ahead of the curve. Had he waited a year and done it with Facebook, it would have more impact today.

WHERE IS IT ?
BEVERLY HILLS,
LOS ANGELES,
USA.

Latitude: 34.0769ºN
Longitude: 118.3907ºW

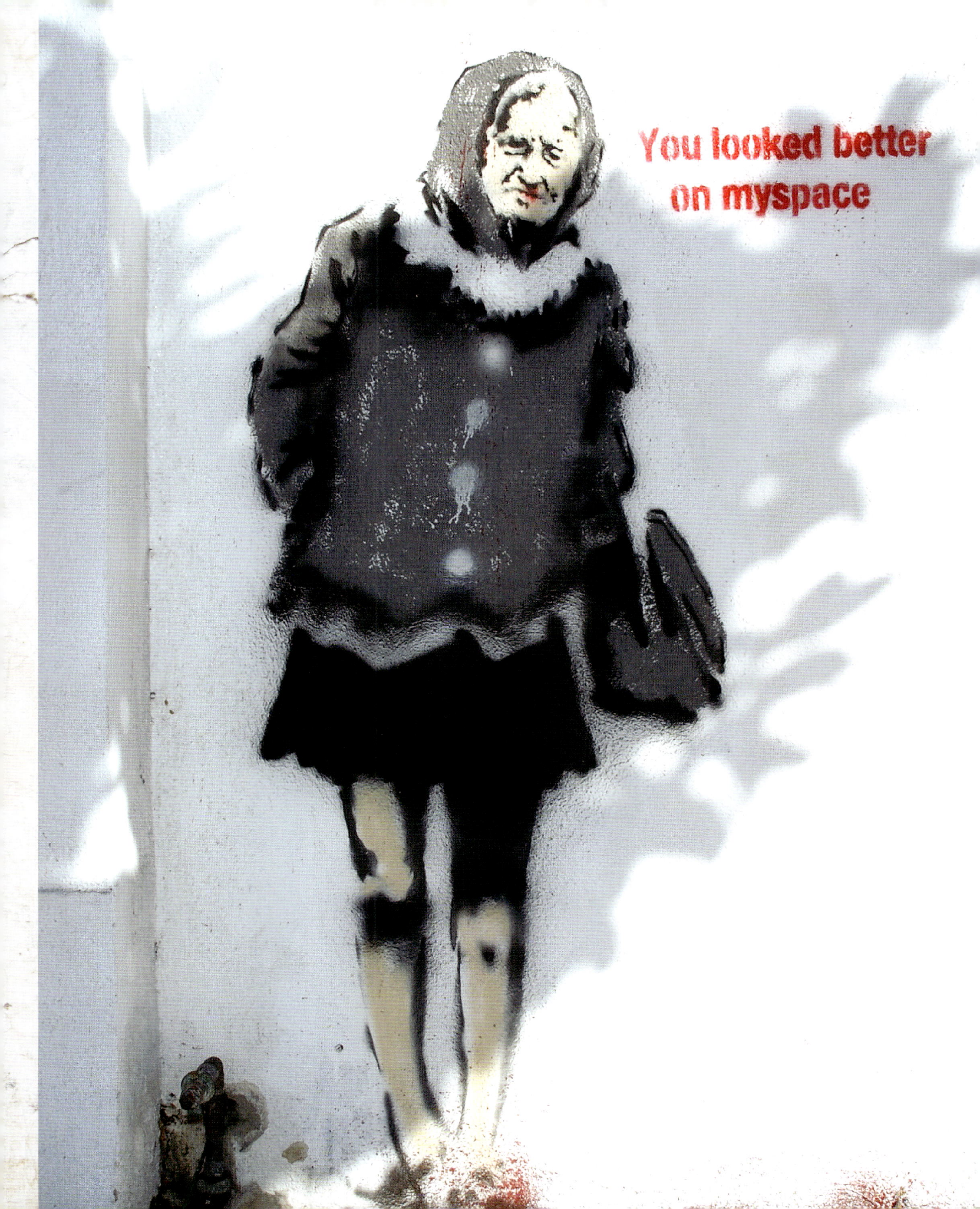

You looked better on myspace

GIRL SEARCHING SOLDIER

"Ill treatment of Palestinian children in the Israeli detention system appears to be widespread, systematic and institutionalized." UNICEF report.

A brilliant example of Banksy's powers of juxtaposition. This piece was created on the Palestinian side of the West Bank wall. It shows an Israeli soldier being frisked by a young girl.

In one simple image Banksy has captured the horror of being a child in the middle of the Palestinian-Israeli conflict, where an oppressive military presence has denied any of the expected innocence of normal childhoods.

As ever with Banksy, however, there are more layers of meaning than at first meet the eye. Despite being created in the Occupied Territories, this is not a typical Palestinian little girl. This is a very Western child, dressed in a pink pinafore dress, wearing pigtails. She even has what look like patent leather shoes and white socks with edging. A child from a secure, well-off English home.

So, this is Banksy, as with so much of his West Bank work, speaking to the West. He is saying, tangentially, imagine if this was your precious daughter, if your children had to be constantly searched at checkpoints in their own land? It's a very effective call to prick Western consciousness for just letting the conflict run and run.

Whilst the image is delightfully absurd, there is also a warning for the Israeli occupying forces. One day, Banksy seems to be saying, our children will be investigating you for what you have done.

WHERE IS IT ?
BETHLEHEM,
WEST BANK.

Latitude: 40.6197ºN
Longitude: 75.3785ºE

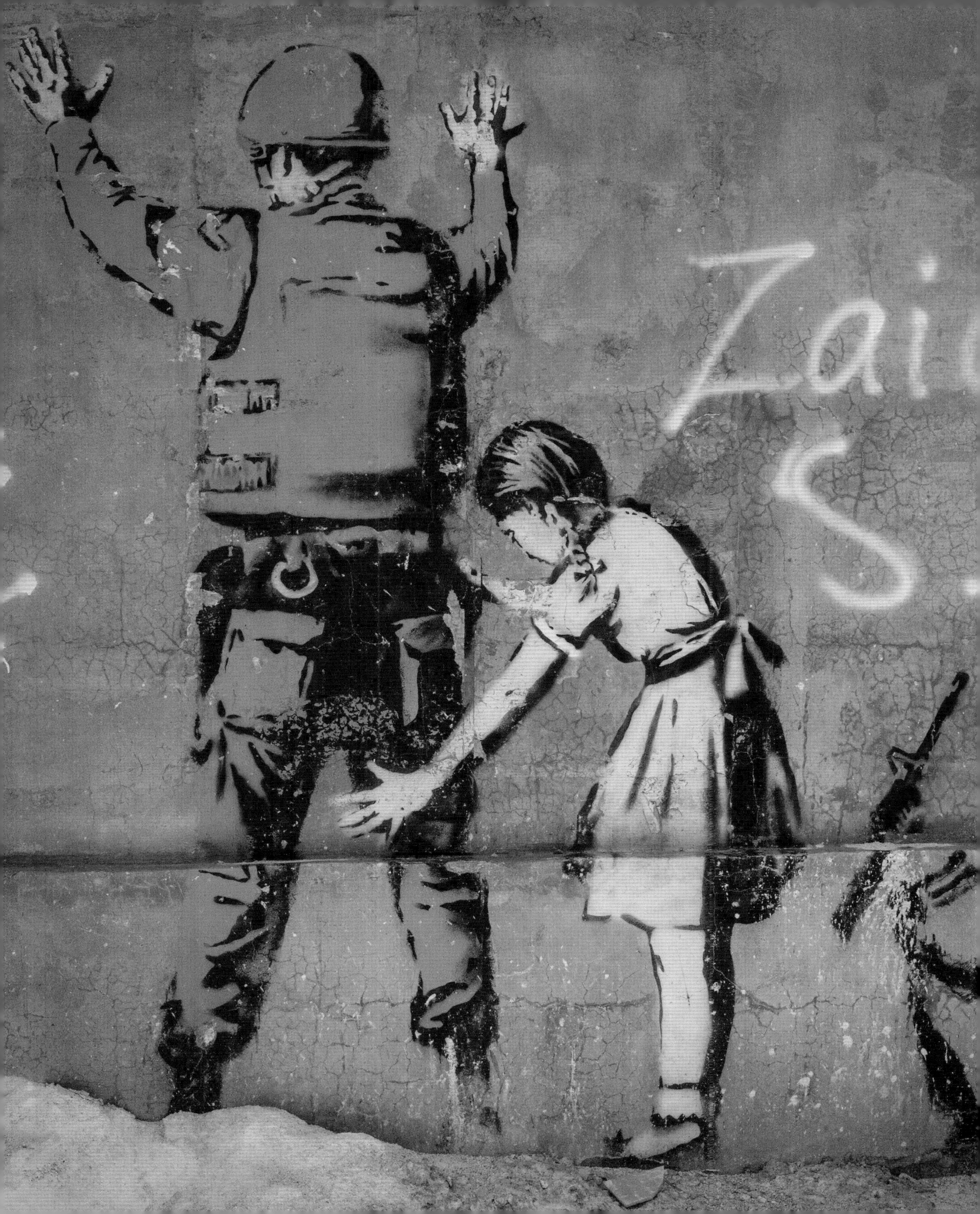

DOVE OF PEACE

"For Westerners it's important to see the Palestinian problem interpreted through art..." Palestinian artist, Suleiman Mansour.

After his 2005 works along the West Bank Wall, Banksy returned to Bethlehem at Christmas in 2007. Things politically hadn't improved, as this piece, painted onto the side of a house pock-marked with bullet holes near the Wall suggests.

As so often, Banksy incorporates existing features on walls into this work, this time the air vent or grille, which suggests a prison. A white dove of peace is flying in, carrying an olive branch. This being the West Bank, the dove is wearing a bullet-proof vest. In a sardonic touch, which Banksy has used in other contexts, the cross-hairs of a rifle's sights are trained on the bird (it's unclear whose side the sniper is on). Are the dove and the artist the same thing – that is, is Banksy just saying find some peace? Or is it that peace, once again, could be shot out of the sky?

The dove has, in addition to his brilliant work on the Palestinian side of the Wall, become one of the images featured on the many unofficial Banksy tours around the West Bank and in Bethlehem. Since the Wall was built, the economy on the Palestinian side has suffered hugely, so the revenue that Banksy has brought is really welcomed. (The previous Christmas Banksy had raised money with a temporary gallery called Santa's Ghetto).

There are no Banksys on the Israeli side of the Wall. What there is, rather bizarrely, is a big banner which states in three languages "Peace Be With You." With no trace of irony it says beneath "Israel Ministry of Tourism."

WHERE IS IT ?
BETHLEHEM,
WEST BANK.

Latitude: 31.7178ºN
Longitude: 35.2026ºE

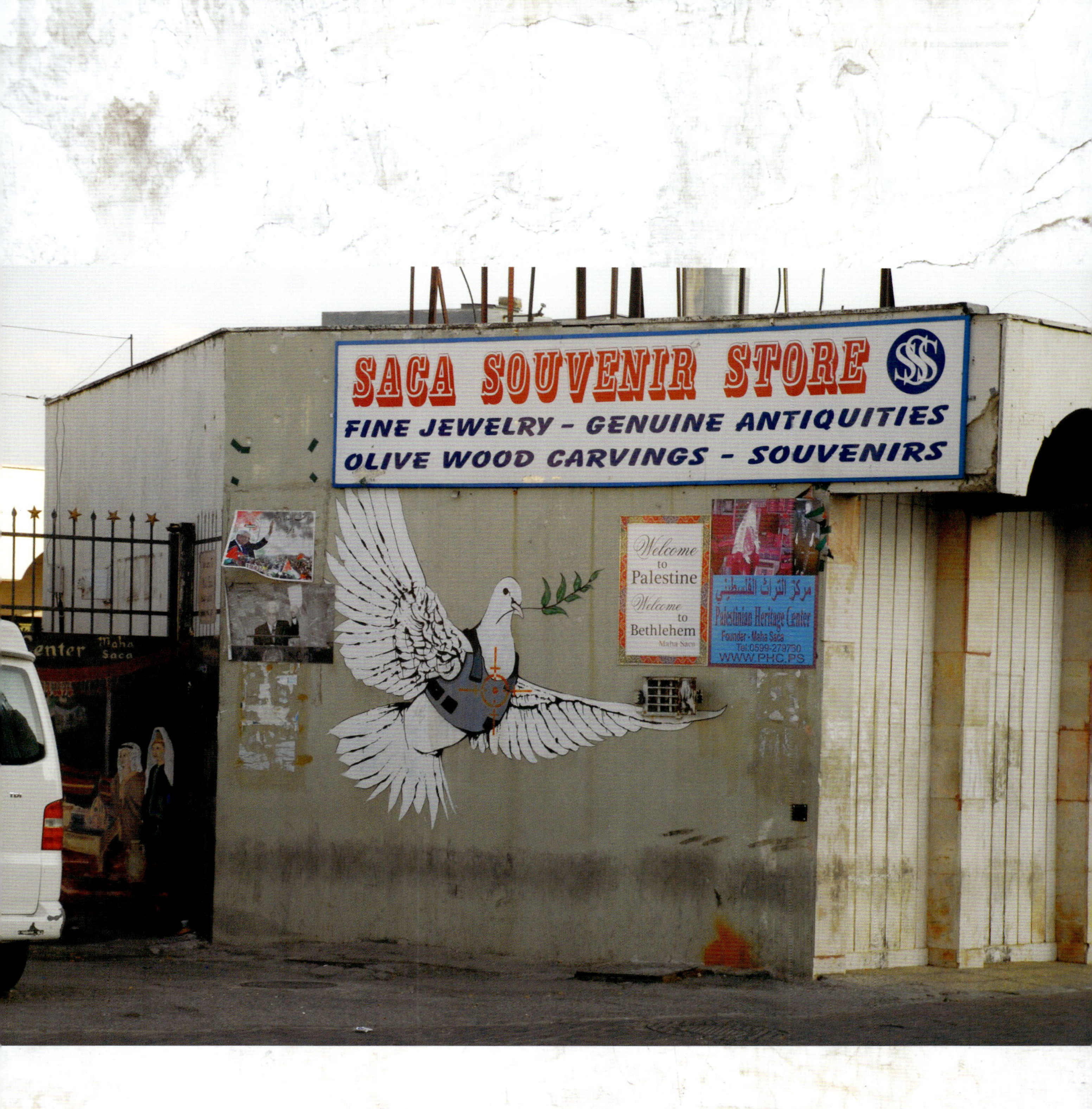

SACA SOUVENIR STORE
FINE JEWELRY - GENUINE ANTIQUITIES
OLIVE WOOD CARVINGS - SOUVENIRS
Welcome
to
Palestine
Welcome
to
Bethlehem
Maha Saca
مركز التراث الفلسطيني
Palestinian Heritage Center
Founder - Maha Saca
Tel.0599-279790
WWW.PHC.PS
Center
Maha
Saca

VERY LITTLE HELPS

"*Every little helps.*" Tesco's slogan since 1992.

Tesco, the UK supermarket chain, has been the subject of a number of Banksy works. When this piece was painted, the company was the most powerful presence in UK retail; around 25% of all spending on food and other goods was within its stores and it was achieving profits of £2 billion a year. This gave it unprecedented power over its suppliers, a power which the customers who worshipped at the Tesco temple for giving them cheap food and goods, clearly enjoyed.

Not everyone was a fan. To some, including this writer, shopping at Tesco spoke of nauseating consumerism, loyalty to the brand driven largely by price. Amazingly the somewhat patronising slogan "Every Little Helps" has been running since 1992; no wonder it has entered the language.

Here Banksy sends Tesco and their consumers up brilliantly in one of his best situationist pieces. A wire fixture is translated into a flagpole, in what could be a scene of 'Breaking the Flag', from the Boy Scouts movement ceremony, with a Tesco carrier bag in lieu of the Union Jack. The Scouts, established at the height of the British Empire, traditionally hold a Flag Break at the start of important meetings; 'The ceremony of 'breaking' (that is to unfold a flag and hang it from a flagpole) the Union Flag...is a sign of respect and reminds us of our duty to Queen and ultimately our country', states the Scouts' manual. Interestingly, the hand on heart gesture is in fact from the US Pledge of Allegiance. This gives the piece more emotional punch, but look closer and you see that the children are using their left hands instead of their right. This is, in fact, an empty gesture.

Here, three traditionally-dressed children pledge their allegiance to the supermarket. Our duty, Banksy almost chides us, is now just to consume; we've created children with no higher purpose...no sign of Queen or Country here.

The model Jerry Hall sold an authenticated canvas of this piece for £82,850, at Sotheby's in 2010.

WHERE IS IT ?
ISLINGTON,
LONDON,
UK.
NOW COVERED IN PERSPEX.
HAS BEEN VANDALISED SEVERAL TIMES.

Latitude: 51.5407ºN
Longitude: 0.0962ºW

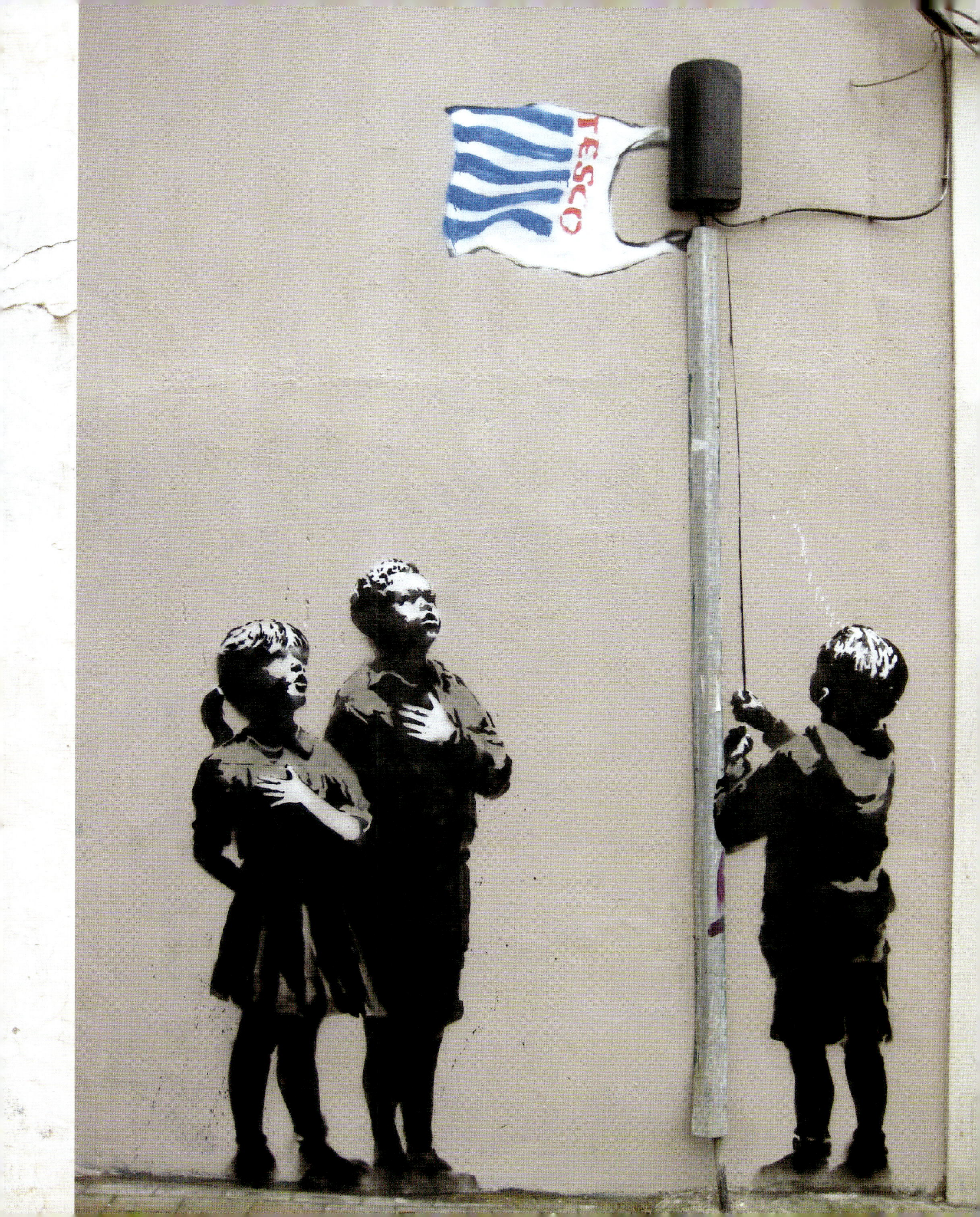
TESCO

BUBBLE SLIDE GIRL

"Any fame is a by-product of making something that means something." Banksy.

Painted on the side of a youth centre, this piece shows Banksy in an unusually simple mode. The piece is delightful, somewhat whimsical, not making any political or social points and with no clever word-play: just bubbles.

It really comes to life in heavy rain, when the water rushing out of the gutter gives the impression of the girl shooting down a water-slide. Banksy shows his usual situationist skill. Where there was a drab wall and a gutter, a simple stencil can create art.

WHERE IS IT ?
HACKNEY,
LONDON,
UK.
BUFFED

Latitude: 51.5483ºN
Longitude: 0.0686ºW

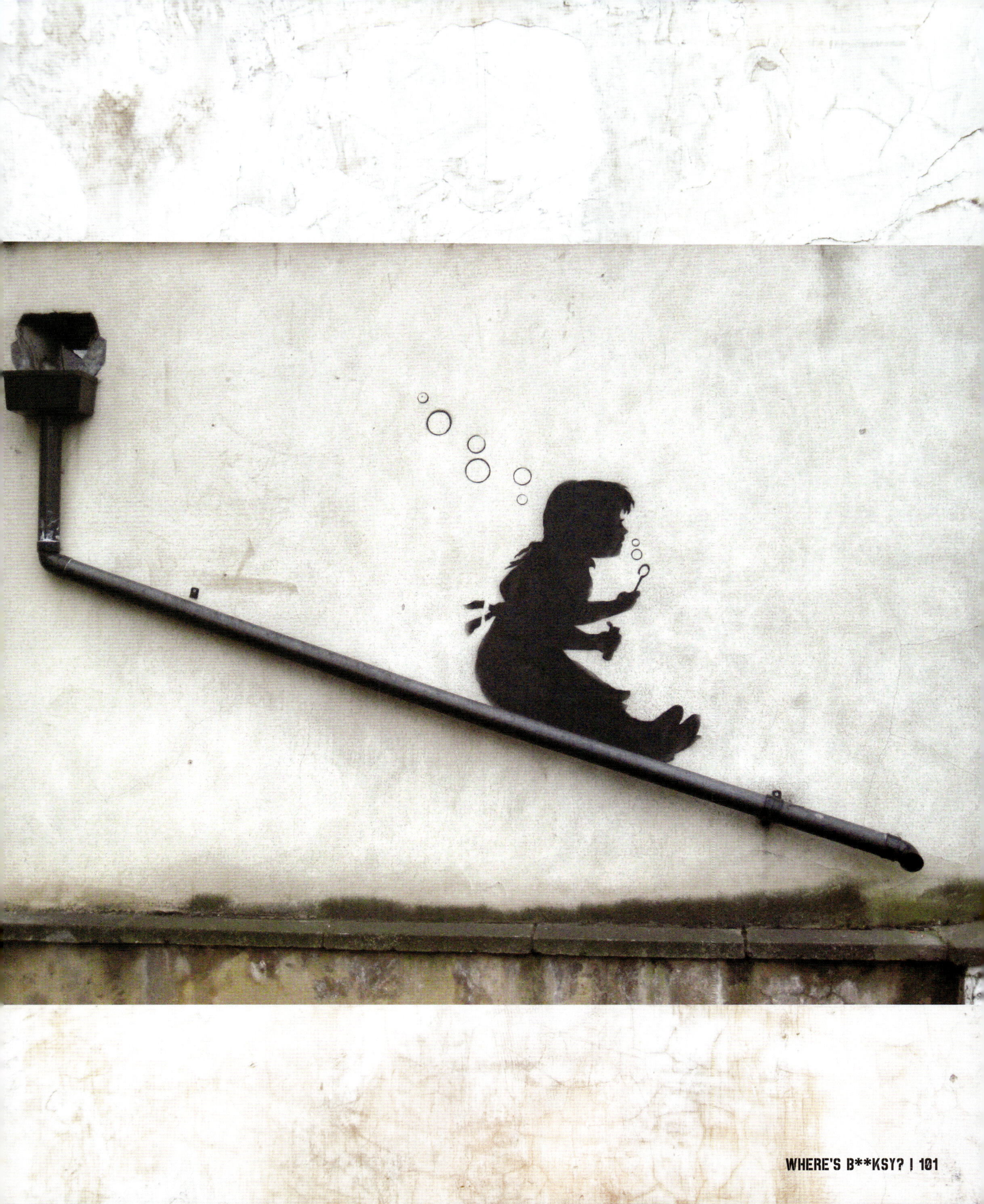

CAVEMAN

"The holy grail is to spend less time making the picture than it takes people to look at it." Banksy.

The start of Stanley Kubrick's *2001 A Space Odyssey* has that unforgettable opening scene, where an ape throws a femur into the air which spins into space and morphs into a rotating nuclear satellite in outer space. It's a magnificent evocation of evolution, of mankind's achievement, of how far we have come.

Kubrick sprang to this writer's mind when first looking at the Banksy piece. We don't know whether Banksy had him in mind, but it really makes this caveman in L.A. resonate. This caveman hasn't thrown the bone, he's holding onto it almost as though evolution has been arrested. In his other hand he has a tray of fast food. The profile does suggest a Big Mac Meal, with fries on the left, the decahedral box, and the drink on the right. Banksy has had a few digs at McDonald's at other times. This is modern man, really still just a caveman feeding his appetite. If anything, in evolutionary terms, he's gone backwards – far from hunting for his prey, he just goes for fast food when hunger bites.

His expression, a "what are you lookin' at?!" grumpy stare, is brilliant. Cavemen we were and, given our addiction to corporate-produced fodder, cavemen we remain. If only Banksy had painted this outside a school teaching Creationism; now that would have been even funnier.

WHERE IS IT ?
BEVERLY HILLS,
LOS ANGELES,
USA.

Latitude: 34.0769ºN
Longitude: 118.3907ºW

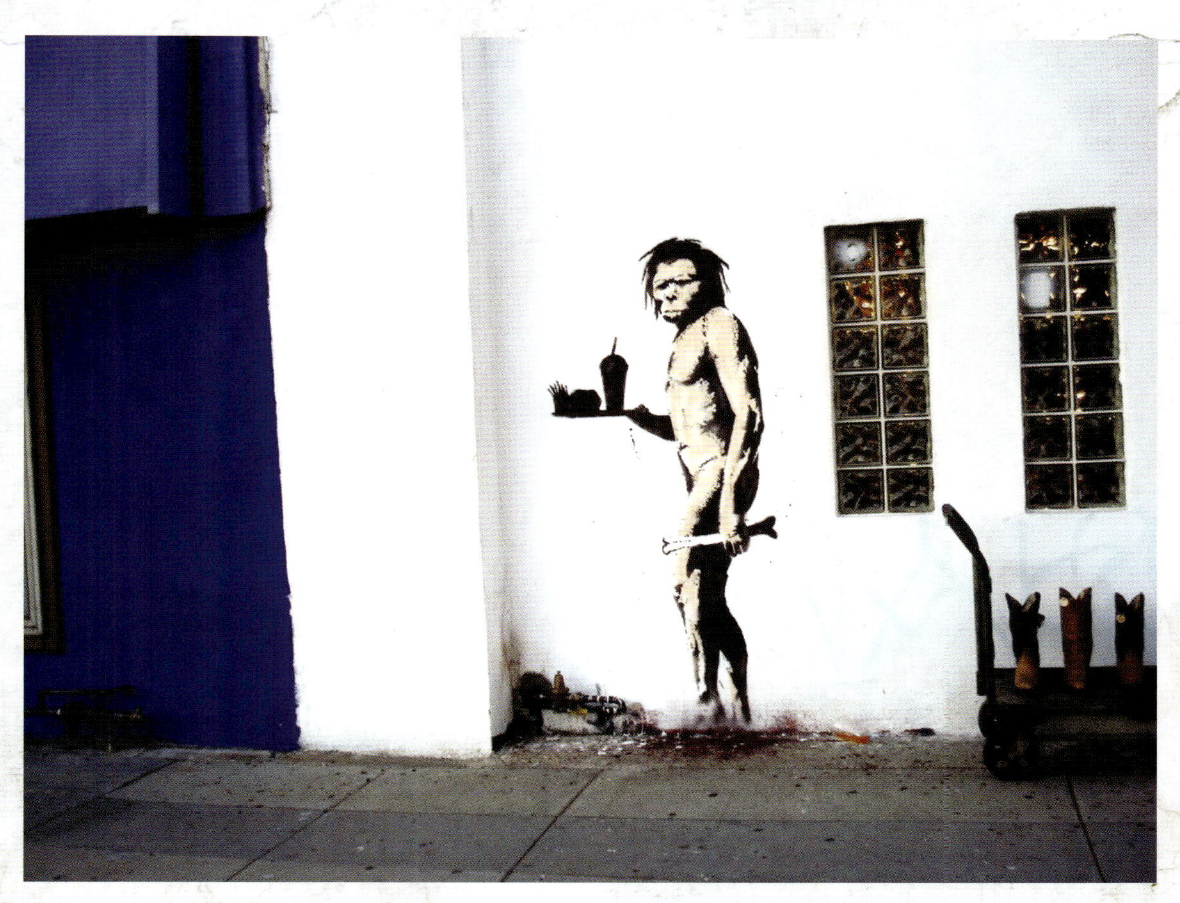

AERIAL FLOWER GIRL

"Los Angeles is a constellation of plastic." Norman Mailer.

One of Banksy's relatively rare silhouette pieces, this is a wonderfully redolent image, of a girl with a watering can. It's straight out of an idyllic English childhood. She has a hat that would not be out of place in Edwardian Sussex, her hair is tied with a long bow, and the watering can is heavy. She is walking, seemingly, in a border of flowers.

There is something so English about much of Banksy's imagery that it is hard not to see this as a comment on over-urbanised L.A. It's unclear whether the girl has just watered the plant that sprouts an aerial, but what a desolate plant it is, how ugly compared to her.

So everything in L.A. is about broadcast TV and media, right? Well, it's a bit of a wooden interpretation, but Los Angelenos aren't really known for their love of gardening for its own sake. A clever and memorable image – perhaps best not to over-intellectualise it.

WHERE IS IT ?
LOS ANGELES,
USA.

Latitude: 34.0145ºN
Longitude: 118.3416ºW

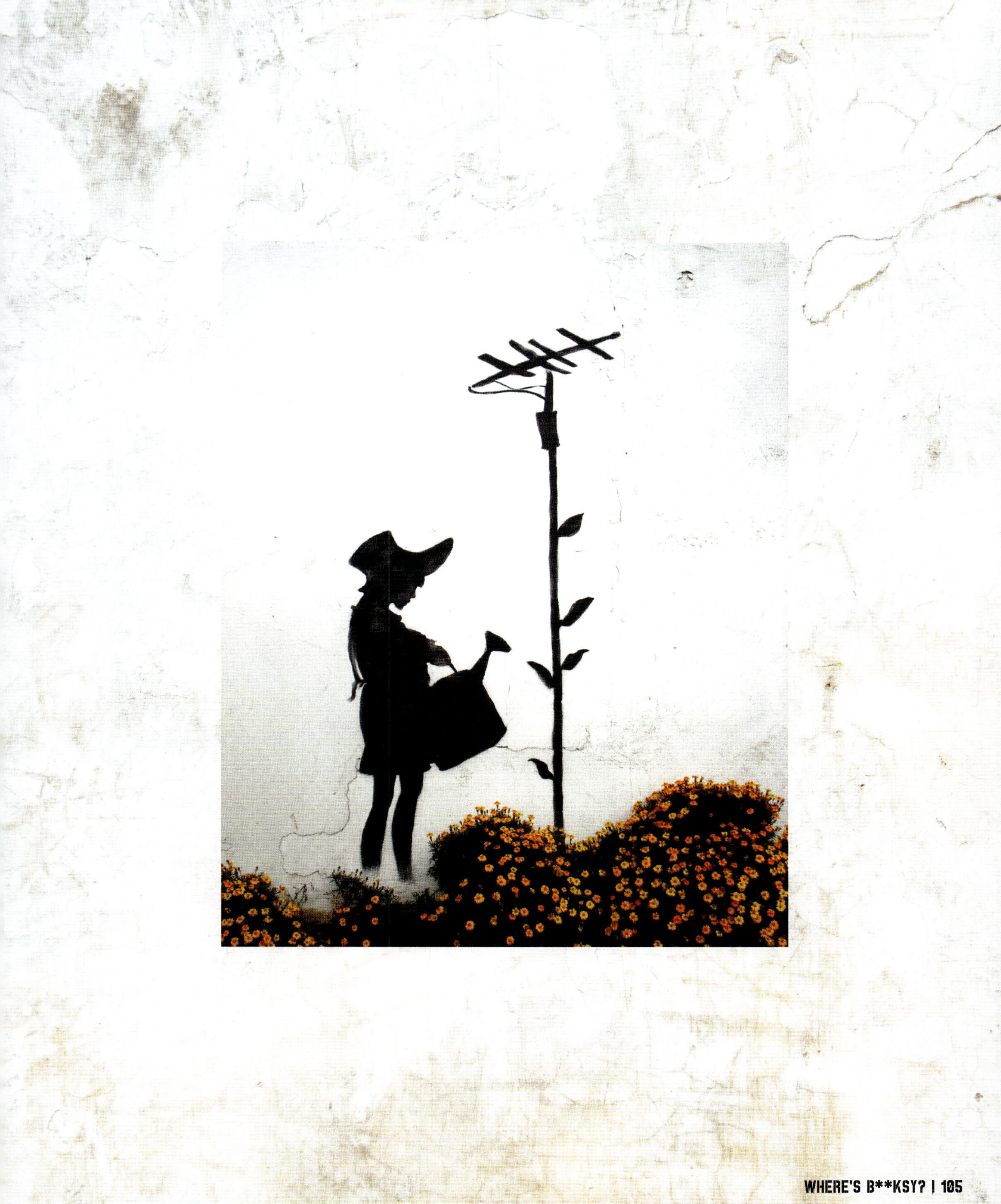

ONE NATION UNDER CCTV

"One nation under God." US Pledge of Allegiance.

"I pledge allegiance to the flag of the United States of America, and to the Republic for which it stands, one Nation, under God, indivisible, with liberty and justice for all." So runs the USA's Pledge of Allegiance, which, thanks to countless Hollywood movies, has entered common parlance the world over. Interestingly the "under God" phrase was not added until 1954, during Eisenhower's presidency, in part a desire to distinguish capitalist USA from atheistic Soviet communism (1954 was the height of the Cold War).

Banksy has made use of US symbols and language in a British context with other pieces. This has everything we love in a Banksy. A brilliant twist to language, and visual wit in spades. It was painted in a secure area belonging to the Post Office, a few feet from a security camera, highlighting the fact that Great Britain is the most surveilled country on the planet. It is three stories high, needing the erection of a pretty tall scaffold in double-quick time one night. Simultaneously Banksy shows how pointless security cameras can be. The small boy, with his red hoody and rucksack up a precarious ladder, is the picture of mischievous innocence, ironically painting a message which the surveillance industry would surely love. The private security guard (also a creeping menace in Britain at the time), is collecting his evidence in pencil-neck fashion. For good measure he has a large threatening dog. The sheer size of the letters, a declaration framed by the sky, really packs a punch.

London has an estimated 422,000 security cameras, according to recent research conducted by Tory MP David Davis. That translates into one for every fourteen people. Across England, the figure is around two million. Over 500,000 people are employed in the UK private security industry, compared to 127,000 police officers.

WHERE IS IT ?
NORTH OF OXFORD STREET,
LONDON,
UK.
NO LONGER THERE;
WESTMINSTER CITY COUNCIL ORDERED ITS REMOVAL.

Latitude: 51.5175ºN
Longitude: 0.1355ºW

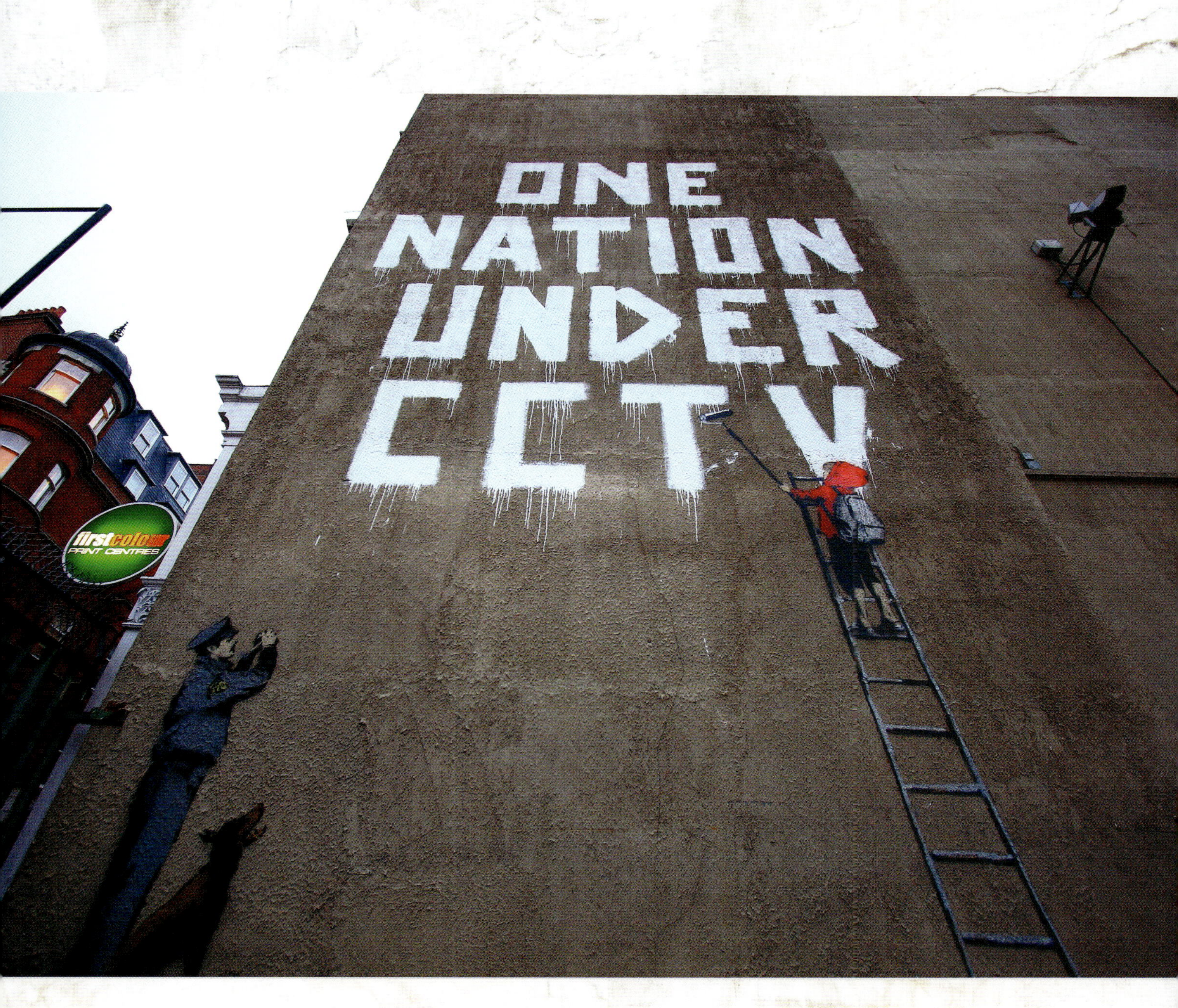

ONE
NATION
UNDER
CCTV
firstcolour
PRINT CENTRES

LET THEM EAT CRACK

"Let them eat cake."
Unfairly attributed to Marie Antoinette in 1788.

Marie Antoinette, so the popular false legend goes, said this when told French peasants were starving due to a harvest failure, on the eve of the French revolution. Fast forward two hundred and twenty years, and Banksy created this piece at the height of the financial meltdown.

This time it's Rat as Wall Street financier, in his white-collared shirt and tie. He has an umbrella, to protect him from bad (financial) weather. Like most bankers following the crash, he is leaving with his money, possibly now off-shore, intact. He has so much (effectively stolen) that it is bulging and spilling out of his attaché case. The look over the shoulder is that of the proverbial rodent leaving the sinking ship.

The reference to the Marie Antoinette mis-quote, catches just the right spirit of contempt the bankers felt for regular Americans in 2008, who were having their mortgages foreclosed, whose houses were collapsing in value, together with, in so many instances, their life savings. "You having trouble coping with that?" he seems to be saying, "well, there's always crack." Meanwhile the Bush administration asked Congress, without embarrassment, for $700 *billion* from those same taxpayers, to bail out Wall Street.

This is another big, provocative piece, and, given the context, rather restrained. It's worth recalling some of the events of 2008. In March the US Federal Reserve (ie US taxpayers) guaranteed $30 billion of Bear Stearns' assets. In July, IndyMac Federal Bank failed. In September Fannie Mae and Freddie Mac were taken over by the US government ($187 billion); Merrill Lynch was days from collapse (although they still paid out $3.6 billion in bonuses), had to be bought by Bank of America; Lehman's went into bankruptcy protection; AIG was bailed out with $85 billion of US government cash; Washington Mutual Bank was closed by regulators; the Bush administration injected $426 billion to save Wall Street. Did any bankers repay any of their mega bonuses? Stupid question!

The Banksy was painted over three weeks after it appeared. Hardly surprising as the rats wanted more. And they got it – $20 billion to Bank of America in January 2009. Over one million Americans lost their homes to the crash during the same period. Another 5.3 million were in negative equity and at risk of foreclosure. 2.6 million lost their jobs. Sales of crack? Through the roof!

WHERE IS IT ?
SOHO,
NEW YORK,
USA.
PAINTED OVER BY NOVEMBER 2008.

Latitude: 40.7199ºN
Longitude: 74.0015ºW

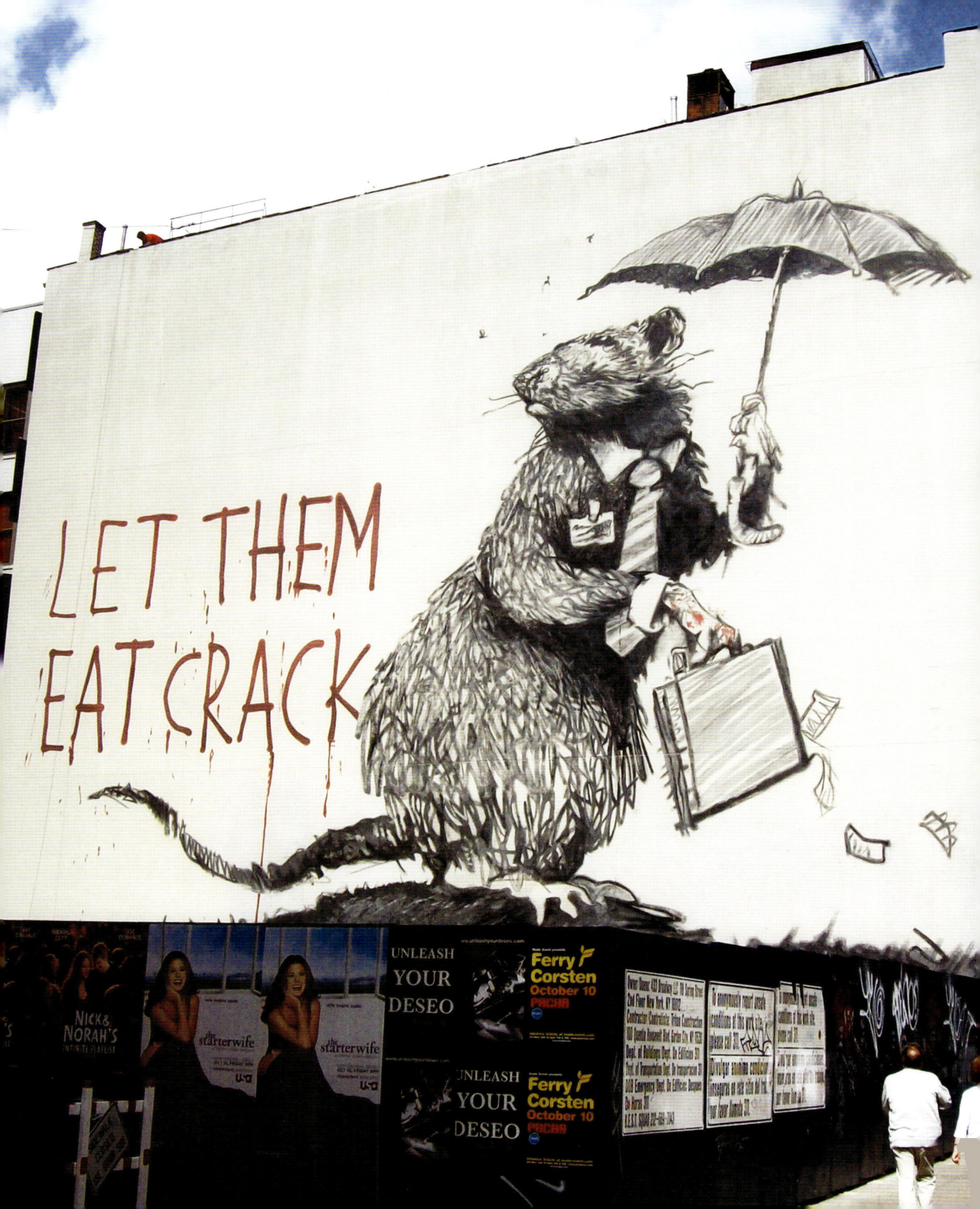

LET THEM
EAT CRACK

FLOWER GIRL

"I remember he was wearing a black hoodie and jeans that were covered with black and white paint." **Banksy (maybe) described by Eytan Rosenberg, owner of Valero gas station on Beverly Boulevard.**

Another clever positional piece from Banksy's time in L.A. in 2008. Painted on the wall of a gas station in Hollywood, this belongs to the series of silhouette girls, of which *Girl with Aerial* is another. It was a style that Banksy subsequently used relatively rarely. Both pieces work well against L.A.'s harsh sunlight.

The piece looks good in this instance with the tree to suggest a forest, although this being L.A. it is a bit stumpy and in a pot. The girl could be taken from a children's story book of Little Red Riding Hood. She is, as it were, wandering down to the woods and will be in for a big surprise. But it's not the big, bad wolf, it's a security camera. Behind the tree, the piece includes a flower stalk with leaves, in the same style as *Girl with Aerial*.

Surveillance is a theme Banksy returns to on a regular basis. Even in the woods, Big Brother is keeping an eye. The strange juxtaposition of this country girl in L.A. and the context, also serves to highlight the absence of nature, of respite from the massive sea of concrete, in this dystopia of urbanism.

In 2013 this piece became the first Banksy mural to be auctioned in the US, at Julien's Auctions in Beverly Hills. It fetched $209,000.

WHERE IS IT ?
HOLLYWOOD,
LOS ANGELES,
USA.

Latitude: 34.0416ºN
Longitude: 118.2380ºW

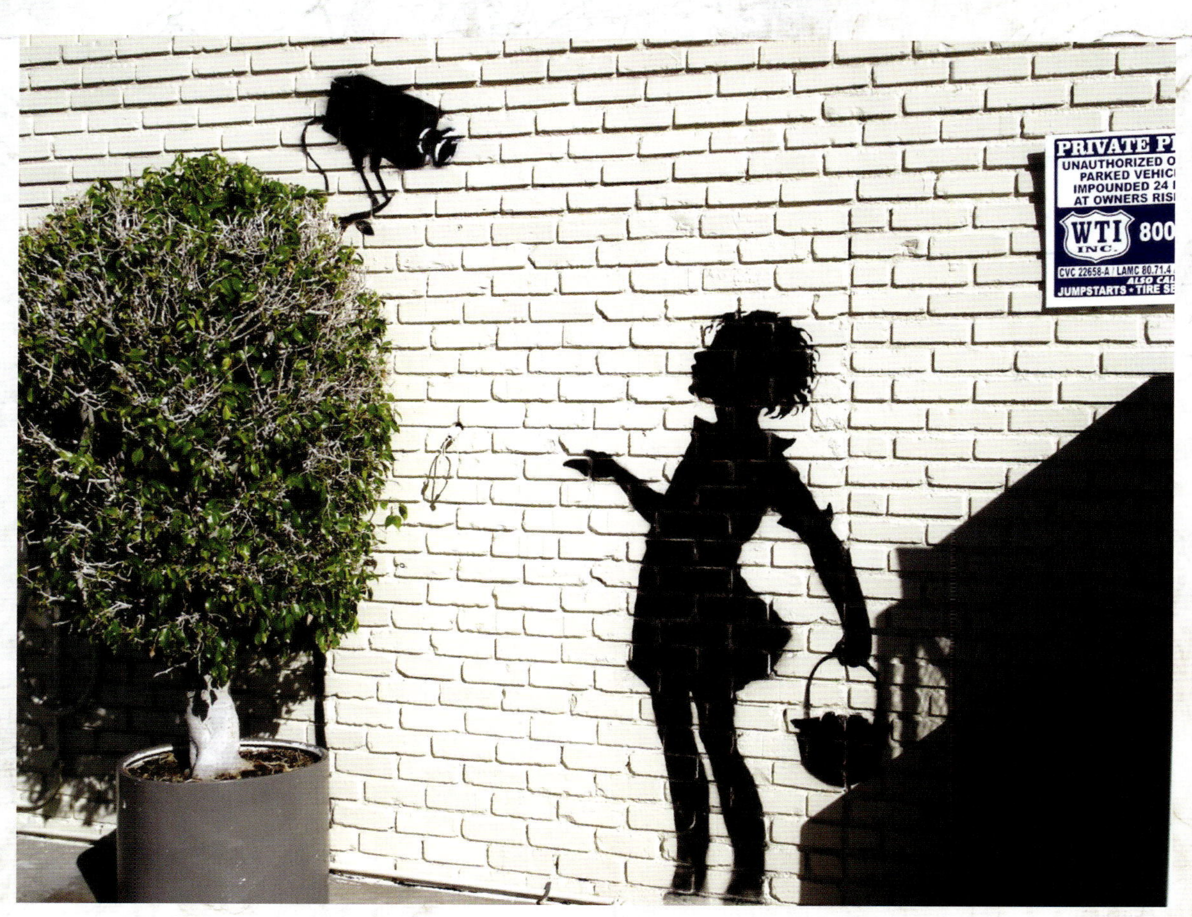PRIVATE P
UNAUTHORIZED O
PARKED VEHIC
IMPOUNDED 24
AT OWNERS RIS
WTI
INC. 800
CVC 22658-A / LAMC 80.71.4
JUMPSTARTS • TIRE SE

WHITEWASHING LASCAUX

"In the space of a few hours with a couple of hundred cans of paint I'm hoping we can transform a dark, forgotten filth pit into an oasis of beautiful art." **Banksy.**

One of Banksy's wittiest, most brilliant pieces, created as part of the Cans Festival, a three-day street art street party hosted and organised by Banksy. The festival took place in a tunnel under Waterloo Station in London and, in addition to Banksy, included works by such uber talents as BTOY, C215, Dolk, Eine, Faile, MBW, Sam3, Sten and Lex, and Vhils.

For this writer, this Banksy was the outstanding piece, a brilliant commentary on the vandalism of local government clean-up gangs eradicating great art. Recreating the UNESCO World Heritage 20,000-year old Palaeolithic cave paintings in the Dordogne, Banksy shows a hilariously diligent council employee with his pressure-washer, spraying out this invaluable wall art as if it was so much graffiti. Today's wall daubings are tomorrow's invaluable artworks... another one of those inadvertent prophecies, given the prices Banksy works would subsequently achieve.

The detail of the paint-drips as the original is dissolved is a brilliant touch.

WHERE IS IT ?
LEAKE STREET TUNNEL,
WATERLOO STATION,
LONDON.

Latitude: 51.5021ºN
Longitude: 0.1160ºW

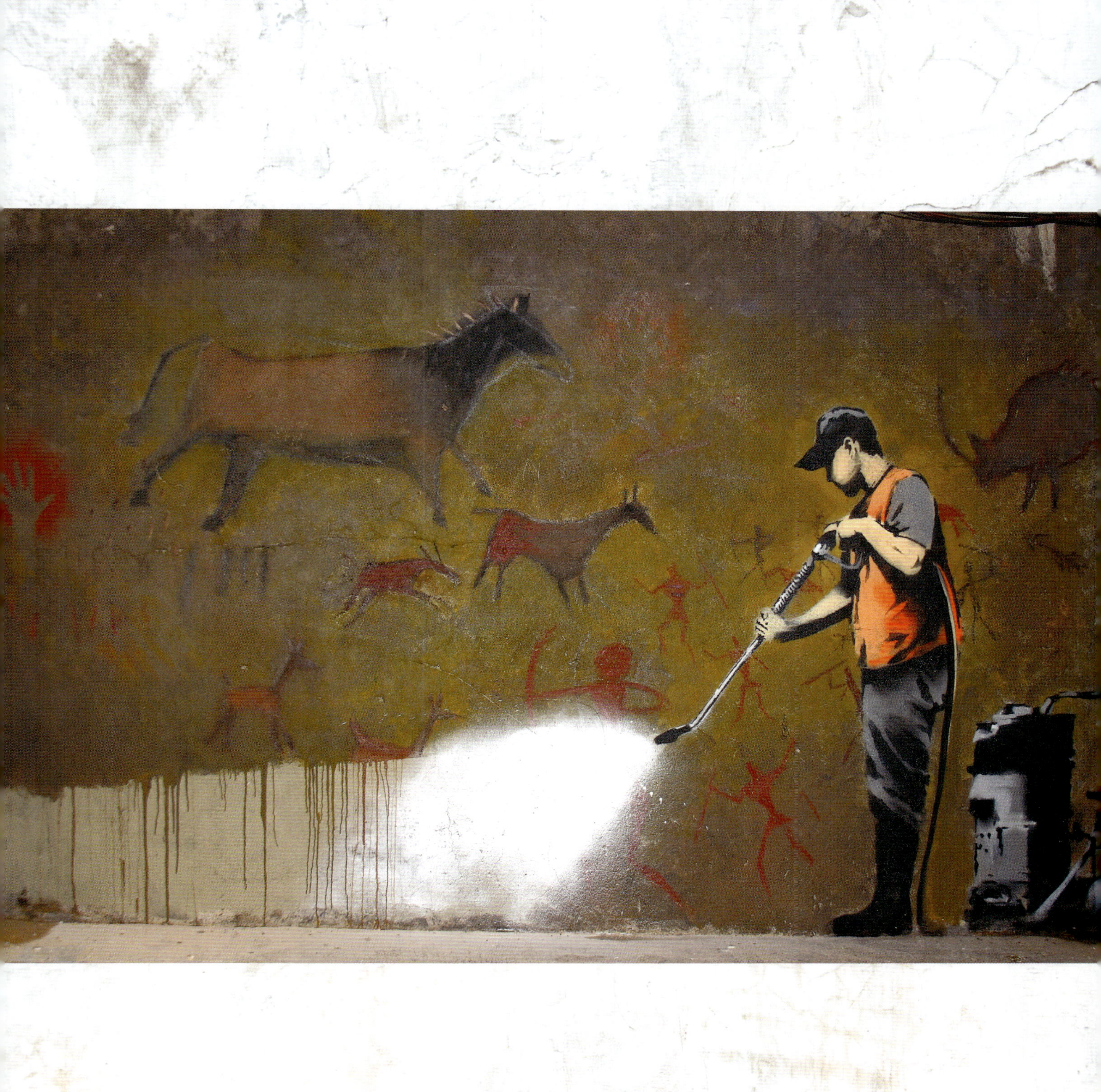

NOLA GIRL WITH UMBRELLA

"I don't think anybody anticipated the breach of the levees."
President G.W. Bush, speaking after Katrina.

A sad but brilliant image, this Banksy is perhaps the most eloquent of his works in New Orleans, from his visit in 2008. A devastating critique of the failures that led to the destruction following Hurricane Katrina, Banksy again uses the image of a child, a little girl in a pinafore dress. She has wisely brought an umbrella to protect her from the rain, but far from protecting her, it is raining inside the cover of her umbrella. With the instinctive gesture of sticking a hand out to feel for rain, she sees that outside it is dry and sunny. The expression on her face feels almost like that borderline between childhood and the evils of the adult world: with much sadness and some puzzlement she is beginning to understand she is not protected.

Banksy is arguably at his best when he encapsulates a burning political issue and comment on injustice in an image like this. Katrina represented a massive district and federal failure, which without doubt led directly to loss of life in the wake of the hurricane. New Orleans' Mayor Nagin had failed to establish an evacuation plan, despite having received $20 million to do so. Despite knowing the storm was on its way (and that poorer, mostly black residents did not have cars), he sent Amtrak trains away from the city empty. When the storm hit he waited a full two days before ordering an evacuation. 53 levees failed in the wake of the storm. Even knowing this, the Federal Emergency Management Agency (FEMA) had only two workers on the ground, rather than the 1000 needed. 30,000 people evacuated to the Superdome on Nagin's orders spent a week in a living hell of sewage, deplorable heat, darkness and without food and water. Meanwhile President Bush, who was on holiday, ignored Governor Blanco's initial requests for help, and then, realising that he might face major criticism, commissioned a PR campaign to blame local officials for the disaster. Over 1800 people died as a result of Katrina.

Given the circumstances, Banksy's piece is remarkably gentle and without rancour. It shows him at his most sensitive, acknowledging the suffering that the citizens of Louisiana and Mississippi had gone through, without making any clever jokes.

WHERE IS IT ?
NORTH RAMPART AND KERLEREC,
NEW ORLEANS,
USA.
STILL THERE, PROTECTED BY A PERSPEX COVER,
IT HAS BEEN JOINED TO THE LEFT BY A STENCIL,
BY A DIFFERENT ARTIST, OF A LITTLE BOY. THIS HAS,
IRRITATINGLY, SENTIMENTALISED BANKSY'S SERIOUS WORK.

Latitude: 29.9706ºN
Longitude: 90.0679ºW

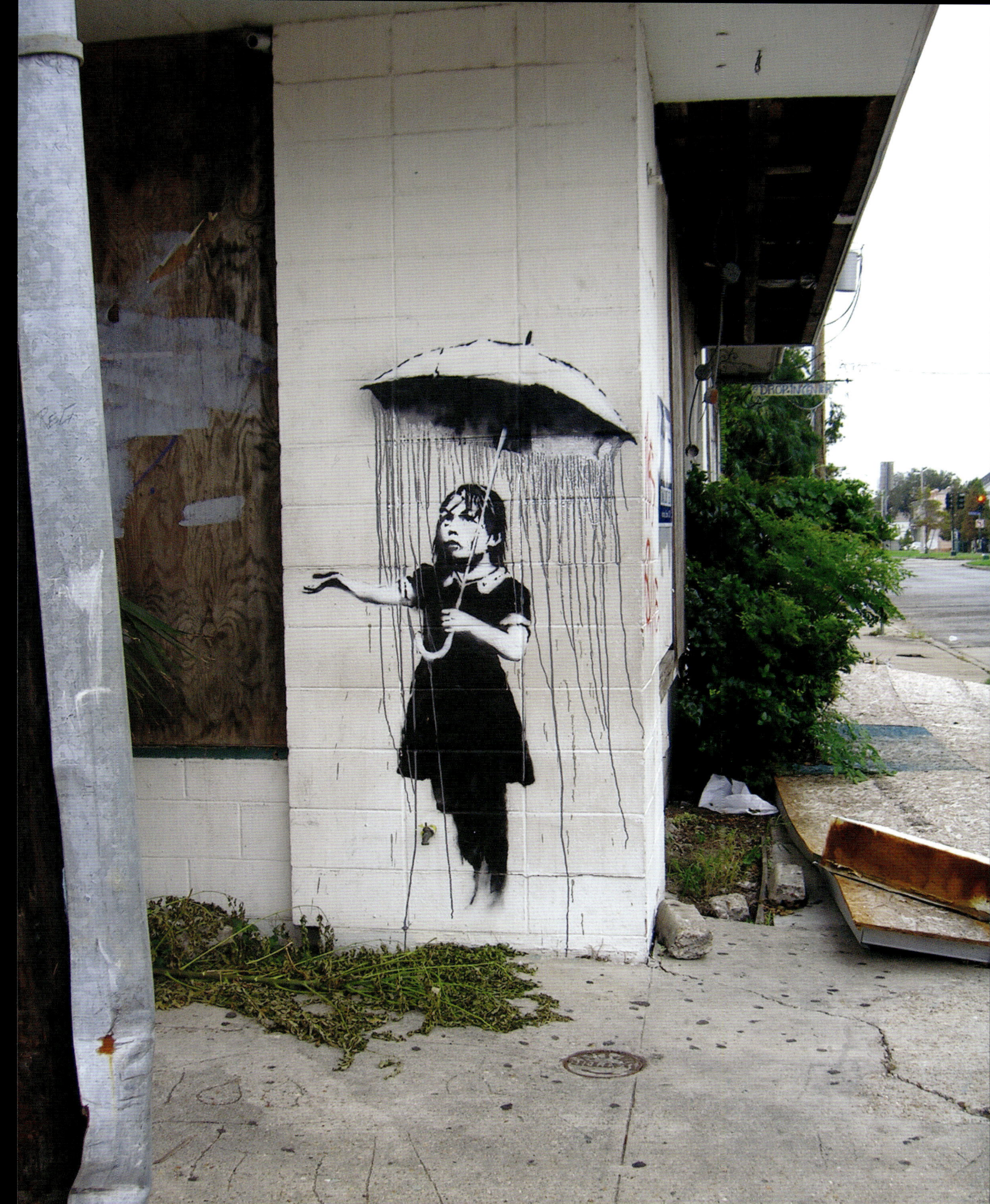

ABE LINCOLN

"Government of the people, by the people, for the people, shall not perish from the earth." **Abraham Lincoln, Gettysburg Address.**

Abraham Lincoln, the 16th President of the USA, the man who led the northern states to win the Civil War and thus achieved the abolition of slavery throughout the Union, walking the streets of New Orleans as a homeless man.

It is no accident that Banksy picked Abe in this role, as a way of illustrating the moral and political bankruptcy that the Bush administration's reaction to Hurricane Katrina represented. Firstly Abe was a Republican, like George W. Bush. Compare the Republican party then and the Republican party now, the piece seems to be saying. Most of those who died and were made homeless by Katrina were from the poorer Black neighbourhoods. By enlisting the figure of Abe, the emancipator of the slaves, Banksy is saying that these were Americans whose right it was to be protected, no matter what the racist view from some parts of Washington. By making Abe homeless, walking the streets, the suggestion is that, with the then administration in power, all Americans were now metaphorically homeless.

It's not hard to find signs in New Orleans saying 'Private Property Keep Out.' Here the sign is apposite: private interests now rule, with government "of the people, by the people, for the people" an obsolete concept, effectively kicked out into the street.

WHERE IS IT ?
NEW ORLEANS,
USA.
SURVIVED UNTIL 2010.
WAS PAINTED OVER AND THEN THE BUILDING
WAS DEMOLISHED TO MAKE WAY FOR THE
UNIVERSITY MEDICAL CENTER.

Latitude: 29.9545ºN
Longitude: 90.0770ºW

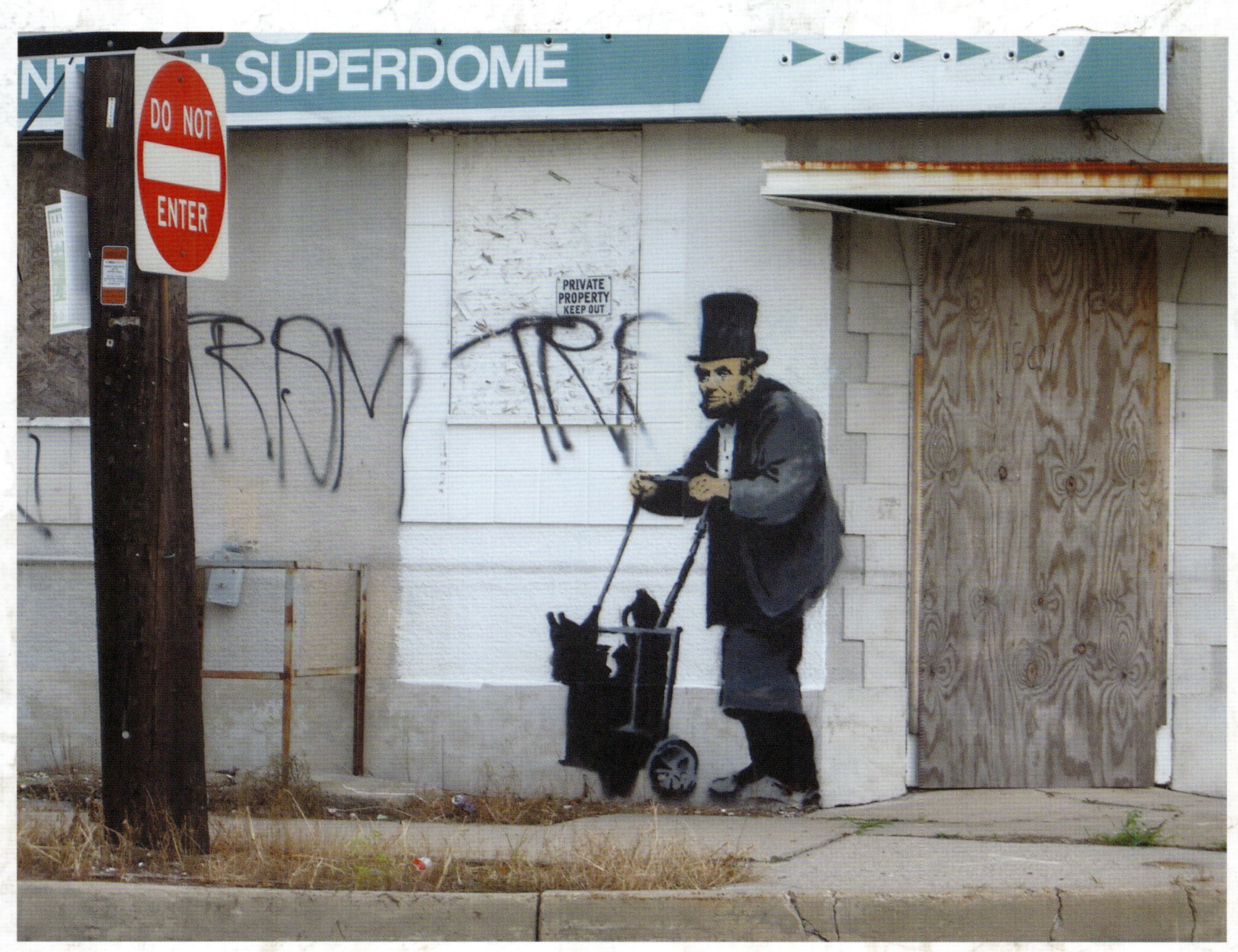
SUPERDOME
DO NOT ENTER
PRIVATE
PROPERTY
KEEP OUT

LOOTING NATIONAL GUARDS

"Go to hell, it's every man for himself."
One NOPD policeman to tourist requesting help during Katrina.

Another astute piece, commenting on the Bush administration's failures in response to Katrina. Two National Guardsmen, meant to protect citizens, are instead shown niftily looting a home of its boombox and TV, easy to do in a city where one third of the police deserted the city in the wake of the Hurricane.

It's hard to know what precise point Banksy is trying to make here, or if it is just a bit of fun, suggesting that authorities may as well have looted homes given their failures in responding to the crisis. The National Guard did not come out well, unlike the military, in the post-Hurricane assessments.

There were major reports of extensive looting post Katrina. Many of these were later shown to be sensationalist and fabricated by the media, fuelling a state of paranoia and suspicion. Inevitably most of the unfounded media suggestions were that looting was undertaken by poor black residents.

There were a number of arrests for thefts committed by a few NOPD officers after the Hurricane; none of the thefts implicated the military.

WHERE IS IT ?
ELYSIAN FIELDS,
NEW ORLEANS,
USA.

Latitude: 29.9616ºN
Longitude: 90.0566ºW

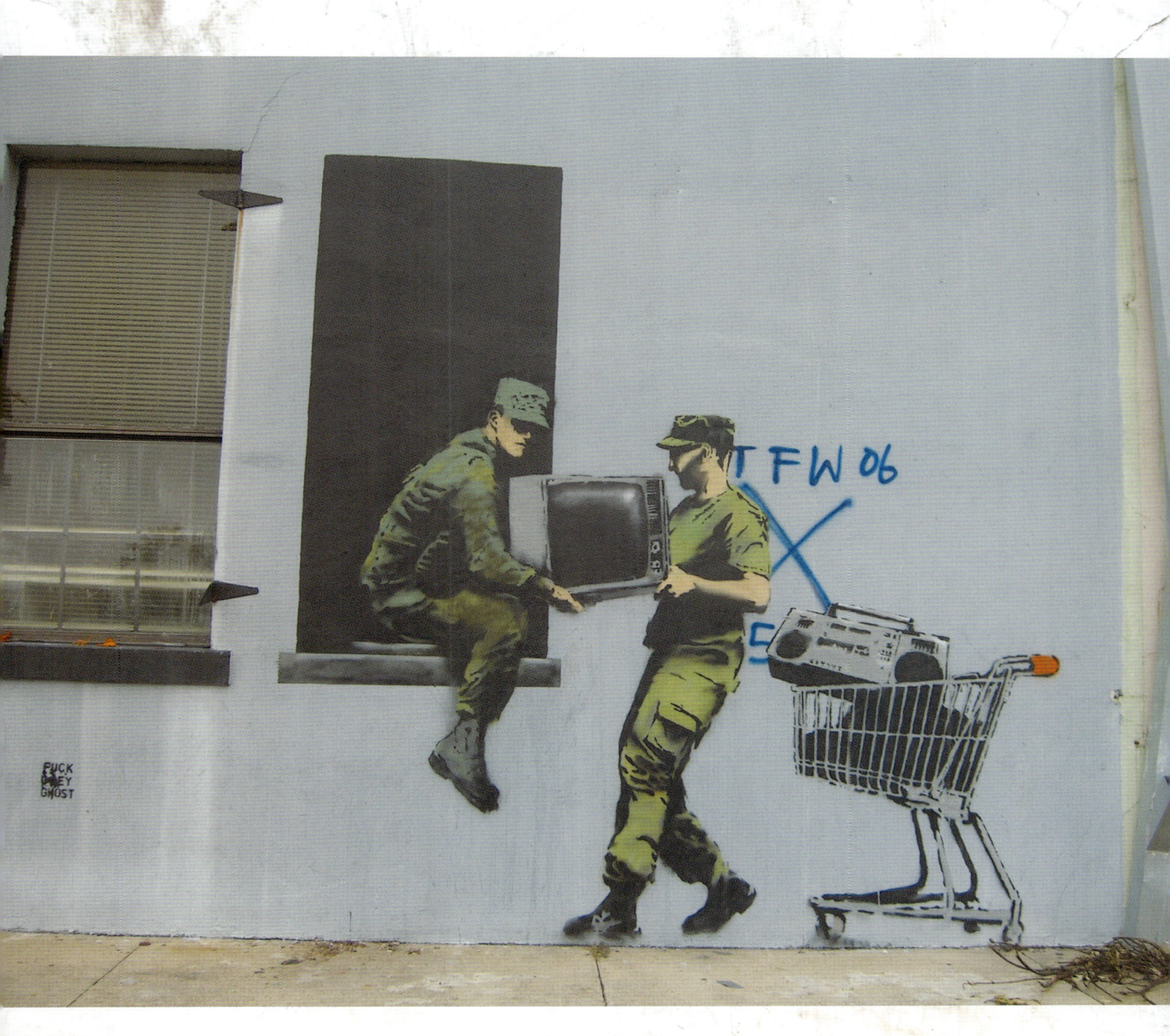

FUCK
MONEY
GHOST
TFW 06

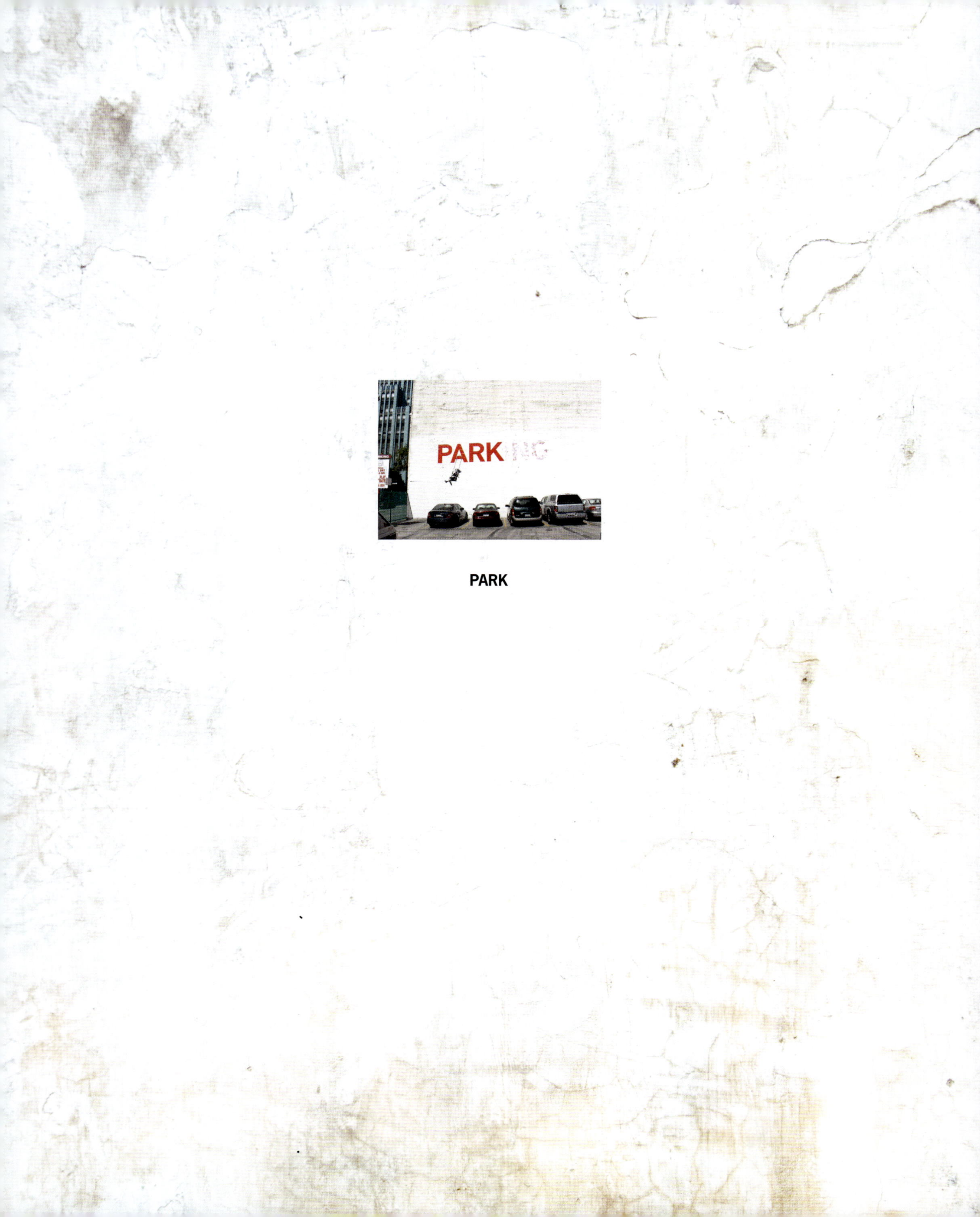

PARK

2009-2010

A brilliantly productive period, with the reach of street art taken to new heights with his documentary *Exit Through the Gift Shop*, nominated for the Best Documentary Oscar. Banksy produces brilliant work in L.A., New York and Detroit. He is again ahead of the game with his criticism of Obama's drone assassination strategy, with *Airstrike*; Obama's popularity does not stop Banksy's searching eye seeing what is really going on in US foreign policy.

LAST GRAFFITI BEFORE MOTORWAY

BOOMBOX BOY

NO FISHING

EXIT THROUGH THE GIFT SHOP

WILL WORK FOR IDIOTS

WHEATPASTER

GUARD ON DUTY

PARK

LIBERTY

TESCO SAND CASTLE

ROLLERHEAD HERON

I REMEMBER WHEN ALL THIS WAS TREES

CALL AN AIRSTRIKE

I LOVE NY

BANKSY 2009-2010

Banksy undertakes a lot of international travel in support of *Exit Through The Gift Shop*. First the launch at the Sundance Film Festival in Utah, then Boston, Toronto, New York and L.A., followed by San Francisco, with a segway to Detroit.

Otherwise it was London again and a seaside trip down to Hastings on the English south coast, for another dig at supermarket giant, Tesco.

SAN FRANCISCO
14. Airstrike,
Chinatown.

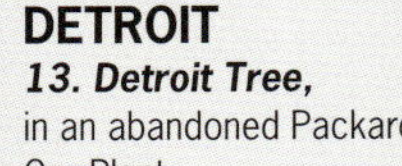

DETROIT
13. Detroit Tree,
in an abandoned Packard Car Plant.

BOSTON
May, 2010

LOS ANGELES
7. Guard on Duty,
La Brea and 4th.

8. Park,
Broadway, Downtown.

UTAH
4. World premiere of *Exit Through the Gift Shop*, Sundance Film Festival, Park City; 24th January 2010.

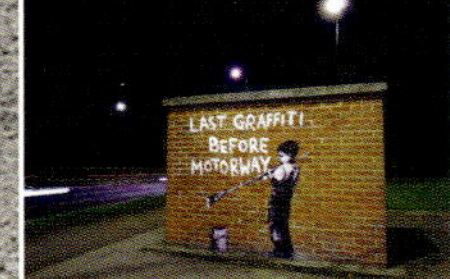

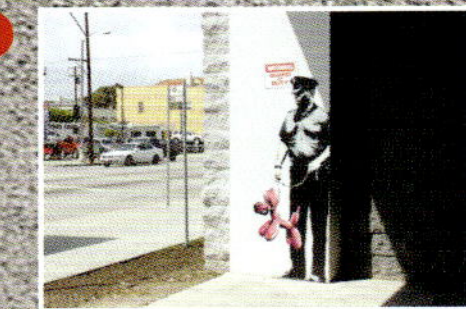

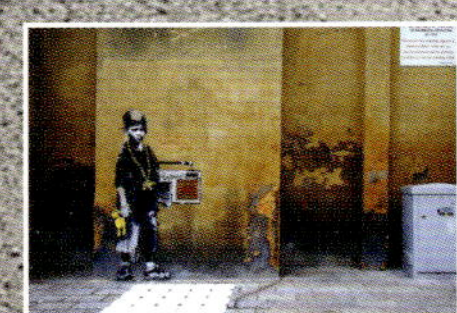

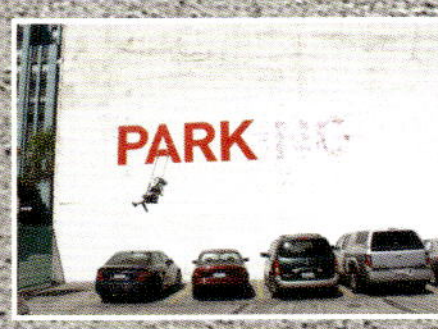

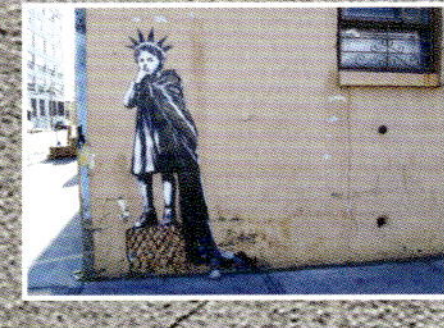

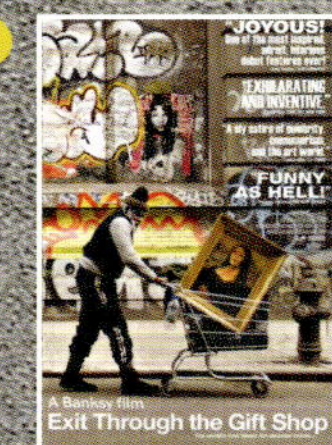

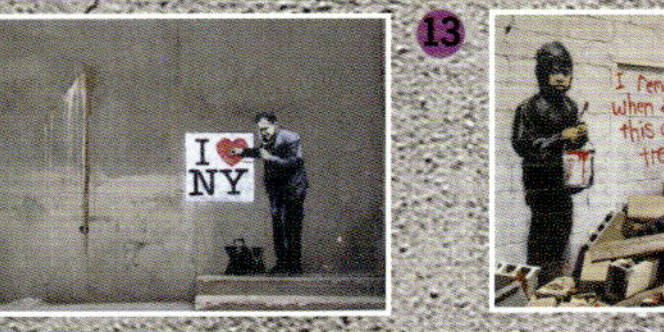

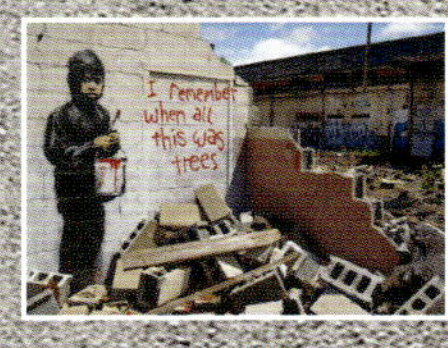

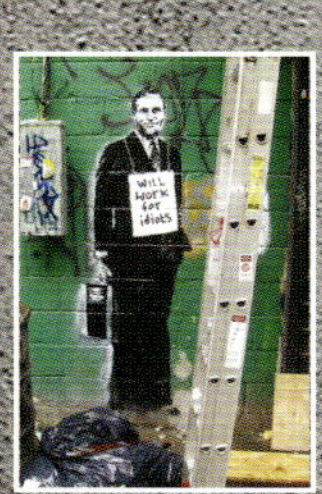

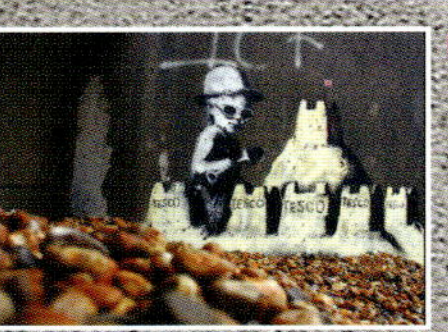

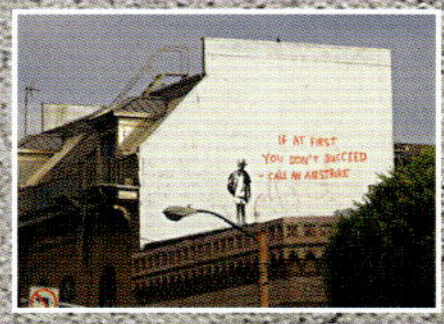

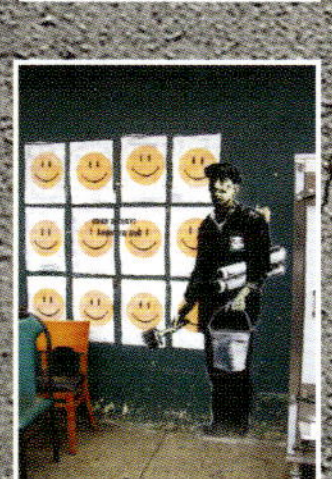

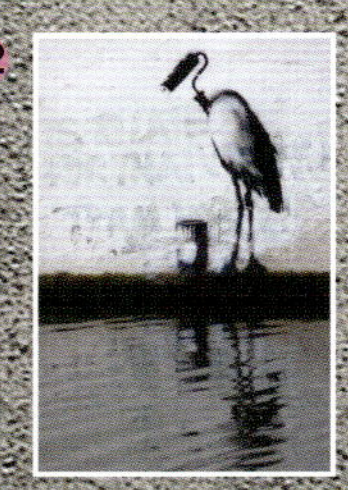

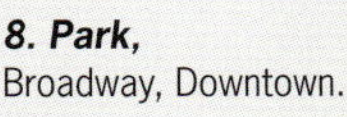

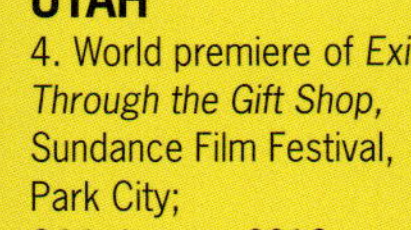

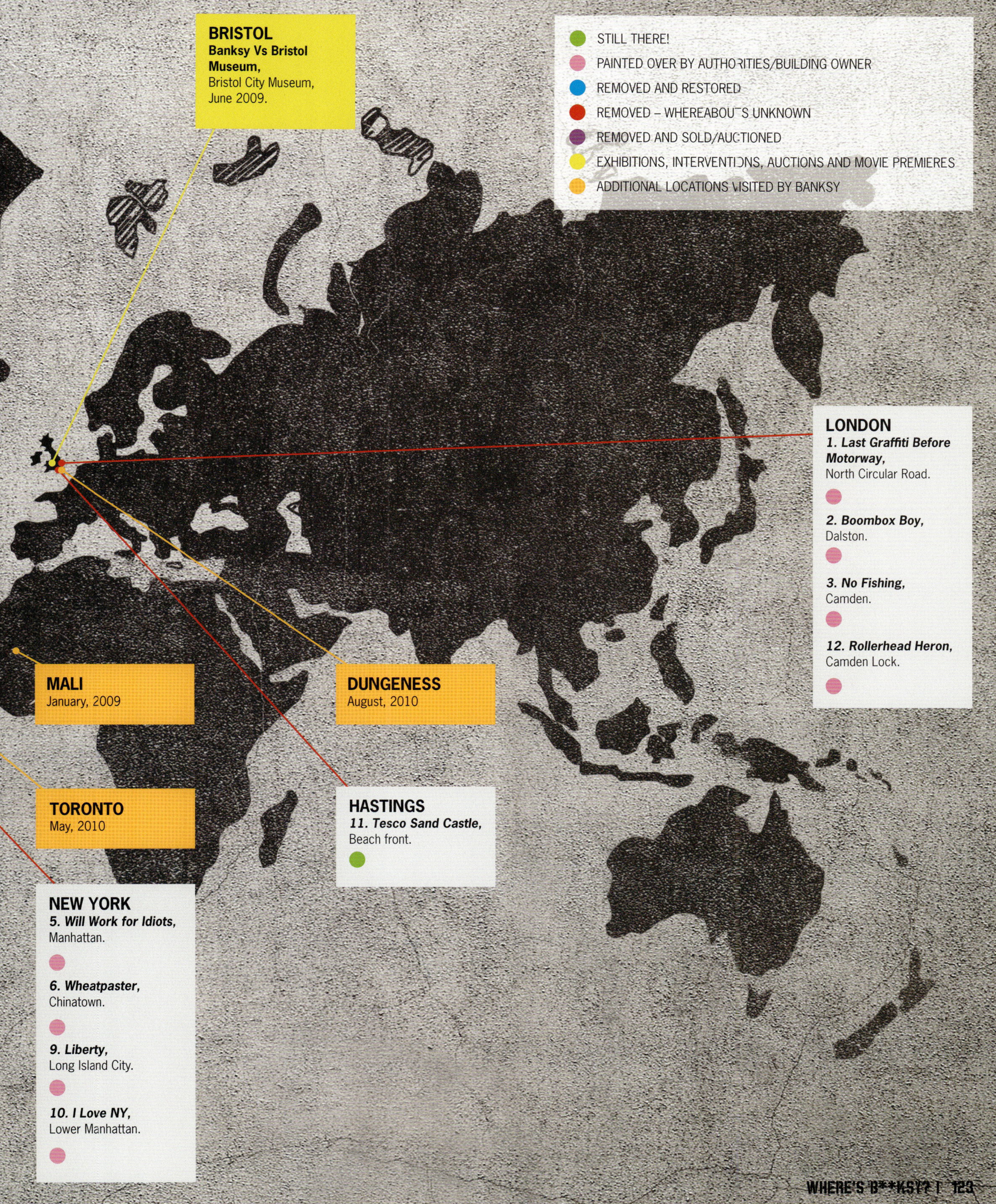

STILL THERE!
PAINTED OVER BY AUTHORITIES/BUILDING OWNER
REMOVED AND RESTORED
REMOVED – WHEREABOUTS UNKNOWN
REMOVED AND SOLD/AUCTIONED
EXHIBITIONS, INTERVENTIONS, AUCTIONS AND MOVIE PREMIERES
ADDITIONAL LOCATIONS VISITED BY BANKSY
BRISTOL
Banksy Vs Bristol Museum,
Bristol City Museum, June 2009.
LONDON
1. Last Graffiti Before Motorway,
North Circular Road.
2. Boombox Boy,
Dalston.
3. No Fishing,
Camden.
12. Rollerhead Heron,
Camden Lock.
MALI
January, 2009
DUNGENESS
August, 2010
TORONTO
May, 2010
HASTINGS
11. Tesco Sand Castle,
Beach front.
NEW YORK
5. Will Work for Idiots,
Manhattan.
6. Wheatpaster,
Chinatown.
9. Liberty,
Long Island City.
10. I Love NY,
Lower Manhattan.
WHERE'S B**KSY? 123

LAST GRAFFITI BEFORE MOTORWAY

"Think outside the box, collapse the box, and take a fucking sharp knife to it." Banksy.

Banksy's art relies as much on the acuity of his sense of language as his visual wit. Always awake to the standard hackneyed phrases used by government agencies to suggest organisation and control, he usurps this language to reveal its essential banality and tedium.

This is a brilliant example. Painted and stencilled on the most nondescript brick box, it sends motorists travelling north out of London on their way with a smile. The language is usually used to provide a helpful warning; 'Last petrol services before motorway', would be typical. The suggestion is that you should pull in, and replenish on some essential supply before proceeding; without it you might be stranded.

That this essential supply is graffiti is, of course, hilarious. It also gives a sense that one is leaving that heartland of great street art, London, for the slightly boring, monocultural country beyond.

As often with Banksy, the use of a small boy, in Huck Finn dungarees, and weighed down by his brush (take note: not the usual roller), but still managing to paint the message despite the difficulty, is both charming but also makes the piece somewhat poignant. How can one object to this helpful bit of information written by this brave, chubby-cheeked young lad?

WHERE IS IT ?
NORTH CIRCULAR ROAD,
A1 JUNCTION,
LONDON,
UK.
HAS BEEN BUFFED.

Latitude: 51.5895ºN
Longitude: 0.2022ºW

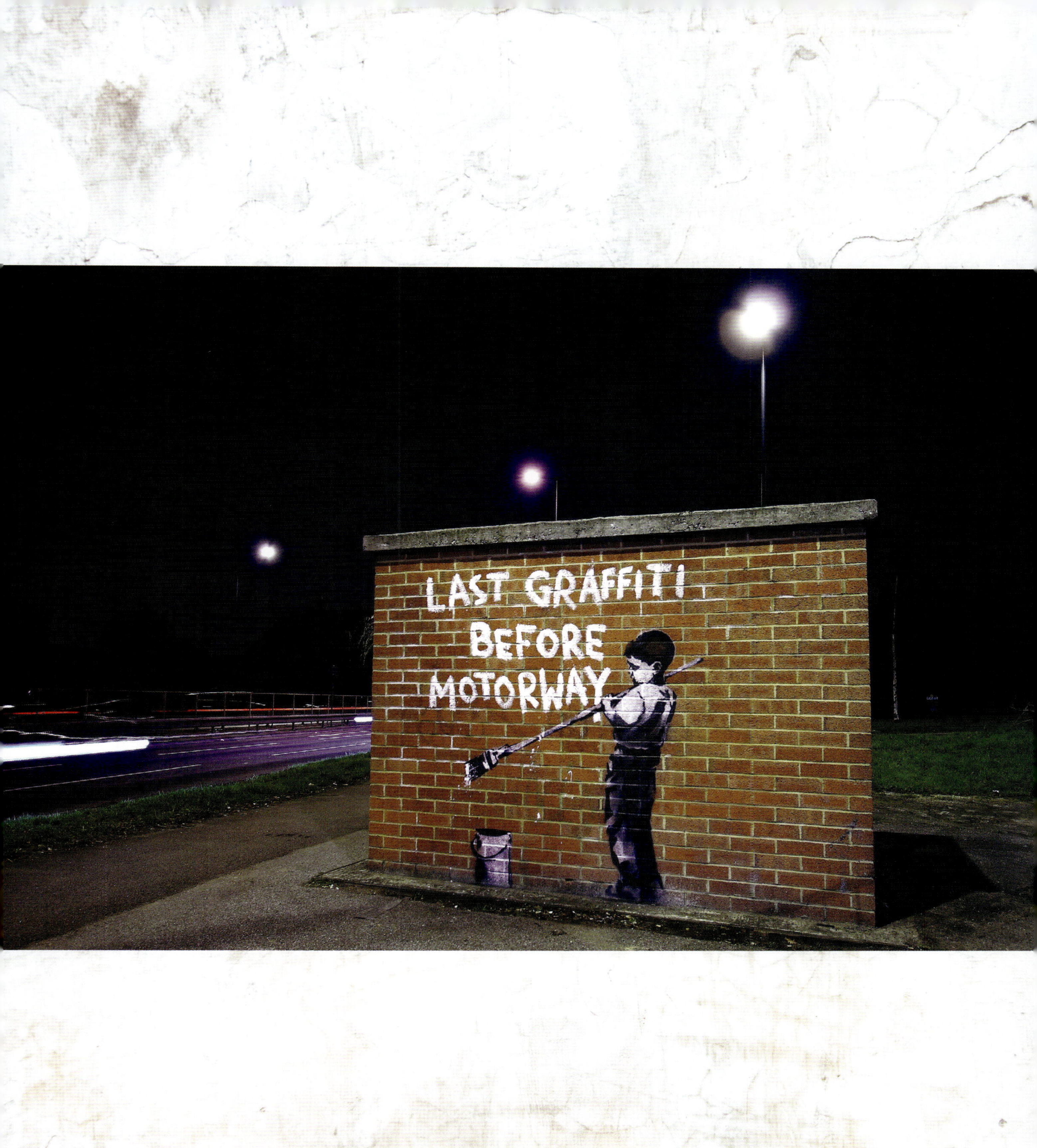
LAST GRAFFITI
BEFORE
MOTORWAY

BOOMBOX BOY

"I felt I needed to prove a point, to be untouchable, to be feared.... I ended up ruining my life."
London boy gang member, imprisoned for stabbing another boy.

Banksy's portrayal of children is usually retro, derived from images of English ideals of childhood, from the 1930s to the 1960s. Very occasionally he strays into new turf, as here.

A very young boy in hip-hop, gangland bling. A massive gold chain around his neck, with a gold sub-machine gun (or is it a water pistol?) hanging from it. On his right wrist, also a chunky gold chain, but hanging from that a soft gold teddy, the sort of teddy one would be given at age 6 months. The child is trying to look mean, but at the same time there is a trace of unhappiness in his expression. In his left arm not quite a boombox, more of one of those big radio-cassette players from the late 1970s. Using the ventilation air-brick as the speaker of the boombox is a brilliant touch, anchoring the piece to the wall, making it part of the building.

This was the first piece that Banksy had created on the street after a six month break, and it is a brilliant piece of stencilling. This boy, and in particular his expression, has real presence. There is no overt message here, other than perhaps that kids are getting into a gangland scene too young. We prefer to think of it as an accurate portrayal of a certain point in growing up, that point of tension between the security of being a kid and simultaneously wishing to be the cool, tough adult.

WHERE IS IT ?
DALSTON,
LONDON,
UK.

Latitude: 51.5489ºN
Longitude: 0.0760ºW

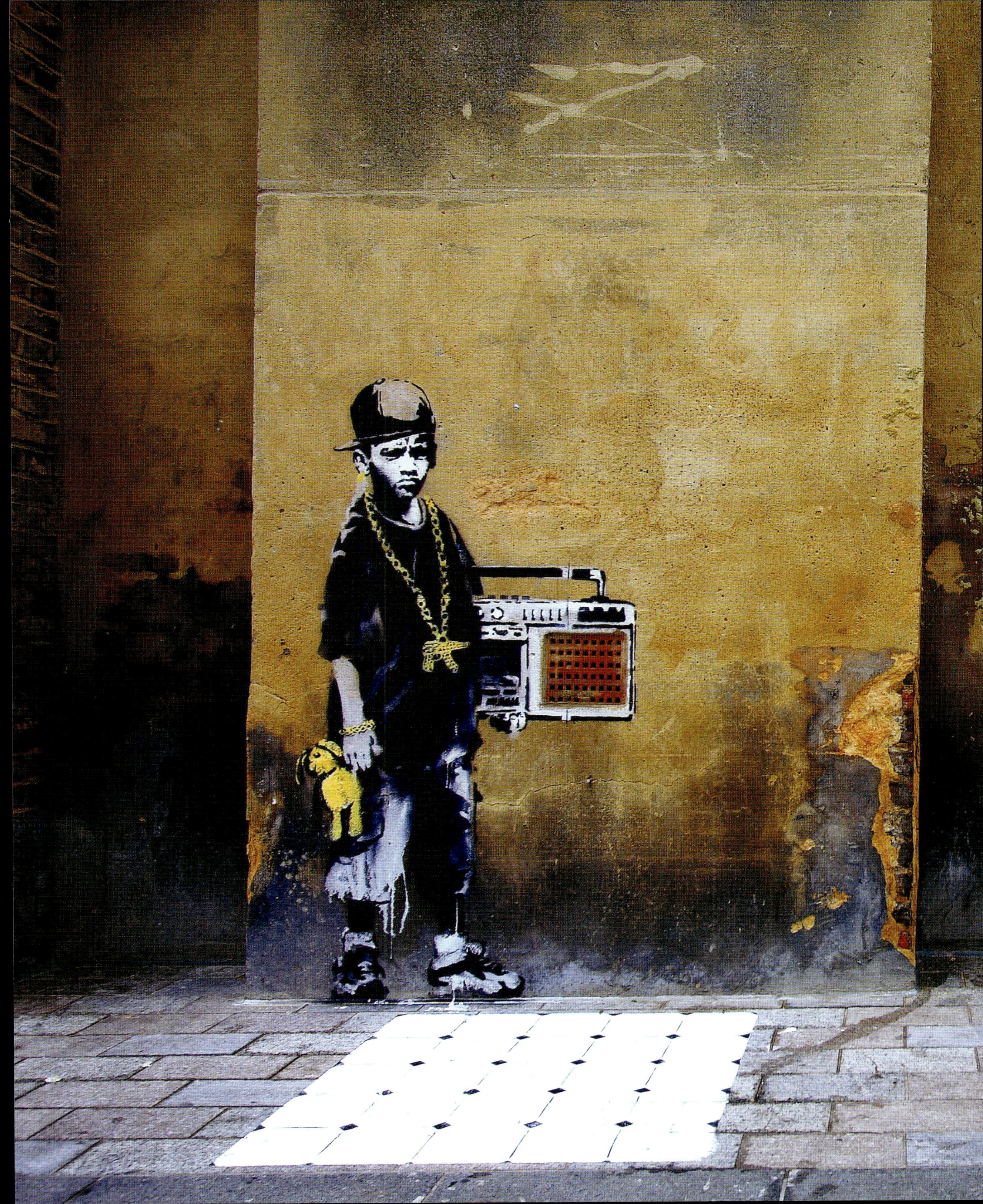

NO FISHING

"We are concerned that Banksy's street art glorifies what is essentially vandalism." Diane Shakespeare, official with the *Keep Britain Tidy* campaign.

One of Banksy's rather charming situationist pieces, featuring a Huckleberry Finn-type child, with his dungarees and straw hat, sitting cross-legged on a folding fishing stool, fishing. Painted in a little-frequented bit of the Regent's Canal on the bank opposite to the one carrying the towpath, this should have made it pretty inaccessible as you would need a boat of some kind to get across. The black patches are where Banksy's self-appointed Bristol rival, Robbo, made the effort to scrawl a number of (not particularly interesting to a wider audience) messages, including 'Banksy, by being in London your [sic] depriving your village of its idiot'. Robbo explained in an interview that Team Robbo represented real freehand graffiti artists, not "your stencil street art middle class art students."

Banksy is here returning to one of his tropes: pointing out the petty signage which is the mark of the quietly oppressive state. Here the boy has fished out a 'No Fishing' sign, making a nonsense of the restriction. The slightly bemused expression on the boy's face shows his puzzlement that anyone should seek to restrict such an innocent pleasure. The drip of paint on the sign has also, inadvertently, caused the image to look like a mini DV camera. A classic case of a Banksy acquiring an extra layer of meaning: even in this dank corner of London, the altered image suggests, you are under surveillance.

WHERE IS IT ?
REGENT'S CANAL,
CAMDEN,
LONDON,
UK.

Latitude: 51.5410ºN
Longitude: 0.1458ºW

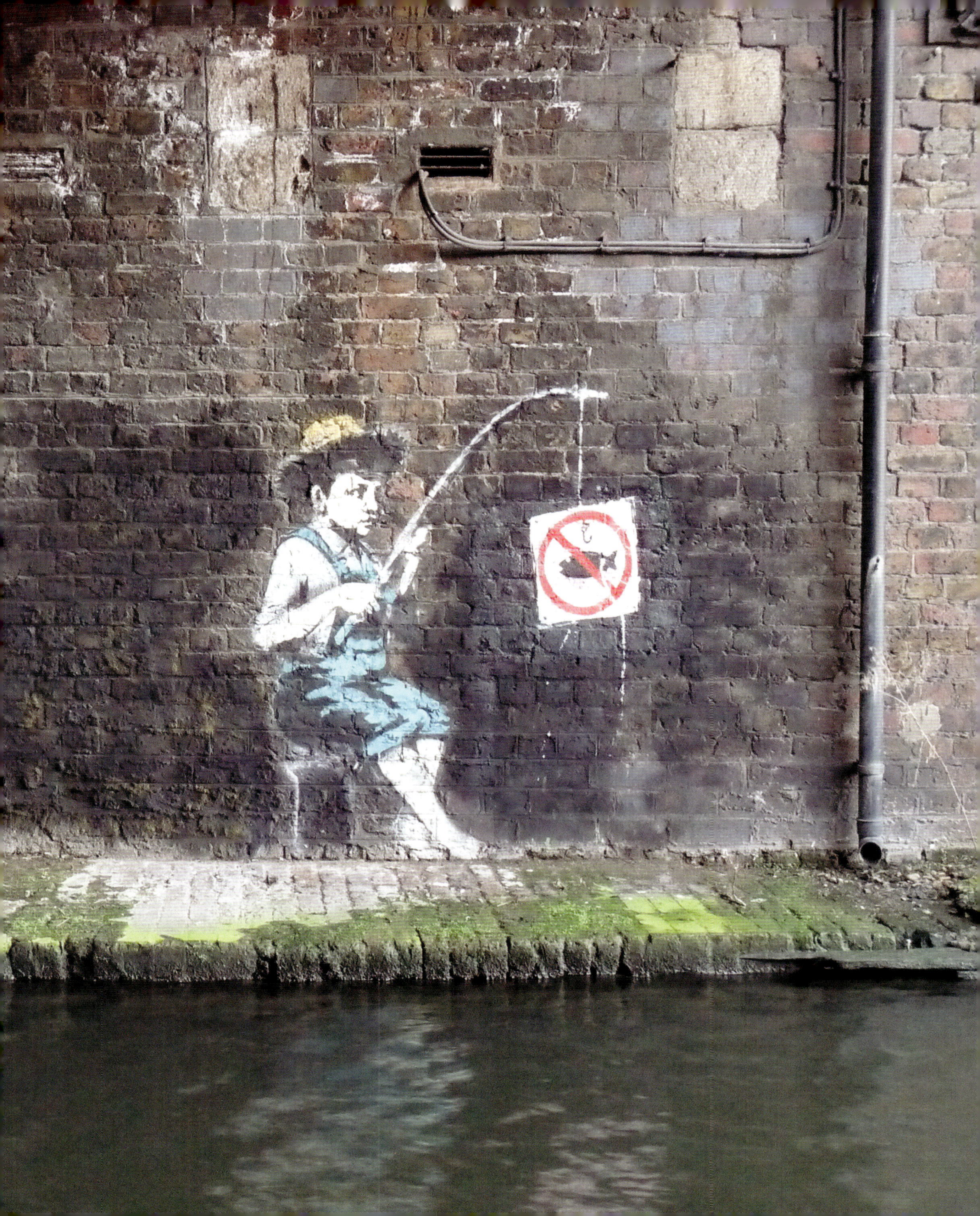

EXIT THROUGH THE GIFT SHOP

"Exit *could be a new subgenre: the prankumentary.*"
The New York Times.

Banksy decides to make a movie and a year later it's nominated for an Oscar at the 2011 Academy Awards for Best Documentary. Another example of a certain Midas touch: what other street artists could have done this?

Except that *Exit Through the Gift Shop* isn't really a documentary, it's part spoof, part information, part stunt. The film purports to examine Banksy and the explosion of street art in Los Angeles. Centre-stage is the friendship between Banksy and L.A.-based Frenchman Thierry Guetta. Thierry, ostensibly, followed street artists around the streets of L.A., shooting tons of footage for no reason. Banksy, so goes the movie, suggests that Guetta should come and use his footage in Banksy's movie and then, why not, just become a street artist himself? So, in double quick time, Guetta adopts the moniker Mr Brainwash, or MBW, and produces a convincing body of Warhol-esque work, which he proceeds to sell at a mega exhibition of his work.

Banksy seems to be deliberately devaluing his own work by suggesting anyone can do it. You can become a mega artist with the right sort of attitude and media manipulation. All it takes is a certain spirit. Talent not required. It's all smoke and mirrors, image subverting image, counterfeit and forgery. If only it were so easy.

The poster for the movie was a triumph, showing art as just another consumer good. In brilliant juxtaposition we see a homeless man, shopping trolley full of black bin bags, walking the streets (a kind of gift shop, given the art on show), about to take the *Mona Lisa* to the checkout – the last man one would see in a gallery shop. And that's the point. Gallery art isn't about art, it's just another form of middle class consumption. It's a delicious irony that galleries are fed up with real art – they would all be in clover if only they could just sell Banksys.

Exit proved too much for the Academy. The Oscar went to the *Inside Job,* a worthy but now forgotten movie on the institutional corruption that led to the 2008 banking crisis. Hollywood is always pious after the event.

WHERE IS IT ?
MOVIE SHOWN AT THE LOS ANGELES THEATER, ARTS DISTRICT, L.A., USA.

Latitude: 34.0464ºN
Longitude: 118.2524ºW

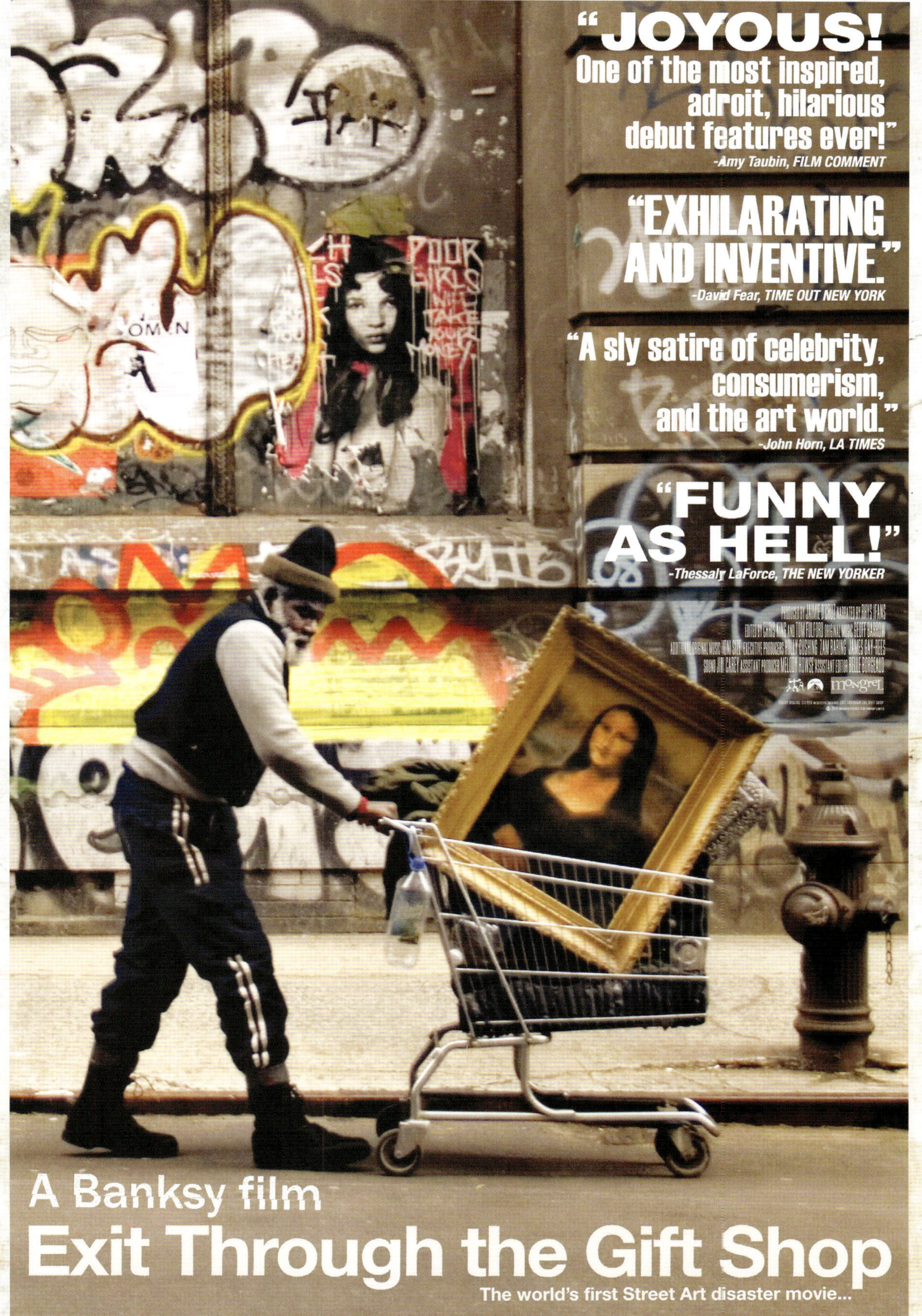
"JOYOUS!
One of the most inspired, adroit, hilarious debut features ever!"
-Amy Taubin, FILM COMMENT
"EXHILARATING AND INVENTIVE."
-David Fear, TIME OUT NEW YORK
"A sly satire of celebrity, consumerism, and the art world."
-John Horn, LA TIMES
"FUNNY AS HELL!"
-Thessaly LaForce, THE NEW YORKER
A Banksy film
Exit Through the Gift Shop
The world's first Street Art disaster movie...

WILL WORK FOR IDIOTS

"Recovery and New Beginning." Theme of the G20 summit in Toronto, 2010.

May 2010 saw Banksy back in North America, in order to promote *Exit Through the Gift Shop,* amongst other things. He first created a version of this image in Toronto at the time of the G20 summit (in an alley near Dundas and Manning), before the one in Manhattan, shown here.

It depicts a smarmy, clean-cut, standard corporate/ bureaucratic type. Banksy's contempt for global corporations and Western governments is pretty clear from most of his pieces. The suited drone is an idiot as is anyone stupid enough to hire him. The ignominious contrast of the small sandwich board and its child-like writing, with that complacent, smarmy, sales-y, confidence-inducing smile, is what makes the image work.

The piece is somewhat ambiguous, however. Is this a comment on all the salarymen thrown on the scrap heap, 1930s depression-style, following the 2007/08 financial crash? Is it a comment on the G20 continuing with the same old formulas in 2010 that caused the crash in the first place? Were he in Wall Street pinstripes, the message might be clearer. Banksy recycled the idea again (also in New York), but with a 1960s salaryman sporting a pork-pie hat.

The piece was painted in an alleyway favoured by taggers. It was painted over by their irrelevant daubs within three days. Maybe they weren't fond of Banksy, or did they think the piece was somehow aimed at them?

WHERE IS IT ?
BOWERY,
NEW YORK,
USA.
WAS TAGGED OVER AFTER THREE DAYS.

Latitude: 40.7252ºN
Longitude: 73.9924ºW

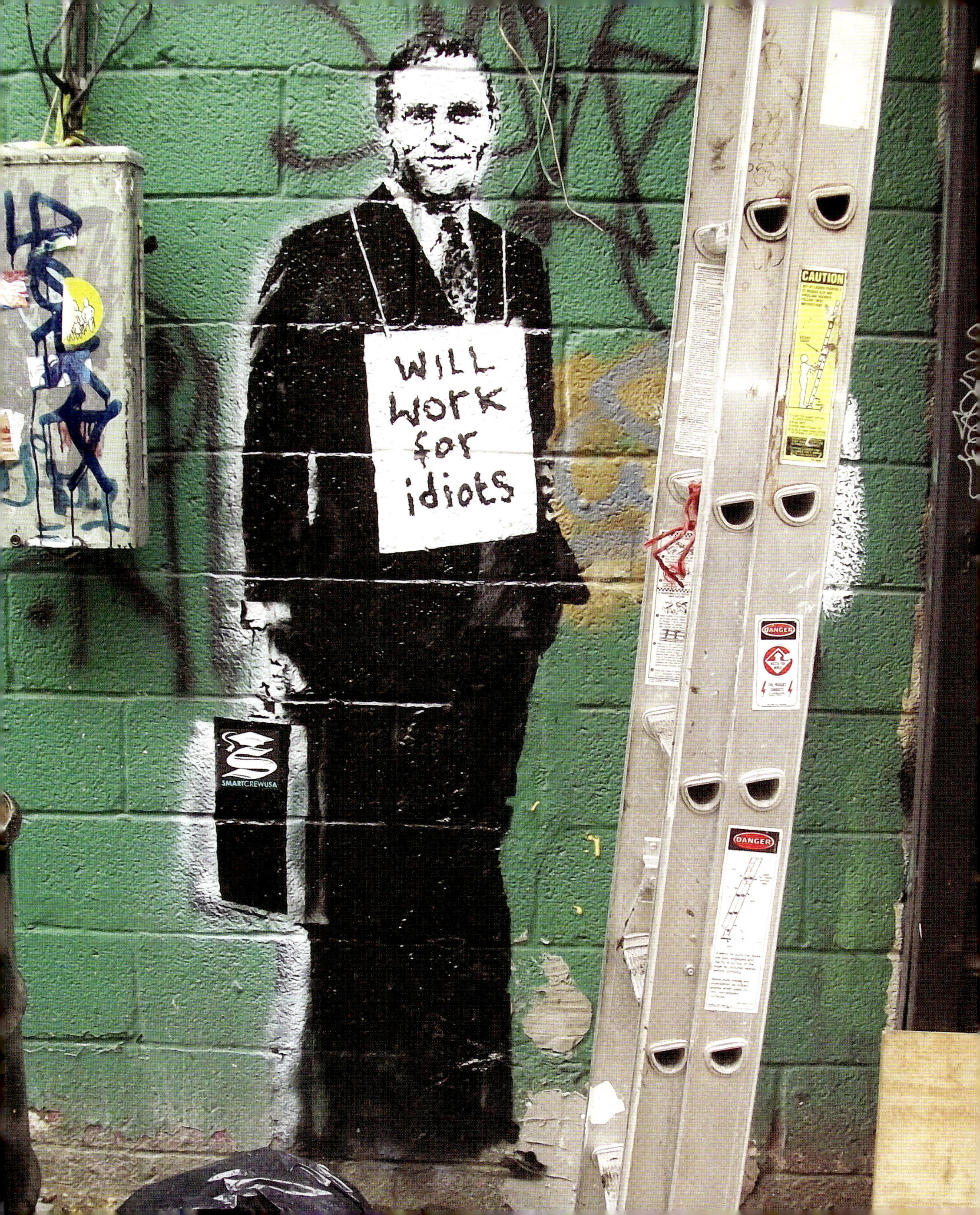

WILL
WORK
for
idiots
SMARTCREWUSA
CAUTION
DANGER
DANGER

WHEATPASTER

"He is among the most clever fellows I've ever encountered, however I've never encountered him."
John Sloss, US indie mogul and distributor of *Exit*, on Banksy, in *The Boston Globe*.

Sometimes we imagine that Banksy has got a great book of 1930s depression-era photos, which he takes as inspiration for his retro cast of characters. This wheatpaster seems to fit that bill. Dressed with his regulation flat cap, wearing a suit but with a cravat as befits someone who will sweat on the job, carrying his tin bucket and brush, he is a somewhat paradoxical stand-in for a present-day wheatpaste artist.

Here he has posted an unlikely set of acid house happy faces. Banksy has used these many times, notably on the faces of riot policemen and on a figure of the grim reaper. Here the juxtaposition with the retro wheatpaster, and the line 'Free Entry, Poster Boy' – suggesting that he will be offered a few E-tablets – is hilarious.

Banksy has used 'Poster Boy' in other cities, notably in his Boston Chinatown piece, *Follow Your Dreams*, which generated loads of interest at the time of the launch of *Exit*.

WHERE IS IT ?
CHINATOWN,
NEW YORK,
USA.

Latitude: 40.7089ºN
Longitude: 74.0112ºW

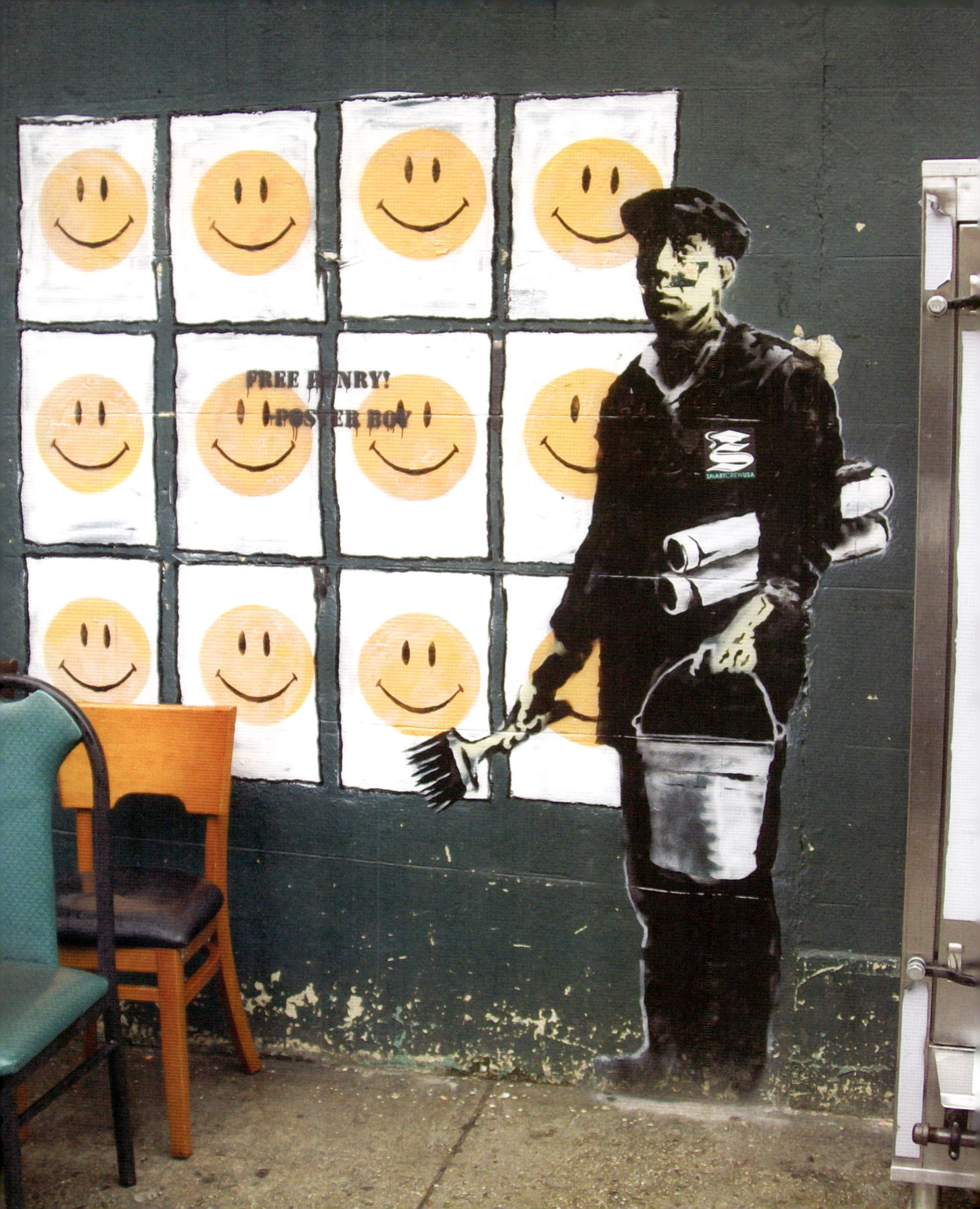

FREE HENRY!
POSTER BOY

GUARD ON DUTY

"US private security spending is estimated to rise to $68 billion annually by 2019." **Freedonia Group report.**

The first version of this piece, with the dog on the right of the guard, appeared on a wall of the old Ontario Provincial Police headquarters in Toronto, in May 2010. That building was slated for demolition, but the Banksy was preserved. The developer was planning to build a big 66-storey condo development and clearly thought a Banksy on the premises would appeal to some of his wannabe hipster clientele.

A month later, Banksy recreated an almost identical piece in L.A.. Brilliantly positioned, inside a security fence, right by a "Warning, Guard on Duty" sign, this has echoes of Banksy's *One Nation Under CCTV* and *Designated Graffiti Area* pieces, re-configured for a North American setting.

Banksy effortlessly sends up the serious, butch security guard, with his emasculating pink balloon dog. The dog has a touch of Jeff Koons about it and is depicted with a leaping stance. However the leash is limp and he is muzzled. It's one of Banksy's most satisfying works.

WHERE IS IT ?
LA BREA AND 4TH,
LOS ANGELES,
USA.
REMOVED A FEW DAYS
AFTER IT WENT UP.
WHEREABOUTS UNKNOWN.

Latitude: 34.0669ºN
Longitude: 118.3440ºW

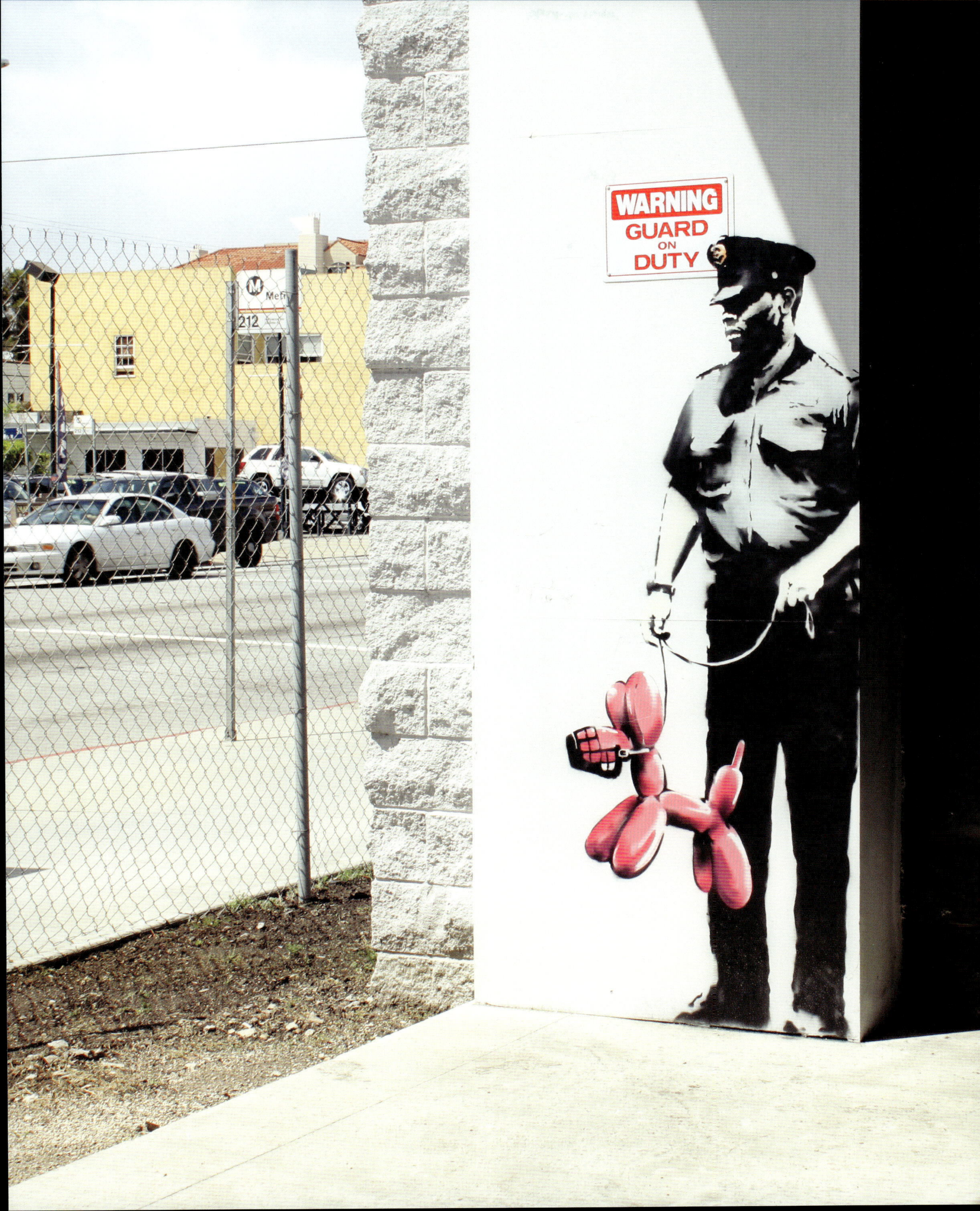

WARNING
GUARD
ON
DUTY

PARK

"Good artists copy, great artists steal." Pablo Picasso.

Another great situationist piece from Banksy's time in L.A. promoting the release of *Exit Through the Gift Shop;* this appeared a few days before the premiere, a few blocks from the Los Angeles Theater.

In broad terms, Banksy is here criticising our addiction to the automobile, an apposite statement in L.A., which, as cities go, is the ultimate car junky. The traditionally-dressed little girl on the swing, the top loops cleverly passed through the crossbar of the 'A', is wonderfully conceived, her legs and hair giving the whole composition motion. It's an admonishment to society and to adult selfishness: how come it's so easy to find car parking, so hard to create a park?

As it happened, a neighbourhood group just a block away were trying to convert a parking lot into a grassy space with a small playground when this was created. Perhaps Banksy had heard of this, perhaps it is coincidence. The piece was painted on the side of designer Tarina Tarantino's showroom, and we know she attended the premiere of *Exit.* Maybe she was the source for the idea?

WHERE IS IT ?
BROADWAY,
DOWNTOWN,
LOS ANGELES,
USA.

Latitude: 34.0430ºN
Longitude: 118.2560ºW

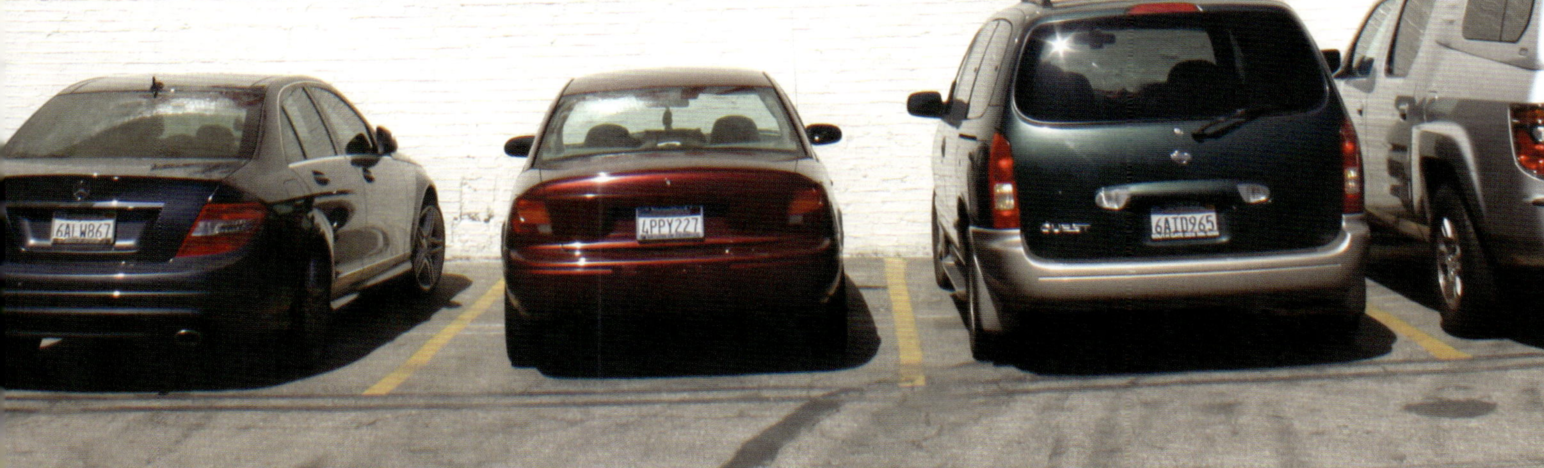

PARKING

LIBERTY

"*I used to think other graffiti writers hated me because I used stencils, but they just hate me.*" Banksy.

Not the happiest Banksy image, it has been interpreted as an anti-American piece. A young tomboyish girl is shown as the Statue of Liberty, picking her nose, with a pretty cussed expression on her face. To gain height she stands on a crate in her small boots. The cloak is way too big for her.

It could just be an image of a naughty kid. It could also be seen as a commentary on what attitudes and messages the US is projecting to the outside world. The once mighty nation, that welcomed lost souls from Europe into her heart, is now mean-spirited and shrunken, needing to stand on something else to achieve any stature. The cloak, for which read her grandeur and noble history, is now too big a legacy for her to wear. In place of the torch of freedom, there's a bogey, a touch of 'Fuck you'. Perhaps Banksy was just wanting to really piss off a few locals.

If so, he succeeded. Quite a few graffiti writers in Long Island City didn't like it, and it was destroyed within 24 hours. Comments on the piece on LTV Squad's website included: "LIC Natives like real graffiti, Banksy is Street Art"; "Banksy=sellout"; "These tourists need to go back over the Pulaski Bridge [connecting LIC to Queens] and keep their 'art' where it belongs"; and, "Banksy destroyed art".

Others had a different view and rejoindered: "Banksy is a fekking genius"; "piggybacking on Banksy is the only way anyone would see these talentless hacks"; and "Fuck all you critics who say Banksy and Obey are sellouts." One small image, not his best, but so much reaction....

WHERE IS IT ?
LONG ISLAND CITY,
NEW YORK,
USA.
PAINTED OVER WIITHIN 24 HOURS.

Latitude: 40.7447ºN
Longitude: 73.9485ºW

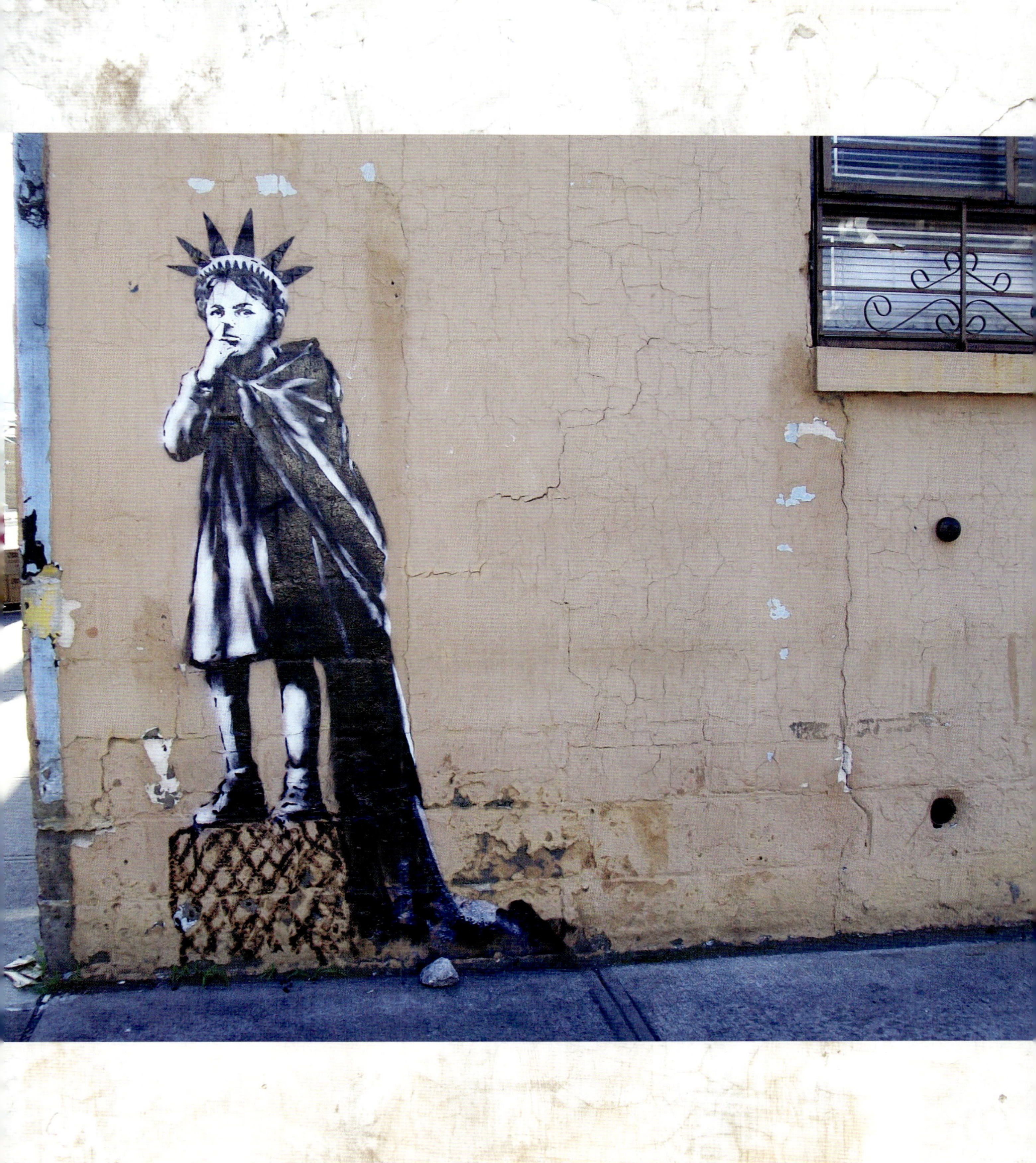

TESCO SAND CASTLE

**"We have a zero tolerance policy on graffiti and that is absolutely right...
I have agreed that Banksy can be an exception to our rule and can stay."**
Councillor Jay Kramer, Hastings Borough Council.

The British supermarket mega chain, Tesco, has been a major target for criticism from Banksy. At the time this piece was painted, on a wall fronting the beach in the characterful seaside resort and ancient fishing town on England's south coast, Tesco was extending its corporate tentacles into every corner of Britain, with the sort of strong-arm tactics that owning some 25% (that's around £30 billion per year) of all UK grocery spending gives you. Amongst major supermarket chains, Tesco in particular faced major opposition from some communities over its plans to build new mega-stores in out-of-town centres, using its muscle to force through planning decisions. Tesco also had a policy of buying land in strategic locations in expectation of further expansion, or to prevent competitors being in a position to challenge its future plans.

In this wonderful image, a small boy, looking rather sinister in his shades and what looks like a beachwear version of a pith helmet, is shown steadily building his forts, as he proceeds with a plan to eventually surround and control the castle in the centre. The castle, with its little Union Jack, represents Britain. The word 'Tesco' has been pricked into the sand on each turret. The boy, we suspect, signifies the Tesco corporate machine, aiming at constant capitalist expansion.

As so often with Banksy, this piece turned out to have an unexpected prophetic quality. In 2014 Tesco faced a UK Serious Fraud Office investigation over its overstatement of £263 million in profits. Some of its success did look as though it was built on sand.

WHERE IS IT ?
BEACH FRONT,
HASTINGS,
UK.

Latitude: 50.8510ºN
Longitude: 0.5592ºW

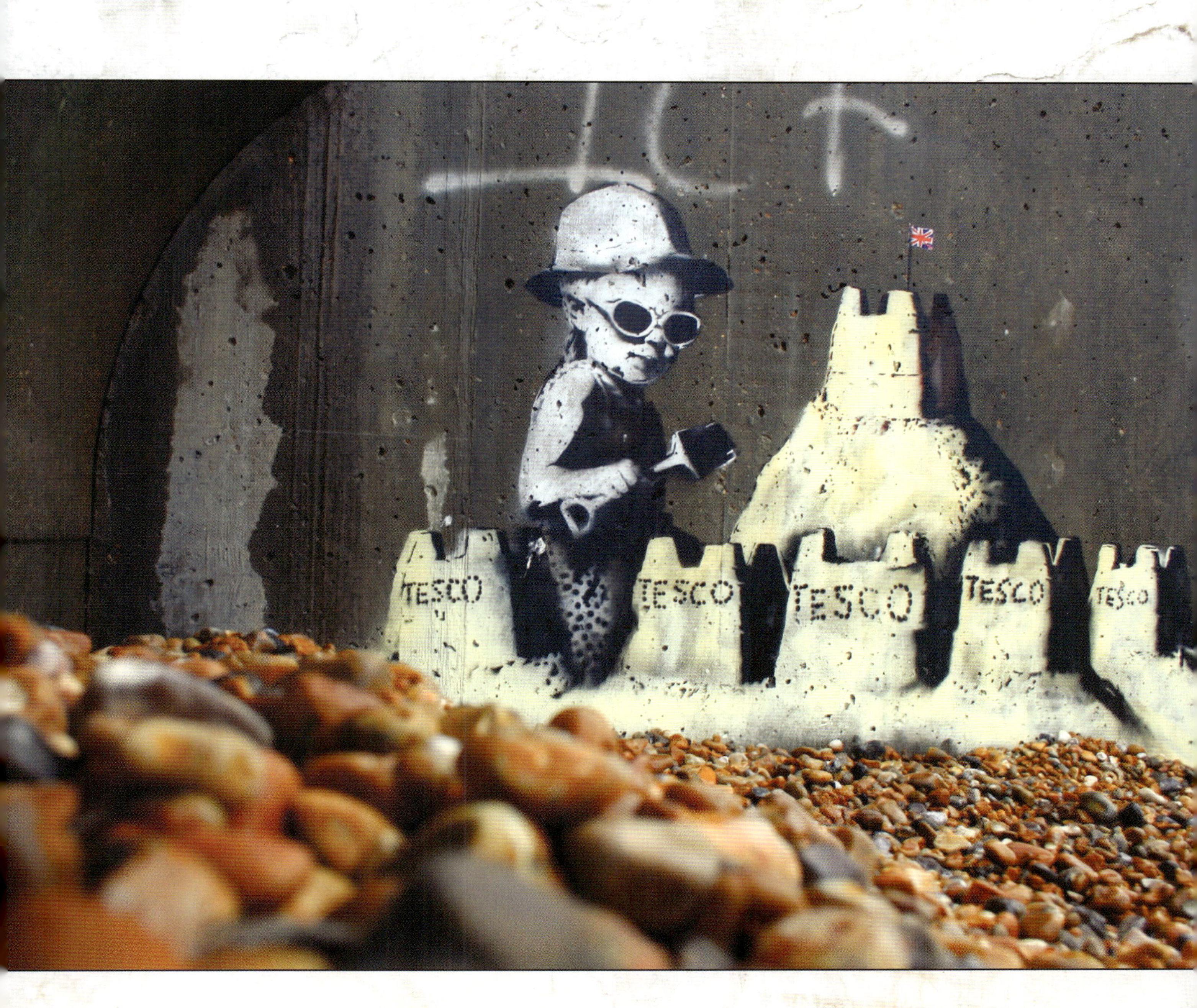

TESCO
TESCO
TESCO
TESCO
TESCO

ROLLERHEAD HERON

" If you're the type who gets sentimental about people scribbling over your stuff, I suggest graffiti is probably not the right hobby for you."
Banksy, in *Time Out*.

One of four pieces created by Banksy along the Regent's Canal in Camden, north London, which again makes perfect use of the water. This time it's a heron, who has just flown in, with a paint roller for neck and head, sitting patiently by the can of paint he has just used to whitewash a wall covered in graffiti. The piece took the place of a previous Banksy *I Don't Believe in Global Warming*, which was covered in water at different times of day (depending on the activity in the lock at Camden), making its ironic point about the dangers of global warming eloquently and effortlessly.

The Banksy pieces were all subject to attack by Team Robbo, with their, as usual, rather prosaic messages. Banksy then swooped in with replacement pieces as a riposte. Here, a Team Robbo tag over the previous *Global Warming* piece has been partially whitewashed by the bird. Some local street artists speculated that the feud between the two was a publicity stunt, designed to raise the profile of Robbo (who is respected in underground circles) as well as Banksy, who had recently released *Exit Through the Gift Shop* in the UK. Who can tell?

WHERE IS IT ?
CAMDEN LOCK,
REGENT'S CANAL,
LONDON,
UK.

Latitude: 51.5416ºN
Longitude: 0.1448ºW

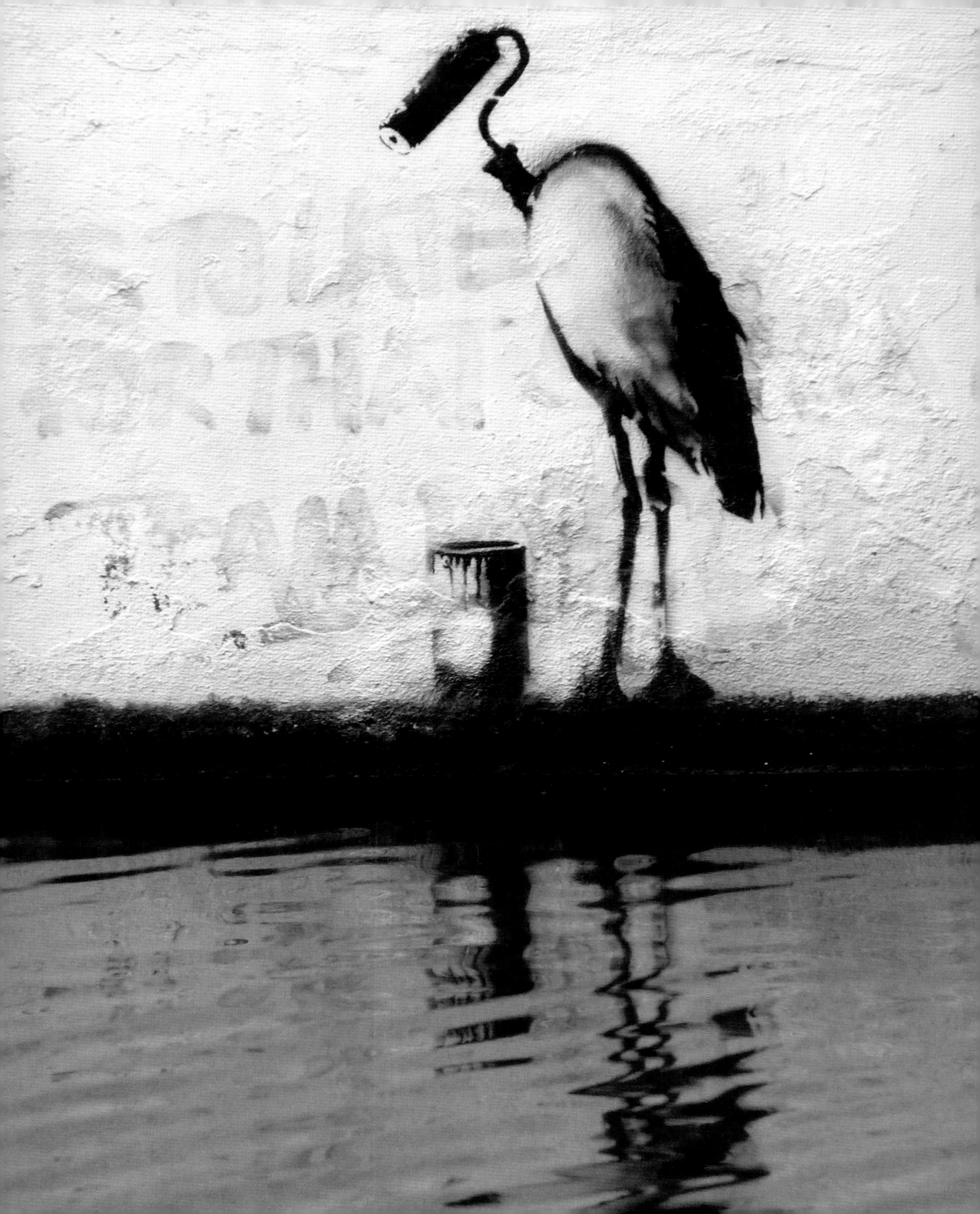

I REMEMBER WHEN ALL THIS WAS TREES

"Speramus meliora; resurget cineribus. (We hope for better things. It will rise from the ashes)." **Motto on Detroit's flag.**

Detroit is the most dramatic example of a US rust-belt city, and of the viciousness of American capitalism. Once the famed home of the 'Big Three' – Ford, General Motors and Chrysler – and a host of others, the city grew from 280,000 residents in 1910 to nearly two million by 1950 and boasted stunning skyscrapers and handsome homes. Following the rise of global competition and the decisions to move motor manufacturing to cheaper locations in search for ever greater profits for Wall Street, the population of Detroit collapsed, to around 700,000 today. Huge swathes of the city were simply abandoned, crime rates rocketed to some of the highest in the US and, in 2013 (three years after this piece was painted), Detroit filed the largest municipal bankruptcy case in US history. This being the US, capitalism was allowed to take its course.

The rise of the car plants also saw a big influx of African-American workers from the South. This Banksy shows an African-American boy, in a slightly strange hooded jacket, looking rather dejected in the ruins of the Packard car plant. This was built on East Grand Boulevard, a road inspired by Haussmann's urban plans for Paris, which was lined with trees. Packard arrived in 1903 and bought a 35-acre site, to build the then largest auto factory (3.5 million square feet) in the world. It lasted 55 years, closing on Packard's bankruptcy, in 1958. Today the site is in a state of ruin.

So, the boy can't literally remember when it was trees, but Banksy's piece does succeed in making a point about the hugely destructive and ephemeral nature of Darwinian capitalism, and of US corporations in particular. Notwithstanding a number of attempts at the redevelopment of the plant, it rather looks, from the image opposite, as though the trees could soon be back.

WHERE IS IT ?
ABANDONED PACKARD CAR PLANT,
DETROIT,
MICHIGAN,
USA.
THE BANKSY WAS REMOVED AND SOLD TO A PRIVATE BUYER IN 2014.

Latitude: 42.3794ºN
Longitude: 83.0287ºW

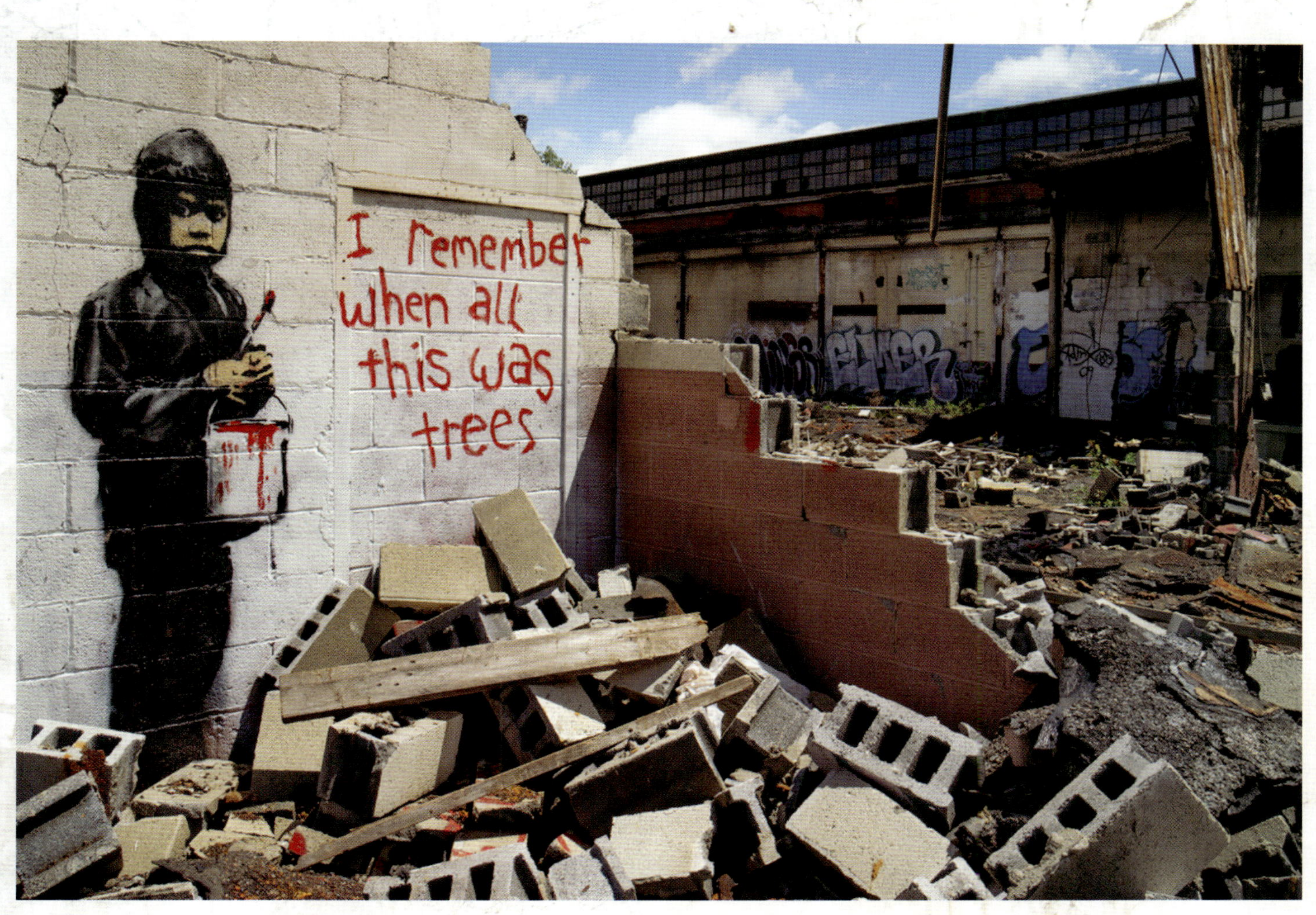

I remember
when all
this was
trees

CALL AN AIRSTRIKE

"We must define our effort not as a boundless 'Global War on Terror', but rather as a series of persistent, targeted efforts to dismantle specific networks of violent extremists." **President Barack Obama, 2010.**

After his stint in L.A., effectively promoting *Exit Through the Gift Shop*, Banksy spent time in San Francisco, where he created ten pieces, of which this is the most memorable, attacking US foreign policy.

As so often with Banksy, we have the usurpation of a common piece of language together with an image that takes some deciphering. The quote could be from various sources, although the most probable is its use in the Bond movie *Diamonds Are Forever,* where the villain Blofeld's henchmen, the seedy Mr Kidd and Mr Wint, come up with some trite shared quote after each assassination (on the occasion of this quote, after they blow up a helicopter).

So the quote suggests, if this is a nod to Kidd and Wint, that an airstrike by the US has just taken place, giving the whole piece added significance. In 2010, Barack Obama was in office with a commitment to end the US wars in Iraq and Afghanistan, an admission the Bush administration's ground troop invasions had failed. The flip side of troop reductions was, however, a major increase in US air strikes, particularly from drone attacks. This shows Banksy at his most politically prescient. He seems to be saying to the American public: look, the war is still very much going on, just with different tactics; don't be fooled into thinking otherwise.

The figure of the boy is ambiguous. He looks like a regular high school kid, with his book bag and baseball cap worn sideways. He's sporty and in shorts. Is this meant to personify US foreign policy as teenage, jokey, a sort of game, never mind the consequences? But the figure wears a gas mask. This could be an Iraqi kid on the ground, making a sardonic statement about what's really going on in US foreign policy. Or an all-American kid tangentially reminding us about the civilian casualties: think for a moment, how would you feel if it was American high school kids who were the collateral damage?

WHERE IS IT ?
CHINATOWN,
SAN FRANCISCO,
USA.

Latitude: 37.7979ºN
Longitude: 122.4067ºW

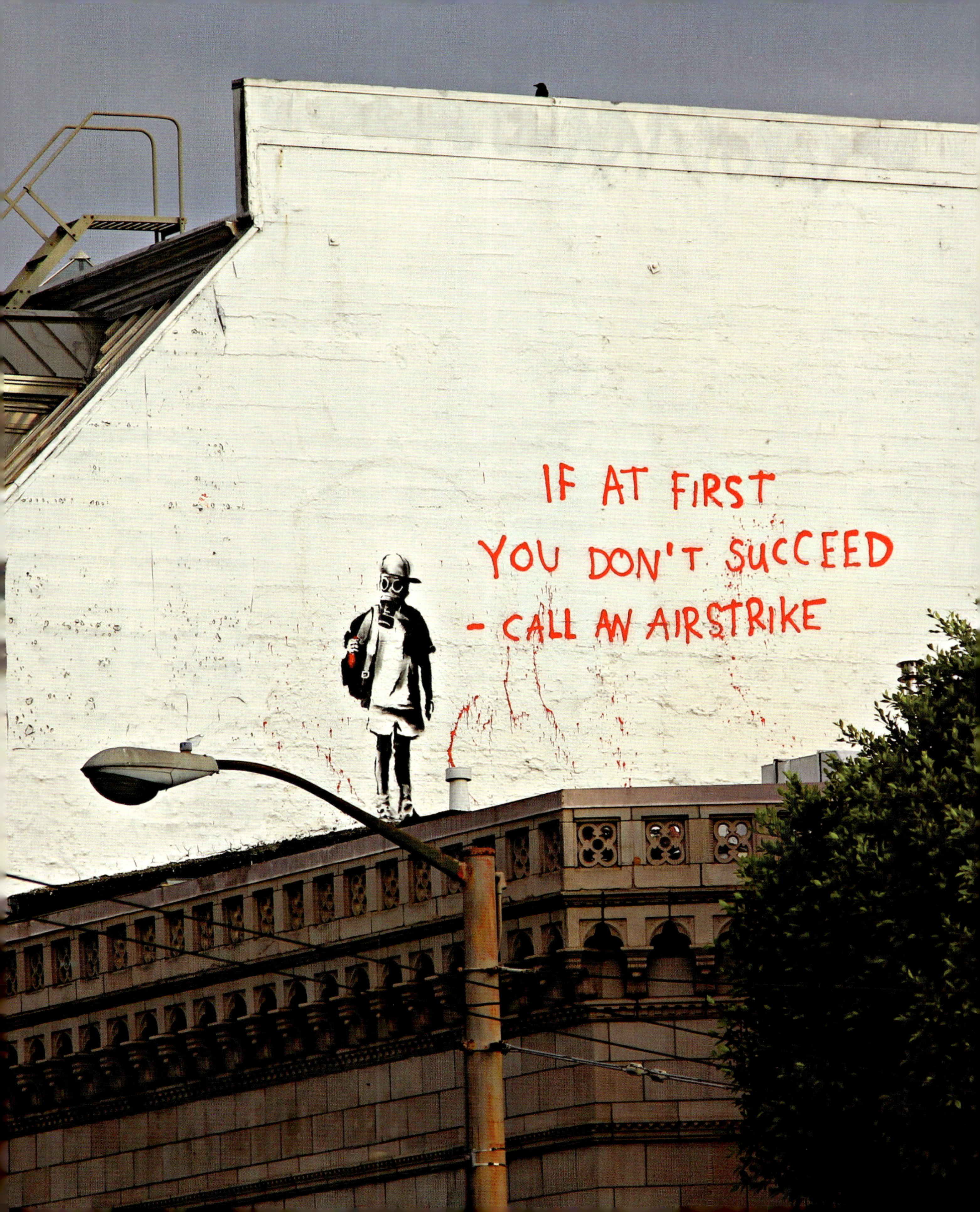
IF AT FIRST
YOU DON'T SUCCEED
- CALL AN AIRSTRIKE

I LOVE NY

*"No one is a bigger supporter of the arts than I am...
defacing somebody's property... is not my definition of art.
Or it may be art, but it should not be permitted."*
New York Mayor Michael Bloomberg.

A development of a similar piece created earlier the same year in San Francisco, this has all the qualities of juxtaposition, anachronism, mocking of common cliché and subliminal irony which define a classic Banksy.

At a top level the image and message are immediate: one of the most ubiquitous symbolic messages – I [heart] New York – is juxtaposed with a doctor listening for a heartbeat with his stethoscope, suggesting that there are reasons to be concerned about New York's health. Look a little more deeply and several other readings are possible. The doctor is from another era: the monocle is suggestive of the 1930s, the suit and brogues similarly so. This is a classic English image – the gladstone bag was standard for UK general practitioners of the period.

Is this a comment on the past judging the present? New York isn't what it used to be? A wry comment on a British judgement on the state of the world's previously culturally dominant city, asking perhaps, 'is there any heart left?' Its location – on Cedar Street, just above Wall Street – might give another clue. Wall Street, after the appalling destruction of the 2008 financial crash, is still as sick as ever, carrying on just as before.

A level of drama is introduced by the situation and the open gladstone bag. In movies from the '30s and '40s, the doctor would be urgently called to the stricken patient and would immediately open his bag and make his assessment. The image is suggestive of this rush. The stairs are the perfect podium to give the image prominence on the street. Altogether, this is one of Banksy's most satisfying images. The stencil, apparently, took just 45 seconds.

WHERE IS IT ?
LOWER MANHATTAN,
NYC,
USA.

Latitude: 40.7089ºN
Longitude: 74.0112ºW

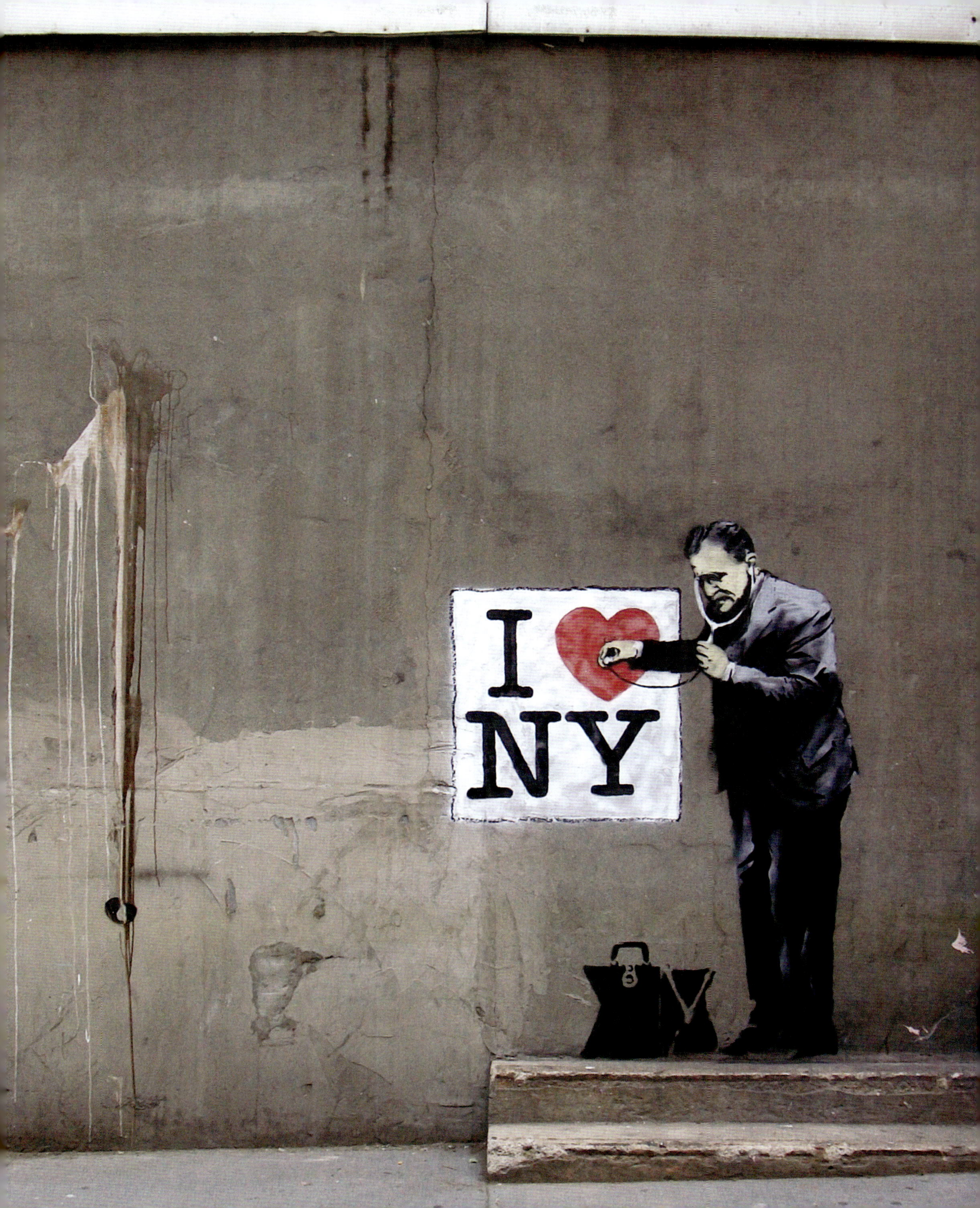

I
NY

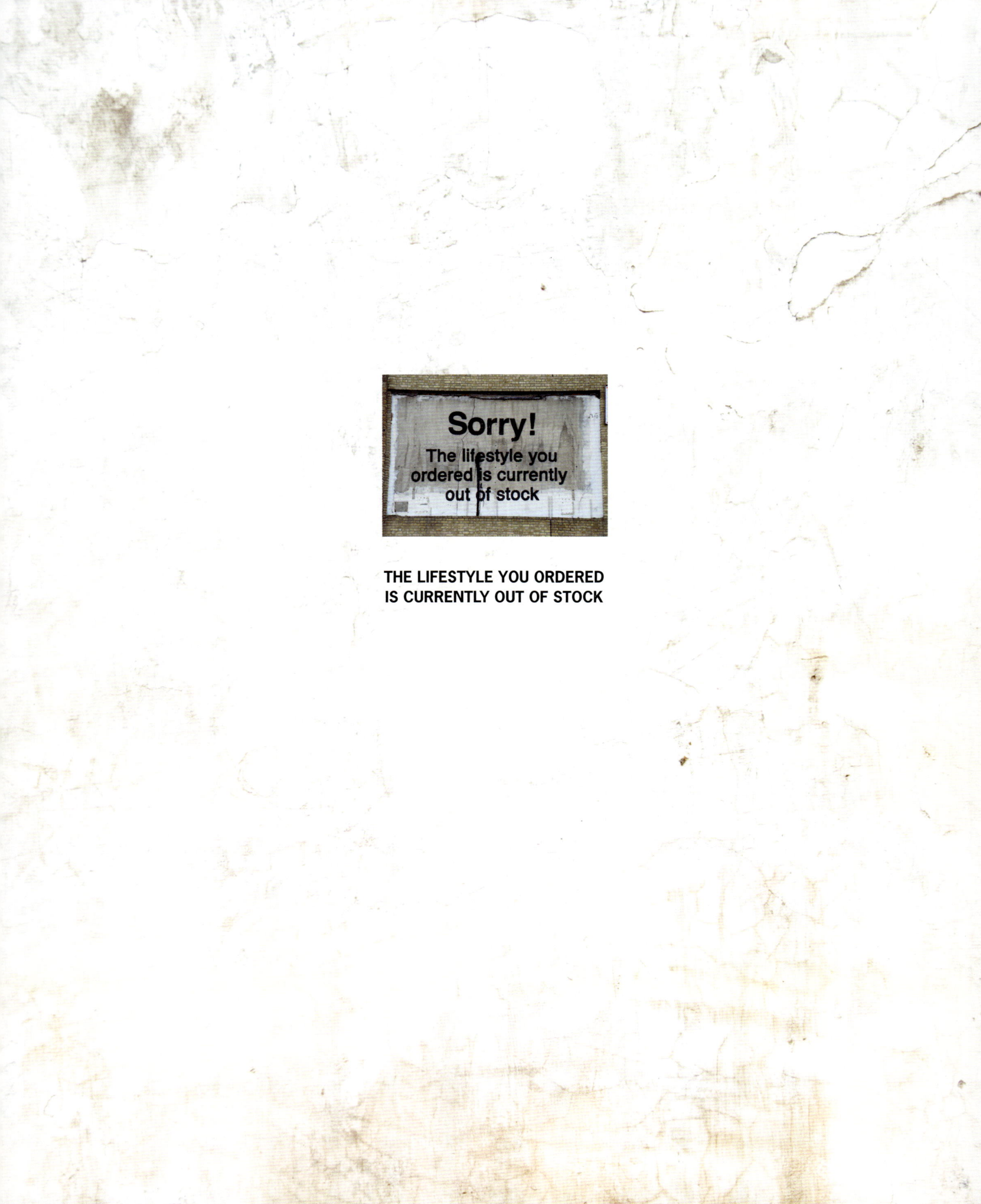

THE LIFESTYLE YOU ORDERED
IS CURRENTLY OUT OF STOCK

2011-2012

Great work in London and L.A. dominates this period. In L.A. side-swipes at the Disney Corporation. Back in London the humbug around the Queen's Jubilee celebrations inspires the anti-child labour piece outside a north London Poundland. Banksy returns to themes of the global financial crash and its austerity aftermath. We also note for the first time a concern over immigration, which would be a recurring theme going forwards.

CHARLIE BROWN FIRESTARTER

CRAYOLA SHOOTER

DRUNK MICKEY

SHOP TILL YOU DROP

SLAVE LABOUR

THE LIFESTYLE YOU ORDERED IS CURRENTLY OUT OF STOCK

SPERM ALARM

BANKSY 2011-2012

In this period new works in the US are limited to Los Angeles. Banksy does create some fantastic new pieces in London, focussing on child labour, migration, consumerism and post-crash economic austerity. A number of these end up being sold in the US.

Banksy also takes what is beginning to look like a habitual trip to the English south coast, this time to Lyme Regis, where he creates his somewhat whimsical *Origami Crane*.

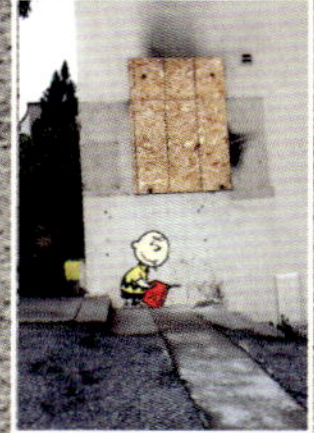

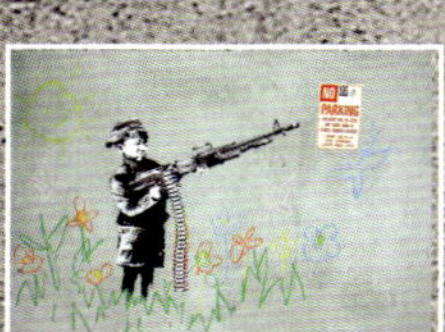

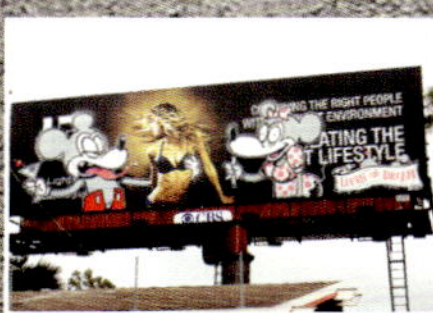

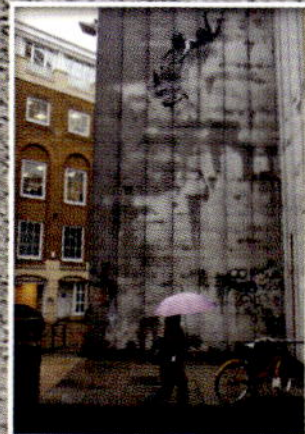

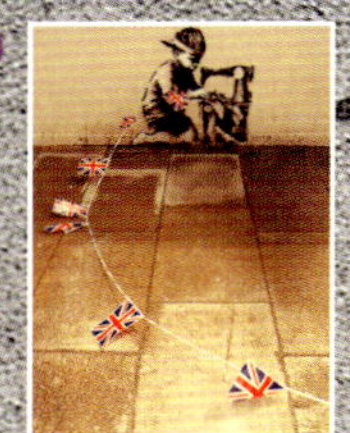

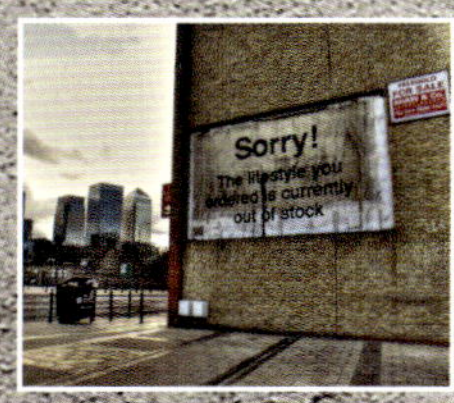

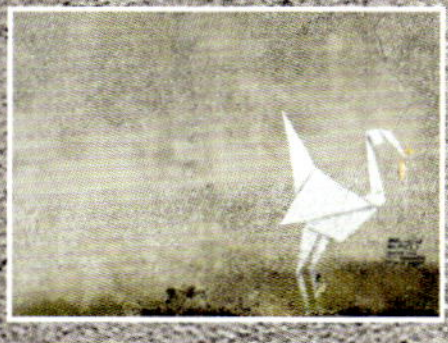

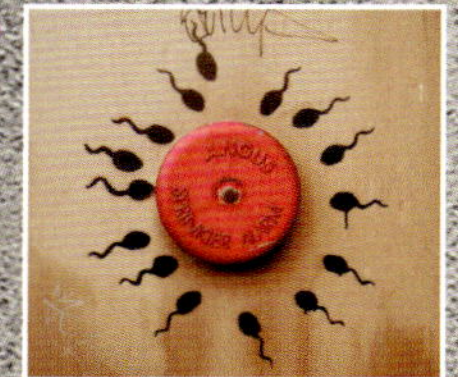

LOS ANGELES

1. Charlie Brown Firestarter, Beverly Hills.

2. Crayola Shooter, Westwood.

3. Drunk Mickey, Sunset Strip.

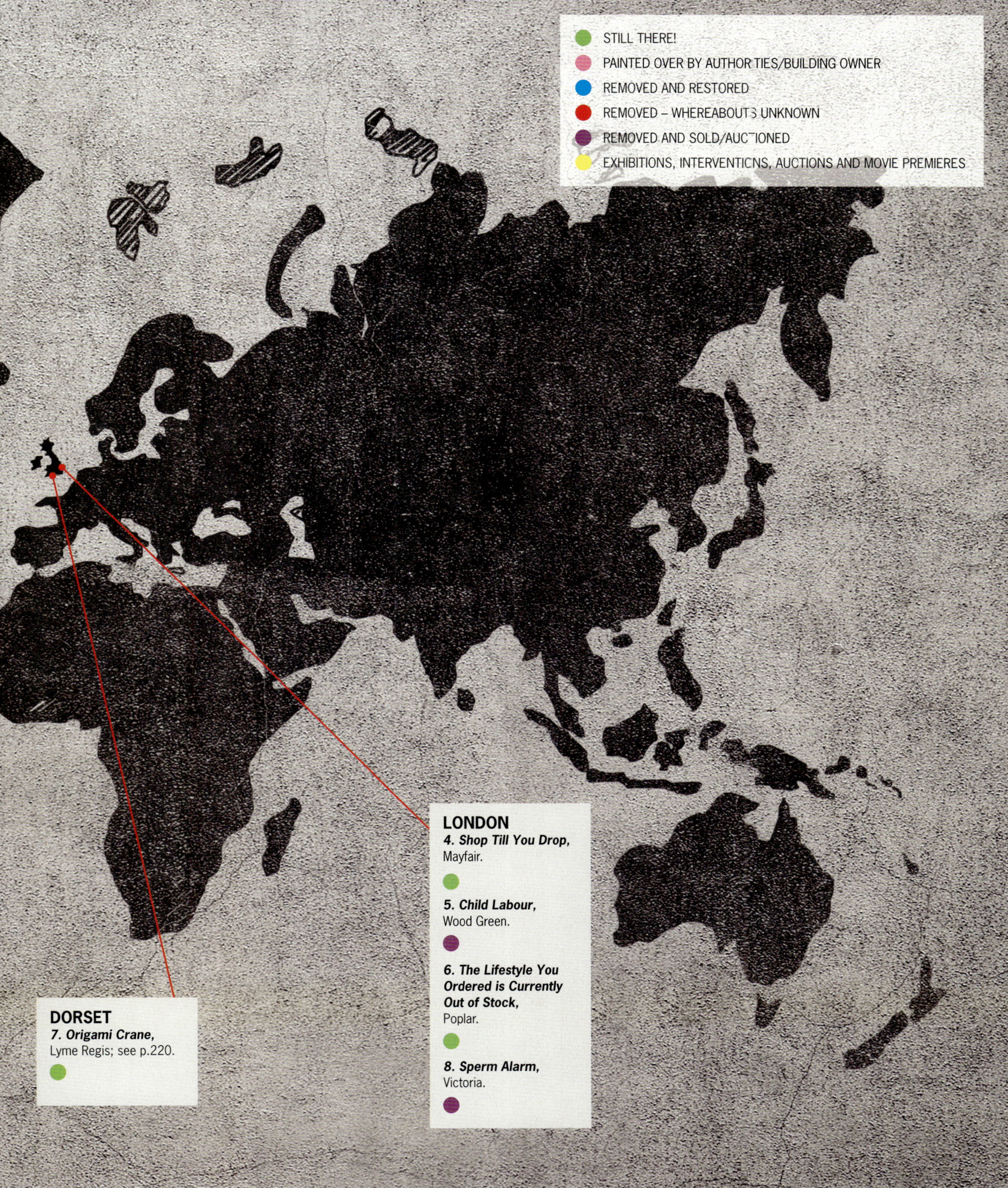

STILL THERE!
PAINTED OVER BY AUTHORITIES/BUILDING OWNER
REMOVED AND RESTORED
REMOVED – WHEREABOUTS UNKNOWN
REMOVED AND SOLD/AUCTIONED
EXHIBITIONS, INTERVENTIONS, AUCTIONS AND MOVIE PREMIERES
LONDON
4. Shop Till You Drop, Mayfair.
5. Child Labour, Wood Green.
6. The Lifestyle You Ordered is Currently Out of Stock, Poplar.
8. Sperm Alarm, Victoria.
DORSET
7. Origami Crane, Lyme Regis; see p.220.

CHARLIE BROWN FIRESTARTER

"What's the good of living if you don't try a few things?"
Charles M. Schulz, *The Complete Peanuts*, 1959-1960.

In L.A. for Oscar season – *Exit Through the Gift Shop* had been nominated for an Oscar for Best Documentary – Banksy spent many nights in the city adding to its cultural attractions. This was his second piece on that trip and, as ever with Banksy, situation and context is everything.

This hilarious image of Charlie Brown, the *Peanuts* cartoon character who, in a way, defines the all-American kid, is shown petrol can in hand, fag in mouth, about to commit arson. The piece was stencilled on the side of a fire-damaged building in Beverly Hills.

Banksy has, in many of his pieces, been adept at conveying the mischievous character of kids, usually juxtaposing them in serious grown-up situations to great effect. He gets Charlie Brown perfectly: the not-quite-knowing smile, the positioning at street level, the naïvety of having a lit fag in his mouth (Charlie Brown would of course burn to a cinder in the ensuing fireball).

The piece was cut out and stolen within 48 hours if its appearance. The thieves had some sense of humour, posting a label saying 'Goodbye' on the board they left covering the resultant void.

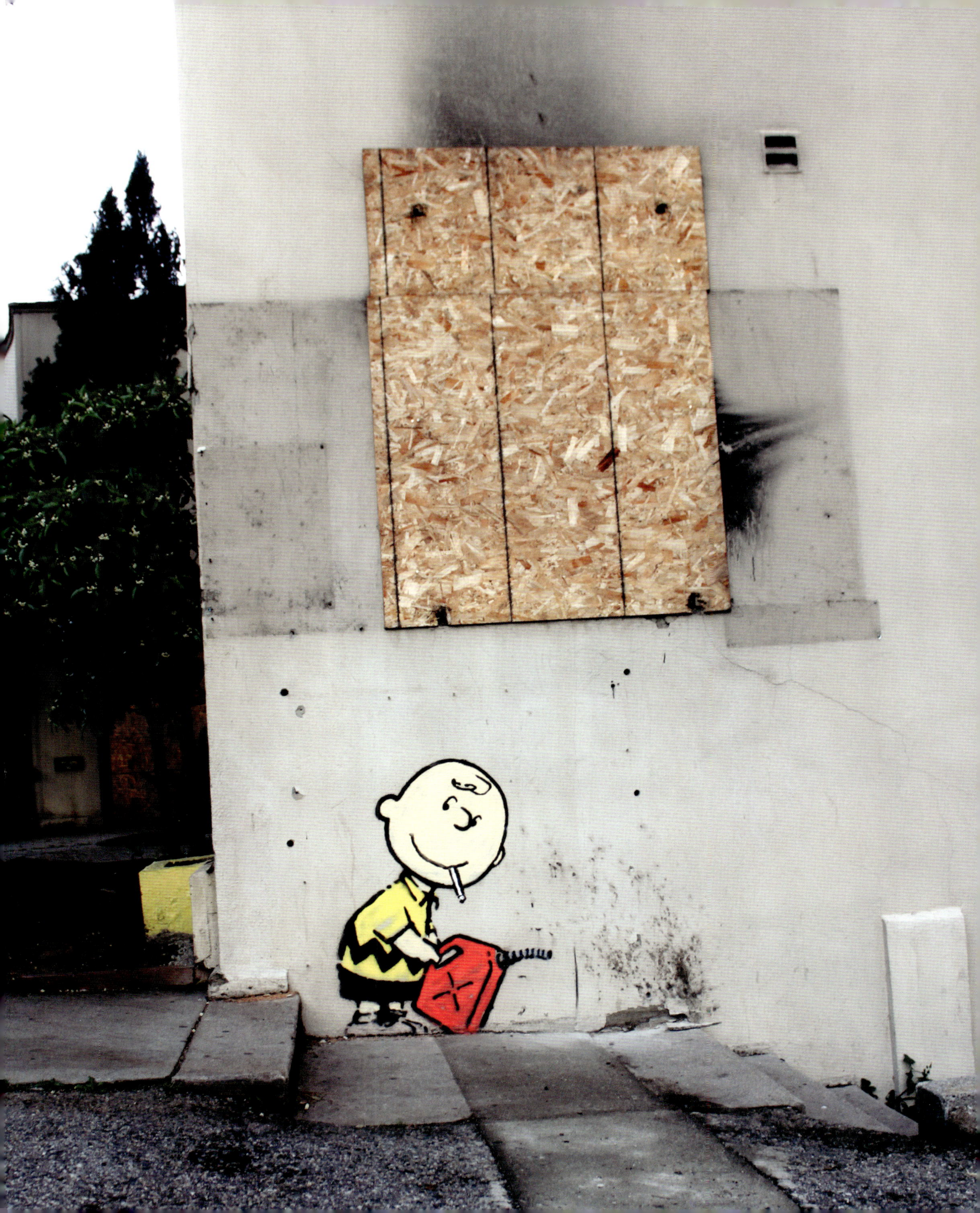

CRAYOLA SHOOTER

"There are an estimated 250,000 child soldiers in the world today."
War Child Charity.

Another Banksy taking a pop, literally, at petty local authority restrictive signage. This time it's a kid brandishing a submachine gun, with a multi-coloured crayola belt of ammunition pointed at a NO PARKING sign. We don't know the exact source of the image, but this does remind us of one of those pictures of VietCong kids from the Vietnam war in the '60s. The expression is pretty determined, the strain of manning the weapon evident.

The contrast with the kid's drawings makes this wonderfully effective. The sun, birds and butterfly are particularly well observed. There appears to be no overt political message here, unless a reference is intended to kids getting ensnared and brutalised in wars in the developing world, or, closer to home, L.A. gangland kids getting into gun crime too young. That all feels a bit serious; a kid with a Crayola submachine gun is just funny.

This was Banksy's first piece in L.A. at Oscar time in 2011; *Exit Through the Gift Shop* was up for Best Documentary. Banksy didn't do anything as crass as attending the ceremony. The pieces he created at night, however, got mega publicity. Sadly, *Crayola Shooter* was buffed over almost immediately after its creation.

WHERE IS IT ?
WESTWOOD,
LOS ANGELES,
USA.
BUFFED SHORTLY AFTER IT APPEARED.

Latitude: 34.0619ºN
Longitude: 118.4452ºW

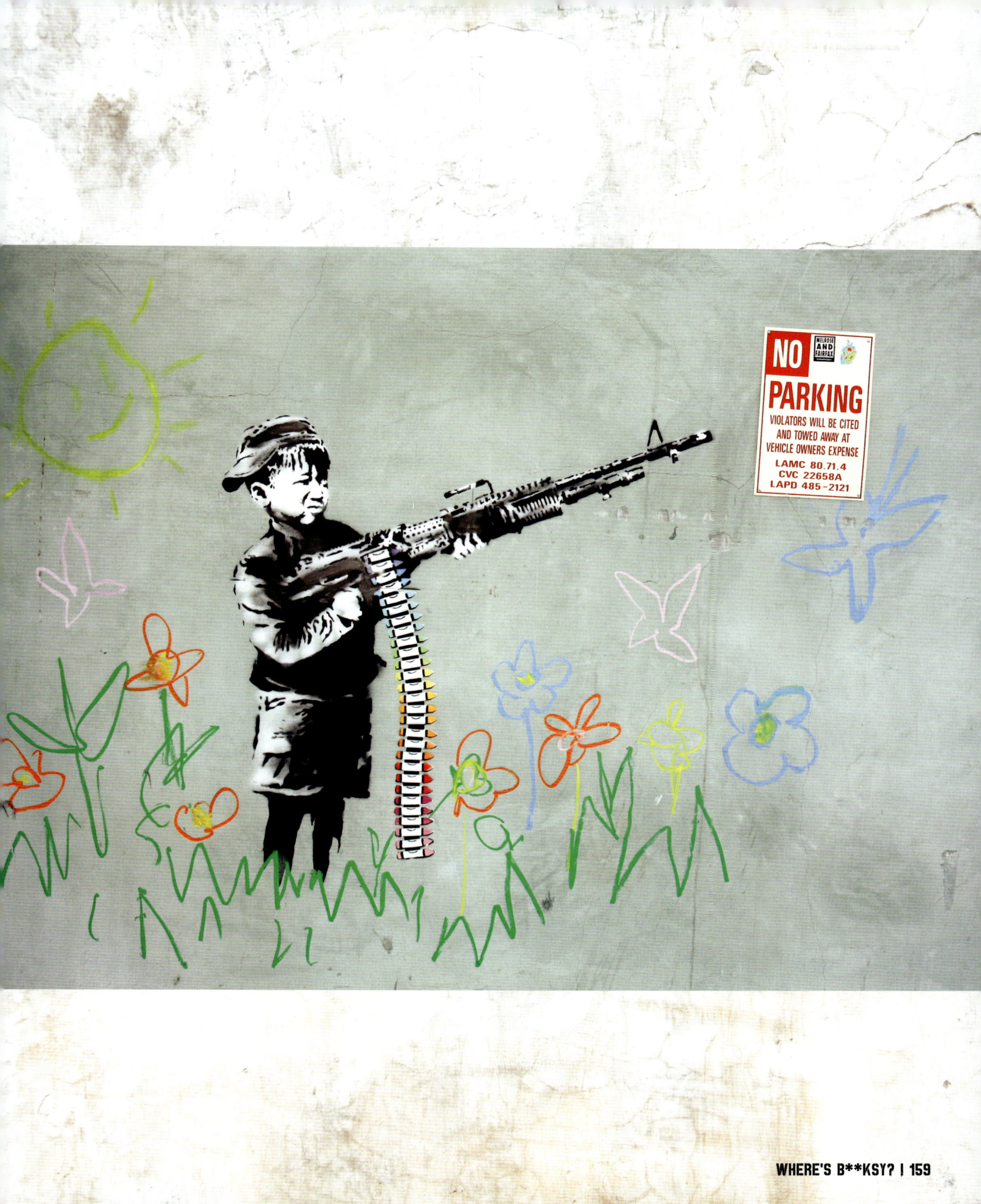

NO PARKING
MELROSE AND FAIRFAX
VIOLATORS WILL BE CITED
AND TOWED AWAY AT
VEHICLE OWNERS EXPENSE
LAMC 80.71.4
CVC 22658A
LAPD 485-2121

DRUNK MICKEY

"When people laugh at Mickey Mouse, it's because he's so human."
Walt Disney.

Banksy has form with Disney, and this is a very funny, brilliant early example. Having usurped an all-American icon in the form of Charlie Brown, it seemed only natural that in L.A. Mickey and Minnie Mouse should be next.

Choosing a billboard advertising Las Vegas company, the Light Group (whose clients include the Bare Pool Lounge – the clue's in the name – in Vegas), Banksy shows Mickey completely drunk, empty martini glass in one hand, bikini-clad girl's tit in the other, lechy tongue dripping with anticipation. Minnie is looking on, with bloodshot eyes and about to snort another line of coke through her rolled-up dollar bill, joining in the party fun. A banner announces that they are 'Livin' the dream'. It's hilarious, and amusingly mocking.

It caused outrage and delight in equal measure. How could a children's icon be shown drunk, in a state where the legal drinking age is 21? How is it OK to show Minnie thinking this behaviour was OK, funny even? And Minnie shown as a coke-head? At the same time Los Angelenos turned up in droves to photograph the billboard. Many celebrated Banksy for showing up, in their view, corporate hypocrisy and greed.

The piece was a huge publicity success. CBS, the owner of the billboard, however, did not find it funny and took it down within 48 hours. They turned down a $10,000 offer from the garage next door for the piece, and workmen were very careful whilst removing it. CBS, we suspect, also realised it was worth so much more than $10k and, of course, claimed ownership. We wouldn't be surprised, one day, to find the work reappearing at a Sotheby's auction.

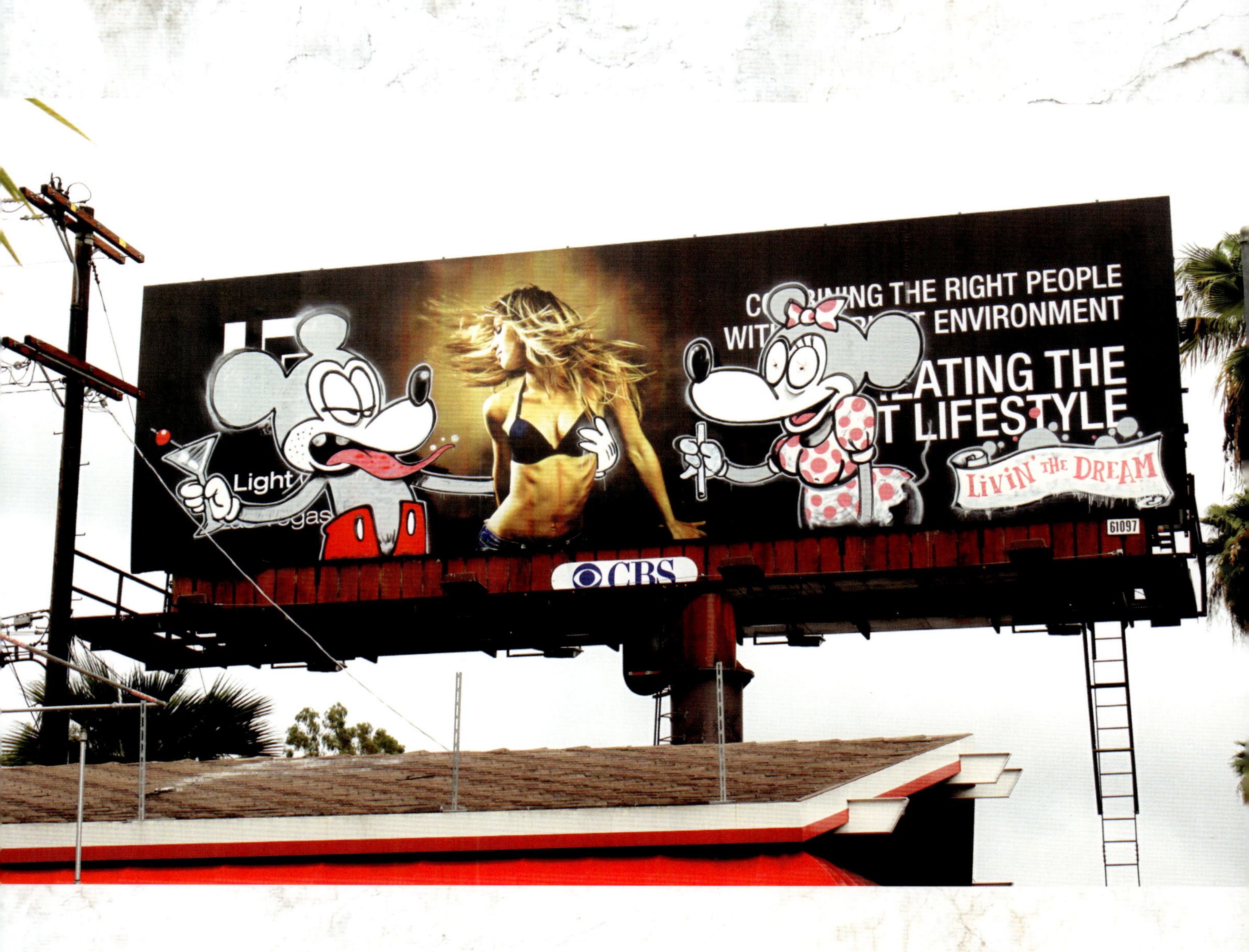
Light
COMBINING THE RIGHT PEOPLE
WITH THE RIGHT ENVIRONMENT
CREATING THE
RIGHT LIFESTYLE
LiViN' THE DREAM
CBS
61097

SHOP TILL YOU DROP

"Governments...regard it as a sacred duty to encourage the most revolting spectacle: the annual feeding frenzy...in which shoppers...stampede into shops...to be the first to carry off some designer junk which will go into landfill before the sales next year."
George Monbiot, *Guardian* columnist, eco warrior.

There's an anti-consumerist streak running through some of Banksy's work, not least his pieces critical of Tesco the supermarket giant. This piece appeared on the side of a building which was shortly to be redeveloped in Bruton Street in London's Mayfair. A literal representation of the clichéd phrase, it depicts a woman dropping off a building clutching her shopping trolley, inevitably plunging to her death.

Unusually for Banksy, the message and depiction does not have any particular resonance with the location. Mayfair's Bond Street is a few minutes away, but that specialises in high-end brands (Vuitton, Hermes, Gucci and their ilk), rather than supermarket stuff; in branded luxury shopping bags rather than trolleys. Interestingly the trolley looks relatively empty, apart from a wine bottle – regularly quaffed Chardonnay? – which is about to fall out.

As a more generalised comment on pointless consumerism, it bears all of Banksy's usual wit. It was also painted at the end of November: was Banksy also tweaking a few tails as the mad splurge in the run up to Christmas was about to take off?

WHERE IS IT ?
MAYFAIR,
LONDON,
UK.

Latitude: 51.5117ºN
Longitude: 0.1478ºW

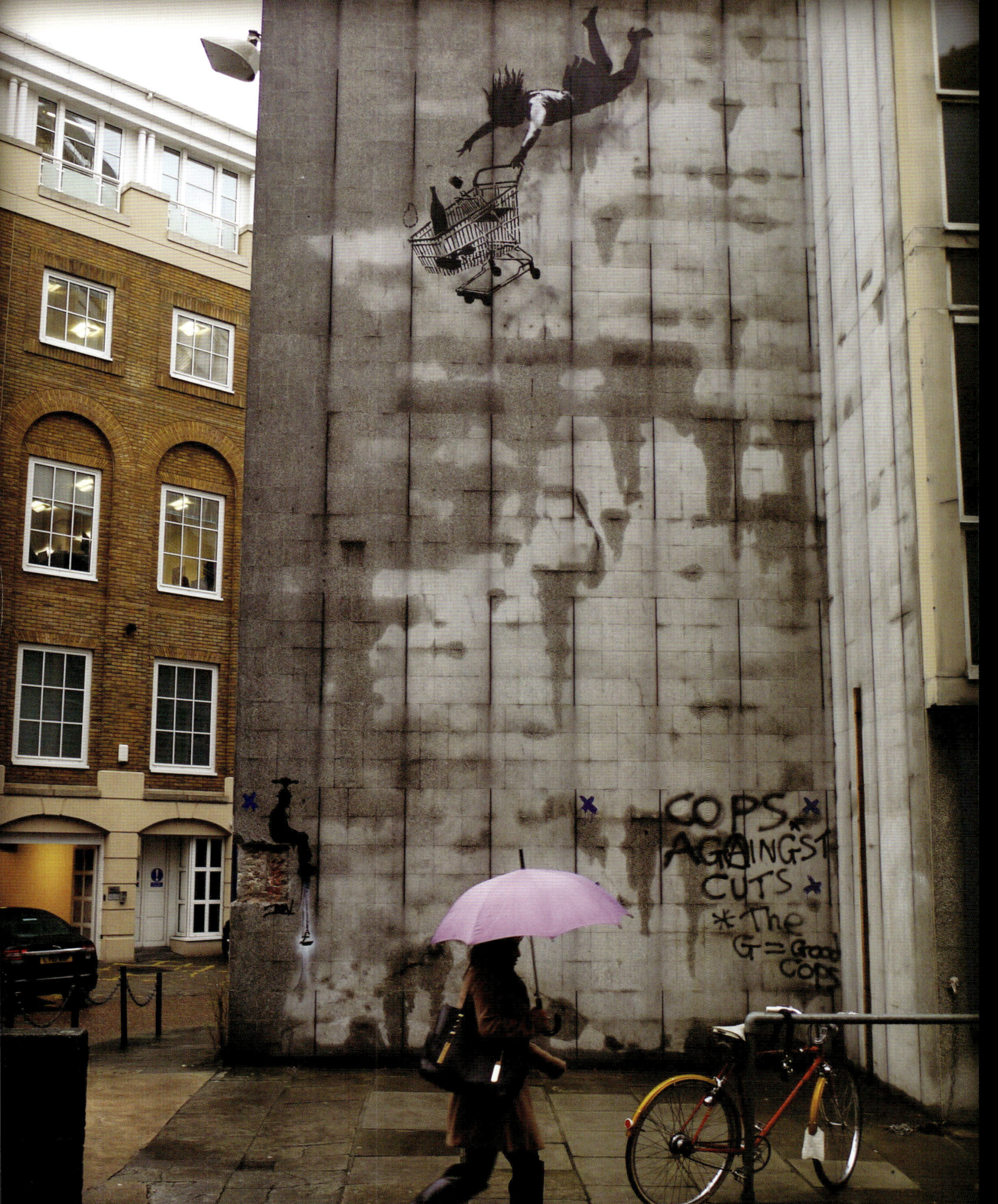

COPS
AGAINGST
CUTS
* The
G = Good
COPS

SLAVE LABOUR

"You have deprived a community of an asset that was given to us for free...I call you, and your consciences, to pull the piece from both potential sales and return it to its rightful place." **Wood Green MP Lynne Featherstone.**

2012 was the year of both the Queen's Jubilee and of the London Olympics. This piece, painted with brilliant positioning, on the side of a tacky Poundland shop in the north London suburb of Wood Green, was Banksy enjoying a pop at the royals and all the schmaltz culture around patriotism. In the midst of all the props and tat produced to celebrate 60 years of feudal monarchial rule, have the British paused to think why their Union Jack bunting is so cheap?

Poundland is jammed, as its name suggests, with uber-cheap goods, produced under who knows what conditions in India and China. If stuff is so cheap, well then someone is, by Western standards, being grossly underpaid, the piece suggests.

So many of Banksy's cleverest techniques are on display in this, one of his most memorable images. The piece is about child labour sweatshops, of which there are still so many in India and Bangladesh. The boy looks Asian, but could so easily be one of those Victorian urchins working the mills in nineteenth century England. The sewing machine is certainly turn of the 20th Century, with the suggestion of gold patterns on shiny black. He is on his knees, the most painful of positions. He wears a reversed sun visor, suggesting intense heat. And this child is working at slave rates, to produce rubbish for idiotic, sentimental, dreaming-of-the-old-days-of-Empire British consumers. It's searing in its effect. That it appeared in May 2012, a month before the Queen's celebrations, gave it added punch.

The piece was 'removed' in 2013, and appeared for auction in Miami. After legal concerns the piece was withdrawn from sale, only to reappear at auction in London where it was sold by Bankrobber London, for $1.1 million.

WHERE IS IT ?
WOOD GREEN,
LONDON.
WAS 'REMOVED' AND EVENTUALLY SOLD AT AUCTION IN LONDON. A REPLICA, NOT QUITE EXACT, IS NOW UNDER PERSPEX IN THE ORIGINAL LOCATION.

Latitude: 51.5905ºN
Longitude: 0.1034ºW

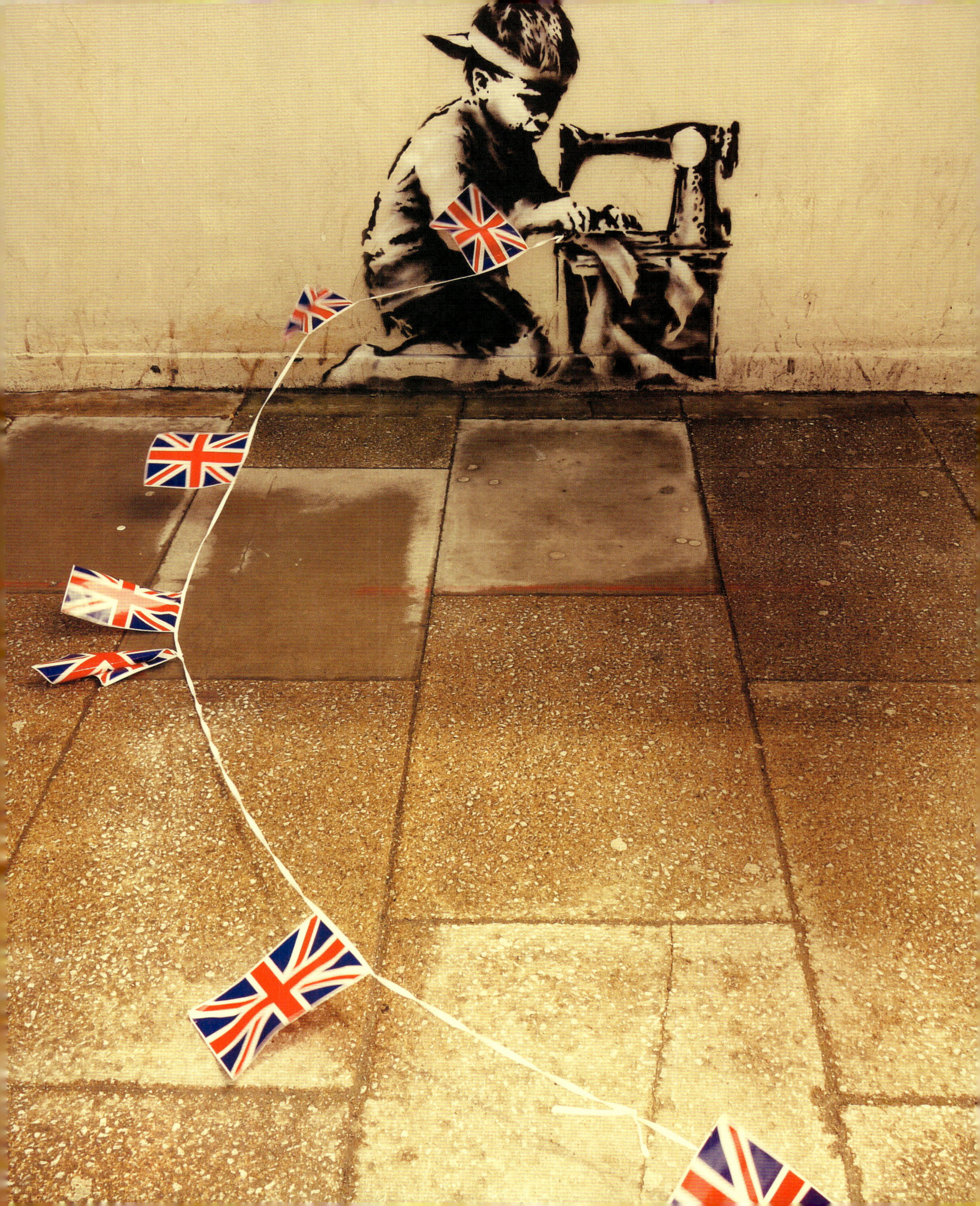

THE LIFESTYLE YOU ORDERED IS CURRENTLY OUT OF STOCK

"We're all in this together." George Osborne, UK Chancellor of the Exchequer.

One of the most effective bits of positioning of any Banksy, when viewed from this angle. A painted sign outside a foreclosed building on East India Dock Road, takes a swipe at our lifestyle obsessions and belief in instant consumer gratification. In the distance are the towers of some of the biggest global banks – HSBC, Barclays, JP Morgan Chase, Citi. It almost feels as though this message is coming from them: we screwed up, but guess what, it's you guys who are going to pay. It's no accident that the sign is painted on a building where the freehold is for sale, possibly a result of the financial crisis.

The location of the piece in Poplar, an area with high levels of social housing and many residents on benefits, is somewhat ironic, and takes the anti-consumerist surface meaning of the piece onto another level. For many locals, there was never a question of buying into a lifestyle. In this context, lifestyle means just about getting by with the help of public services, which are suffering dramatic cuts due to the UK government's austerity policies. Austerity, yup you guessed it, to pay for the debts of the guys in the skyscrapers, whose lifestyle, of course, remains very much in stock.

It's always useful to remember how much the banks have cost the UK taxpayer, because they would, of course, prefer we forget. According to *The Guardian* in 2012:

In cash terms the UK government has so far spent £123.93 BILLION [on the bailout of the UK banks], but has at various points since the crisis began been exposed to a sum 10 times larger [yup, £1.2 TRILLION].

Don't hold your breath; these lifestyles won't be back in stock for a helluva long while.

WHERE IS IT ?
POPLAR,
LONDON,
UK.

Latitude: 51.5067ºN
Longitude: 0.0178ºW

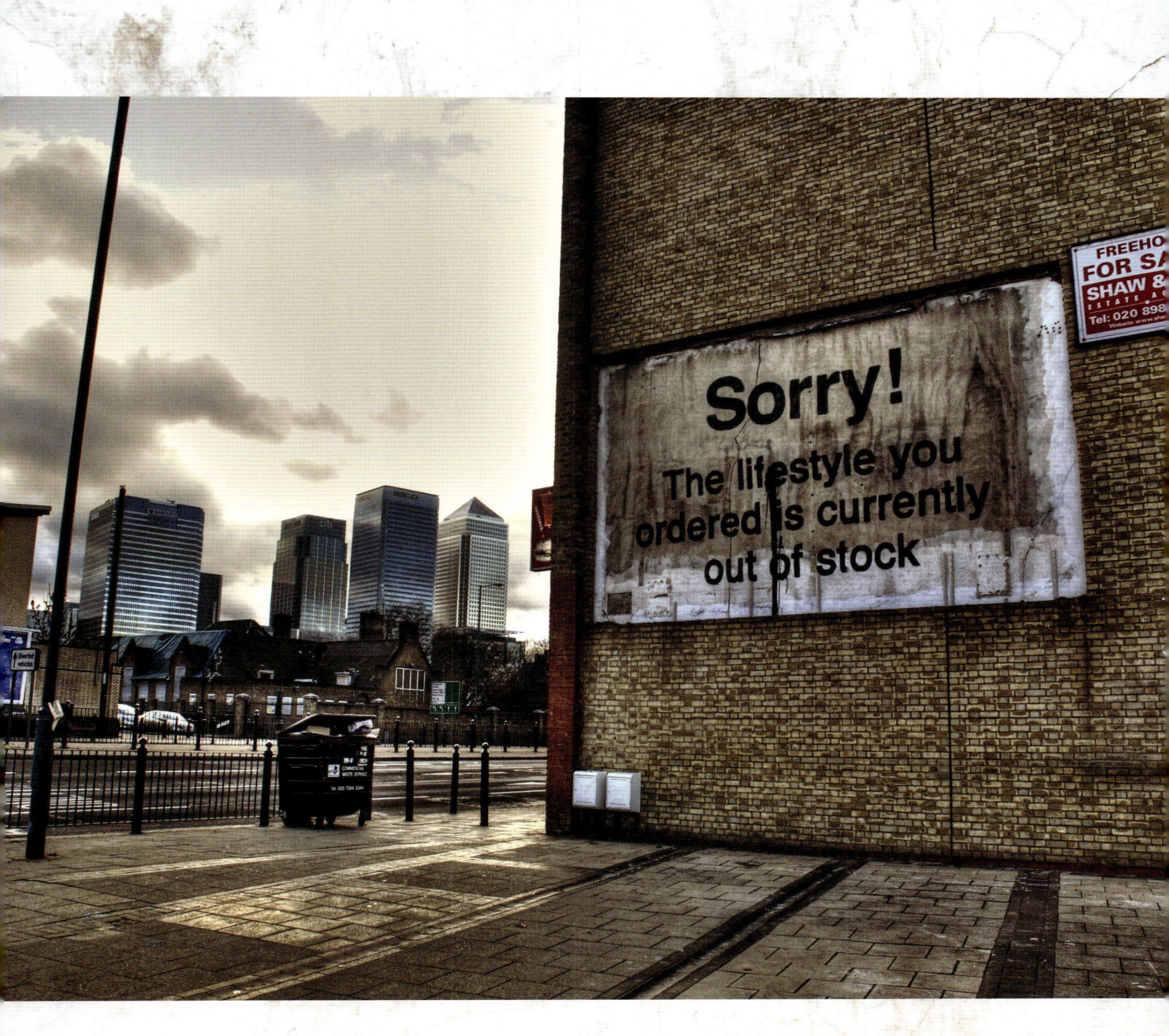
Sorry!
The lifestyle you ordered is currently out of stock
FREEHO
FOR SA
SHAW &
ESTATE A
Tel: 020 898

SPERM ALARM

"I think it's disgusting people are allowed to go around displaying art on walls without getting permission."
Banksy, commenting on the Stealing Banksy show, (which he did not sanction).

Banksy has a wonderful way of usurping the most tedious of street fittings and incorporating them into brilliant, instant works of art. Quite often it's street signs, telling us not to do something, sometimes it's airbricks, or strange architectural features on the sides of buildings. Where he is perhaps most successful is in his mocking of CCTV cameras, or his adoption of alarms of one sort or another to brilliant effect, as in *Girl With The Burst Eardrum* of 2014, or in this piece here, which appeared outside the Hesperia Hotel near London's Victoria Bus Station.

We see fifteen very eager, wriggly sperm gunning for the egg represented by the red alarm. Banksy clearly remembers his human biology lessons as there is a fit one who is ahead of the race and will manage to break in. Presumably the alarm will then go off, as in the case of an illegal entry. Except that this sperm will fertilise the egg and life will carry on.

When interpreting any Banksy, location usually has a bearing on the idea of the piece. The Hesperia Hotel is next to London's passport office, where everyday queues of people apply for passports. Extend the analogy, and these are fit immigrants about to do great things. But the alarm will go off because we are paranoid, as though our virgin land is being invaded.

The piece was cut out by a Londoner with previous form in stealing art. The staff at the hotel noticed its absence, saw it was for sale on Ebay for £17,000 and, somewhat unsportingly, contacted the police. He was tried in court for attempting to 'convert or transfer' criminal property. Interestingly the judge, a man of taste clearly, stated that the piece constituted 'graffiti art'; how times have changed. The piece disappeared from view for a number of years, before turning up at the Stealing Banksy show (not sanctioned by Banksy) in 2014 and then at Julien's Auctions of Beverly Hills in 2015.

WHERE IS IT ?
VICTORIA,
LONDON,
UK.
WAS CUT OUT SHORTLY AFTER IT APPEARED.

Latitude: 51.4961ºN
Longitude: 0.1420ºW

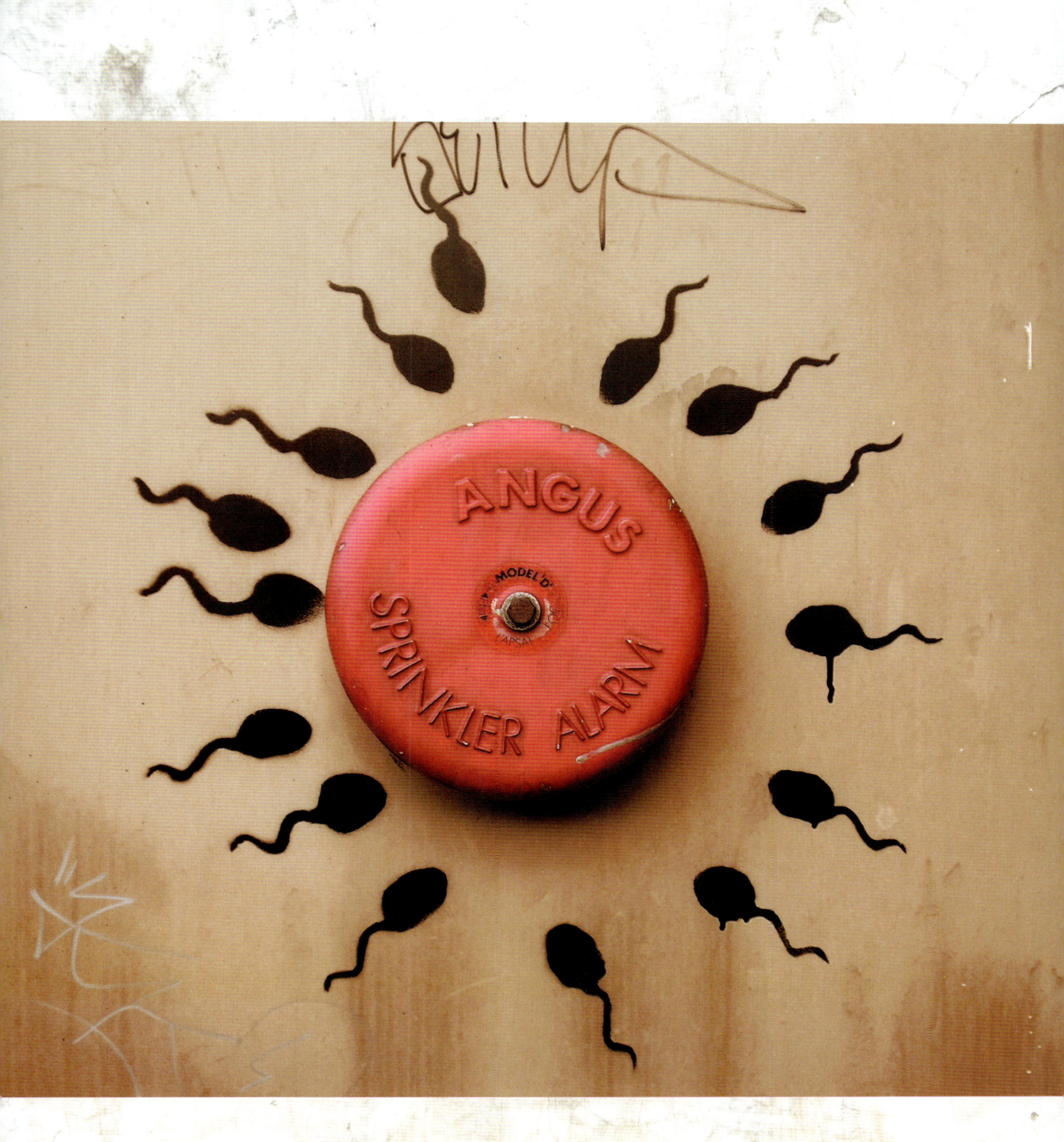

ANGUS
SPRINKLER ALARM
MODEL 'D'

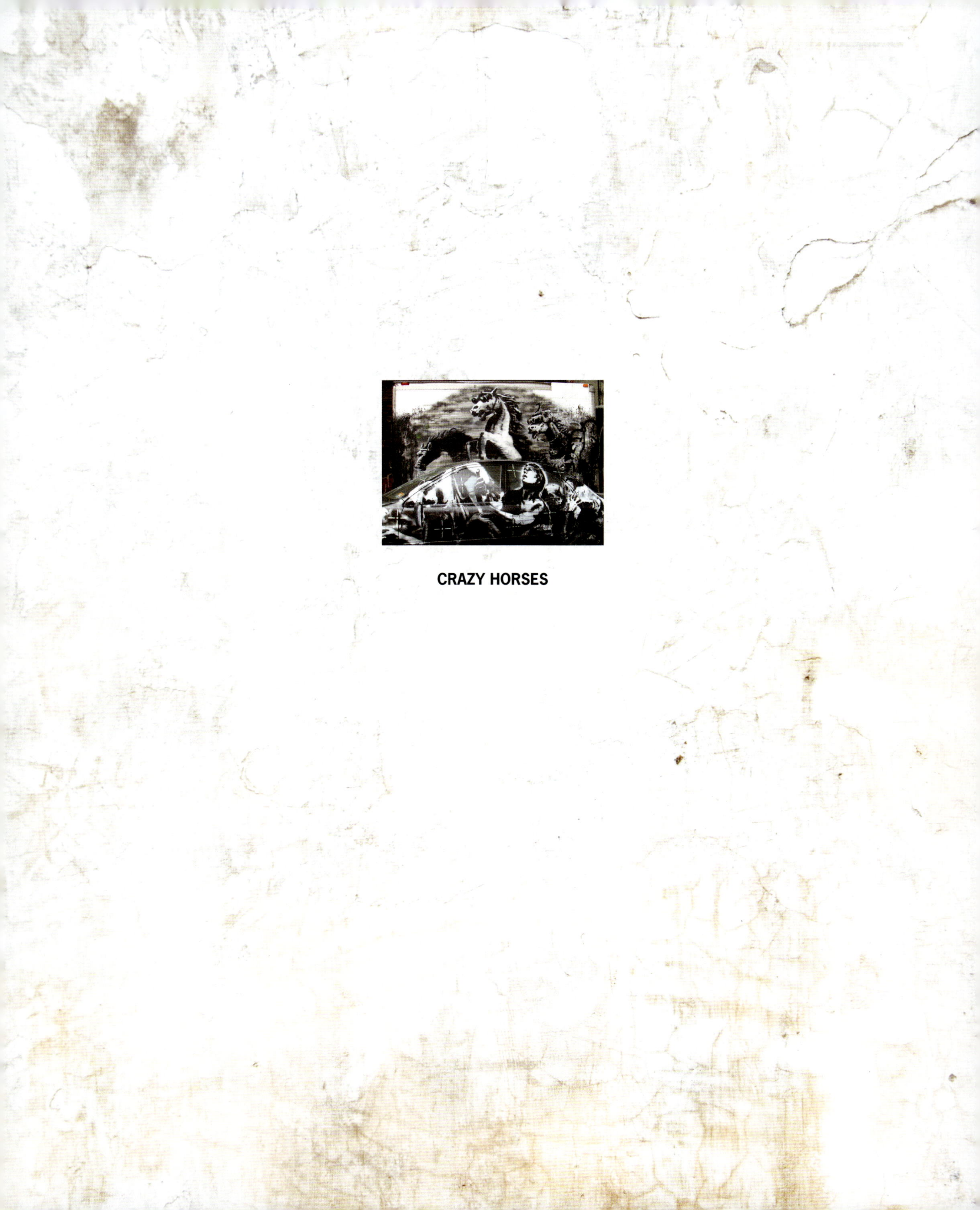

CRAZY HORSES

2013

The year of the triumph of the New York residency. 31 days, and 30 works around the city revealing again high wit and visual eloquence outstripping, by far, any other street artists. Themes include individual freedom, the evils of Nazism, animal cruelty, overbearing corporate power (this time McDonald's) and a risky tribute to 9/11. His anti-war *Crazy Horses* raises the bar – Banksy's most searing anti-war piece to date.

THE STREET IS IN PLAY

YOU COMPLETE ME

BOY WITH HAMMER

GHETTO 4 LIFE

WAITING IN VAIN

THE BANALITY OF THE BANALITY OF EVIL

JAPANESE SCENE

CRAZY HORSES

SHOE SHINE

SIRENS OF THE LAMBS

TWIN TOWERS

ETERNITY

OS GEMEOS COLLABORATION

BANKSY 2013

The year of the brilliant New York 'residency', entitled *Better Out Than In*. Most works were created in mid and lower Manhattan – Soho, Hell's Kitchen and the East and West Villages. However Banksy also ventured to the smart Upper West Side, did his stall in Central Park and created works in The Bronx, Queens, Brooklyn and Staten Island. Some of the installations were on trucks, which drove all over Manhattan. The Day 16 piece also moved to various McDonald's around the city.

- 🟢 STILL THERE!
- 🔴 PAINTED OVER BY AUTHORITIES/BUILDING OWNER
- 🔵 REMOVED AND RESTORED
- 🔴 REMOVED – WHEREABOUTS UNKNOWN
- 🟣 REMOVED AND SOLD/AUCTIONED
- 🟡 EXHIBITIONS, INTERVENTIONS, AUCTIONS AND MOVIE PREMIERES

Day 1:
The Street is in Play, Allen Street, Lower East Side.

Day 2:
This is My New York Accent, Allen Street, 11th Ave and 25th St.

Day 3:
You Complete Me, 6th Ave and 24th St.

Day 4:
Occupy, The Musical; Dirty Underwear, The Musical; Playground Mob, The Musical. Lower East Side, Williamsburg and Bushwick.

Day 5:
3-D Mobile Waterfall; mobile garden (includes rainbow, waterfall and butterflies) created in delivery truck.
East Village and various locations throughout the city during the residency.

Day 6:
Rebel Rocket Attack, Video, showing Dumbo shot down by Syrian rebels, posted on Banksy's YouTube channel.

Day 7:
Battle to Survive a Broken Heart, Van Brunt St & King St, Red Hook, Brooklyn.

Day 8:
I Have a Theory That You Can Make Any Sentence Seem Profound by Writing the Name of a Dead Philosopher at the End of it. Plato. 255 Freeman St, Greenpoint.

Day 9:
Crazy Horses, 159 Ludlow St, Lower East Side.

Day 10:
Beaver With No Parking Sign, 274 Bradford St, East NYC.

Day 11:
Sirens of the Lambs, stuffed animals in a slaughterhouse truck.
Started in the Meatpacking District, then toured the city for two weeks.

Day 12:
Concrete Confessional, Cooper Square & East 7th St, East Village.

Day 13:
Spray Art for Sale. Banksy sells authenticated works for $60 a pop at a stall in Central Park.

Day 14:
What We Do in Life Echoes in Eterni..., 69th St & 38th Ave., Queens.

Day 15:
Twin Towers Tribute, Jay St & Staple St, Tribeca.

Day 16:
Ronald McDonald Shoe Shine, 839 Westchester Ave., South Bronx and various other McDonald's locations.

Day 17:
Japanese Footbridge Scene, Graham Ave & Cook St, Bed Stuy.

Day 18:
Banksy x Os Gêmeos Open Air Gallery, W 24th St, under the Highline.

Day 19:
Vaginal Anthill, Staten Island.

Day 20:
Boy With Hammer, Upper West Side.

Day 21:
Ghetto 4 Life, Elton Avenue and 153rd St, South Bronx.

Day 22:
Everything but the Kitchen Sphinx, 127th St & 35th Ave.

Day 23:
Today's art has been cancelled due to police activity.
Message on Banksy's Instagram page. Rumours of his arrest proved unfounded.

Day 24:
Waiting in Vain, Larry Flynt's Hustler Club, West Side Highway, Hell's Kitchen.

Day 25:
Grim Reaper in a Bumper Car, E Houston St & Elizabeth St.

Day 26:
The Grumpier You Are, the More Assholes You Meet, Message on back of truck which departed from Sunset Park.

Day 27:
This Site Contains Blocked Messages, Banksy's response to the *New York Times* rejecting his op-ed column. It was published instead on Banksy's website.

Day 28:
Tagging Robot, Coney Island.

Day 29:
The Banality of the Banality of Evil, Housing Works thrift shop, 23rd St.

Day 30:
Bronx Zoo Leopard, Yankee Stadium.

Day 31:
Inflatable Throw-Up, Banksy tagged his name in inflatable bubble writing on the last day of his residency.
Borden Ave & 35th St, Queens.

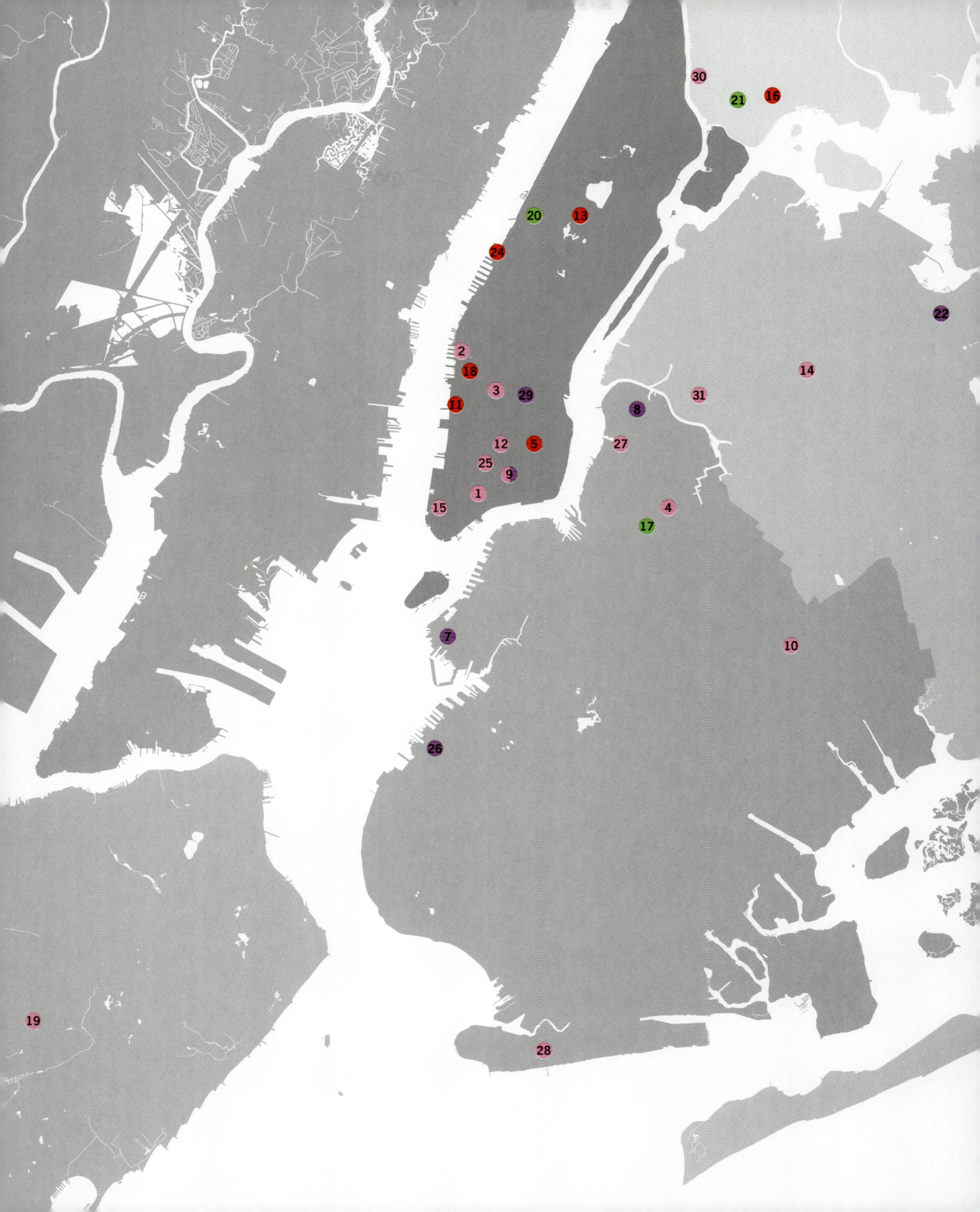

THE STREET IS IN PLAY

**"People say graffiti is ugly, irresponsible and childish...
but that's only if it's done properly."** Banksy.

Also known as *Graffiti is a Crime,* this was Banksy's first work for his month-long New York residency, the title announcing that this particular street art event had just kicked off. It was apposite that it was an absolutely classic Banksy, and one of his best works to date. As the residency went on, Banksy was to introduce many new concepts, which would be fully developed by the time of his *Dismaland* show in 2015.

The theme of children in somewhat retro dress returns, this time with two boys who, with their flat caps, could be taken straight out of the streets of an English mining village in the 1930s. One, the slightly older one, has boots and is wearing a jacket. The younger one, standing on his back, is a bit more of an urchin – unshod, but wearing braces, with his sleeves purposefully rolled up. The lower boy appears to be smiling at the naughtiness of the crime; the younger lad looks serious and tentative as he grasps the aerosol.

The usurpation of the sign is quite brilliant, integrating the art into the street, cocking a snook at city authorities (whilst making them accessories to the work), and making the viewer delight with glee at the cleverness of it all.

It is a charming comment on the anti-establishment yet young nature of street art, but also of the camaraderie and team effort often involved in getting illicit art onto walls. In the context of New York it was brilliant. The city seemed pretty split down the middle in its attitude to street art, and in reaction to Banksy. Half seemed convinced, po-faced, no-matter-what, that street art is, very simply, a crime; the other half delighted in the art. The city authorities expressed their view, buffing the work after 24 hours.

WHERE IS IT ?
LOWER EAST SIDE,
NYC,
USA.
BUFFED WITHIN 24 HOURS.

Latitude: 40.7172ºN
Longitude: 73.9913ºW

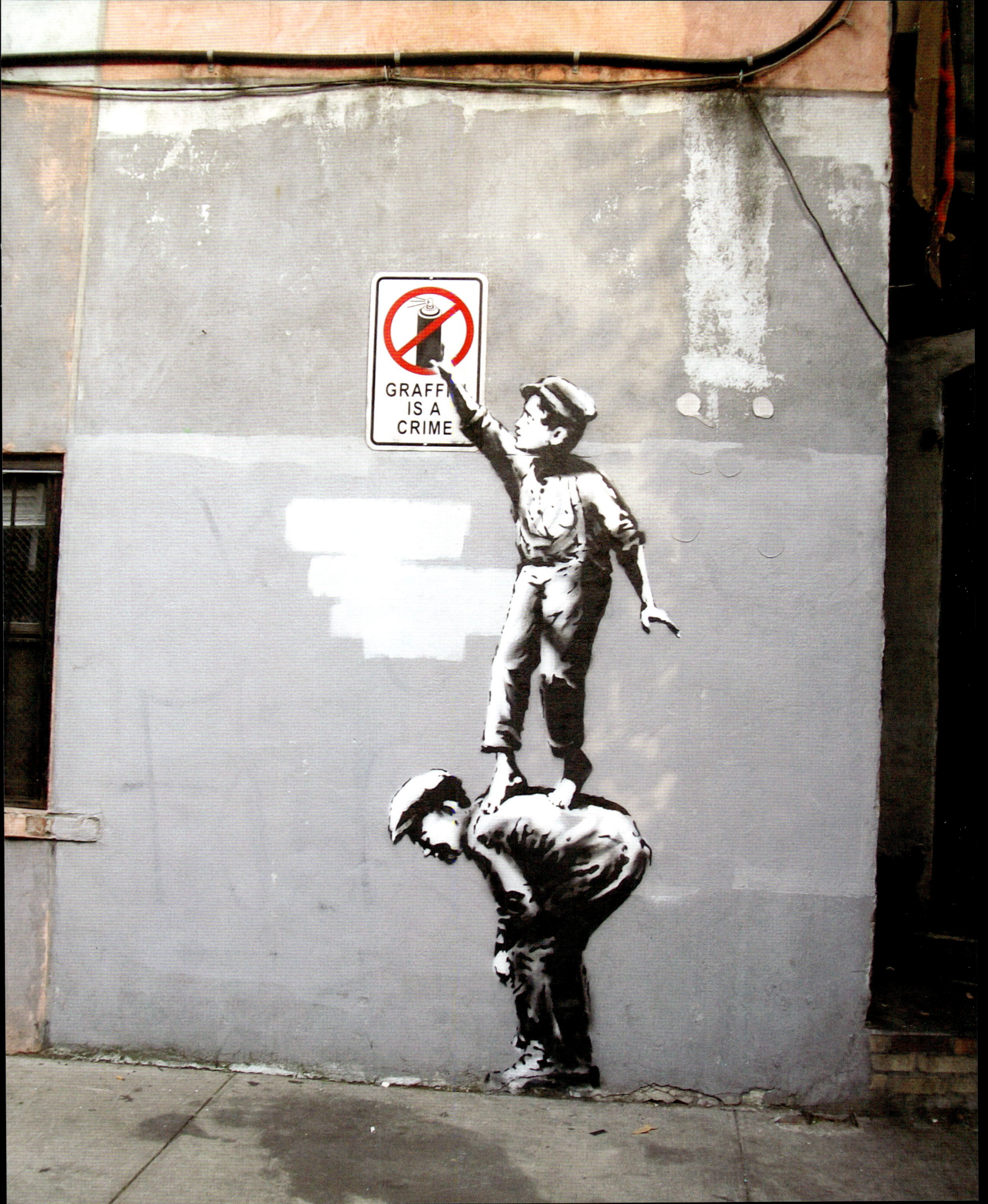

GRAFFITI
IS A
CRIME

YOU COMPLETE ME

"*Dogs are the original graffiti artists.*" Banksy.

Day 3 of Banksy's New York residency. Language and image in brilliant fusion. The one thing that would have made this even wittier would have been an actual fire hydrant. The dog, we think, is a labrador retriever. As with the other pieces of *Better Out Than In*, a freephone number was stencilled on the pavement. Calling it would give the reader additional information, although the commentary (was it recited by Banksy in a faux American accent?) might have driven people nuts by suggesting, tangentially, that it was in Mid-town rather than Chelsea.

The schmaltzy piece of language 'you complete me' is hilarious, the fire hydrant (think city authorities) loving being peed on. The recording asked "Wouldn't the architecture foisted on our cities be incomplete without the maverick stains of those answering back?" So, the dog and street artists are associated, the function of their 'art' here perfectly encapsulated, and satirised, in image form.

The piece was vandalised, or added to, with the tags of many street writers, within a few minutes of being painted. Some New Yorkers were outraged. There was speculation on some social media that Banksy may have been behind, or encouraging, some of the tagging. It certainly added to the frenzy and happening nature of his residency.

There's nothing that gets people mad like art being defaced.

WHERE IS IT ?
24TH STREET & 6TH AVENUE,
NYC,
USA.

Latitude: 40.7436ºN
Longitude: 73.9923ºW

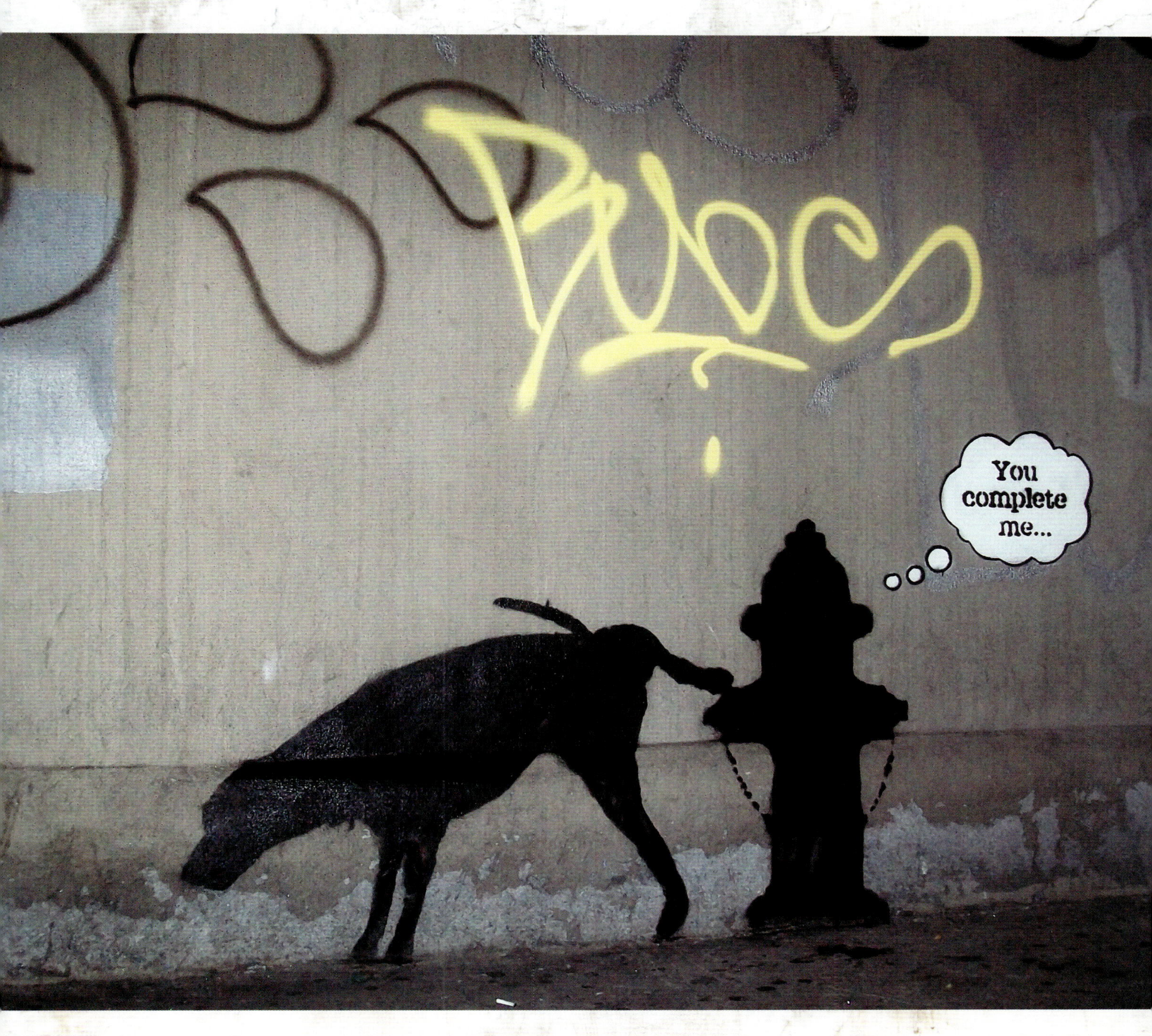
You
complete
me...

BOY WITH HAMMER

"Nothing is black and white." Banksy.

One of the successes of Banksy's 31-day New York residency, was New Yorkers having no idea where he would strike next. This time it was in the upscale Upper West Side, on 79th Street.

A wonderfully simple piece of situationism, Banksy sees beyond everyday objects, to see what they could be. Here a fire bell, a metal sleeve protecting the connecting wire and a fire hydrant are transformed into the classic fairground game, high striker. The game involves hitting a panel with a heavy hammer to see how high the indicator will go. If you get it high enough, the bell goes and you win a prize!

The simplicity of this silhouette is enchanting. It is a wonderful evocation of childhood and its pleasures. It suggests the brilliant ability of children to play with the simplest props. What is striking too is the range it demonstrates in Banksy's work – from this, to the elaborate truck installations, also part of his residency.

On the day the piece appeared there was an attempt to deface it; onlookers then intervened to defend it. The owner of the building on which it was painted declared that for him it was art, and quickly protected it with a sheet of plexiglass.

WHERE IS IT ?
UPPER WEST SIDE,
NEW YORK,
USA.
STILL THERE, PROTECTED WITH PLEXIGLASS.

Latitude: 40.7838ºN
Longitude: 73.9799ºW

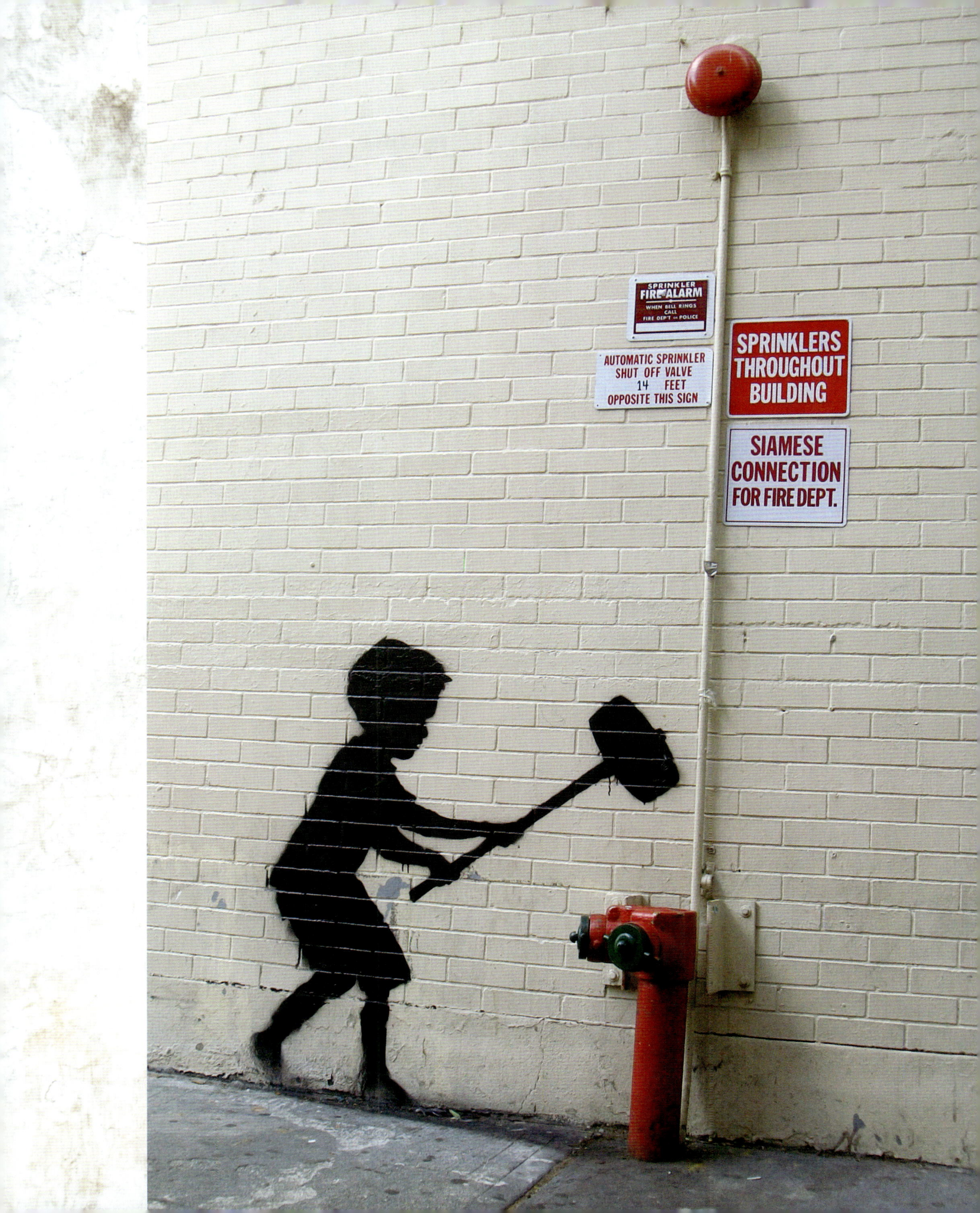

SPRINKLER
FIRE ALARM
WHEN BELL RINGS
CALL
FIRE DEP'T or POLICE

AUTOMATIC SPRINKLER
SHUT OFF VALVE
14 FEET
OPPOSITE THIS SIGN

SPRINKLERS
THROUGHOUT
BUILDING

SIAMESE
CONNECTION
FOR FIRE DEPT.

GHETTO 4 LIFE

"Many Bronxites are upset at Banksy's choice of words, and they are right to be upset." Ruben Diaz Jr., President Bronx Borough.

A wonderfully provocative piece, which elicited just the right sort of righteous indignation which further enhanced publicity for day 21 of the residency. Diaz added "Banksy should be aware that graffiti art and graffiti culture originated in the Bronx. Perhaps it would be better to use his talents to help us tell the story of the 'New Bronx'." Jeffrey Guard, director of the Bronx Art Exchange gave a short admonitory lecture: "What Banksy, who is presumed to be both white and English [a double crime], may not have realised is that in American culture a white person using the word 'ghetto' can be perceived as racially charged."

Did he not look at the piece? What it reveals is that Banksy is *completely* aware. It shows a schoolboy, immaculately dressed in the manner of the top private prep schools in England, being waited on by the family butler, holding his spray cans on a silver tray. This is such a witty send-up of the white adopters of graffiti culture, toffs who like to make out they're from the street. Perhaps Banksy is even sending himself up a little here. In that sense it is an homage, a desire that street culture will not be anaesthetised and cleaned up. It is also a fantastic rendition of childhood rebellion; the absurd contrast between the language, the scruffy writing and the neat, stiff stance of the good schoolboy together with the utterly obsequious butler, are brilliant.

The piece drew big crowds and generated endless column inches. The owner of the building loved it: "It's beautiful, it's a nice work of art. More power to him. As long as it doesn't hurt anybody, it's fine."

WHERE IS IT ?
BRONX,
NYC,
USA.

Latitude: 40.8184ºN
Longitude: 73.9148ºW

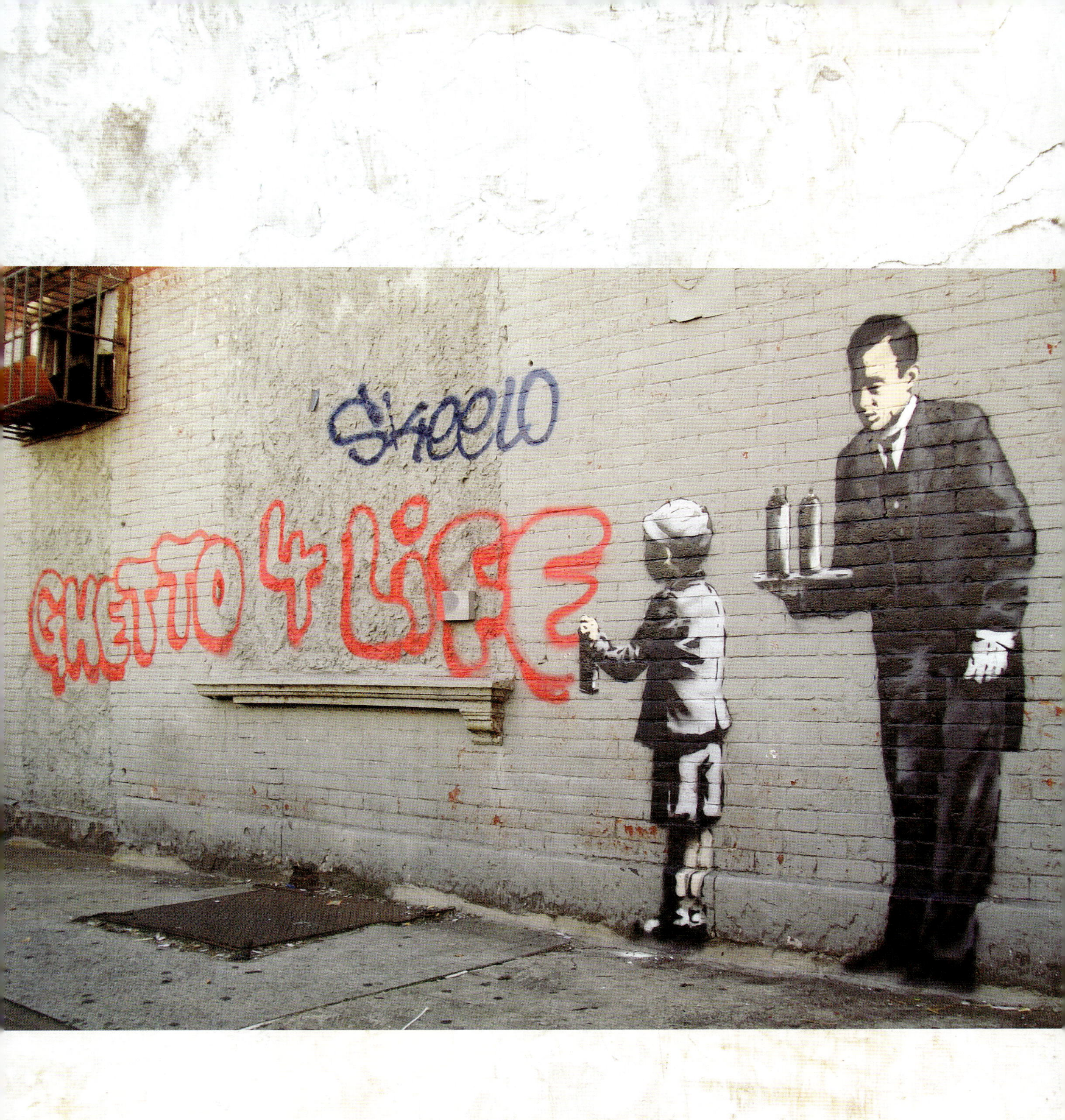
SKEELO
GHETTO 4 LIFE

WAITING IN VAIN

"There are four basic human needs: food, sleep, sex and revenge." Banksy.

Created on day 24 of Banksy's New York residency, this appeared the day after Banksy had taken a break in creating artworks around the city "due to police activity," as he said on his website, cleverly making the police, rather than the street artist they were hunting down, sound illegal.

As ever with Banksy, context is everything. This appeared on a roll-down shutter covering the entrance to Larry Flint's Hustler strip club on 51st Street in Manhattan. This stage-door Johnny is wearing a Humphrey Bogart-era suit, possibly a tux. The bouquet of flowers is a romantic gesture, suffused with pathetic hope. He is waiting for a stripper who presumably worked the night (the Hustler Club shuts at around 6.15 am; the piece was painted shortly after it shut). The leaves falling off the flowers suggest he has waited quite a while and any potential for romance here is wilting, fast. The falling red petals are redolent of blood spilt. Not a happy scene.

Shortly after the piece appeared, beefy security guards emerged to protect it from crowds of New Yorkers photographing frantically, in order to prevent anyone from tagging or defacing the work. The Hustler Club's marketing director said, without irony, "We're honoured that Banksy chose the Larry Flint Hustler Club New York to share his art." Several dancers from the club came out and posed with the work before the gate was removed 'for safekeeping' that evening. A spokesman from Hustler suggested the work could one day be displayed inside the club. Could be a bit of a mood-killer.

WHERE IS IT ?
HELL'S KITCHEN,
MANHATTAN,
NYC,
USA.

Latitude: 40.7673ºN
Longitude: 73.9959ºW

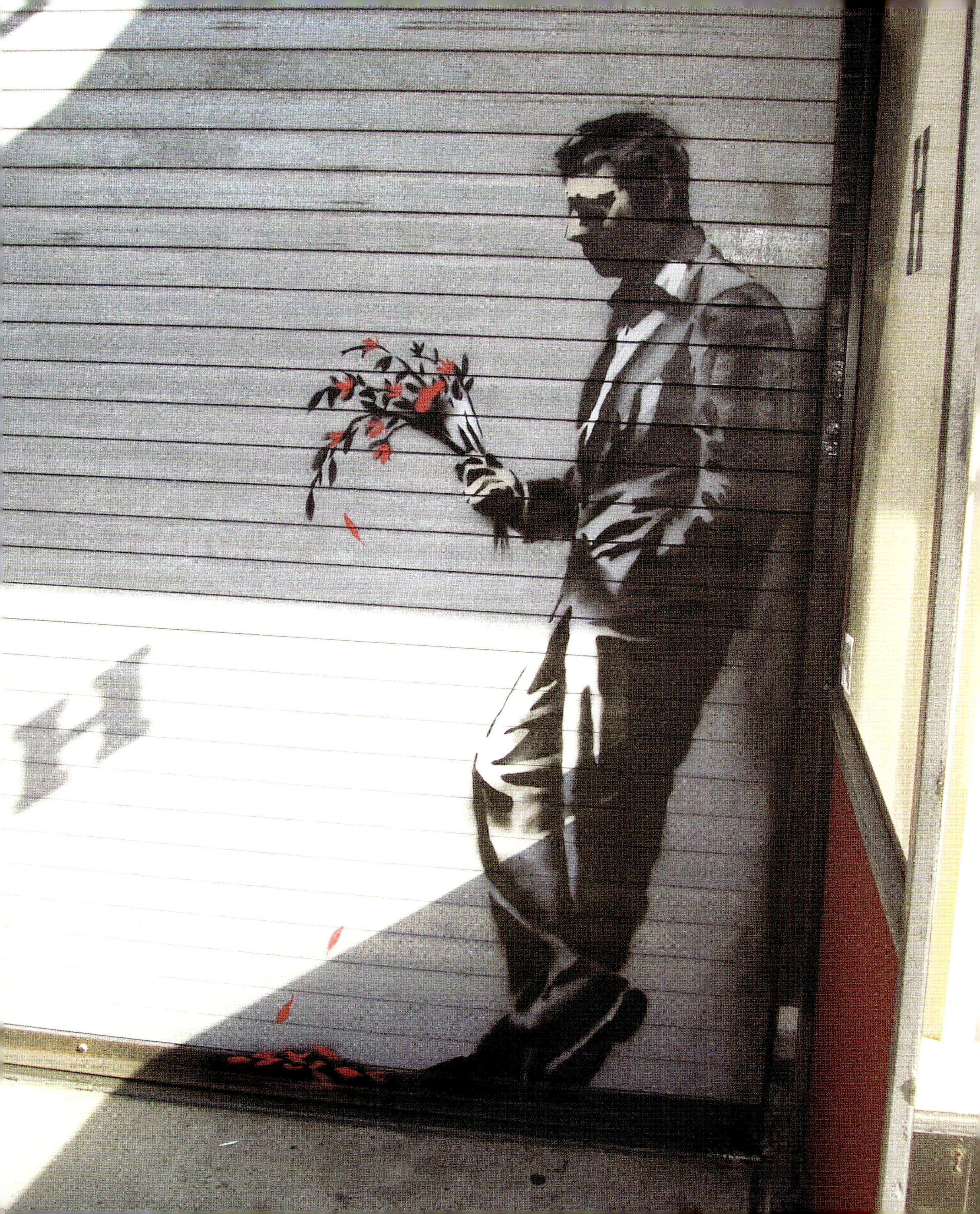

THE BANALITY OF THE BANALITY OF EVIL

"When I hear the word 'culture' I reach for my revolver."
Hermann Göring.

This piece was created for day 29 of the residency. Banksy purchased a painting from the Housing Works thrift store on East 23rd Street, 'vandalised' it by adding a Nazi and then donated it back to the store to be sold.

The original painting was indeed a banal cliché. To us it looks like a piece from someone who might have followed a show such as the 1970s *The Joy of Painting,* depicting a scene of autumnal foreground with wintry mountain peaks in the background. To this banal scene Banksy has added a banal Nazi officer, gazing at it in banal fashion. Nazis loved these romantic nature scenes, considered acceptable and morally suitable for consumption by the Master Race, rather than the 'degenerate' Modern art which they considered 'depraved'. An exhibition was held in Munich in 1937 showing acceptable art, in The House of German Art in Munich, soon daubed by the wittier locals as 'Palazzo Kitschi'.

It's hard to decipher this piece, but is Banksy suggesting that people who love this sort of kitsch have traces of white supremacist attitudes? Is a point being made about the denial of the presence of First Nation peoples in this 'virgin' landscape? The title (a reference to the title of Hannah Arendt's book about the trial of Adolf Eichmann) perhaps is a better guide: Banksy has simply doubled the banality and put it back where it belongs – in a thrift store full of other trash.

Shortly after its return, a representative of Banksy's called the store, authenticated the work and suggested it be auctioned. It sold for $615,000, the money going to Housing Works, who provide support for homeless patients living with HIV/AIDS in New York.

WHERE IS IT ?
GARMENT DISTRICT,
MANHATTAN,
NYC,
USA.
SOLD AT AUCTION TO PRIVATE COLLECTOR.

Latitude: 40.7391ºN
Longitude: 73.9834ºW

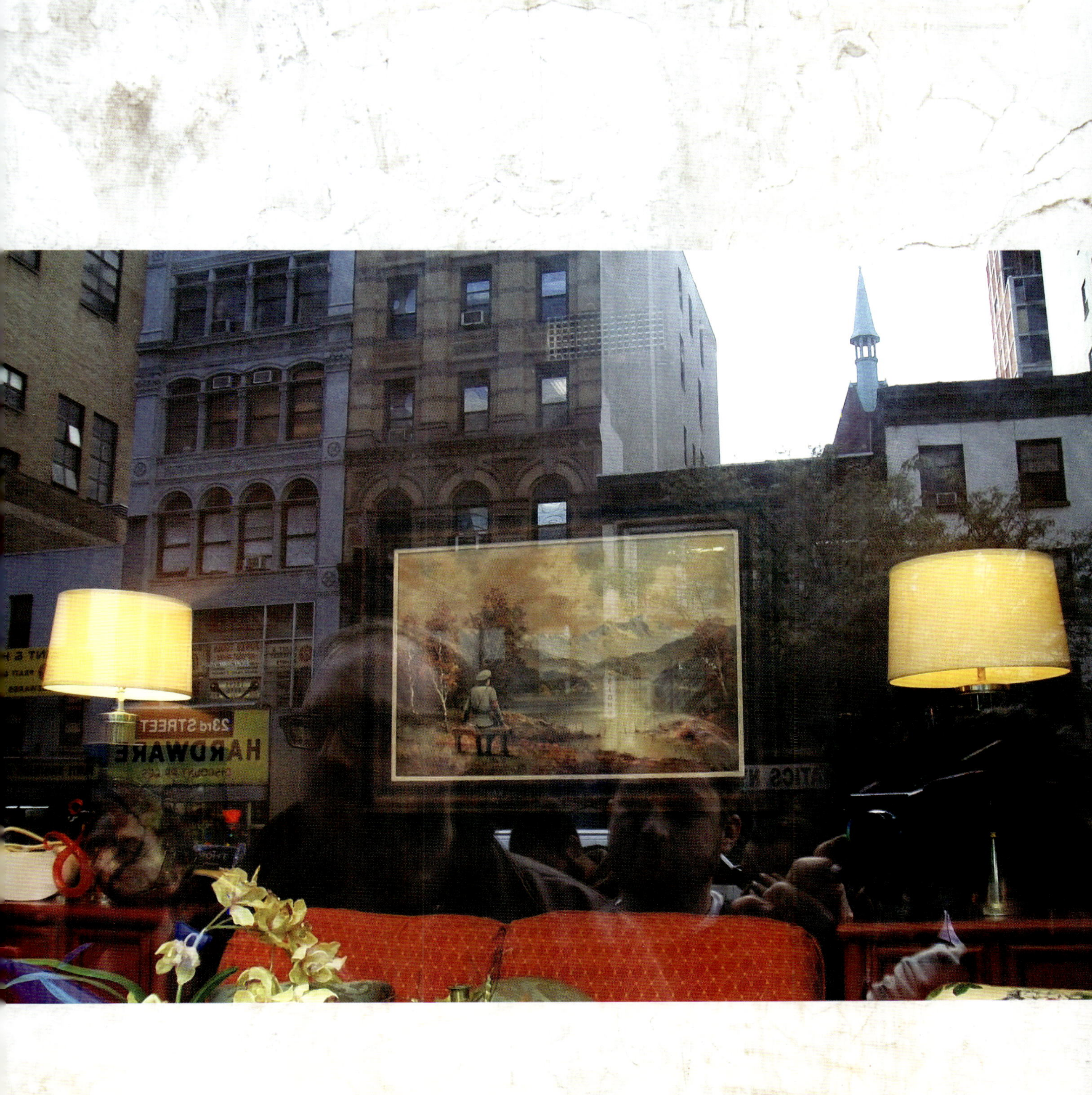

JAPANESE SCENE

"One original thought is worth 1,000 meaningless quotes."
Banksy, quoting Diogenes the Cynic.

A wonderful scene of silhouettes of two Japanese ladies conversing, wearing full kimonos with traditional obi sashes. The presence of a parasol and fan, suggest that this is a scene in a relaxing garden. Banksy used a bizarre existing arch feature on the side of this building, for his Japanese garden bridge, and the scene is completed by the bonsai tree, possibly with Spring's first cherry blossom, to the left.

This was created on day 17 of Banksy's residency, a sharp contrast with the previous day's Ronald McDonald shoe-shine boy live installation. Loads of interpretation has been loaded onto this piece, but to us it's just a charming and clever use of an architectural feature, a pause before the day 18 gallery installation with Os Gemeos.

Ignoring the image of peace, repose and spring-time optimism, a tagger managed to deface the stencil within an hour of it going up. He was quickly thrown to the ground by a crowd that had assembled. Three Banksy fans, with quick reactions, managed to remove his spraypaint with alcohol wipes. The owner of the building has since, slightly bizarrely, placed a roller shutter covering the bonsai and the women, but leaving the right-hand side of the bridge exposed.

WHERE IS IT ?
WILLIAMSBURG,
NYC,
USA.
NOW OBSCURED UNDER A
PROTECTIVE ROLLER-SHUTTER.

Latitude: 40.7012ºN
Longitude: 73.9432ºW

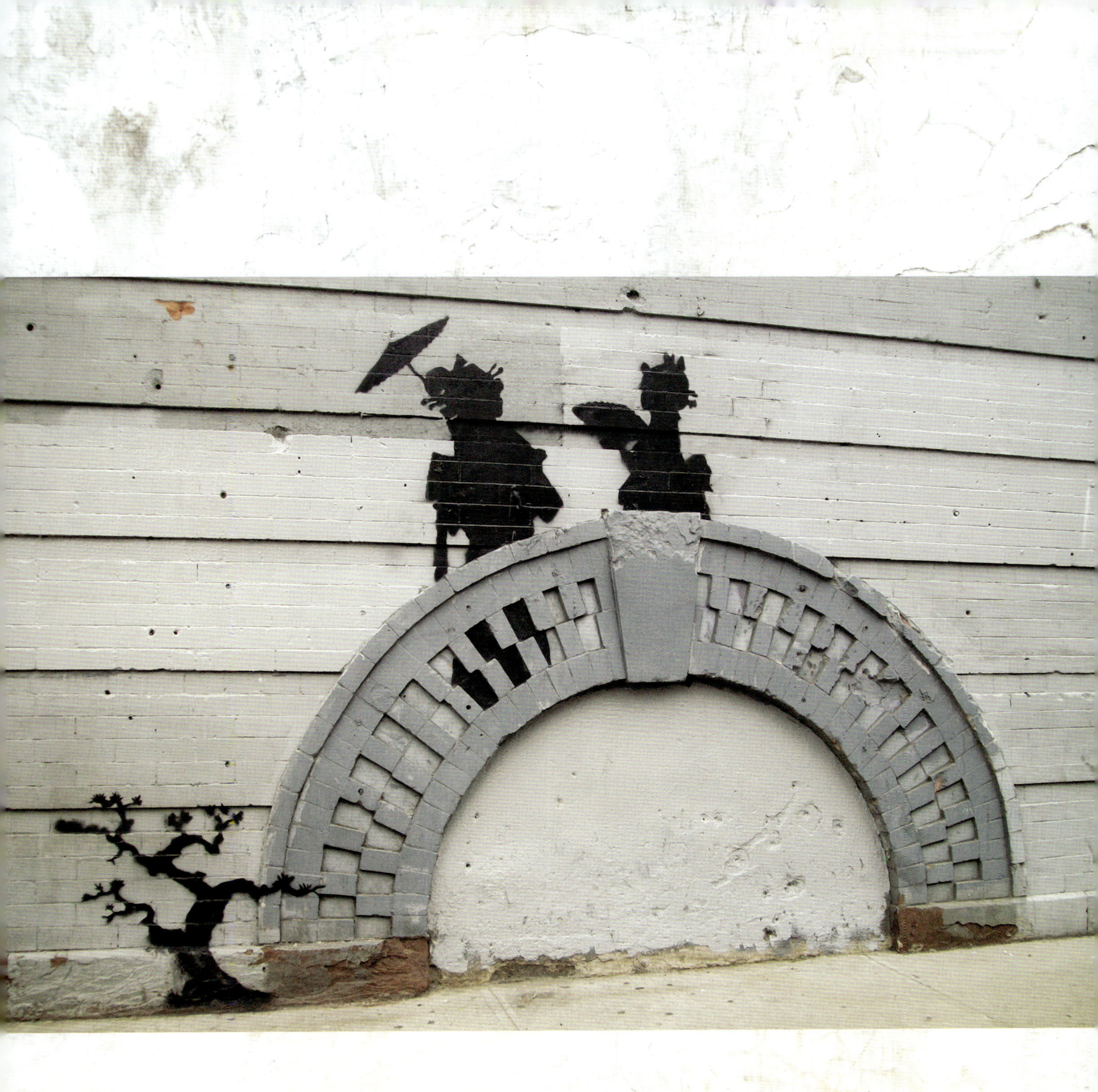

CRAZY HORSES

"There is, I am certain, among the Iraqi people a respect for the care and precision that went into the bombing campaign."
Donald Rumsfeld, US Secretary of State for Defense.

Perhaps Banksy's most emotive political work to date, this astonishing installation appeared in Manhattan's Lower East Side, on Ludlow Street, on day 9 of his New York residency.

The scene is a direct reference to, and evocation of, a US air-strike on Baghdad in 2007. On an oil drum Banksy stencilled a 1-800 number, which took the caller to a 39-minute recording, taken from the *Collateral Murder* video – released by Bradley Manning through Wikileaks in 2010 – of the air-strike. The contents are truly disturbing, showing an Apache helicopter gunning down two children, some combatants, a Reuters news agency photographer and a number of civilians who came in to help the wounded; in all it's estimated 18 people died in the attack. As well as the sound of gunfire, we hear an exchange between the helicopter crew and some soldiers, mentioning that children were being rushed to hospital, to which the soldier says, of the Iraqis, "Well, it's their fault. They shouldn't have brought a kid to a gun battle."

The crazy horses galloping through, riderless, in the background, with their night-vision goggles, are a reference to the US military and give the piece a powerful classical flavour: there's a touch of Delacroix here. Banksy is saying that the horror of war has not changed. The trapped figures in the car, placed in poses of terror and despair, are also reminiscent of the grand masters. Their figures are marked by the cross-hairs of snipers' rifle sights; this is the moment before they're shot dead. The oil drum says it all: oil is what this war is mostly about.

WHERE IS IT ?
LOWER EAST SIDE,
MANHATTAN,
NEW YORK,
USA.

Latitude: 40.7205ºN
Longitude: 73.9882ºW

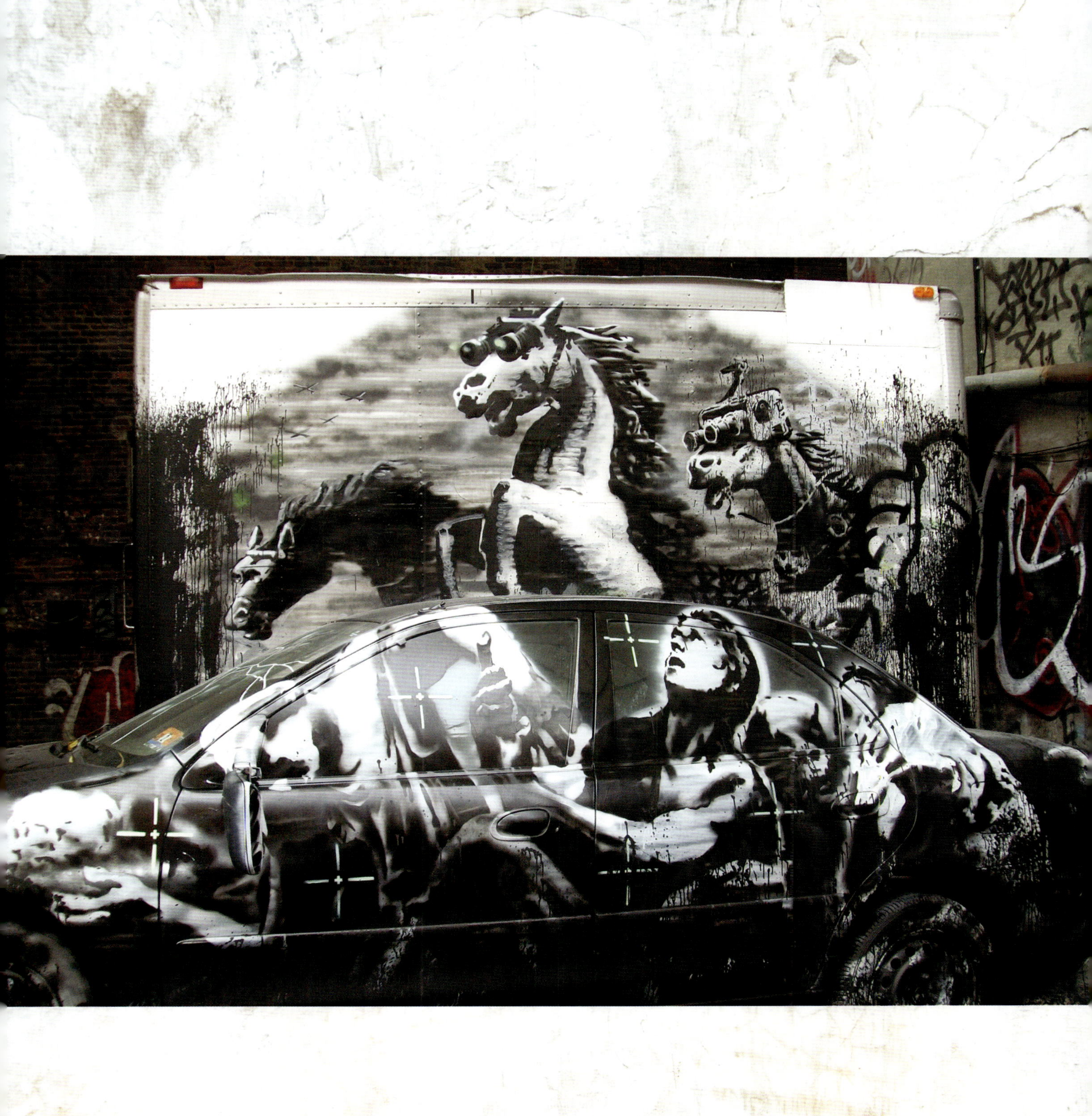

SHOE SHINE

"The most sculpted figure in history after Christ." Banksy.

On day 16 of the residency, this 'live' installation appeared outside a McDonald's in Westchester Avenue in the South Bronx. The installation appeared again on day 21, in Manhattan's Lower East Side.

This ultra-eloquent dig at a major global corporation has it all. Ronald McDonald is having his boots shoe-shined by a man from the lower orders. The look on his face is one of total aristocratic disdain and entitlement. The face was apparently modelled by Banksy after the bust of Hermes by the Ancient Greek sculptor, Praxiteles. Global corporations, the piece seems to say, are the aristocracy of our era. The boots are hugely outsized, a comment on McDonald's bestriding the globe, its global carbon footprint, or its ability to keep the workers down. They also beg the question, are these feet of clay? The actor, dressed in the collarless shirt and flat cap of the 1930s English working class man, suitably grubby and unshod, wears the cussed expression of the downtrodden.

Banksy's audio guide to the piece on his website stated: "Ronald was adopted as the official mascot of the McDonald's fast food corporation in 1966. Fibreglass versions of his likeness have been installed outside restaurants since, thus making Ronald arguably the most sculpted figure in history after Christ."

WHERE IS IT ?
BRONX,
NYC,
USA.

Latitude: 40.8287ºN
Longitude: 73.8782ºW

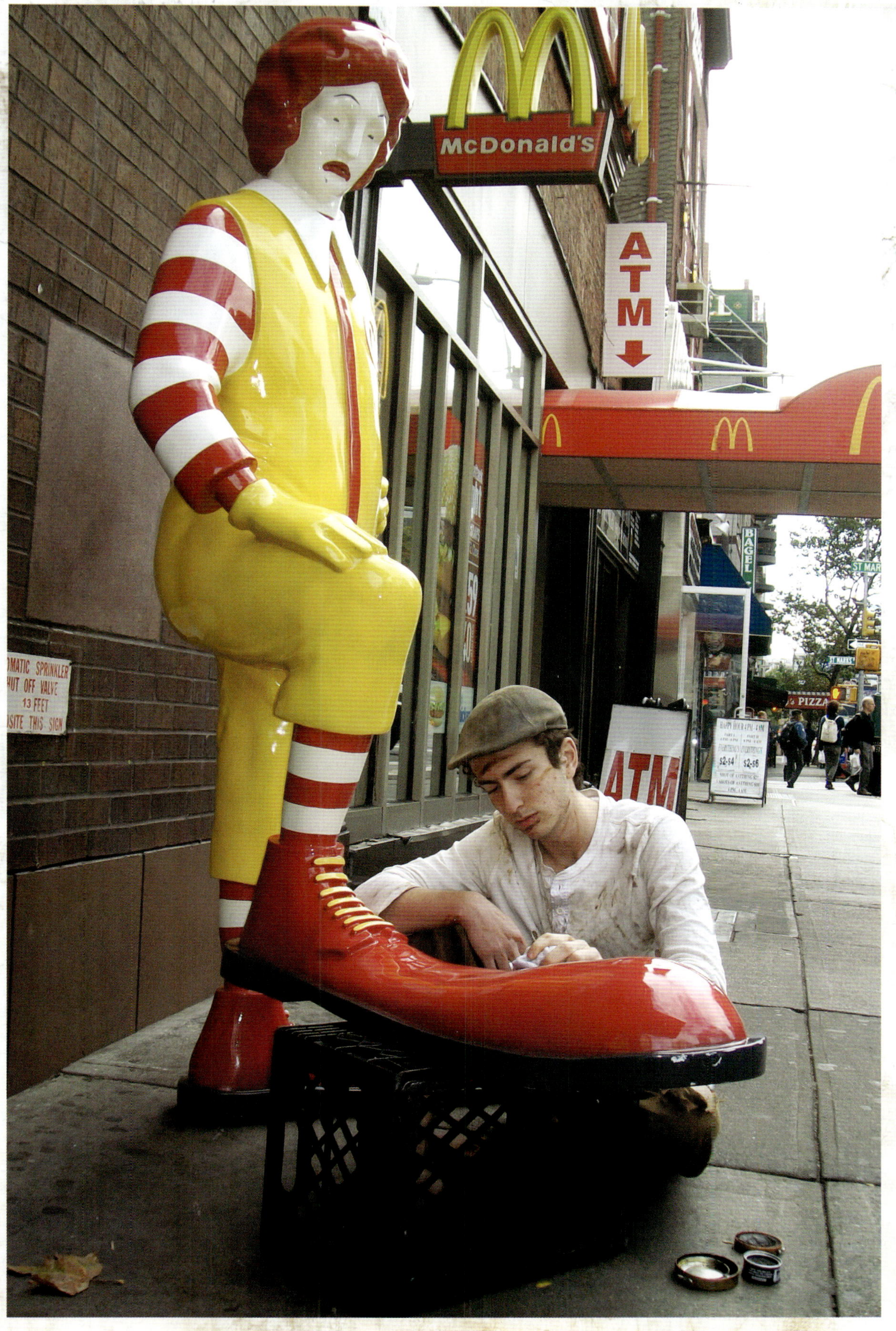

McDonald's
ATM
M
BAGEL
ST MARKS
PIZZA
ATM
AUTOMATIC SPRINKLER
SHUT OFF VALVE
13 FEET
OPPOSITE THIS SIGN

SIRENS OF THE LAMBS

"*I am having an old friend for dinner.*"
Dr Hannibal Lecter, *Silence of the Lambs.*

A regular, weathered green slaughterhouse truck, labelled 'Farm Fresh Meats' appeared, jam-packed with cuddly stuffed toys – not just of lambs, but of pigs and cows also – on day 11 of the residency in (appositely) Manhattan's Meatpacking district. It toured the streets of New York, with screams and squeals emanating from inside, at intervals for the following two weeks.

The play on words brings into sharp focus the psychopathic sadism man is capable of, as revealed by Hannibal Lecter in *Silence of the Lambs.* The Sirens were, famously, the women in Homer's *Odyssey* who lured sailors onto their island's rocky shores, and thus to death in shipwrecks, with their seductive songs. More prosaically, sirens are loud, high-pitched warnings. So, not only are these animals highlighting their plight on their way to slaughter, but also warning us of the heinous consequences of our factory-farming activities. In his usual, multi-layered fashion, Banksy is giving normally helpless animals a true voice.

Banksy has made several references in his work to animal cruelty, both on the practices of the processed food industry and in the human penchant to train performing animals in captivity (see *Dismaland* on page 208). Here, the cosy comfort of food industry branding and euphemistic language ('Farm Fresh') is in sharp contrast to the violence and horror which will befall these animals very soon.

New Yorkers see these slaughterhouse trucks wandering their streets every day. The animals within don't scream so we don't notice them. Perhaps next time, Banksy will have made us think twice?

WHERE IS IT ?
MEATPACKING DISTRICT,
MANHATTAN,
NYC,
USA.

Latitude: 40.7397ºN
Longitude: 74.0068ºW

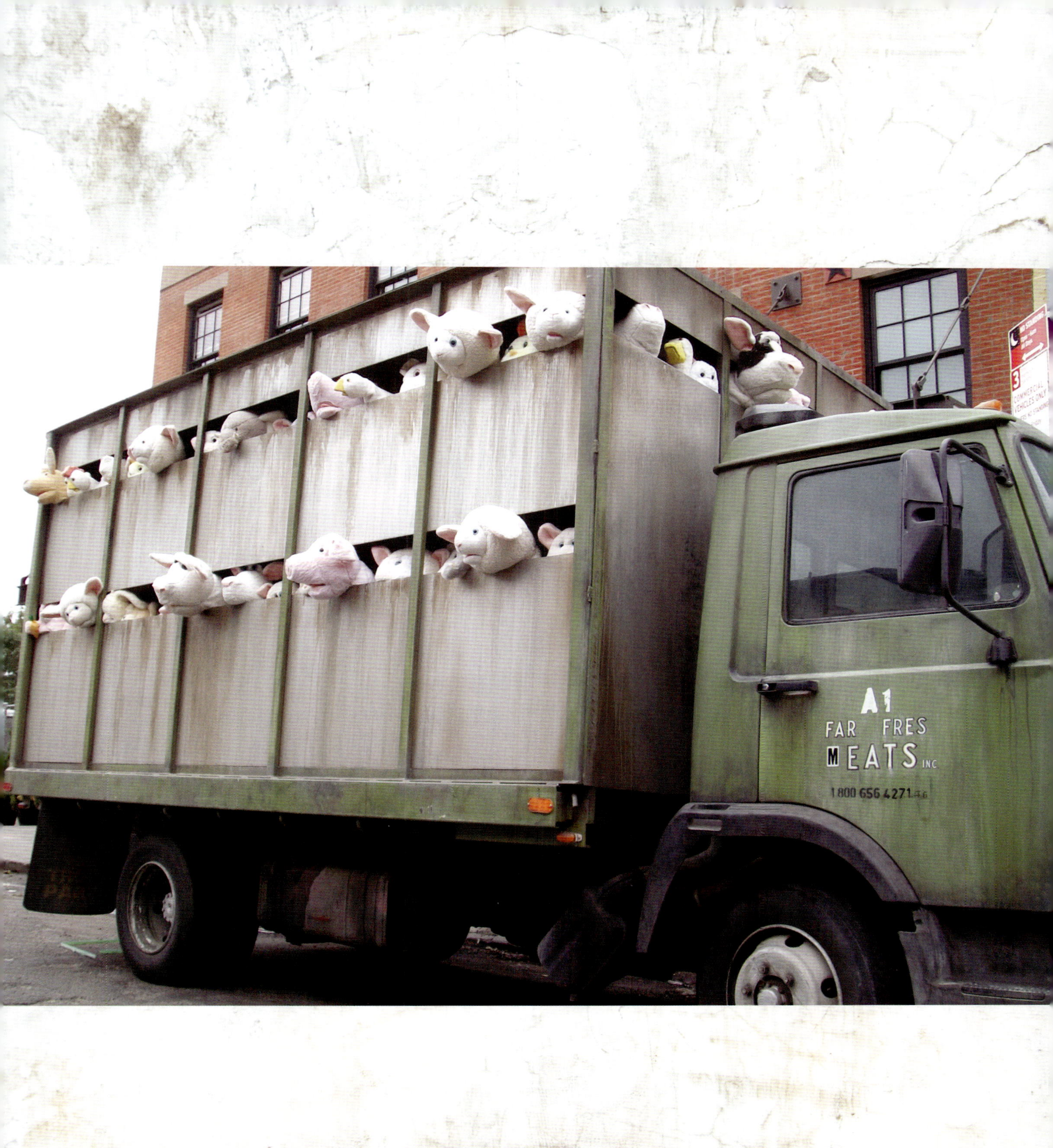

A1
FAR FRES
MEATS INC
1 800 656 4271 46

TWIN TOWERS

"The attacks of September 11 were an attack on all of us and we will live out our lives in their shadow.
But it is also how we react to adversity that defines us."
Banksy, part of intended op-ed piece for the *New York Times*."

There's no subject more sensitive, more personal to New Yorkers, than the attacks on the Twin Towers on 9/11, 2001. Even twelve years later, when Banksy created this piece on day 15 of his residency, the scars on the city were there for all to see; the subject remains as serious as ever.

It was therefore an act of great bravery to create this piece, which was intended as an homage to the 2,996 victims who lost their lives as a result of the attacks on that clear September day. It shows a silhouette of lower Manhattan as seen across the East River from Brooklyn Heights. An orange chrysanthemum flower marks the spot where the American Airlines Flight 11 from Boston hit the North Tower of the World Trade Center. In some cultures, the flower symbolises bereavement.

New Yorkers responded well to the piece. The site in Tribeca was soon turned into a shrine, with candles and flowers. Messages went out on social media asking that Banksy-haters not disturb the image. The request was sadly ignored, with one conspiracy theory idiot writing 'Inside Job' next to the piece. It was then protected by plexiglass, which was then covered in black paint.

A second piece, painted in Brooklyn Heights that same morning, survived less than a week before being buffed by the city.

Some New Yorkers took less kindly to Banksy's subsequent aesthetic criticism of the New World Trade Center, published on his website on day 27, after the *New York Times* snootily refused to run the story. "One World Trade Center is a non-event. It's vanilla, it looks like something they would build in Canada." He added, very provocatively "it's a shy skyscraper" that "so clearly proclaims the terrorists have won."

WHERE IS IT ?
TRIBECA,
MANHATTAN,
NYC,
USA.
PLEXIGLASSED, THEN PAINTED OVER.

Latitude: 40.7163ºN
Longitude: 74.0086ºW

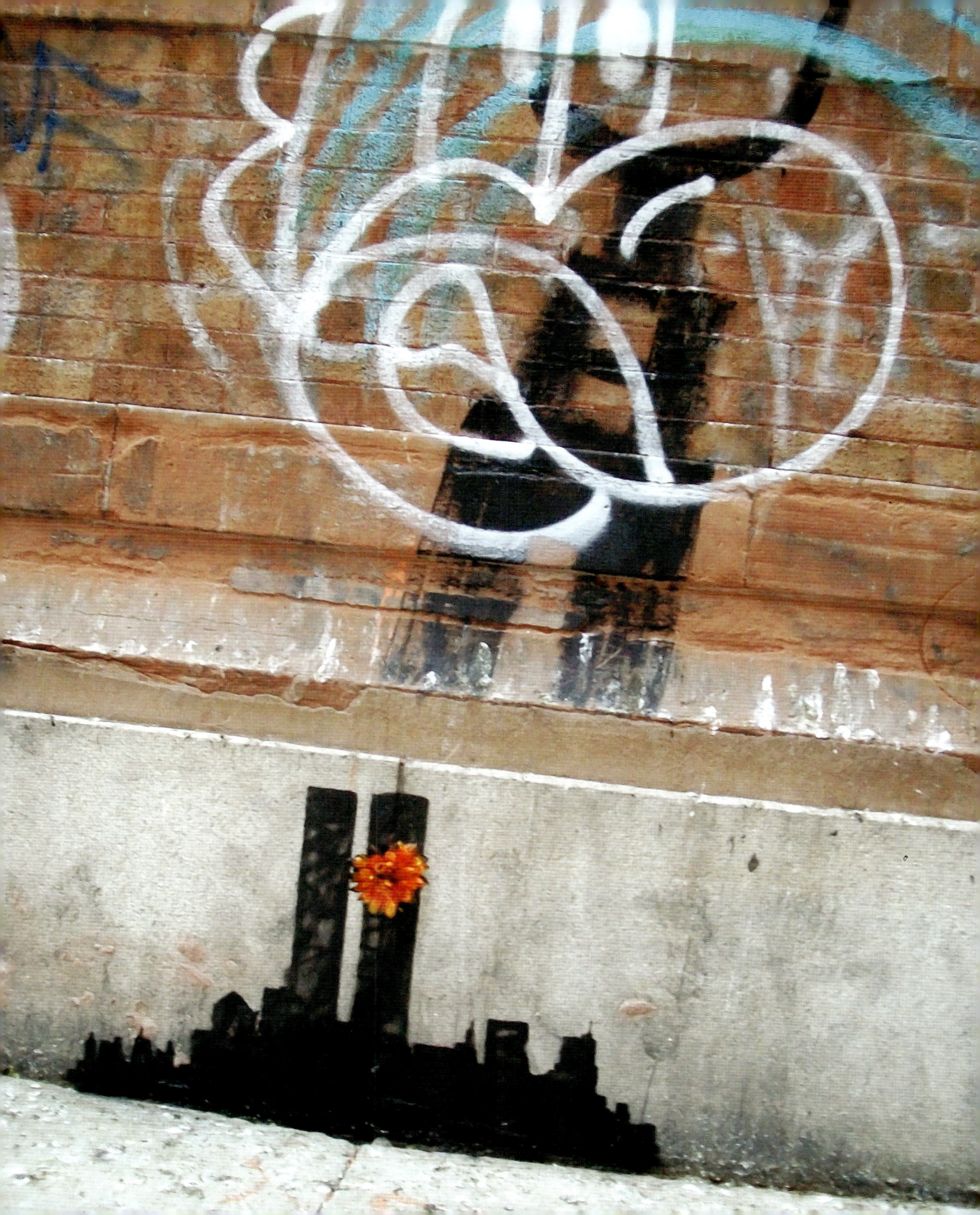

ETERNITY

"What we do now echoes in eternity."
Marcus Aurelius, *Meditations*, written c.170–180 AD.

"What we do in life echoes in Eternity," so says Maximus Decimus Meridius (Russell Crowe) as he rallies his troops before battle in *Gladiator*. Banksy had said he was often accused of using slightly lowbrow sources, but that in this instance he would use that hostility to make him stronger. In fact this was an in-joke, as the *Gladiator* quote is a lift from the *Meditations* of philosopher-Emperor Marcus Aurelius.

Banksy wittily takes the quote, written in the neat hand you might be expected to write in a detention at school, and turns it into a piece on the transience of all things, the most transient of which is street art. The chap washing the graffito off the wall is dressed in a boiler suit with the essential flat cap, and looks as though he is doing his job calmly, methodically and at his own pace. The piece acquires extra resonance given that Banksy painted his *Twin Towers* pieces the following day.

It didn't take long for this Banksy to prove its point. By 8pm on the day after its appearance it had already been defaced. *Sic transit gloria mundi*, as Maximus Decimus Meridius might say.

WHERE IS IT ?
WOODSIDE,
QUEENS,
NYC,
USA.
DEFACED SHORTLY AFTER ITS APPEARANCE.

Latitude: 40.7512ºN
Longitude: 73.9036ºW

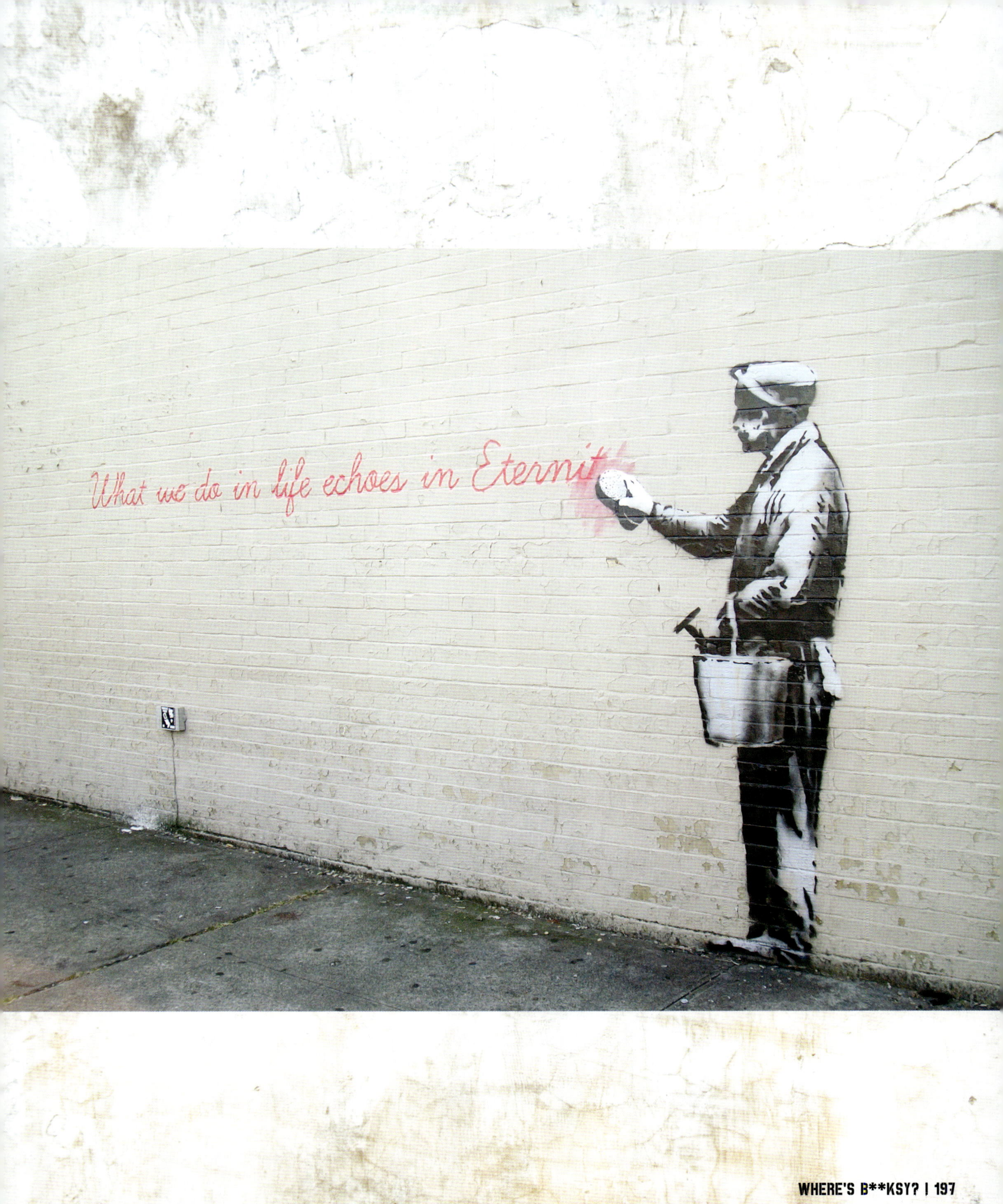

What we do in life echoes in Eternity

OS GEMEOS COLLABORATION

"This is our country. We will occupy it. These are our streets. We will occupy them. We are the 99%." Occupy movement chant.

Brazilian superstar street artists Os Gemeos (translation: The Twins), collaborated with Banksy on these two mega canvases which appeared on day 18 of the residency in Chelsea, under the Highline. The neighbourhood is jammed with art galleries, making it the perfect location. Of all the *Better Out Than In* pieces, this one perhaps lived up the most to the residency's title.

One canvas depicts a crowd of regimented riot police in black and greys, in the middle of which is one of Os Gemeos's brightly coloured figures, head wrapped in a scarf. The second canvas is the obverse: one solitary riot policeman amidst a sea of Os Gemeos figures. The telling thing is, though, that all the riot police look the same, whilst every Os Gemeos figure is an original, wearing their scarves in different fashion, one sporting a beard and shades, some looking left, others looking right or up, and so on; a brilliant comment on the robotic, mindless, inhuman nature of so much authority. Hilariously the piece had a 'museum' guard, in peaked hat and uniform, sitting on a stool (to the left of the picture), guarding the works. A bench was provided, and refreshments: cheap wine from a water cooler.

Banksy stated on his website that the 'gallery show' was inspired by the Occupy movement, the first significant demonstration of which was Occupy Wall Street, in NYC's Zuccotti Park in 2011.

Nothing has changed since. At the time of writing, the richest 1% of Americans own 37.1% of the nation's wealth, and rising; 20% of Americans own 87.7% of the total, and rising. Inequality is back to levels of disparity last seen in the US in 1928. The guys who employ the guys on the left-hand canvas are more powerful then ever.

WHERE IS IT ?
HIGHLINE,
CHELSEA,
NEW YORK,
USA.
THE INSTALLATION WAS REMOVED, WE ASSUME BY BANKSY OR OS GEMEOS, THE SAME DAY.

Latitude: 40.7480ºN
Longitude: 74.0048ºW

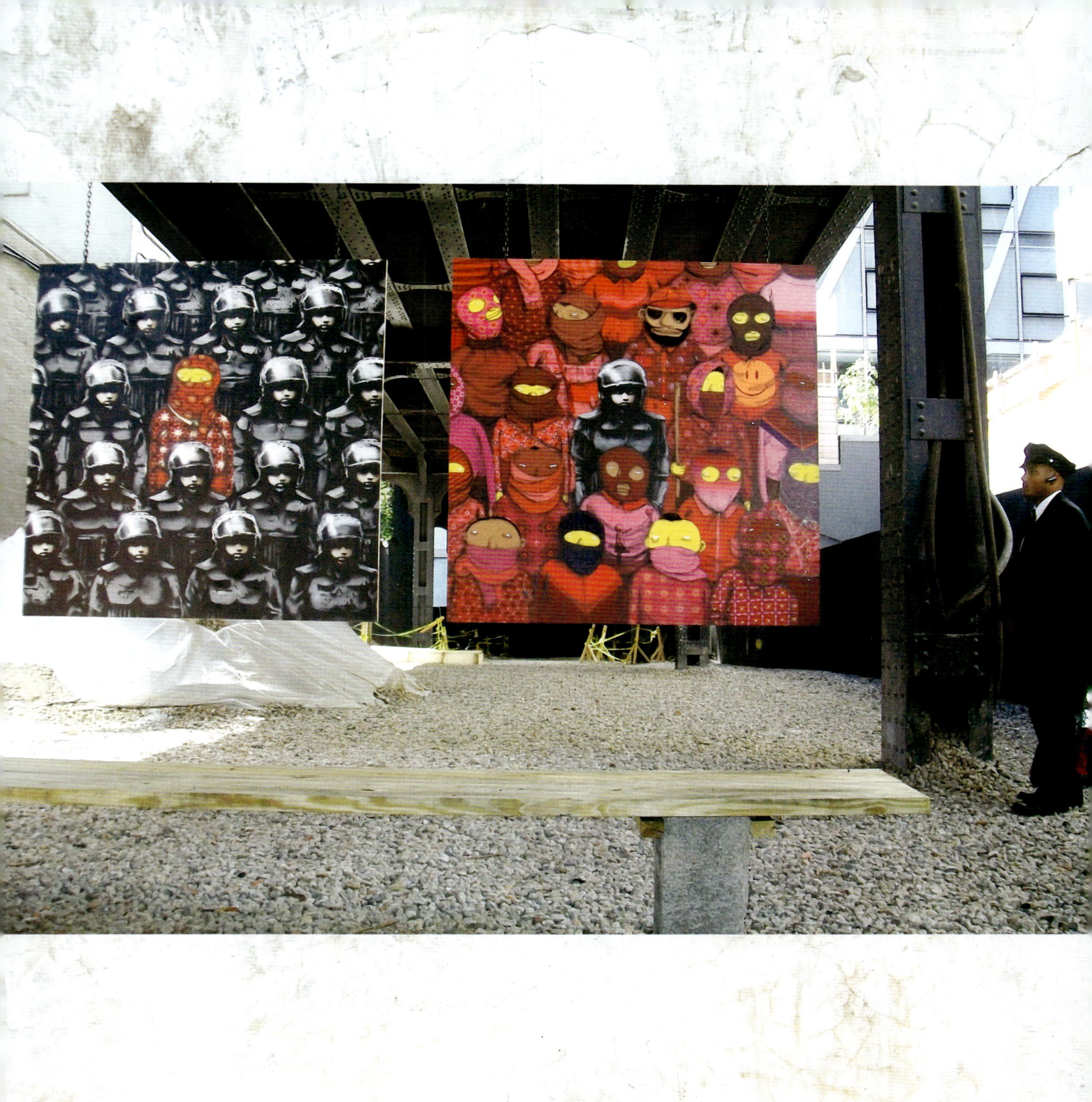

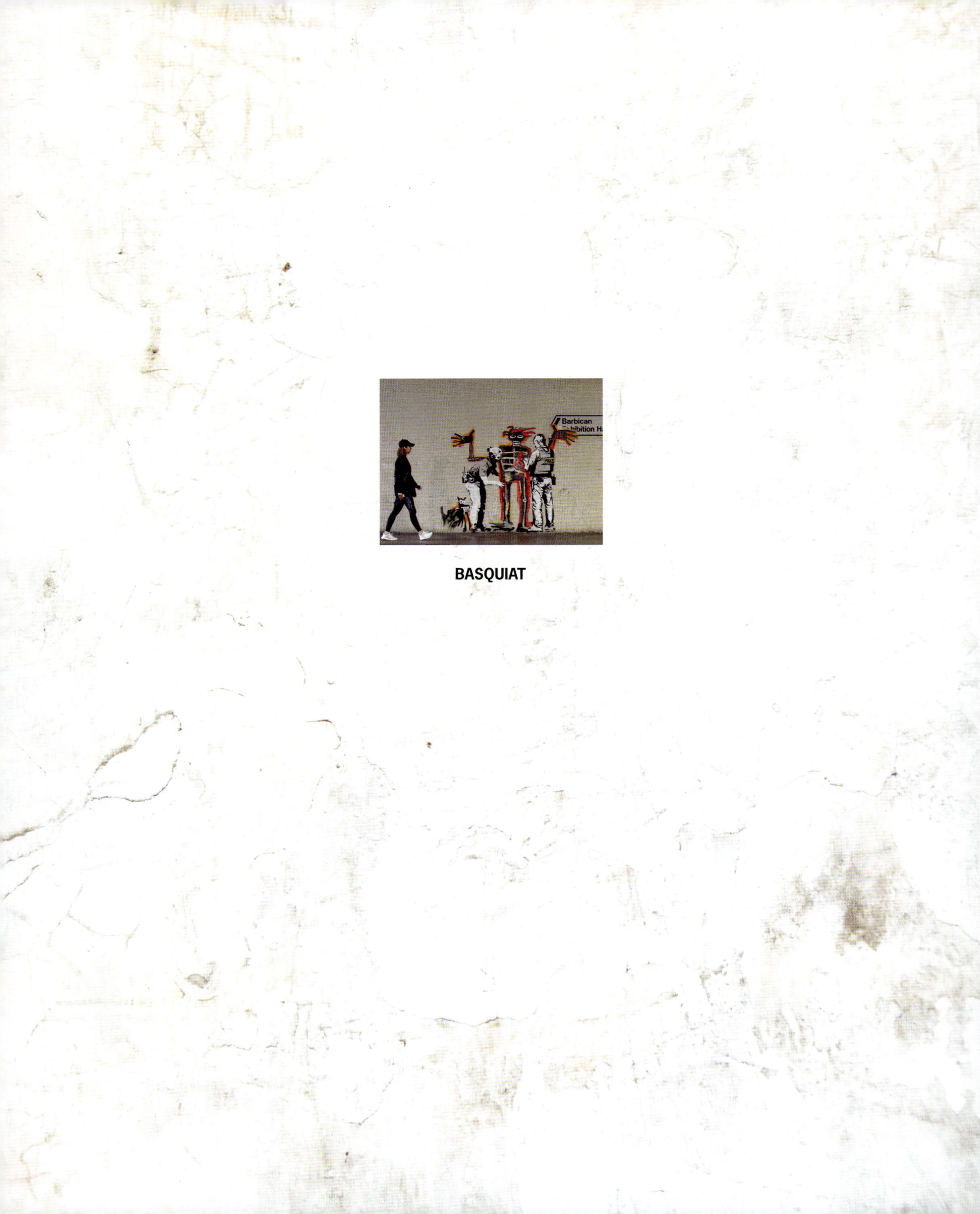

BASQUIAT

RECENT WORKS

Banksy achieves the unthinkable – a Grade II* listing – for his Cheltenham surveillance phone box. Then, proving that his impresario powers are far from diminished, the astounding Dismaland show, featuring Banksy and 58 other artists. Political themes remain at the forefront of his work – the plight of poor migrants inspire the brilliant *Son of a Syrian Refugee* featuring Steve Jobs. Whilst everyone has forgotten the Palestinians, Banksy shows that he has not, returning to Gaza for *Kitten* and creating The Walled Off Hotel. Then the amazing *Love is in the Bin,* which makes headlines around the world. Banksy, uber eloquently, now turned his attention to how the lure of money leads us to trash our environment, with the typically witty *Venice in Oil.* More recently Banksy has returned to creating wonderful, clever works featuring children, including *Valentine's Day* and *Hula Hoop Girl*; his ACHOO!! was a witty commentary on the Covid pandemic. One of its effects – the absence of travel – was brilliantly referenced in his *Great British Spraycation.*

GIRL WITH A PIERCED EARDRUM

EAVESDROPPING

DISMALAND

SON OF A SYRIAN REFUGEE

KITTEN

BRIDGE FARM PRIMARY SCHOOL

THE WALLED OFF HOTEL

BREXIT

BASQUIAT

LOVE IS IN THE BIN

VENICE IN OIL

MIGRANT CHILD WITH PINK FLARE

DEVOLVED PARLIAMENT

GOD BLESS BIRMINGHAM

VALENTINE'S DAY

HULA HOOP GIRL

AACHOO!!

CREATE ESCAPE

WE ARE ALL IN THE SAME BOAT

SEAGULL AND CHIPS

HIGH STREET SANDCASTLE

LUXURY RENTALS ONLY

BANKSY RECENT WORKS

Recently, Banksy's major works have been created in the UK, France and Italy, with *Kitten* (Gaza Strip) and The Walled Off Hotel (West Bank) the exceptions. This period is striking for the absence of works in the USA, after the brilliantly effective New York residency.

In England, Dismaland was a triumph, *Brexit* perfectly captured the self-destructive nature of the in/out EU referendum, Banksy paid homage to the brilliant Basquiat and effortlessly mocked the art market and its true values with *Love is in the Bin*. He also created in Bristol, Cheltenham, London, Birmingham and Nottingham. One of Banksy's other preoccupations during this period has been the plight of refugees, with pieces in Calais and Venice. He also intervened directly, financing a boat helping to rescue refugees in the Mediterranean.

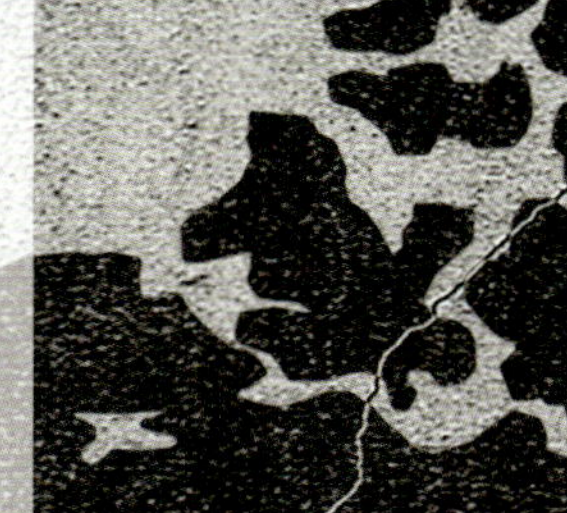
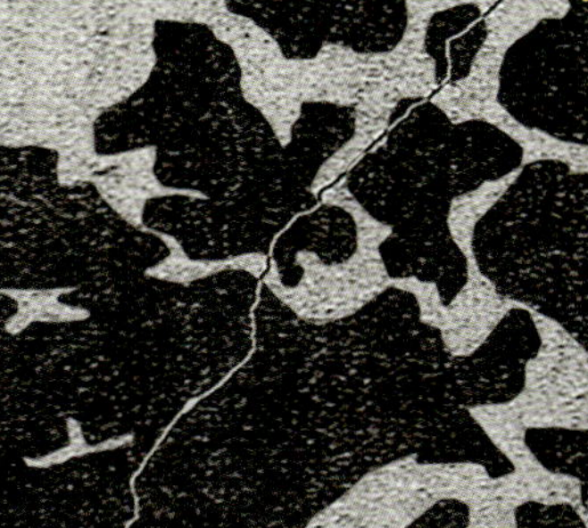
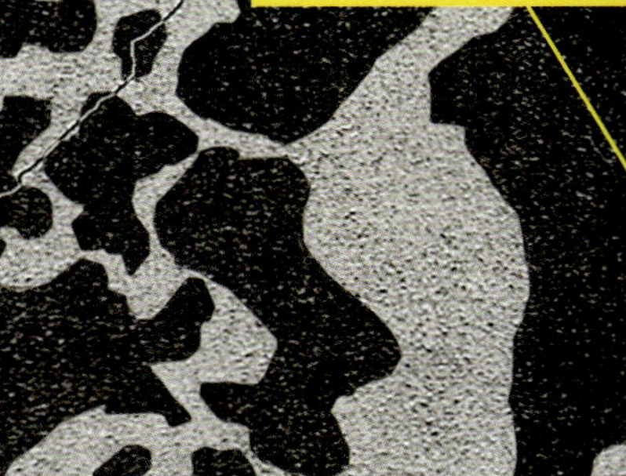
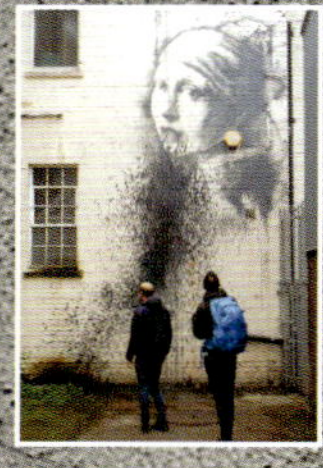
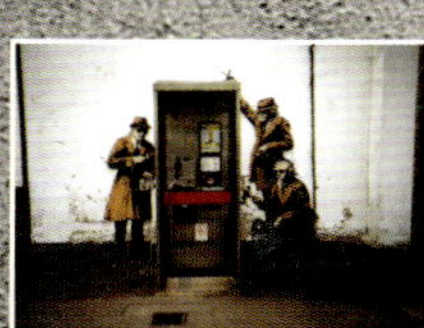
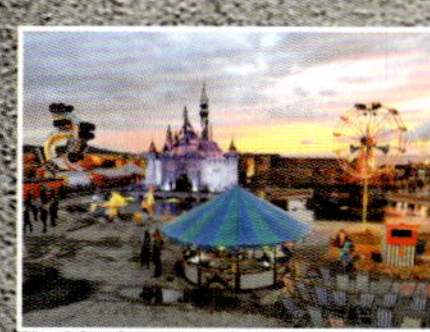
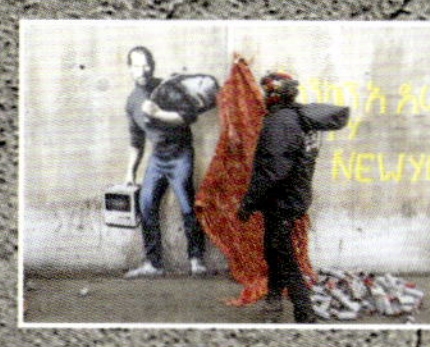
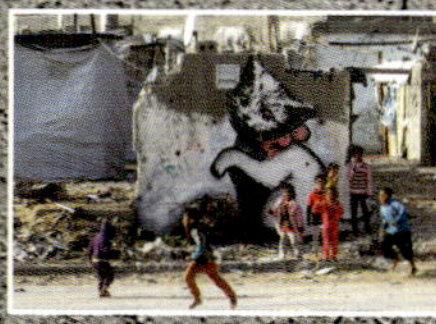
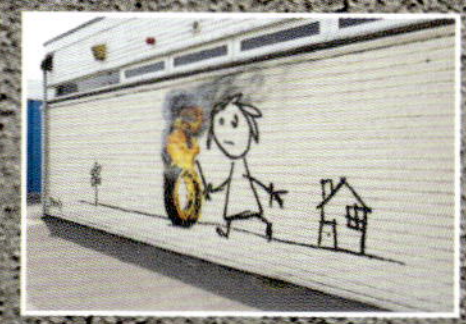
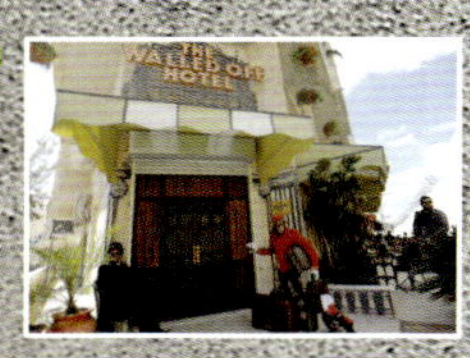
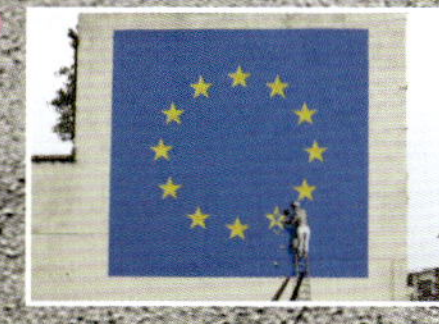
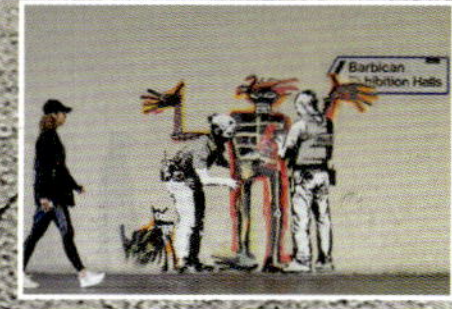
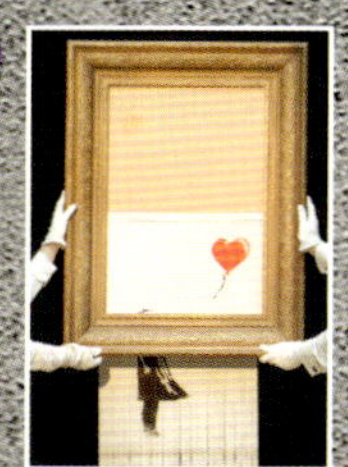
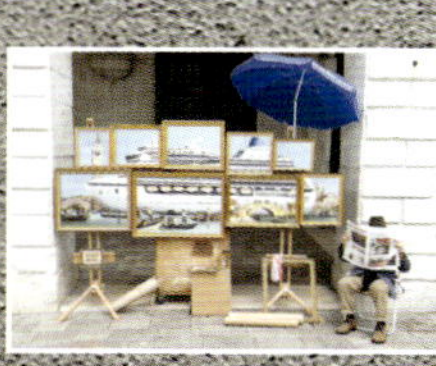
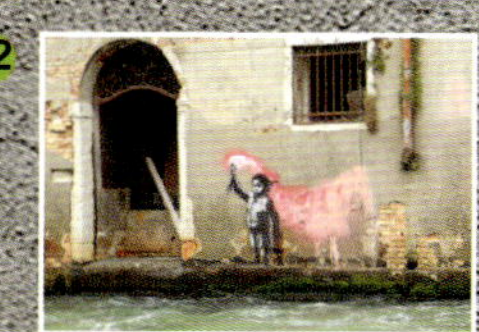
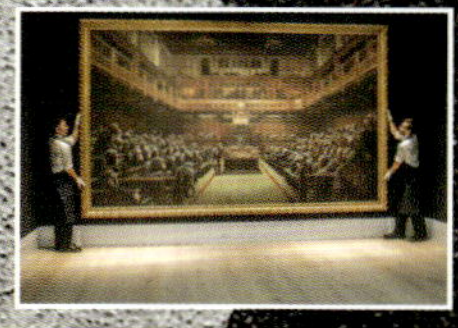
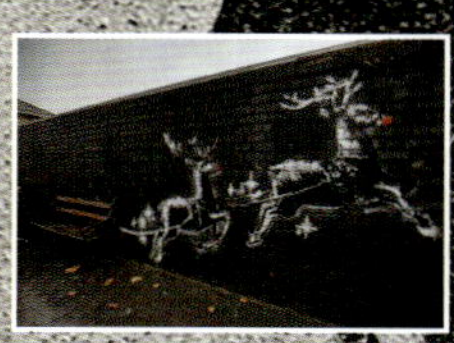
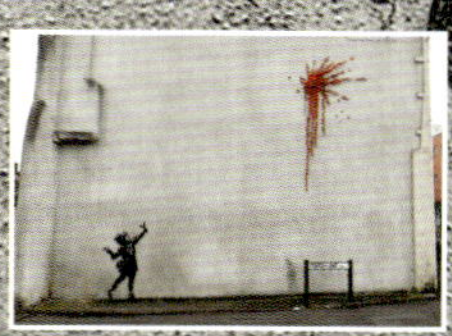
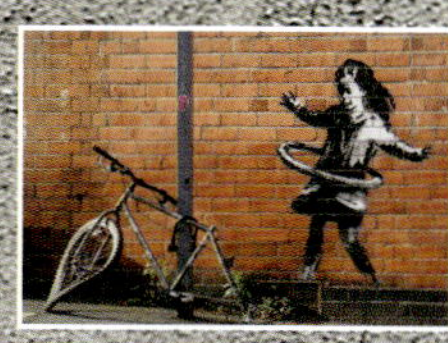
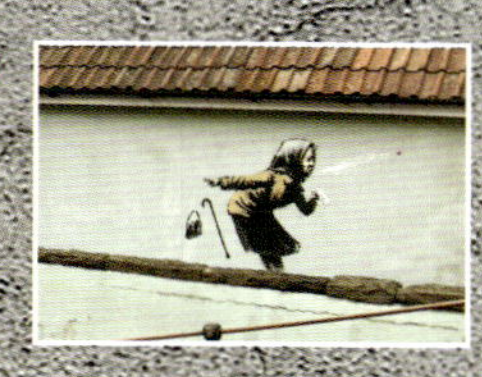
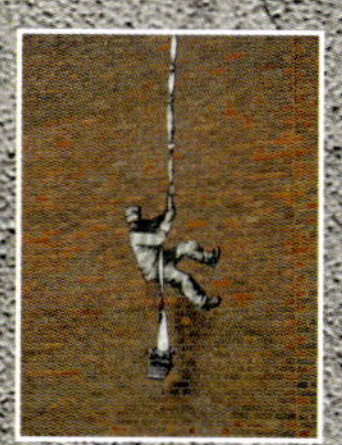
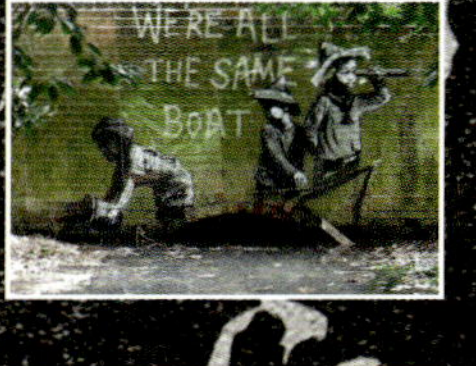
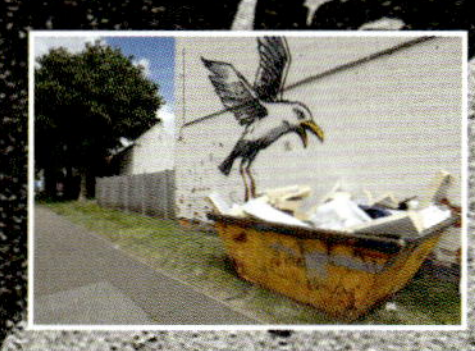
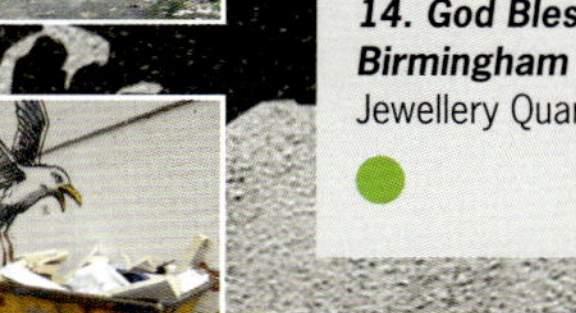
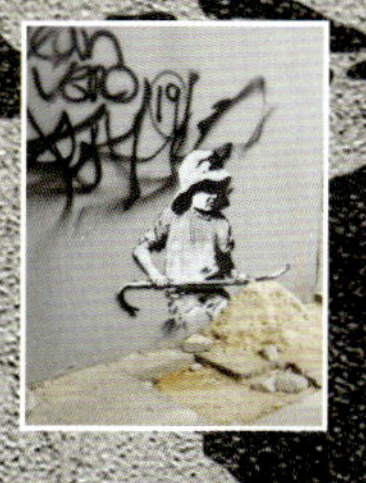
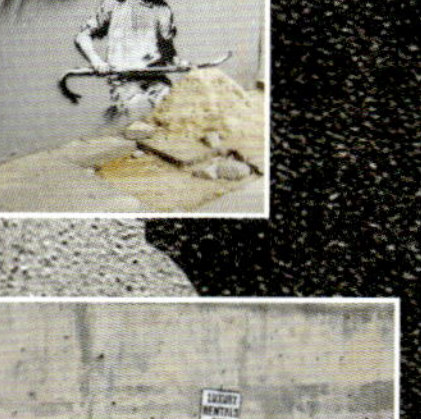
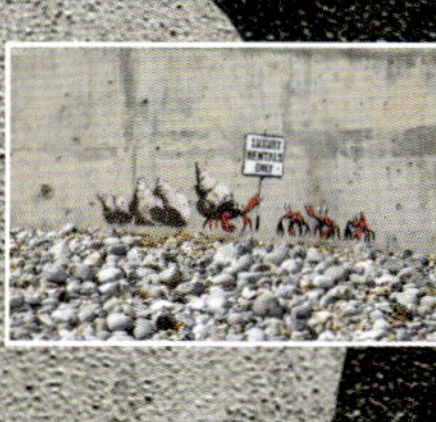
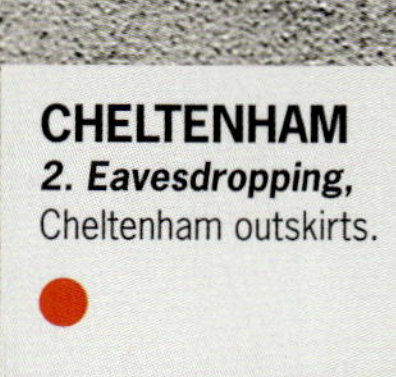

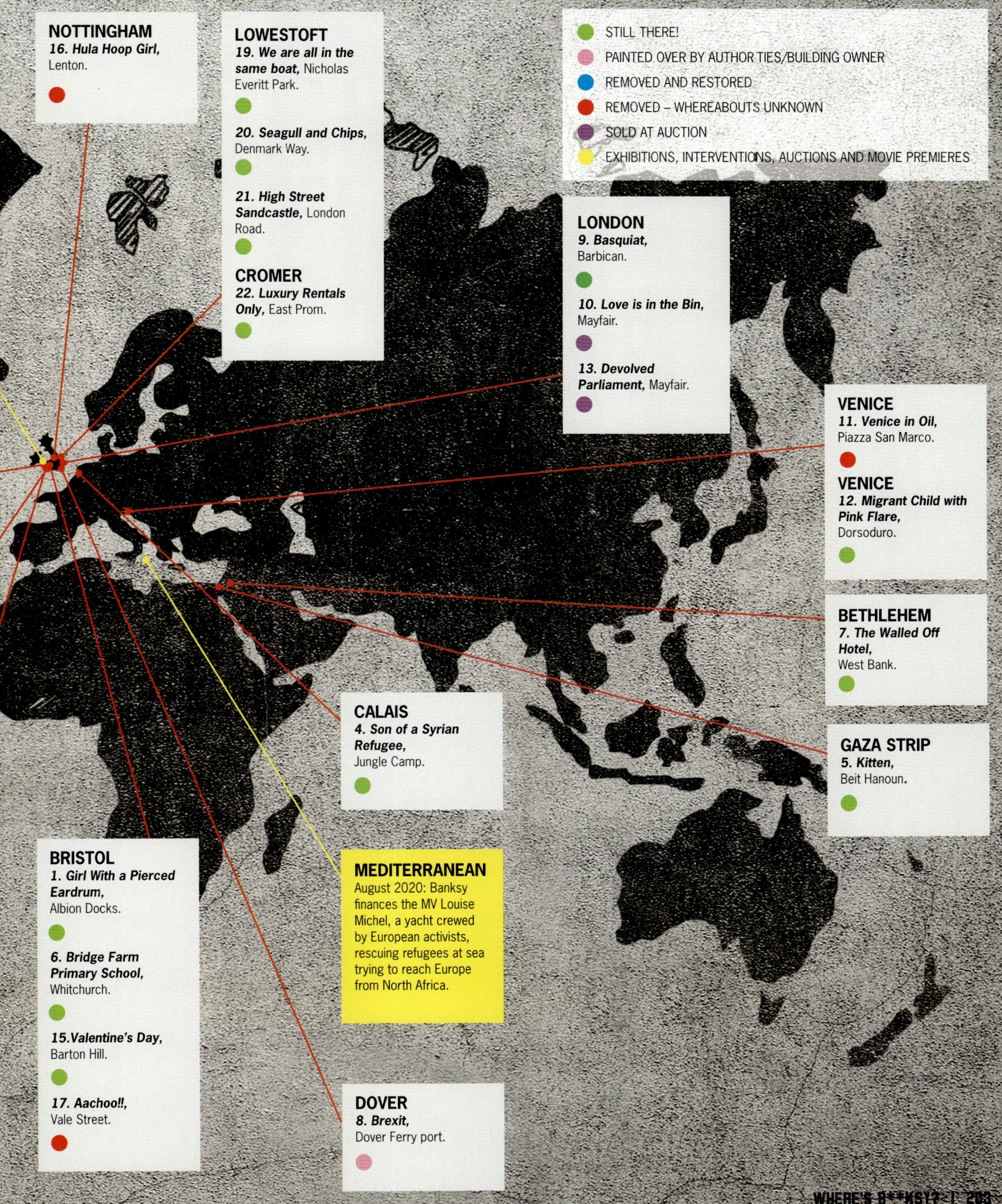

STILL THERE!
PAINTED OVER BY AUTHOR TIES/BUILDING OWNER
REMOVED AND RESTORED
REMOVED – WHEREABOUTS UNKNOWN
SOLD AT AUCTION
EXHIBITIONS, INTERVENTIONS, AUCTIONS AND MOVIE PREMIERES

NOTTINGHAM
16. Hula Hoop Girl, Lenton.

LOWESTOFT
19. We are all in the same boat, Nicholas Everitt Park.
20. Seagull and Chips, Denmark Way.
21. High Street Sandcastle, London Road.

CROMER
22. Luxury Rentals Only, East Prom.

LONDON
9. Basquiat, Barbican.
10. Love is in the Bin, Mayfair.
13. Devolved Parliament, Mayfair.

VENICE
11. Venice in Oil, Piazza San Marco.

VENICE
12. Migrant Child with Pink Flare, Dorsoduro.

BETHLEHEM
7. The Walled Off Hotel, West Bank.

GAZA STRIP
5. Kitten, Beit Hanoun.

CALAIS
4. Son of a Syrian Refugee, Jungle Camp.

BRISTOL
1. Girl With a Pierced Eardrum, Albion Docks.
6. Bridge Farm Primary School, Whitchurch.
15. Valentine's Day, Barton Hill.
17. Aachoo!!, Vale Street.

MEDITERRANEAN
August 2020: Banksy finances the MV Louise Michel, a yacht crewed by European activists, rescuing refugees at sea trying to reach Europe from North Africa.

DOVER
8. Brexit, Dover Ferry port.

GIRL WITH A PIERCED EARDRUM

"The artist has also made a tongue-in-cheek reference to the burger van opposite, with the caption 'Gallery cafe open Monday to Sunday 8am to 2pm'."
Bristol Post

Back on his home turf, a brilliant parody of Vermeer's wonderful *Girl with a Pearl Earring*, using a yellow ADT security alarm box in place of the pearl, and retitled, appositely, *Girl With a Pierced Eardrum*. Another Banksy side-swipe at the paranoia associated with the security industry, the use of Vermeer's brilliant image (Banksy's piece manages to recreate, by some clever technique, the stunning, elusive expression on her face, with slightly parted mouth and steady eyes gazing at the viewer) is in sharp contrast to the inner peace that will be shattered when the alarm goes off.

This was created on the side of a recording studio in Hanover Place in Bristol. Within 24 hours some goon came and splattered black paint all over it. The BBC reported: "A spokesman for Avon and Somerset Police said no report of criminal damage had been made and therefore police had not launched an investigation." Whether they were referring, in their usual hackneyed-phrase fashion, to the original, or the paint splatter, was unclear.

Banksy has referenced iconic classical paintings and old masters on a number of occasions, including Delacroix's *The Raft of the Medusa* and Da Vinci's *Mona Lisa*.

WHERE IS IT ?
ALBION DOCKS,
BRISTOL,
UK.
STILL THERE.

Latitude: 51.4470ºN
Longitude: 2.6096ºW

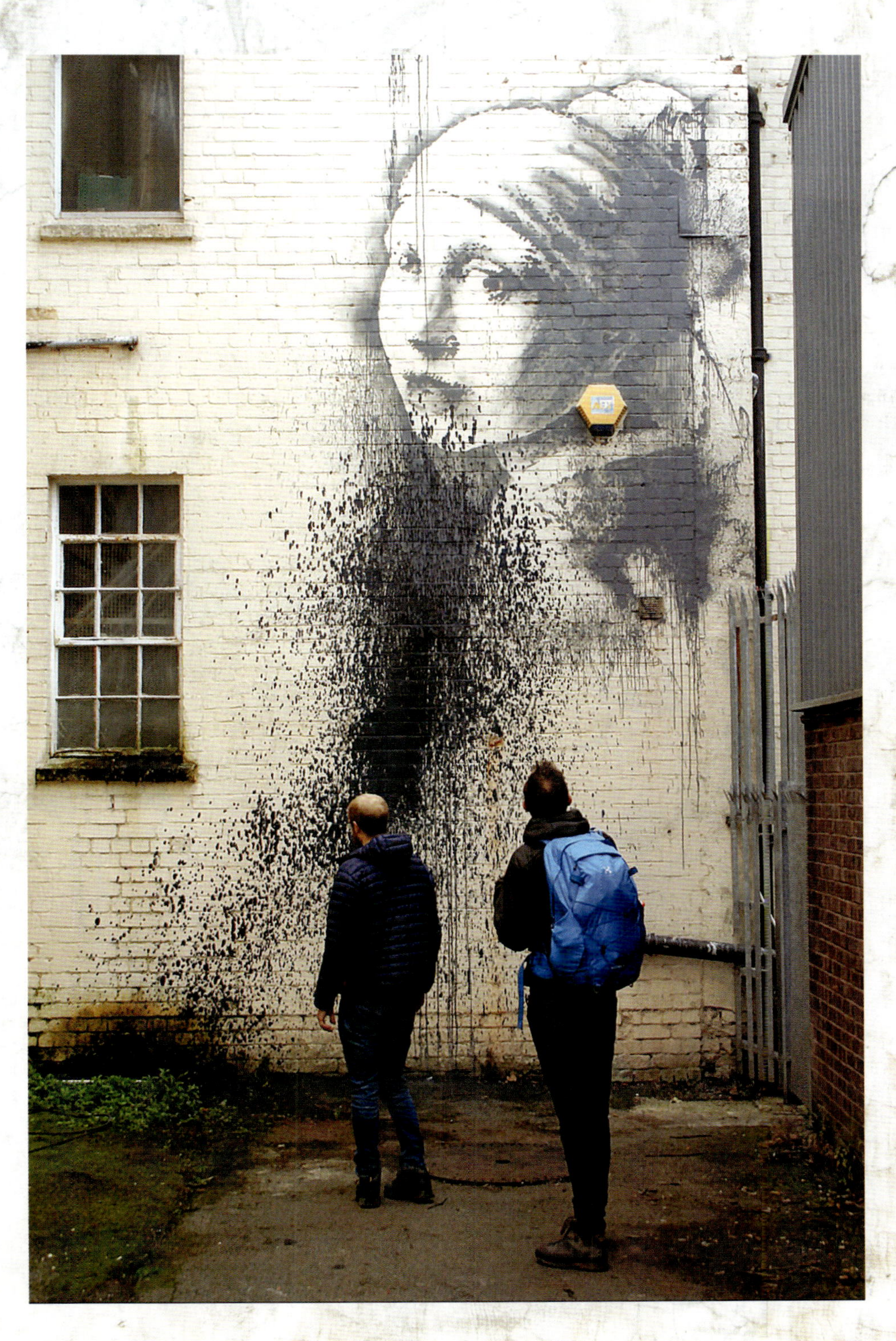

EAVESDROPPING

"Surprised...when I did art at school I got an 'ungraded'."
Banksy, in response to the news that this artwork would be listed Grade II*.

It may seem strange that this surveillance piece should appear by a phone box, painted onto the side of a very ordinary house in Cheltenham, a rather sleepy, conservative, quintessentially English market town in Gloucestershire. Not so strange when you realise that GCHQ (Government Communications Headquarters) is just three miles away.

GCHQ is the UK government's ears and eyes across the globe. It started life in 1919 and then, based at Bletchley Park during World War II, it was responsible for cracking the Wehrmacht's Enigma Code, which allowed Britain to anticipate German military movements. It operates under the direction of Britain's Joint Intelligence Committee, MI5 (homeland intelligence) and MI6 (overseas intelligence). Basically, it's full of really nosy snoops, who monitor whatever digital and other comms traffic they think necessary.

The agency was in the news big time in 2013, when Edward Snowden, the US National Security Agency contractor, revealed that GCHQ was in the process of collecting all UK online and telephone (including text) data, and that it also has access to the US Internet monitoring programme, PRISM. In 2015 it was also revealed in court that the agency conducts computer hacking. Watch out: GCHQ knows what you're doing, right now.

So, it's hilarious to see Banksy depicting the spooks in trench coats, shades and pork pie hats, so they wouldn't look out of place with Michael Caine in the *Ipcress File*, monitoring a public call box, using mega mikes and a very retro reel-to-reel. The absurdity and public nature of the surveillance allows Banksy to make precisely the opposite point. You can't see these guys, but they're everywhere.

As with many other Banksy pieces, this becomes more relevant as time passes, witness the FBI encryption row with Apple in 2016. Questions are also being raised around the erosion of civil liberties, as Western governments seek more snoop powers in order to disrupt Islamist terror plots before they go live. The question is: who else are they checking out?

WHERE IS IT ?
CHELTENHAM,
UK.
DESPITE BEING GRADE II* LISTED, THE PIECE WAS
MYSTERIOUSLY REMOVED IN 2017.

Latitude: 51.8995ºN
Longitude: 2.0656ºW

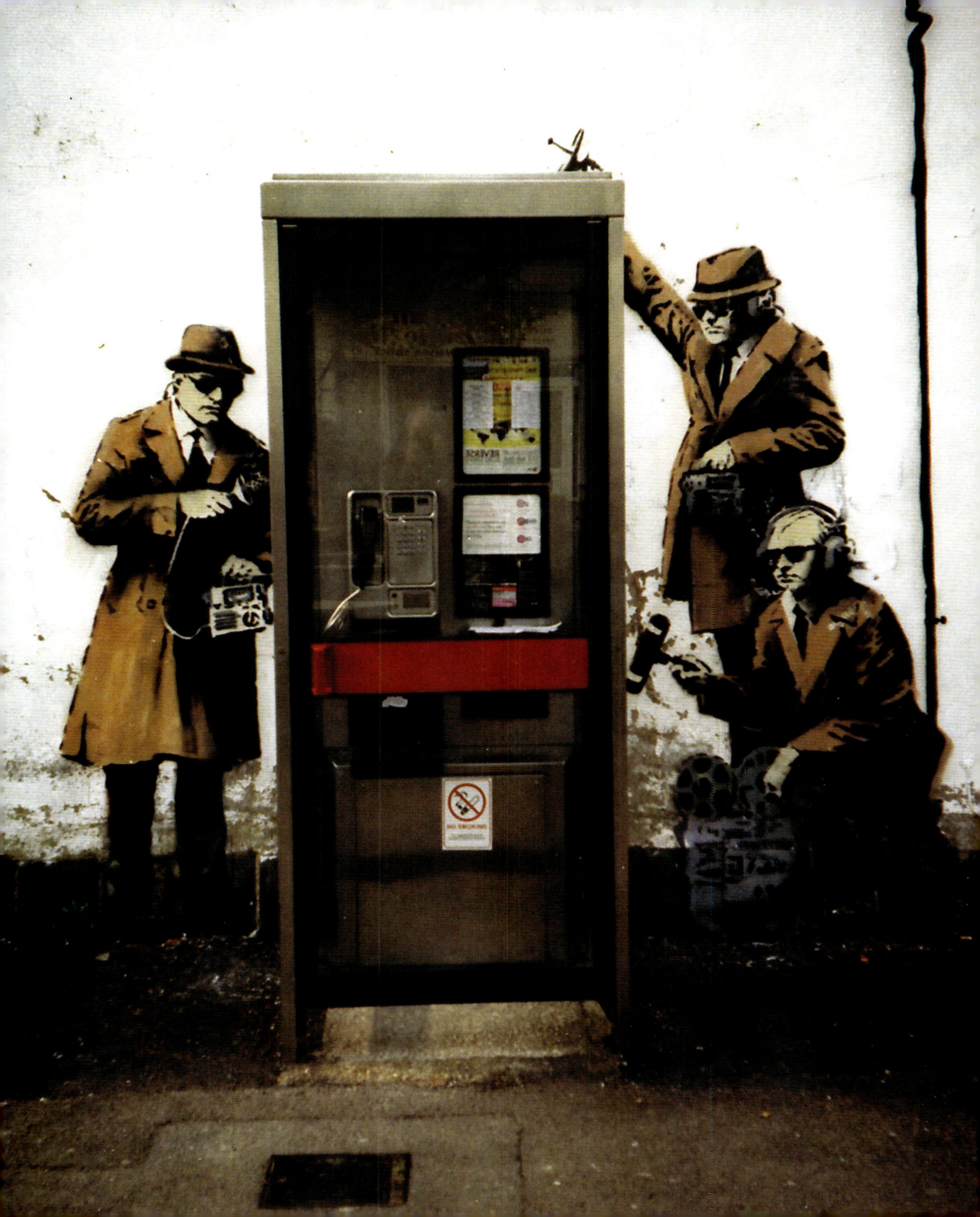

DISMALAND

"The following are strictly prohibited in the Park – spray paint, marker pens, knives and legal representatives of the Walt Disney Corporation."
Dismaland brochure.

Banksy has form as an impresario-provocateur. Think the Cans Festival of 2008, the Banksy Versus Bristol Museum show of 2009 and the New York residency of 2013. Dismaland, however, for sheer invention and bravado, surpassed all of these and proved that, more than a decade after he became really established, his ability to create waves had diminished not one iota.

Located in the Tropicana, a derelict lido in the maudlin and frequently rainy English west country seaside resort of Weston-super-Mare, the five week show was a total triumph. It sold out ultra fast, received 150,000 visitors and contributed over £20 million to the local economy.

Billed as a 'Bemusement Park' and as 'The UK's most disappointing new visitor attraction', the name was a polemical dig at Disney, not just with the play on Disney World, but also with a nightmare recreation of Disney's fairytale castle. Inside the works of 58 artists and activists were on show, including Damien Hirst, Jimmy Cauty, Bäst, Espo and Jenny Holzer. Banksy and his fellow artists highlighted some regular political themes: the plight of Syrian and other migrants to Europe, the vapidness of celebrity culture, nauseating consumerism, financial corruption and animal exploitation. Taken as a whole it was a wonderful critique of the dystopia in which we live.

The final ceremony featured Russian feminist punk band Pussy Riot, with a set including women singing in cages and a choreographed clash between protestors and riot police. That wasn't quite the end of the attraction, however. Dismaland was dismantled and some of the structures were shipped to the Calais migrant jungle, to provide much-needed shelters. The gift was, true to form, entitled Dismal Aid.

WHERE IS IT ?
TROPICANA LIDO,
SEAFRONT,
WESTON-SUPER-MARE,
UK.

Latitude: 51.3404ºN
Longitude: 2.9821ºW

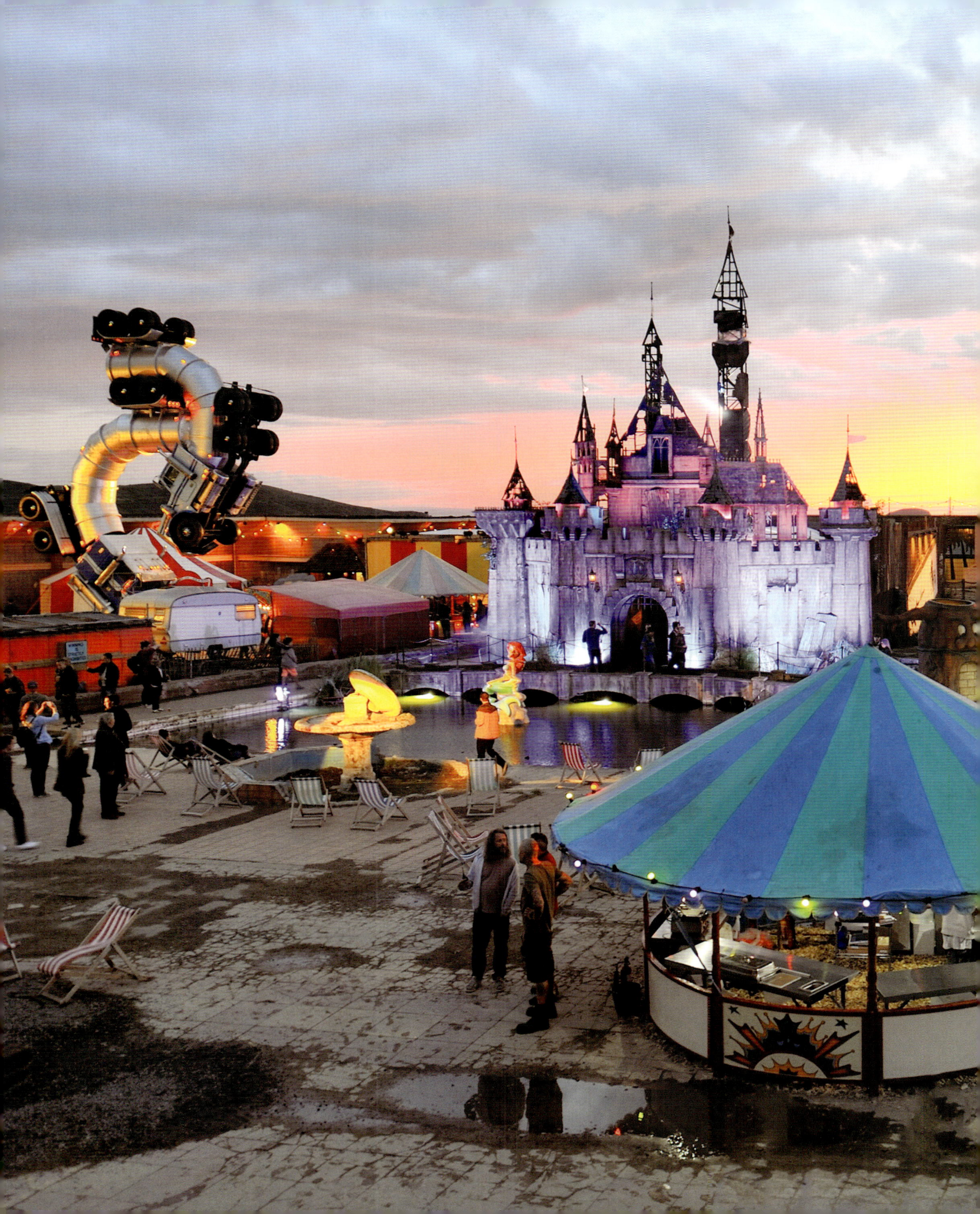

SON OF A SYRIAN REFUGEE

"Being the richest man in the cemetery doesn't matter to me. Going to bed at night saying we've done something wonderful, that's what matters."
Steve Jobs.

Steve Jobs, the legendary co-founder of the world's most successful computer company (and, in 2015 when this piece was created also the world's most valuable company, with a market capitalisation of $772.65 billion), was the son of a Muslim Syrian refugee to the USA. His mother was a German-Swiss Catholic whose father refused to allow her to marry a Muslim, and Steve was put up for adoption whilst still a baby, with a kind couple, Paul and Clara Jobs. The latter he never described as his 'adoptive' parents, but as "my parents 1000%."

Painted at the height of the Calais migrant crisis, when refugees from war-torn Syria were amongst those seeking a better life in Britain, Banksy is highlighting the crassly impersonal nature of the debate, where people are treated as just troublesome numbers. This could have been Jobs' biological father in the 'Jungle', or perhaps there could even be a visionary genius like Jobs amongst the driven individuals with great ambitions for a better life.

The image shows Jobs in his early 50s, in signature dark polo neck, jeans and trainers. In his hand he holds the lovely Macintosh 128k, a completely transformational machine; launched in 1984 it was the first mass-market example of GUI and a mouse. At the time Jobs would have been 29 and with rather more hair. The look of single-minded determination, the contrast between the migrant's overshoulder bag and poised-to-run stance are unmistakable. And the Mac says "Look at me. I am an individual with brilliant ideas. I may be a migrant but I will transform your world for the better."

The press attention this image garnered did much to humanise the debate about the Calais Jungle in 2015. It also provided a small revenue stream – the chap on the right charged 1 euro a time to move the blanket so a photograph could be taken.

WHERE IS IT ?
'JUNGLE' CAMP,
LANDFILL SITE,
CALAIS,
FRANCE.

Latitude: 50.9708ºN
Longitude: 1.9034ºE

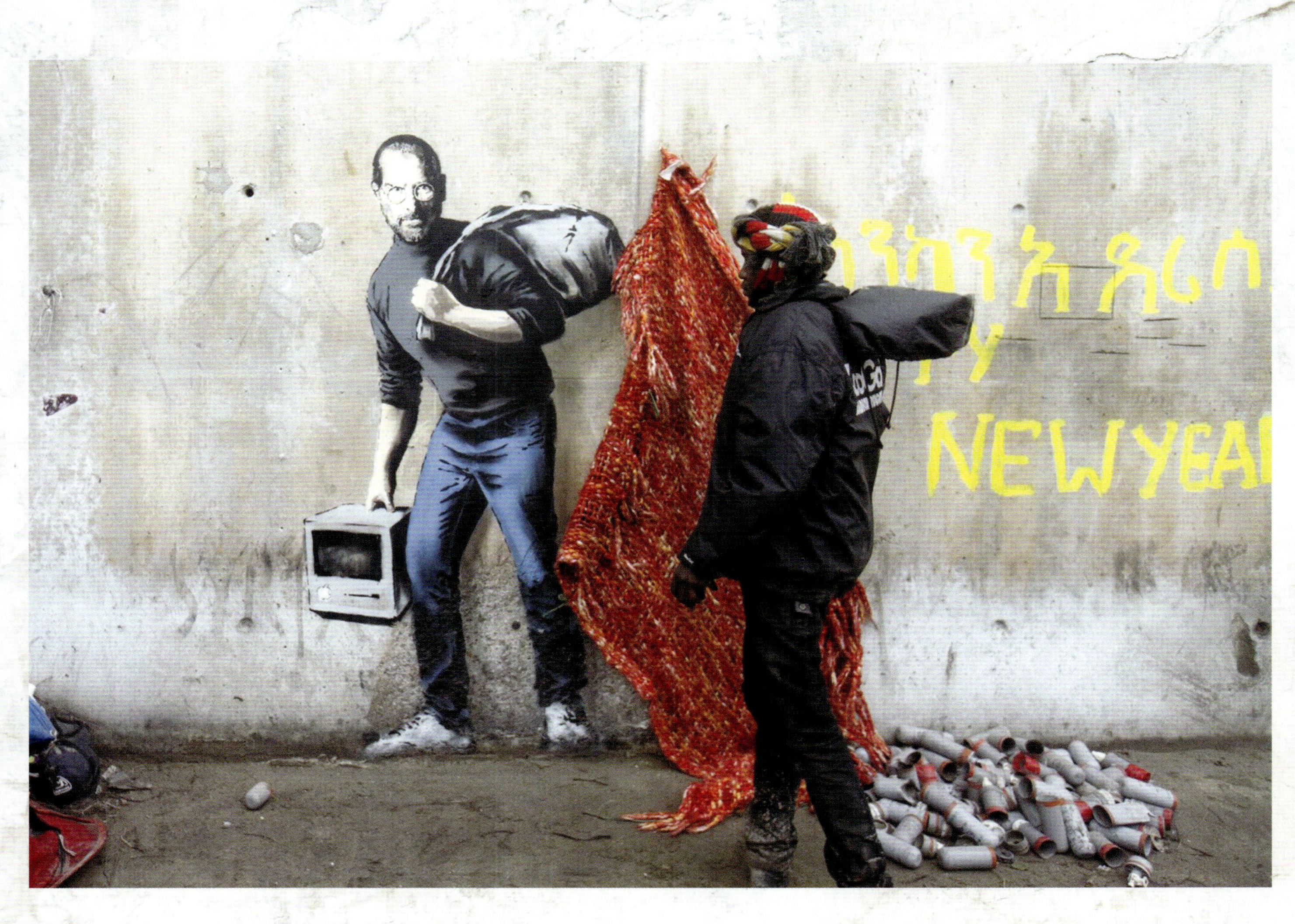
ንክን አዲስ
NEW YEAR

KITTEN

"I wanted to highlight the destruction in Gaza by posting photos on my website – but on the Internet people only look at pictures of kittens."
Banksy's website, 2015.

Banksy shows great consistency in his political causes. He doesn't do a piece highlighting an issue, collect the plaudits and then forget about people. In 2005 he created some of his most memorable images on the West Bank Wall to highlight the plight of the Palestinians. Things had not improved by 2015, so Banksy was back at a time when the Palestinian issue had somewhat dropped off the radar in the West.

In 2014 the Israeli Armed Forces launched an operation, ostensibly in response to Hamas rocket attacks, called Operation Protective Edge. The result was 2,104 people killed in Gaza, with 69% of deaths, according to the UN, being civilians. On the Israeli side 67 soldiers and 6 civilians were killed.

The side of a house on which Banksy created this image was one of 18,000 destroyed in the attacks. Banksy shows the most fluffy and vulnerable of creatures, a kitten, about to innocently stick his paw into a ball of twisted metal, thinking that it will be a soft ball of wool. This is a powerful, deliberately sentimental picture of how wars destroy childhoods, made more poignant by the irrepressible children playing in front of it.

Kitten was one of four works created by Banksy on this trip, together with a film documenting the Israeli militia and bombing campaigns. Entitled sardonically *Make this the year YOU discover a new destination*, it showed the devastation caused by Protective Edge, with heavily ironic, holiday-brochure-speak captions, such as 'Welcome to Gaza. Well away from the tourist tracks (access is via a network of illegal tunnels)' and 'The locals like it so much they never leave (because they're not allowed to)'.

WHERE IS IT ?
BEIT HANOUN TOWN,
NORTHERN GAZA STRIP.

Latitude: 31.5387ºN
Longitude: 34.5385ºE

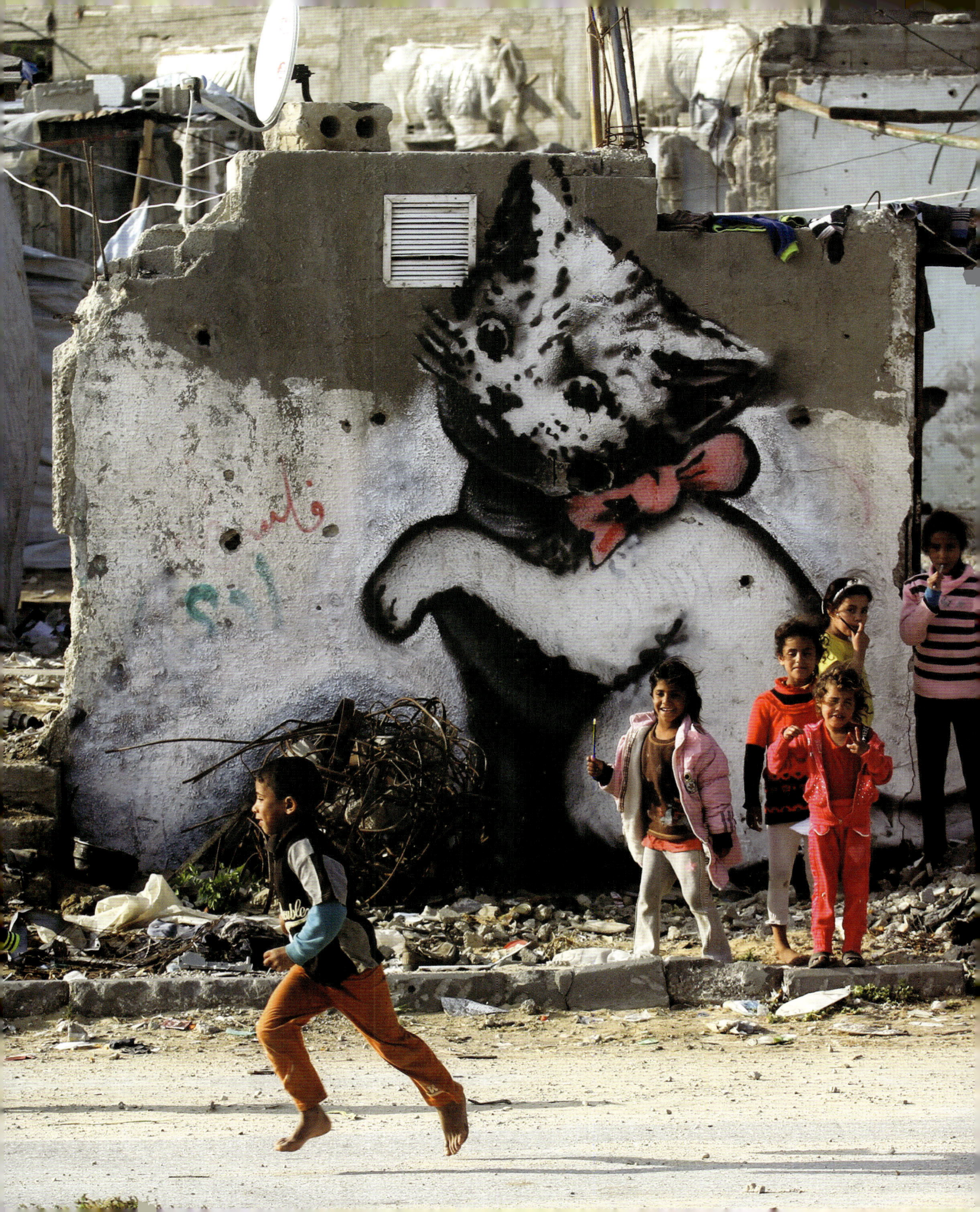

BRIDGE FARM PRIMARY SCHOOL

"Remember it's always easier to get forgiveness than permission".
Banksy's note to the children of Bridge Farm Primary School, Bristol.

In 2016, the pupils from Bridge Farm Primary decided to rename their school houses after renowned Bristolians. They chose 15th-century explorer John Cabot, Isambard Kingdom Brunel (designer of the Clifton Suspension Bridge in the city), in rebellious spirit, Blackbeard (the pirate reputedly born in Bristol) and in really rebellious spirit, Banksy. They sent Banksy a letter telling him of their plans and went away for their half-term holidays thinking no more of it. To their amazement and delight, on their return they found this mural by way of thanks from the artist, who confirmed its authenticity.

Banksy shows a great affinity for sardonic children's humour in some of his work. This piece has distinct echoes of *Charlie Brown Firestarter* of 2011. The juxtaposition of the kid's drawing with the burning tyre is brilliantly effective. It's funny because it has a sinister edge. Like Lewis Carroll, Roald Dahl and Edward Gorey, Banksy gets that kids like real naughtyness and find the 'goodness' forced on them by adults totally tedious.

Together with his mural Banksy left a letter for the pupils: "Dear Bridge Farm, thanks for your letter and naming a house after me. Please have a picture. If you don't like it feel free to add stuff – I'm sure the teachers won't mind. Remember – it's always easier to get forgiveness than permission. With love, Banksy."

The headmaster loved that it was "inspirational and aspirational" for the pupils. We see his point, but it also made us chuckle sardonically.

WHERE IS IT ?
BRIDGE FARM PRIMARY SCHOOL,
WHITCHURCH,
BRISTOL.

Latitude: 51.5478ºN
Longitude: 0.0547ºW

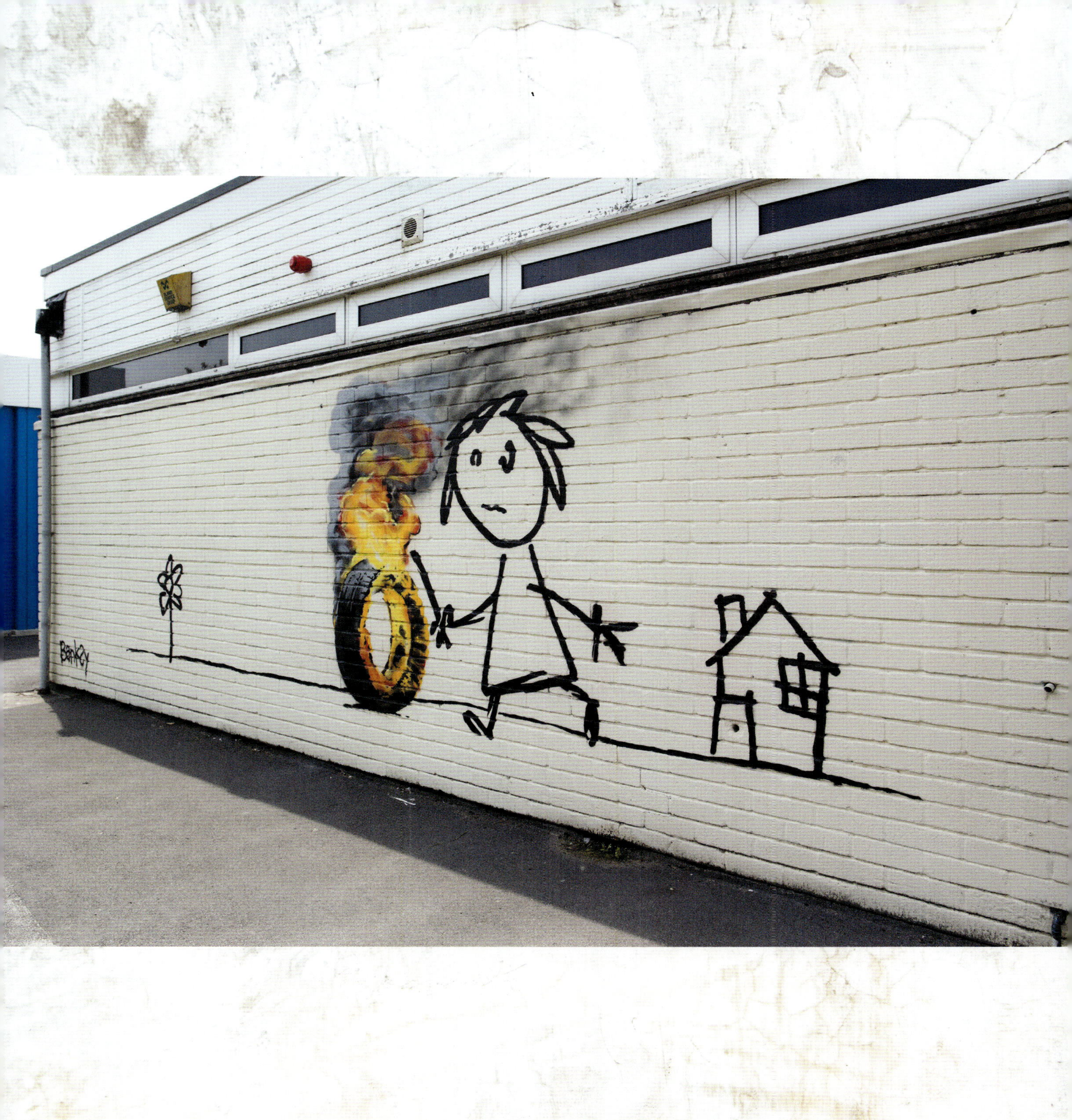

Banksy

THE WALLED OFF HOTEL

"The hotel with the worst view in the world." Banksy

A clear and witty reference to the renowned Waldorf-Astoria hotels, in the lit-up font which suggests jazz-age American luxury. It also references the thinking behind the 1908 opening of William Waldorf Astor's Waldorf Hotel in London, which aimed to bring a bit of US pizzazz into the then stuffy capital of the British Empire. The ironies suggested show Banksy at his best, using wit, humour and sheer cleverness to again highlight one of the causes closest to his heart: the continuing and abysmal plight of the Palestinians living in effective incarceration behind Israel's concrete security wall.

As ever with Banksy, however, when you look deeper the story has several additional layers of meaning. Waldorf originally built his first hotel next door to his aunt's house in Manhattan, as a way of annoying her. Eventually peace ensued between Waldorf and his aunt's son, John Jacob Astor IV; he persuaded his aunt to move, built the Astoria on the neighbouring site and in time the hotels merged to form the Waldorf-Astoria. We don't know if Banksy saw a parallel with the settling of the hotel dispute and the prospect of an Israeli-Palestinian peace based on a federal two-state solution, but it does make one think that that would be a great direction for Israel to start promoting, rather than this inhuman barrier.

Inside, the hotel is full of brilliant witty politically-charged artworks and installations. The 'Presidential Suite' includes a bullet-strafed watertank which feeds the hot-tub, a brilliant burst of anger at successive US presidents' failures to secure peace. A classical bust in empire style is wreathed in tear gas from a canister. There are nods in the furnishings and installations to Britain's former protectorate rule of Palestine, which arguably laid the foundations for the current mess. In many of the rooms there are original Banksy artworks.

The hotel of course is not just a work of art. It is intended to bring visitors and foreign currency into the shattered Bethlehem economy. Book a stay if you can: it's an unforgettable experience.

WHERE IS IT ?
OVERLOOKING THE ISRAELI 'SECURITY BARRIER',
182 CARITAS STREET,
WEST BANK,
BETHLEHEM.
STILL THERE AND YOU CAN BOOK TO STAY!

Latitude: 31.7190ºN
Longitude: 35.2035ºE

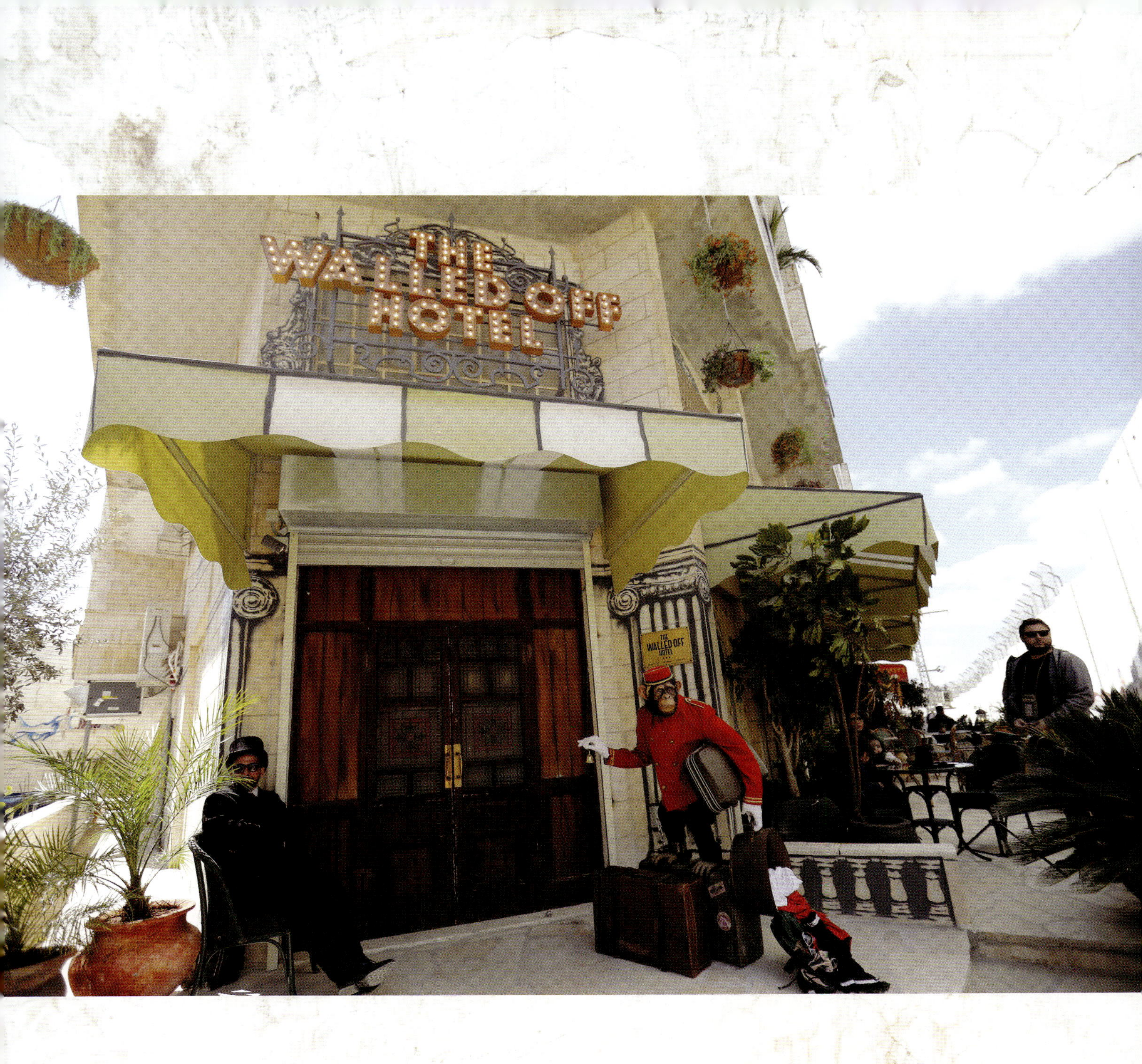

THE
WALLED OFF
HOTEL
THE
WALLED OFF
HOTEL
★★★

BREXIT

"The stars stand for the ideals of unity, solidarity and harmony among the peoples of Europe." EU's website.

On June 23rd, 2016, the UK voted in a referendum to leave the EU. A year later, on 29th March, 2017, Article 50, beginning the formal process of leaving, was triggered by the UK government. This was during the fraught run up to the French presidential elections, which saw the right-wing anti-EU candidate, Marine Le Pen, gaining in the polls. On the morning of the French election, Sunday May 7th, this Banksy appeared in Dover, Britain's gateway to Europe. As usual, Banksy has proved himself a master of paradox. The mural appeared on a building next to the ferry port which was slated for demolition. It was cars and lorries going *to* and trading *with* Europe that would be best placed to see it. And this willful act of self-destruction is being carefully undertaken by a conscientious worker, carefully chipping away at Britain's membership. It was the working class vote, particularly in depressed seaside towns like Dover, which led to the Brexit side winning the vote, by 3.8% (51.9% leave, 48.1% stay).

This is Banksy at his clever, subtle and somewhat prophetic best. Two and a half years on from the creation of this work, the UK had still not exited the EU. Banksy's suggestion that Brexit would not only wreck the ideals of European unity, but would also be an arduous, tedious process, has been confirmed by subsequent events.

WHERE IS IT ?
YORK STREET,
DOVER FERRY PORT APPROACHES.
MYSTERIOUSLY WHITEWASHED IN SEPTEMBER 2019.

Latitude: 51.5478ºN
Longitude: 0.0547ºW

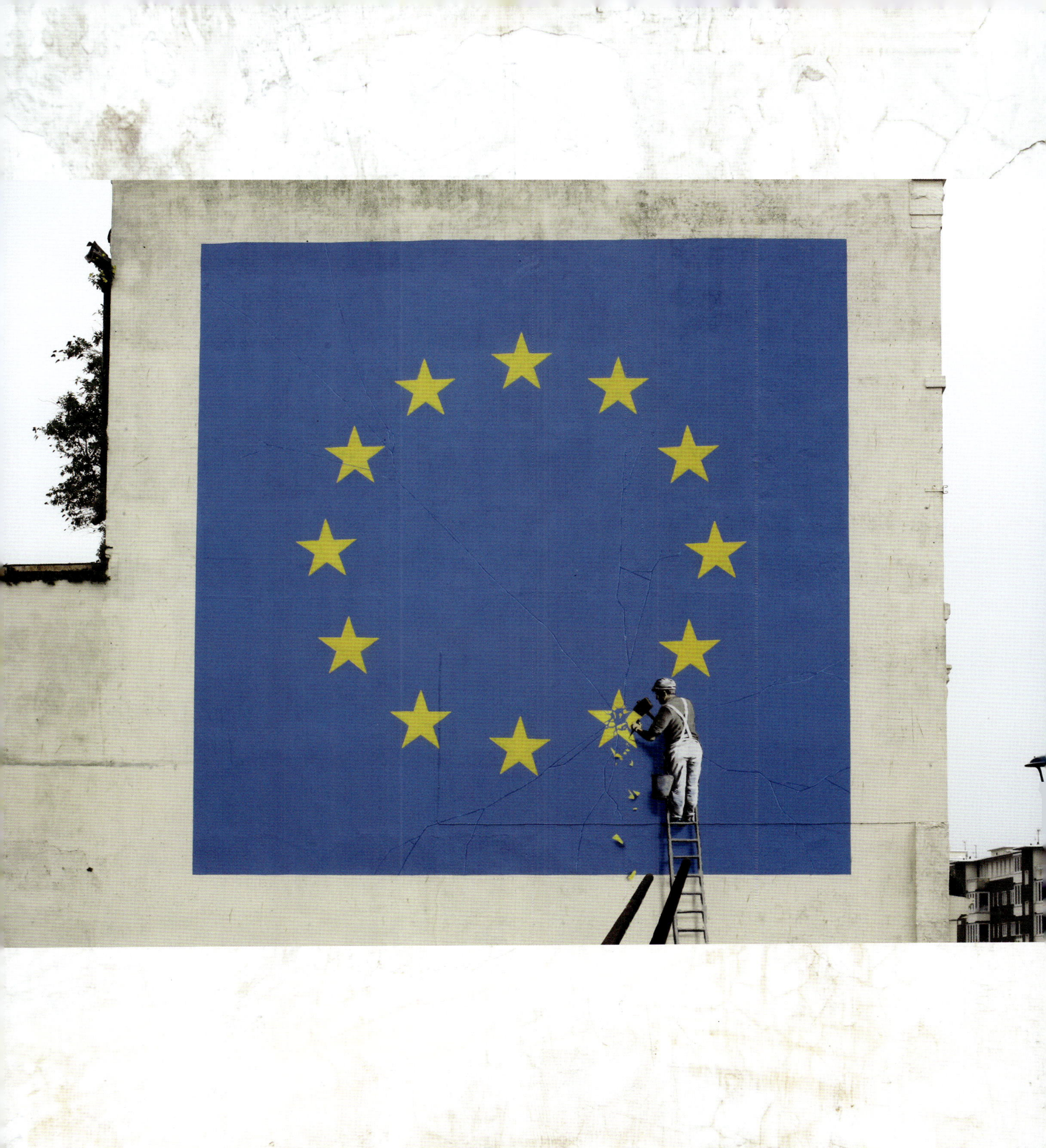

BASQUIAT

"Major new Basquiat show opens at the Barbican – a place that is normally very keen to clean any graffiti from its walls." Banksy's Instagram.

Banksy loves nothing more than mocking the British middle classes for their hypocrisy. This piece appeared before the opening of the first major show of Basquiat's work in the UK, in The Barbican, the City's major art centre, bang in the middle of the financial district. The people now fawning over the New York graffiti artist's work, would have been those who would have applauded the police stopping and searching a black man walking near the gallery just because he looked, in their eyes, 'suspicious' in an exclusively middle class area. Young black guys in London are eleven times more likely to be stopped and searched by the Metropolitan Police than whites, according to the UK's official Equality and Human Rights Commission. Basquiat would have been one of those guys.

The piece, inspired by Basquiat's 1982 *Boy and Dog in a Johnnypump*, is clearly an homage from one brilliant artist to another. Banksy, we suspect, aside from a love of Basquiat's work, would have appreciated the way he used the anagram SAMO©, standing for "Same Old Shit" to sign the graffiti he created in Manhattan's Soho and East Village. The Barbican, effortlessly living up to Banksy's suggestion of middle class hypocrisy, loved the work and recognised its financial and artistic value (the Basquiat show, their most popular ever, benefited from the extra publicity generated by the Banksy) and proceeded to protect it under a perspex covering.

WHERE IS IT ?
BARBICAN,
THE CITY (FINANCIAL DISTRICT)
LONDON.

Latitude: 51.5478ºN
Longitude: 0.0547ºW

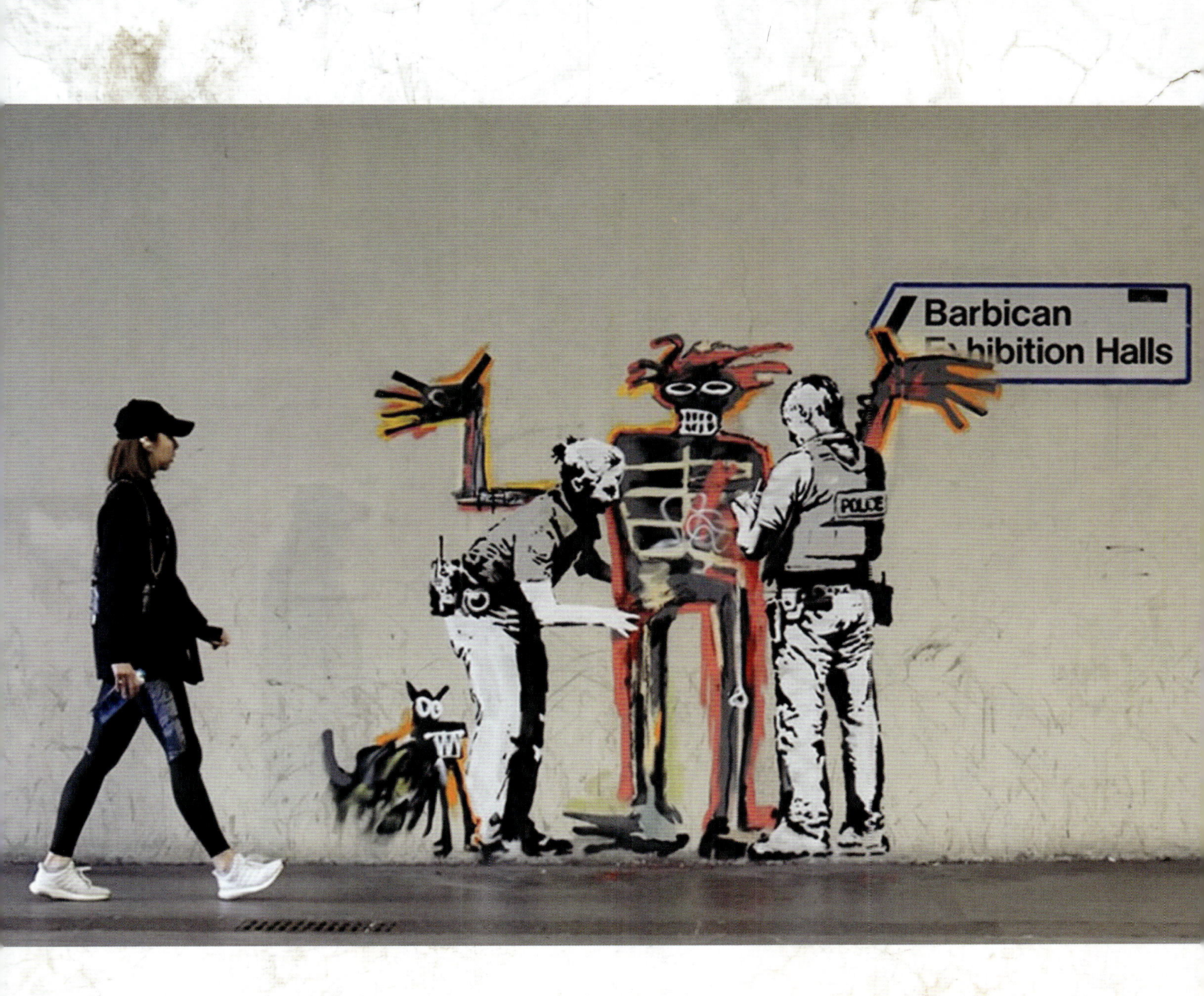
Barbican
Exhibition Halls
POLICE

LOVE IS IN THE BIN

"...in the process of 'destroying' the artwork, a new one was created."
Sothebys.com

The date: the 5th October, 2018; the location: Sotheby's auction house in London. The lot was an authenticated Banksy, *Girl with Red Balloon,* with an estimate of £200,000 – £300,000. Bidding was frantic in the packed auction room, with many bids coming in from the 30 registered telephone bidders. Then, as the hammer went down with the top bid of £1.042 million ($1.4 million), the picture started shredding before the astonished crowd. Banksy had not just pranked Sotheby's, but the entire art world and its bizarre sense of what constitutes art and value. A shredder, hidden in the frame, which got past Sotheby's checks, had been set off remotely. But things didn't go according to plan. The shredder jammed, with only half the picture destroyed, leaving the lonely heart balloon still in frame.

The astonishing stunt made headlines around the world: the first artwork in history to have been created, live, during an auction. Banksy renamed the work *Love is in the Bin*. The buyer, far from being distraught at the wrecking of her purchase, was thrilled. "When the hammer came down...I was at first shocked, but gradually I began to realize that I would end up with my own piece of art history." Estimates immediately following the sale suggested it was now worth twice what she had just paid. The estimates were wrong – the work was subsequently sold at auction for £18,582,000, a record for a Banksy work, at Sotheby's in October 2021.

Banksy again has the last laugh: the world of 'high' art clearly values rubbish more than the art itself.

WHERE IS IT ?
SOTHEBY'S AUCTION HOUSE,
MAYFAIR,
LONDON.

Latitude: 51.3045 ºN
Longitude: 0.08413º W

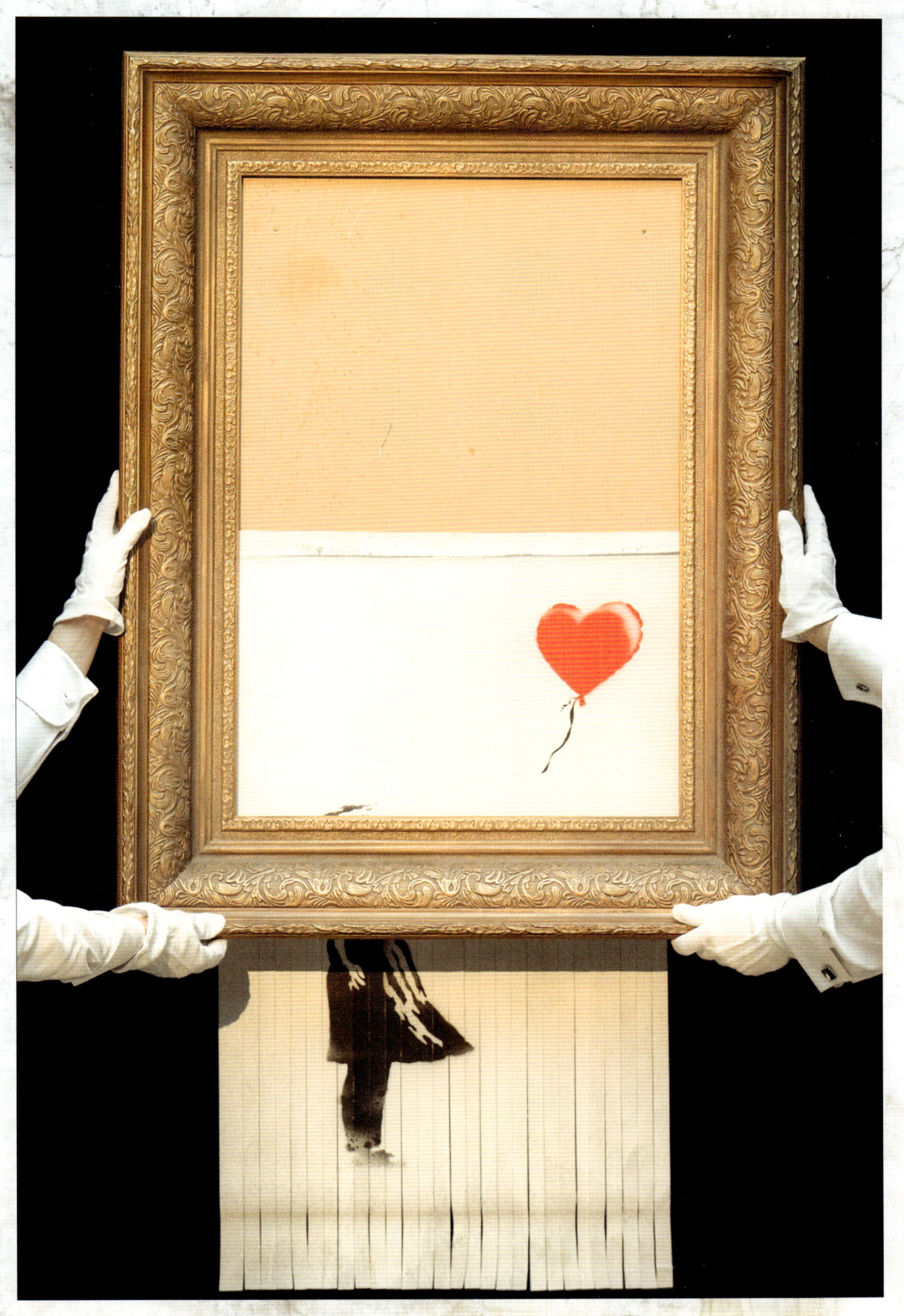

VENICE IN OIL

"Despite being the largest and most prestigious art event in the world, for some reason I've never been invited." Banksy's Instagram, on the Biennale.

On the 22nd May 2019, during the Venice Biennale, Banksy trundled a street vendor's art trolley into St. Mark's Square, opening it up to reveal this series of canvases. Classic scenes from Canaletto of the Rialto, Grand Canal and San Giorgio Maggiore, with gondoliers in the foreground, are swamped by a vast cruise ship. It's a brilliant critique of the Venetian authorities trashing their own – the world's most beautiful – city, for the sake of the two billion euros in revenue that Venice makes from its 25 million annual visitors, many of them day trippers from the cruise ships. Banksy is striking a chord with many Venetians and their *No Grandi Navi* ('No Big Ships') protests, which so far have had little effect. He also makes an environmental point: these vast, ugly cruise liners not only have a huge carbon footprint, they leech oil into the lagoon's sensitive ecosystems. *Venice in Oil* isn't just a deliciously sardonic pun, with its art scholarship overtones; it's also framed in black, in the manner of invitations to funerals.

Banksy (for we think it was he), was bundled off by the police as his display was unauthorized. They didn't bother to look twice at the work. It was all filmed for his Instagram. Effortlessly, Banksy once again cocked a snook at ridiculous authority figures, strutting about in their silly uniforms. As he wheeled his trolley away, Banksy's movie showed a huge liner in the background, entering the Grand Canal, sounding its horn. The movie has, to date, been viewed more than 300,000 times. Banksy proves once again that he is the maestro of both stunt and image, the ultimate artist- prankster-provocateur.

WHERE IS IT ?
ST MARK'S SQUARE,
VENICE,
ITALY.

Latitude: 45.4342 ºN
Longitude: 12.3385 ºE

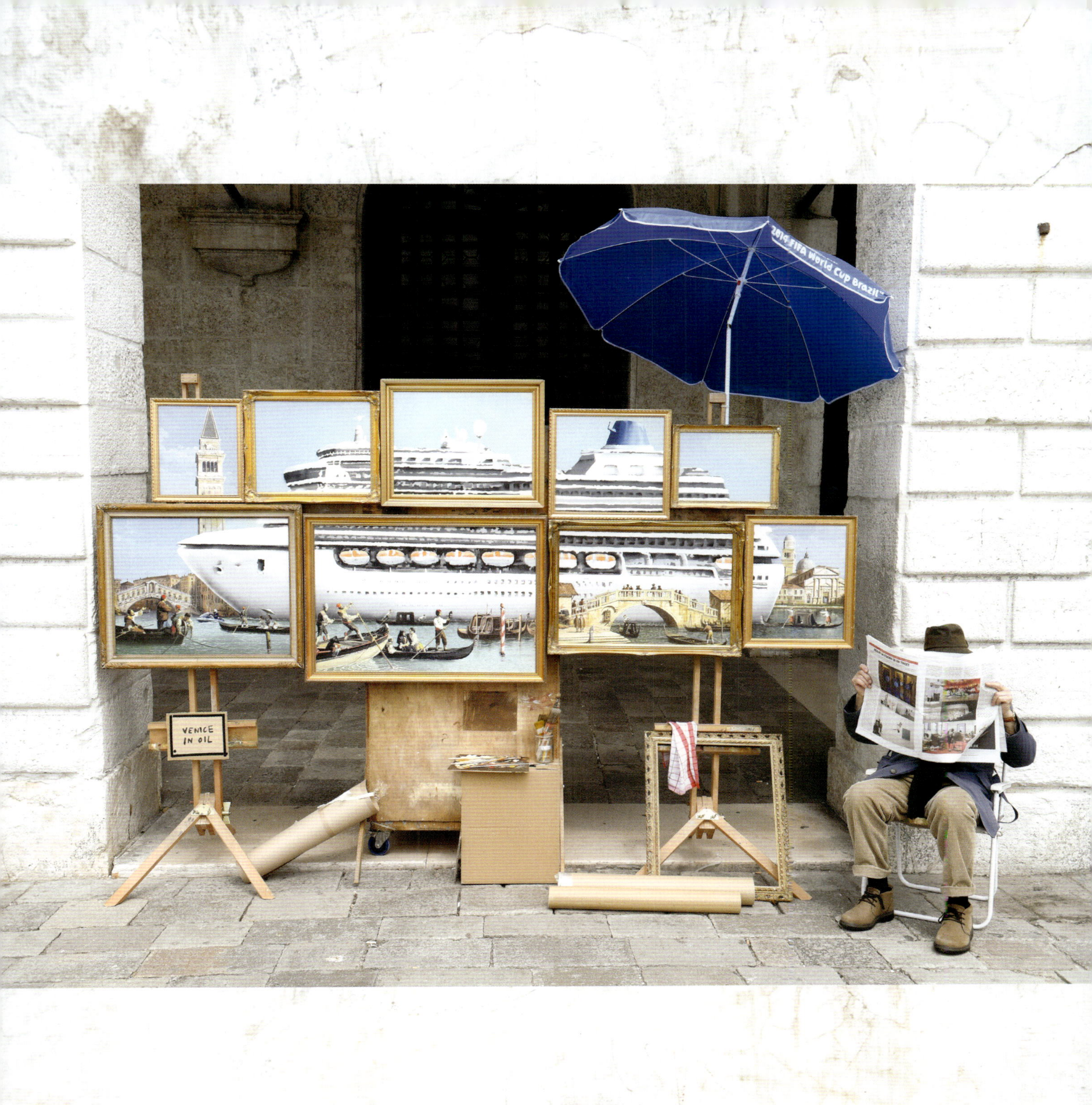

2014 FIFA World Cup Brazil™
VENICE
IN OIL

MIGRANT CHILD WITH PINK FLARE

"5,303 migrants died on their journeys in 2019."
Missing Migrants Project, part of the UN Organisation for Migration.

This, a brilliant situationist work, was the second of Banksy's pieces in Venice during the 2019 Biennale. It eloquently highlights two of his major concerns – the plight of refugees and asylum seekers and rising sea levels as a result of global warming, and how the two are completely connected.

Banksy once again uses the poignancy of a child, in his life jacket, holding a pink flare such as was used by migrants escaping war, political repression, poverty and lack of opportunity for a better life in Europe. The flares were usually released when the small dinghies, in which such children travelled, were on the verge of sinking beneath the surprisingly treacherous waters of the Mediterranean, here represented by the rise and fall of Venetian canal waters. At times during the day, depending on the season, the waters can reach the child's life jacket, giving this piece a life of its own. A further brilliant touch is the windswept hair of the child – he, or is it a little girl? – is in a storm, in danger, at risk of drowning.

The piece also seems to act as a warning. Do nothing about global warming, it seems to say, and these rising waters will also change your lives for ever. That it's a child also warns us that it is the lassitude of the current generation in charge which will create the disaster that will affect our children's futures. Like his other piece, *Venice in Oil*, from the same trip, Venice is the perfect location for this message: the world's most beautiful city is drowning and will eventually be destroyed if nothing is done. Shortly after the piece was completed, Venice suffered one of its worst *acqua altas* ever, with the waters rising up the the child's shoulders.

WHERE ?
RIO DE CA FOSCARI,
DORSODURO,
VENICE.

Latitude: 45.4327ºN
Longitude: 12.3236ºE

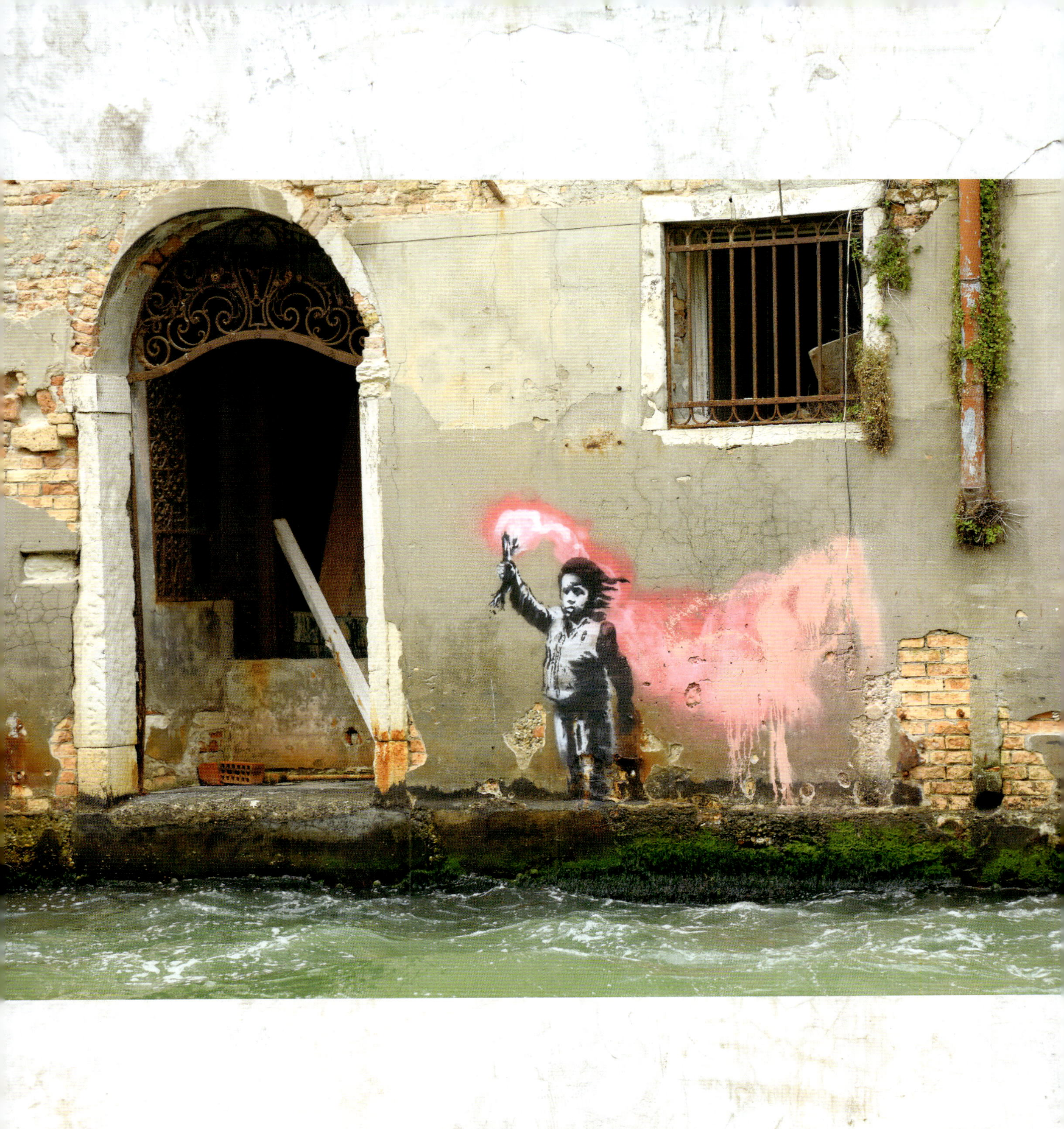

DEVOLVED PARLIAMENT

"Record price for a Banksy painting [£9.9 million] set at auction tonight. Shame I didn't still own it." Banksy's Instagram

Banksy first created this vast canvas – it's over four metres wide – for his Banksy versus Bristol Museum show in 2009. In the style of a fusty Victorian Empire painting, it depicts the 650 MPs in the UK House of Commons chamber as a bunch of chimps, during Prime Minister's Questions, a wonderully statisfying reflection of Banksy's opinion of their general level of intelligence, usefulness and of the quality of their debates. At the time it was called *Question Time*, and after the show sold to a private collector.

Wind forwards ten years and Banksy's uncanny ability to seemingly foretell the future was once again in evidence. Yet little could Banksy have imagined how perfectly the Commons of 2019 had lived up to his depiction of 2009. He, together with the painting's owner, decided to show the piece again, for the tenth anniversary of the original Bristol show, and as a way of marking that the UK was due to leave the European Union in March 2019. Banksy slightly reworked the piece – in the second version, the lamps in the chamber have been turned off, a rather chilling echo of Lord Grey's comment on the eve of the First World War: "the lamps are going out all over Europe." If the MPs seemed simian in 2009, how much more so now, having spent three years endlessly discussing how to rip Britain out of the EU, but without being able to agree on any course of action. Renamed *Devolved Parliament,* this became *the* image that perfectly captured the nation's mood about its rulers. It also appeared to be a comment on how this crop of politicians was totally ill-equipped to rule going forwards. "Laugh now", Banksy quipped, "but one day no one will be in charge." The more the chimps deliberated, the more the piece acquired historical resonance. The owner decided it was time to sell. Sotheby's, the auctioneers, were bullish, and suggested an estimate of £1.5 – £2m. The bidding took place in the same auction room as for *Love is in the Bin*. There were ten bidders, five in the room, the rest on the phone. At one point it looked as though the painting would go for £6.4 million, but bidding resumed and the hammer finally fell on a telephone bid of £9,875,500.00, including fees. It had all taken just 13 minutes.

WHERE IS IT ?
TWO PORTERS AT SOTHEBY'S HANGING *DEVOLVED PARLIAMENT*, PRIOR TO ITS SALE ON OCTOBER 3RD, 2019.

Latitude: 51.5118° N
Longitude: 0.1437° W

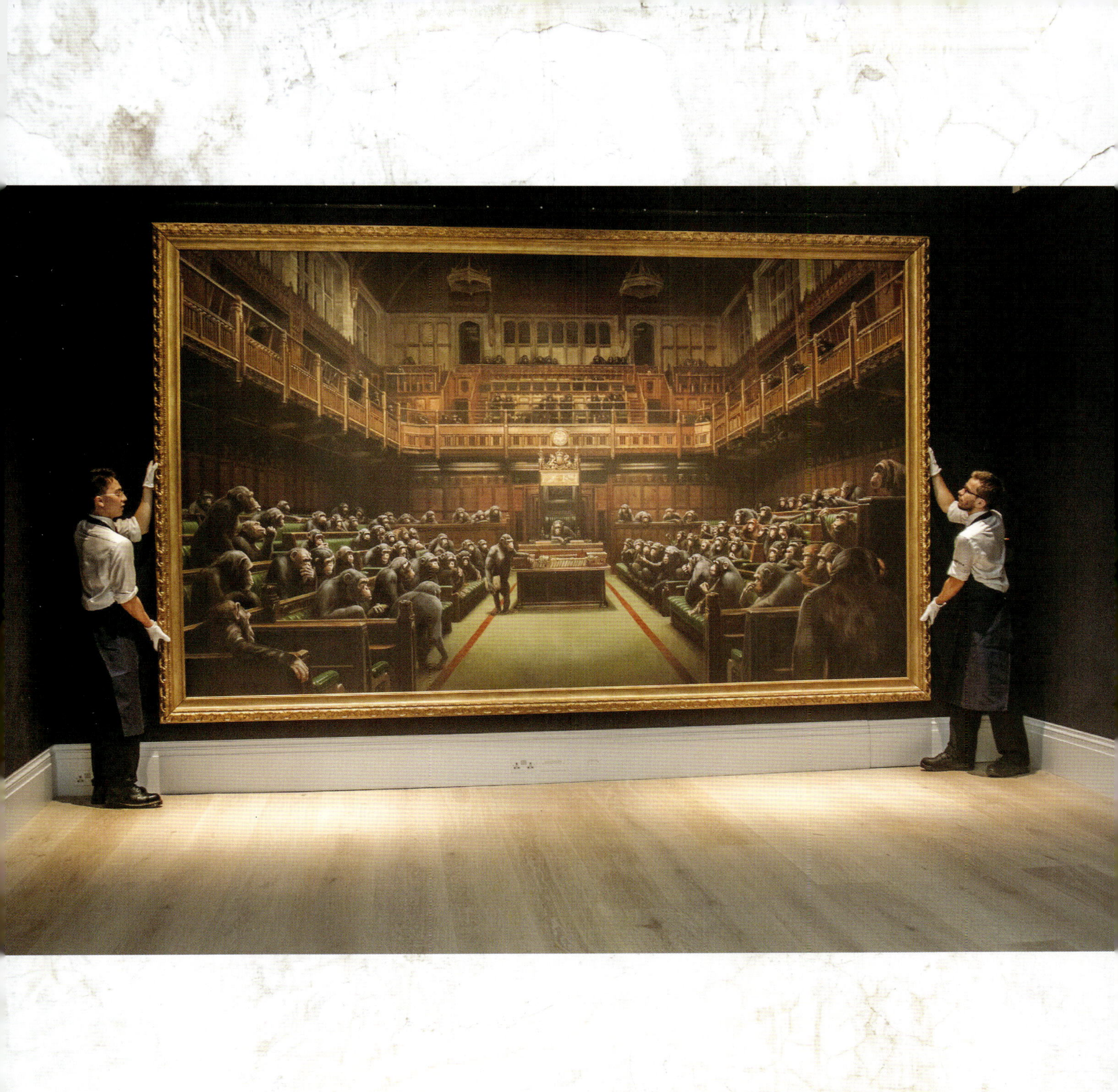

GOD BLESS BIRMINGHAM

"In the 20 minutes we filmed Ryan on this bench, passers-by gave him a hot drink, two chocolate bars and a lighter..."
Banksy's Instagram page

In December 2019, the UK held a general election, the first Christmas election to be held since 1923. The reason was related to the logjam in the UK parliament – the inability of British MPs, the apes of Banksy's previous piece *Devolved Parliament*, to decide on any legislation as it navel-gazed about what to do about Brexit. In typically inspired fashion, Banksy used the political context to create a new piece with deep resonance. On December 9th, three days before polling day, this piece appeared on a wall by the tracks of Birmingham's Jewellery Quarter Station, showing two reindeer towing a park bench regularly used by rough sleepers, as if it were Santa's sleigh. On Banksy's Instagram page a video appeared. A homeless man named Ryan is shown having a quick drink before laying down on the bench, with his head on a large knapsack, his legs stretched out. With the reindeer it made a perfect, slightly dream-like composition, as though he were comfortably getting taken to a better place. Banksy's Instagram, rather ironically, had a backing track of 'I'll be Home for Christmas'. Several people are shown walking, and many cars driving past, indifferent to his presence, although a few passers-by did offer the rough sleeper some sustenance. As ever with Banksy, the whole piece had a great sense of fun, but also made a serious point. When all Parliament could do was bang on for three useless years about Brexit, when the whole election seemed to be only about 'getting Brexit done', no politician was talking about the growing problem of homelessness in England, where the estimate was 4,677 rough sleepers, compared to 1,768 in 2010. Some of these rough sleepers died on cold winter nights, 23 in Birmingham alone in 2018, twice the national average. By the time of the election, on December 12th, the piece had been viewed over three million times, but not before it was defaced by a prankster adding red Rudolph noses to Banksy's piece. It was then protected by a perspex sheet, which, in a fortuitous twist that further highlighted inequalities in the UK, was sold (yes, just the perspex) at auction for £2,300 to a precious metals dealer. He did at least give the money to a local homelessness charity.

WHERE IS IT ?
VYSE STREET,
JEWELLERY QUARTER,
BIRMINGHAM.

Latitude: 52.4369 ºN
Longitude: 1.8464 ºW

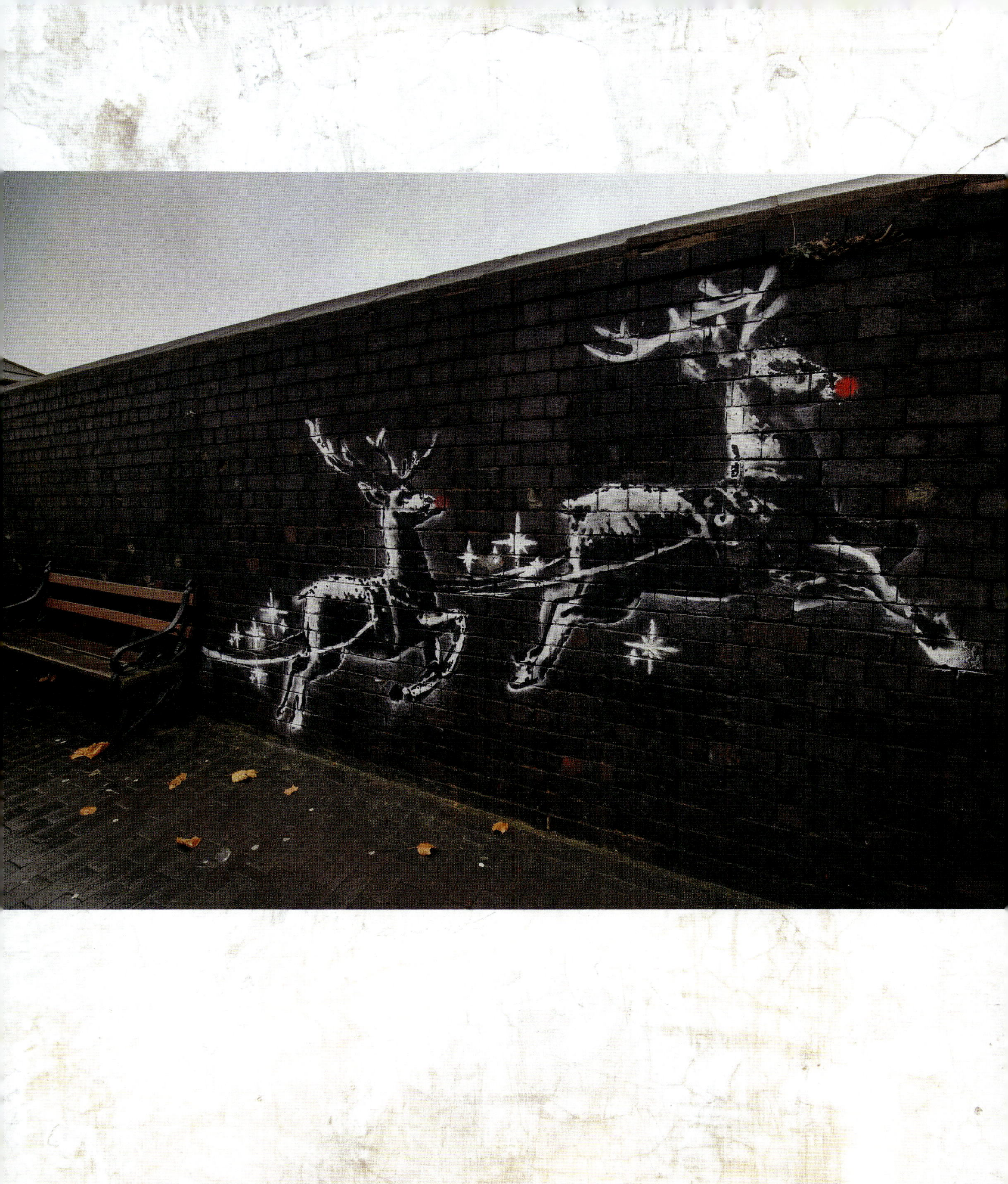

VALENTINE'S DAY

"It's a real, incredible gift...it's a beautiful piece of work and we are genuinely blessed." **Kelly Woodruff, daughter of the house's owner**

On the 14th February 2020, this stunning new Banksy artwork appeared on the side of a house in the Barton Hill area of Bristol. It was Valentine's day morning and this composition just exuded positivity and optimism – a young, carefree girl shooting an explosion of bright red rose petals on an an otherwise rather grey scene on a typically overcast Bristolian day. It was a gift, an expression of love for Banksy's home city.

After all the auction-house cleverness of *Love is in the Bin* and *Devolved Parliament*, this had the freshness of those Banksys from 2002, or 2003 or 2004. Banksy here reprised some of his classic themes. The first was the somewhat retro innocence of the child. She is dressed in a little hooded jacket, with a pleated skirt and thick leggings, and has a charmingly old-fashioned small satchel over one shoulder; there is almost something late Victorian about her look. The trope of the catapult in the hands of a child is not one Banksy has used before, but the idea of 'firing' flowers echoes his *Flower Thrower* from 2003. The sense of something being caught at that split second that it happens, almost like an action photograph, is pure Banksy – *The Street is in Play*, from 2013, is a classic example. The paradox of a childhood weapon usually used to smash windows or bother pigeons, shooting something so lovely at a wall is another pure Banksy twist. It's almost as though Banksy is saying: remember those early images that made you fall in love with my work? I can still do them – seventeen years of extraordinary global success has not dented the freshness of my talent one iota. We expect that it will rival *There is Always Hope* as one of his most memorable, and loved, images.

But just like with the early Banksys, within 48 hours of the piece being up, it was vandalised by some moronic goon, who spraypainted the oh-so-clever phrase 'BCC Wankers' in pink on the piece, partially on the girl. A splash of flowers which had 'fallen' on the sign – part of Banksy's original composition – were also removed. From innocence to innocence abused in a few short hours. But then, just like the earliest Banksys, that sometimes is the nature of street art – so brilliant and life-enhancing, but then also so vulnerable, so ephemeral.

WHERE IS IT ?
MARSH LANE,
BARTON HILL,
BRISTOL.

Latitude: 51.4549 ºN
Longitude: 2.5605 ºW

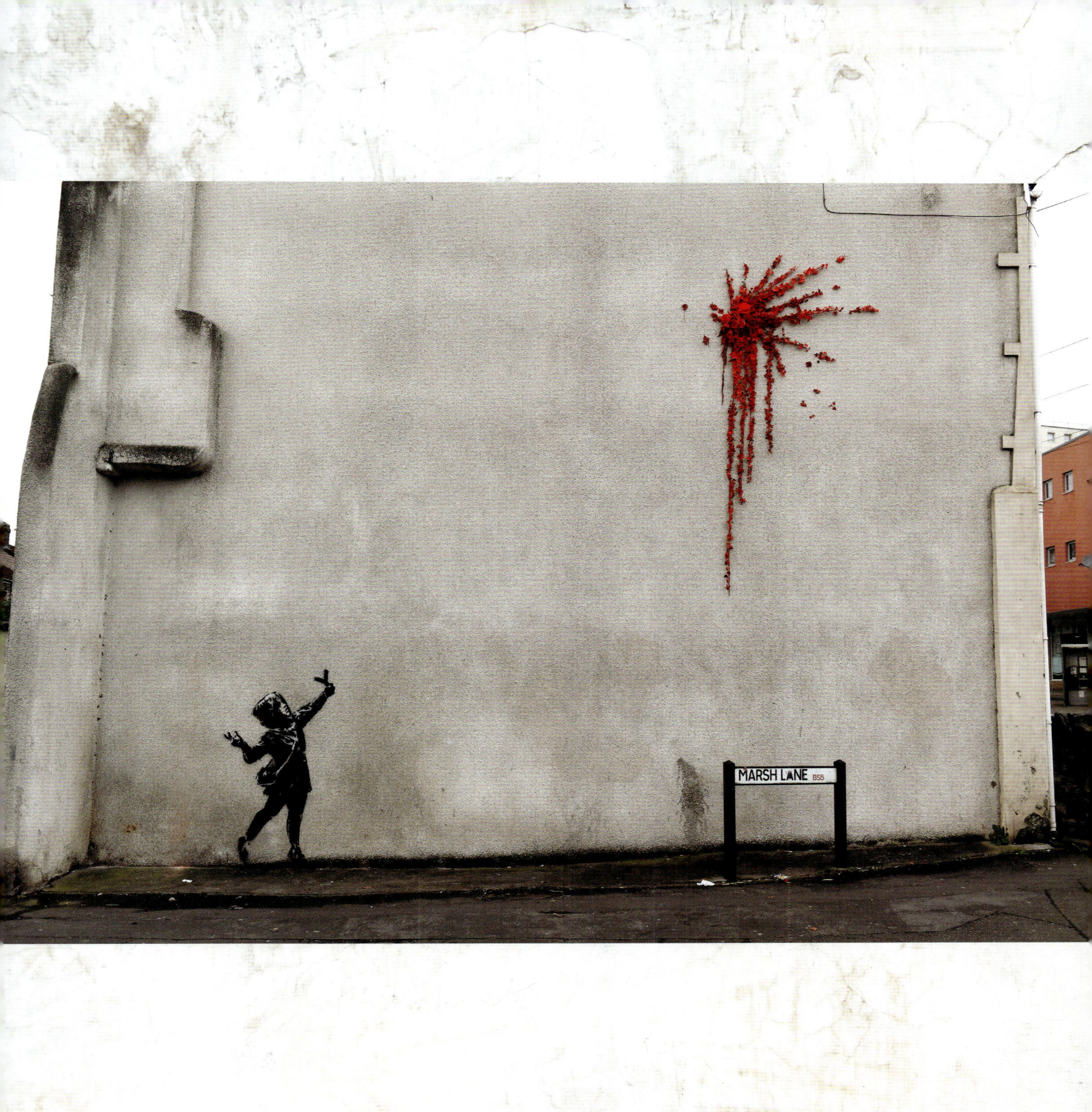

MARSH LANE BS5

HULA HOOP GIRL

"The bike appeared at the same time as the mural."
Surinder Kaur, in The Guardian.

This is Banksy at his wittiest, with a piece that seems to have a desire to simply delight viewers, in a neighbourhood of Nottingham which has had its share of challenges recently. In 2020 Nottingham recorded the highest rate of coronavirus in the UK, with many businesses having to close. This was a blow to an area which had lost many jobs recently, not least with the closure of the Lenton Raleigh bicycle factory in 2002, after 116 years of production, and at one time the world's biggest bicycle plant.

If there's one thing we know about Banksy it is that he likes, and studies, his history, and that he loves making allusions and connections. We're pretty convinced that his choice of a vandalised bicycle (which we suspect he brought along and attached to the lamp post) in Lenton is no accident. It's hard to escape the suggestion that capitalism does not respect communities, but is happy to destroy jobs in search of cheaper manufacturing elsewhere, in this case the Far East. But then Banksy takes something grim and transforms it into an image of childhood fun and quite a bit of mischief. The girl has taken the tyre and turned it into a hula hoop; she is full of energy and concentration. Like many of Banksy's child figures, she is dressed in a somewhat old-fashioned way, wearing a coat with a scarf wrapped around her neck. She seems to have not a care in the world, but is brimming with positivity and charm.

If one purpose of the piece was to cheer people up, in October 2020, in the midst of Covid-19, it certainly worked. The moment it appeared, local residents were queuing around the block to view the work, taking images of their children laughing and hula-hooping in front of Banksy's composition. The local council rushed to protect the piece with perspex, and although that was quickly vandalised, the work beneath remained intact. Sadly, within a few days, some moron decided to steal the bike, removing much of the wit of the composition. The work was then later removed altogether and sold to an art dealer, a real loss for Lenton.

WHERE IS IT ?
ROTHESAY AVENUE,
LENTON,
NOTTINGHAM.
REMOVED, WHEREABOUTS UNKNOWN.

Latitude: 52.9543 ºN
Longitude: 1.1719 ºW

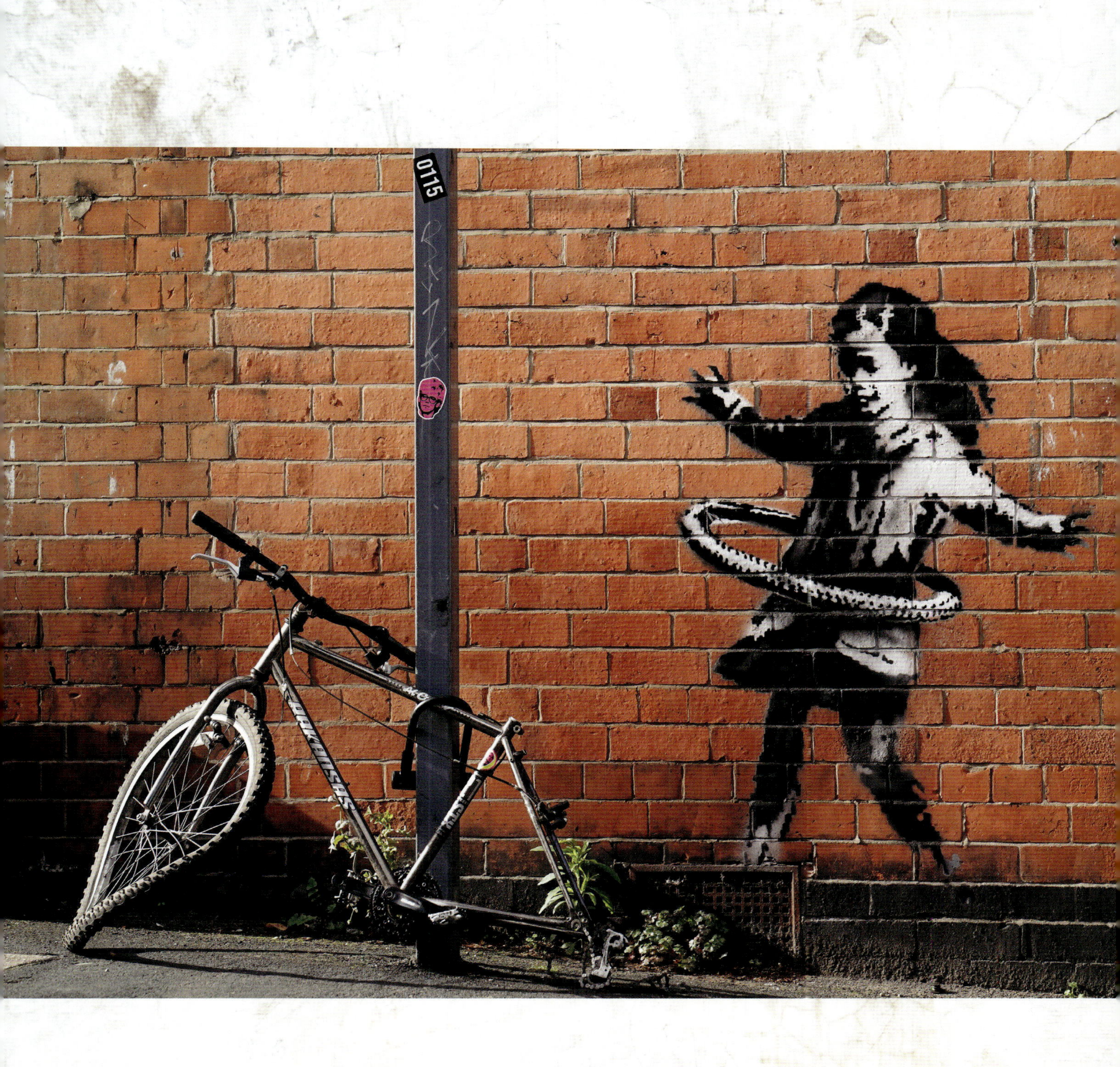

0115

AACHOO!!

"Banksy's "Aachoo!!" post has already been liked over 2 million times on Instagram." CNN, on 11th December 2020.

If there was ever a situation calling for the Banksy treatment, it was surely the global Coronavirus pandemic. Societies overwhelmed, politicians scrambling like headless chickens, social and racial inequalities ruthlessly exposed, celebrities hypocritically breaking lockdown rules, a US President suggesting publicly that drinking disinfectant could provide a treatment, billions of pounds wasted in a land-grab for personal protection equipment, all whilst heroic medical staff were putting their necks on the line to save lives...the list for sardonic humour mixed with acerbic social and political commentary is very long.

Apart from a few interior pieces, including a spray-painted rat in a London Underground train carriage in July, and some images of rats crawling all over his downstairs loo, Banksy hadn't produced a really iconic piece on the pandemic. He did produce *Hula Hoop Girl* in Nottingham in October, a wonderful work, but not a specific comment on Covid-19. But then – at last! – on Thursday morning, 10th December, 2020, a brilliant new work appeared on the side of a terraced house in Totterdown, Bristol.

It was worth the long wait, pure distilled Banksy at his very best. First the location – a very steep hill of houses. Banksy portrays an old lady sneezing so forcefully that her false teeth shoot out of her mouth, followed by a spray of infectious spit and mucus. In the process her body shoots backwards as she drops her stick and handbag. When viewed across the street, the sheer force of her "Aachoo!!" appears to cause a wheelie bin to topple and the houses to lean. But this little old lady is no pushover. As often with Banksy portrayals, she looks tough, possibly cantankerous and the look on her face somewhat dismissive. She seems not to be using her handkerchief to cover her nose or mouth. It's almost as though this is a portrait of sheer anger at the virus, a rejection of all that it means for her generation, a declaration of inner strength, resolve and rebellion. The elderly were overwhelmingly the most at-risk from Covid-19; you wonder, is Banksy making a provocative inter-generational statement here: you made me vulnerable by not wearing a mask, now have it back, see how that feels! As ever, Banksy leaves us guessing, but also smiling at his sheer wit, cleverness and ability to surprise.

WHERE?
VALE STREET,
TOTTERDOWN,
BRISTOL.
REMOVED IN 2021.
Latitude: 51.4410 ºN
Longitude: 2.5719 ºW

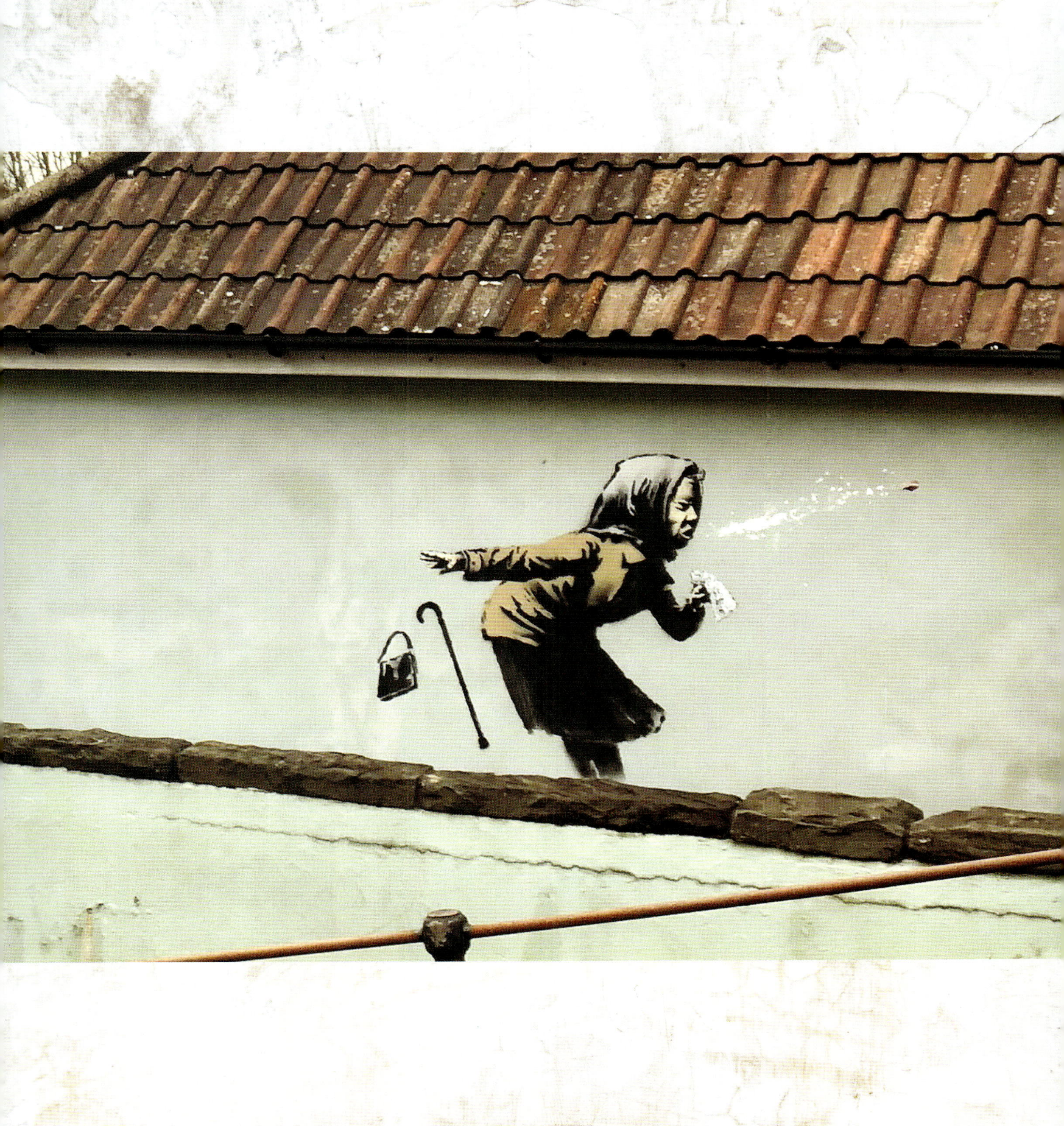

CREATE ESCAPE

"*Society takes upon itself the right to inflict appalling punishments on the individual.*" Oscar Wilde, De Profundis

When notorious Reading Gaol closed in 2014, the philistine British Tory government proposed that the site be sold to property developers. The citizens of Reading, however, wanted it turned into an arts centre and formed a pressure group, Save Reading Gaol. They were given a huge boost when, on the night of 28th February, 2021, Banksy effectively threw the force of his reputation behind the latter with this brilliantly eloquent image. Its title, a pun on the classic Steve McQueen breakout movie, *The Great Escape*, suggested the gaol would be saved for the arts just in time.

The escaping prisoner would seem to be a reference to Oscar Wilde. He was incarcerated here, in cell C.3.3, after being found guilty of "gross indecency" in 1895, following exposure of his affair with Lord Alfred Douglas, the son of the Marquess of Queensberry. It was during his two years incarceration that Wilde wrote *De Profundis* and found inspiration for his classic, *The Ballad of Reading Gaol*.

Banksy's composition is typically brilliant – a heavy typewriter makes the rope made of sheets wonderfully taught. Our escapee has used the sheets as paper – a possible reference to the fact that Wilde – the most successful playwright of his day – was initially denied pen and paper by the vindictive prison authorities. Banksy also had fun revealing that the piece was his, with a hilarious parody of a schmaltzy Bob Ross *Joy of Painting* instruction video released a few days later, showing the work being created. The final image is a celebration of the victory of art and wit over oppressive establishments.

WHERE?
PERIMETER WALL OF READING GAOL,
READING.

Latitude: 51.4410 ºN
Longitude: 0.9667 ºW

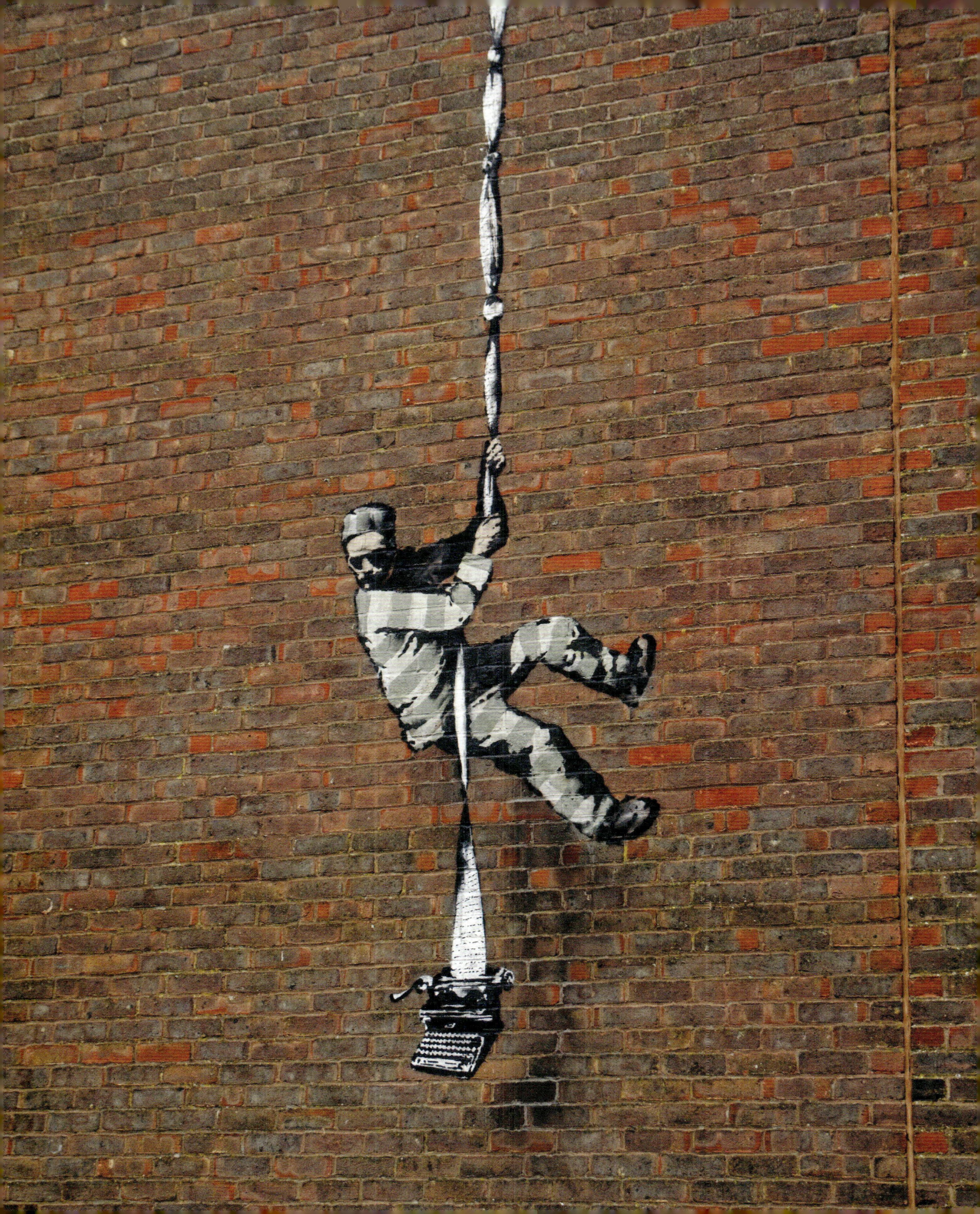

WE'RE ALL IN THE SAME BOAT

"I have only one eye...I really do not see the signal."
Vice Admiral Horatio Nelson, Battle of Copenhagen, 1801.

Banksy has form in picking rather run down English seaside resorts as locations for his artworks. Weston-super-Mare in the west and Hastings on the south coast are both cases in point. The citizens of Lowestoft were completely delighted when, on the morning of 8th August, 2021, not one artwork, but four had appeared overnight. As some wags had it, it was almost a spraycation in the year that the UK government made it almost impossible to take a holiday abroad.

In this smart situationist piece, Banksy returned to themes which past works also featured – namely climate change and the plight of refugees, both of course connected. Originally the piece featured a piece of discarded corrugated iron, which formed the hull of the boat, and blocked the stream. Over-zealous local authorities put safety before art during one of the wettest Augusts on record, and removed the corrugated iron. Like Banksy's Venice piece, the rising floodwaters would have made the point about the effects of climate change very powerfully.

Banksy again shows himself to be master in the portrayal of chidren. All three are dressed in rather old-fashioned clothes, captured in mid gesture. The slightly older boy is in a sailor suit and, in a wonderfully ironic nod to British hero Nelson, is holding his telescope up to his 'blind' eye (Nelson, who was blind in one eye, famously claimed not to see the flag signals ordering him to stop fighting at the Battle of Copenhagen in 1801). With this brilliant historical allusion, Banksy passes a brilliantly sardonic comment on the general public's wilful refusal to acknowledge the devastating effects, both on people and the environment, of man-made climate change.

That this piece appeared in the week that the UN finally produced its IPCC Climate Change report proved again how Banksy's art somehow effortlessly captures the mood of the moment.

WHERE?
NICHOLAS EVERITT PARK,
LOWESTOFT, SUFFOLK.

Latitude: 52.4747 ºN
Longitude: 1.7536 ºE

WE'RE ALL
THE SAME
BOAT

SEAGULL AND CHIPS

"Nothing is scarier than...knowing your fish and chips could fall victim to an angry seagull." **Country Life**

Anyone who has eaten fish and chips on a windswept English beach knows that that omnivore scavanger – the seagull – is a major hazard, shamelessly dive-bombing to grab any food that's going. This is another brilliant situationist piece from Banksy's Lowestoft spraycation. We're pretty sure that this idea would have suggested itself to Banksy, as he drove around Lowestoft in his battered camper van, treating the depressed resort as his canvas.

The discarded insulation do look like so many chips, and the skip almost like a container one might get from a fish and chip shop. The image works on so many levels, in true Banksy fashion. On the surface it's a very amusing image of an English seaside trope. On another level it can be seen as a comment on the amount of mindless rubbish we produce. It also has echoes of Britain's cladding crisis – major corporate and governmental failure which condemned thousands of homes in the wake of the Grenfell Tower disaster, where 'fireproof' combustible cladding which had been passed as OK for lining skyscrapers led directly to the death of 72 people in 2017. One can read too much into it, but one can almost see the seagull representing the rapacious corporations who fed off the sub-standard cladding in their obsessive quest for profits.

But in keeping with the theme of Banksy's 'Spraycation', is this also a comment on a general refusal to accept man-made climate change? Insulation happily discarded? Perhaps, but getting too serious might spoil the English seaside holiday mood.

WHERE?
DENMARK WAY,
LOWESTOFT, SUFFOLK.

Latitude: 52.4747 ºN
Longitude: 1.7536 ºE

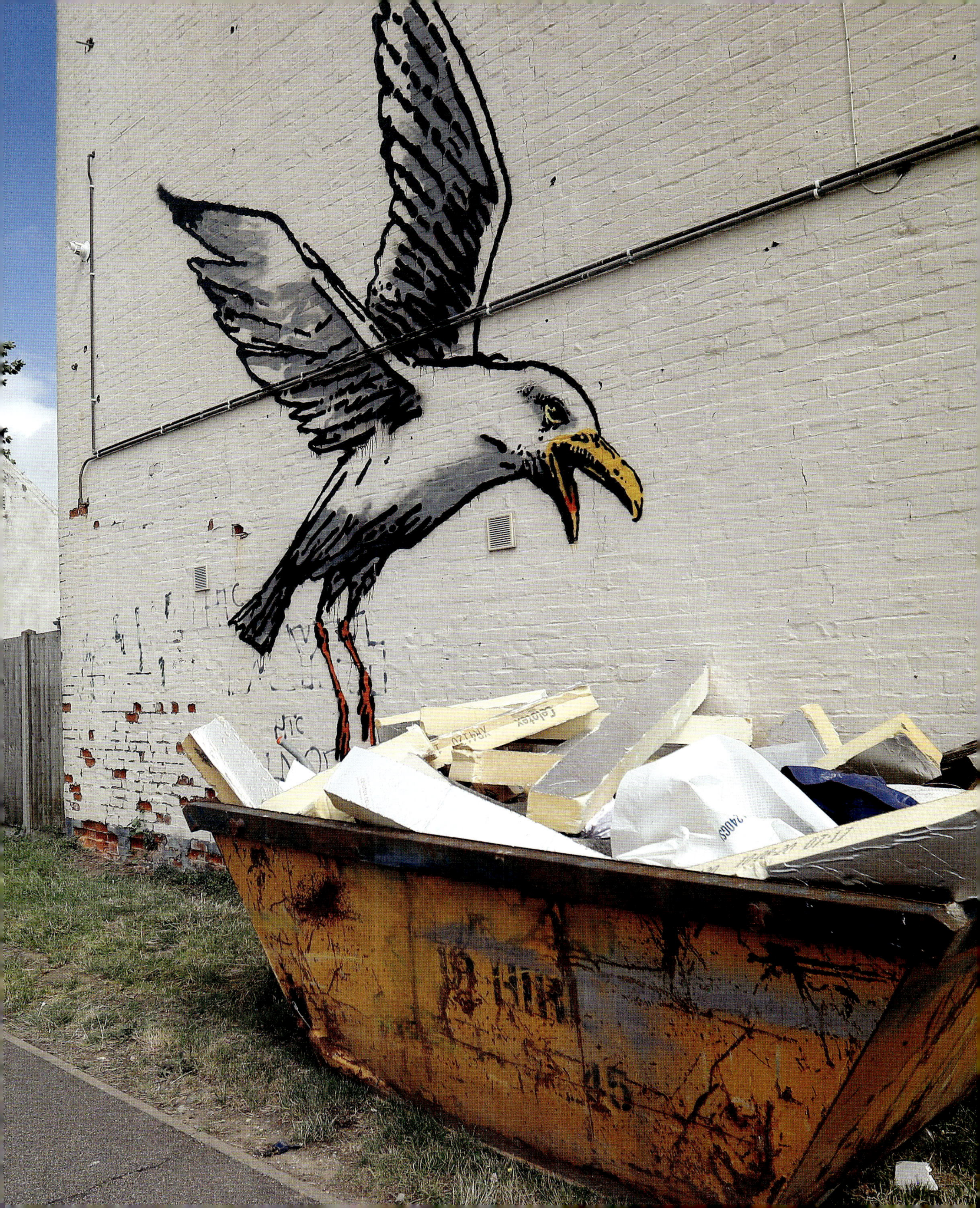

HIGH STREET SANDCASTLE

"Huge swathes of East Anglia will be under water in 30 years."
Eastern Daily Press

You would expect to see a sandcastle being built on the beach, not on the high street. But Banksy's child is well inland and, with a rather serious expression, is building using a crowbar.

This piece is one of Banksy's more puzzling works from the Spraycation, but it does seem to be in keeping with the general theme of man-made climate change and, specifically, rising sea levels. A 2020 report from the Copenhagen-based European Environment Agency showed that Lowestoft would be one of the coastal towns which would be completely inundated by rising sea levels unless action were taken to mitigate rising temperatures. Investment in massive new coastal defences would also be required.

As if to make the point, the original design of this piece showed a neatly-formed sand castle shaped from an upturned bucket. By the time this image was taken, the castle had collapsed. The crowbar would seem to point to the huge amount of effort required, but also that the effort might be pointless – we're in effect building on sand.

The child also points to the fact that there is an inter-generational issue here. The agents of climate change are the adults in the room; it's our children who will have to bear the consequences of our actions.

WHERE?
LONDON ROAD NORTH,
LOWESTOFT, SUFFOLK.

Latitude: 52.4747 ºN
Longitude: 1.7536 ºE

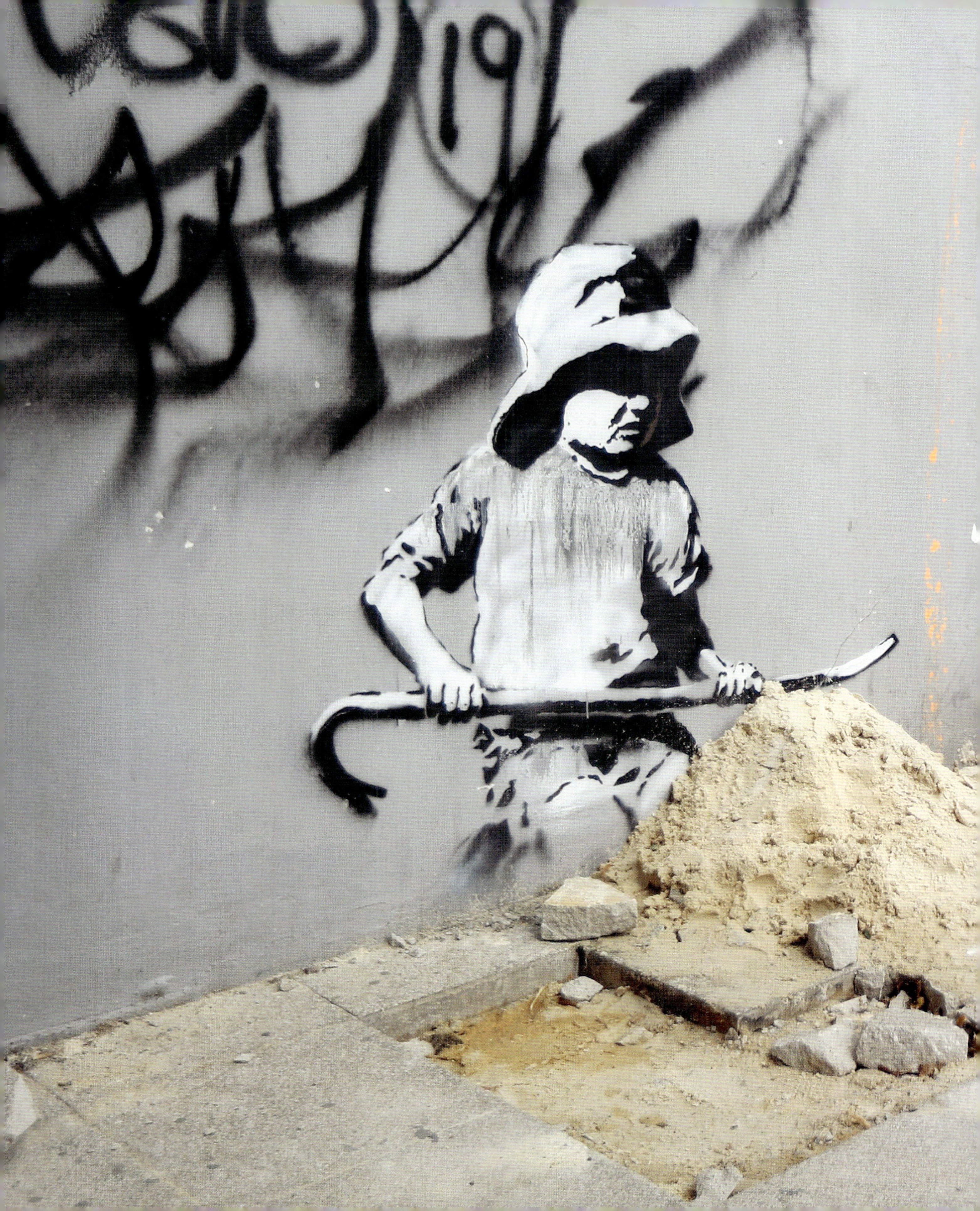

LUXURY RENTALS ONLY

"Locals have been left homeless by soaring property prices and the staycation boom." **The Times**

As part of his Great British Spraycation, Banksy moved up the coast, to Cromer, a seaside resort increasingly a location of choice for moneyed Londoners buying holiday homes, a trend which became particularly intense during the Covid-19 Pandemic and Lockdown.

Along the Cromer seawall, on the East Prom, Banksy created another brilliantly satisfying image. Three shell-less hermit crabs, one carrying a baby on its back, are advancing up the beach towards three empty shells that would provide them with a home. A much bigger, fatter crab stops them in their tracks, with a sign telling them that those shells are reserved for rich crabs.

On first viewing this is another witty image, describing the greed of wealthy holidaymakers, pricing the locals out of homes along England's coastal resorts (a problem particularly accute on the north Norfolk coast ("Hampstead-on-Sea"), Devon ("Chelsea-on-Sea") and Cornwall). But on closer viewing this is a searing commentary on the plight of impoverished and desperate refugees, the image evoking images of them arriving on England's coasts and walking up beaches having risked their lives on flimsy bow-up boats, escaping violence and poverty in Syria, Yemen, Lybia and now, Afghanistan. The fat crab represents the wealthy West, not wishing to have their selfishly comfortable lifestyle bothered by migrants.

The attention to detail is amazing. Each crab is an individual, gesturing or pleading; the crab at the rear is talking to its young. That this was painted in Cromer, renowned for the flavour of its crabs for centuries, reveals Banksy again to be a master of situation and context.

WHERE?
EAST PROM,
CROMER,
NORFOLK.

Latitude: 52.9307 ºN
Longitude: 1.2976 ºE

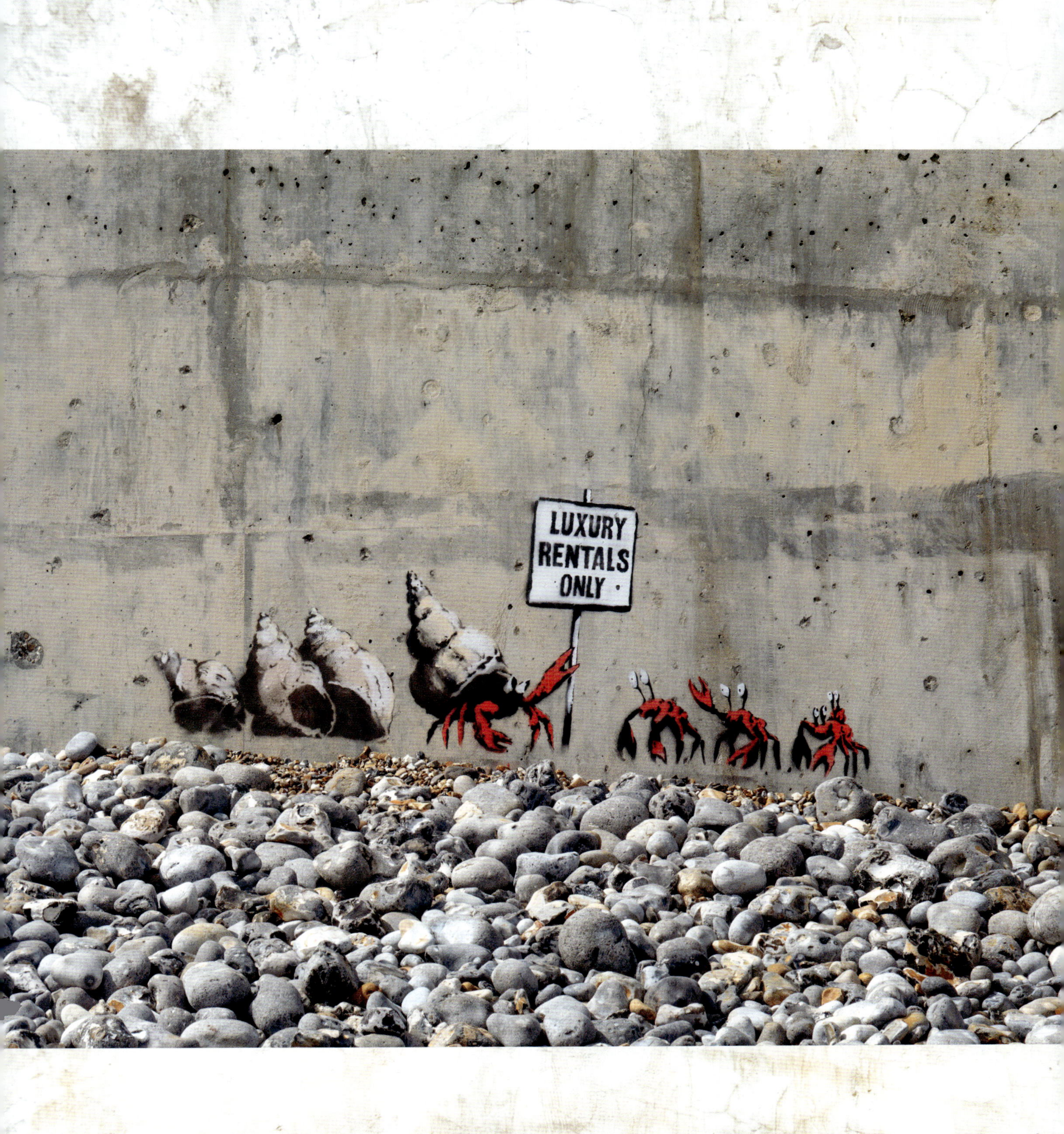

LUXURY
RENTALS
ONLY

CREDITS

XAVIER TAPIES is the author of *Street Art and the War on Terror*, *Street Artists – The Complete Guide* (with Eleanor Mathieson), *Street Artists – The Complete Guide 2* and *Women Street Artists – The Complete Guide*. An elusive writer who shuns the publishing limelight, he divides his time between several European cities.

ALLAN MOLHO and his family live in New York City.

LORD JIM (a.k.a. Stefan Kloo), is an art-dork, maker and collector who figures that someone needs to keep and eye on things. He's been making a case for street art for well over a decade now and can't shake the feeling that there might just be something to it. Originally from Germany, Lord Jim lives with his beloved wife and two champion sons in Los Angeles, where he also does the most damage. His photo collections can be found on flickr.com/photos/lord-jim/.

SAM MARTIN is based in Hastings, England. He is an avid photographer who documents the vibrant counter-culture of his very creative home town, dubbed 'Shoreditch on Sea'.

KEVIN FLEMEN is based in London and has been photographing street art around Europe for the past ten years.

ROSS HOLDSWORTH originally hails from Melbourne, Australia, came to London in 2005 and has been chasing street artists, particularly Banksy, ever since. An avid collector of urban art, his passion has led him from Melbourne to Mile End, Bristol to Bethlehem, Whitechapel to Weston-super-Mare. Armed with a lens and a bike, his hunt for the elusive will never cease.

MARGARET 'MAGS' COBLE is an artist, writer, professional dog walker and avid photo-documenter of her home town of New Orleans. She is a huge fan of street art and utilises spray paint and stencils in her own work: artbymags.com.

This book was made possible by the many photographers around the world who have documented Banksy's work. Apart from their evident enthusiasm for this most brilliant of street artists, they have ensured a valuable record of his work as seen on the street, usually before it has been buffed, defaced or otherwise destroyed. We are particularly grateful to our headline team, Margaret Coble, Kevin Flemen, Ross Holdsworth, Lord Jim, Sam Martin and Allan Molho. Without their enthusiasm, this volume would not exist.

Credits are listed below by name of work, in the order they appear in the book:

CONTENTS AND INTRODUCTION
If Graffiti Changed Anything ROSS HOLDSWORTH
Security Guard SAM MARTIN
No Loitering MARGARET COBLE

EARLY WORKS
Mild Mild West CANIS MAJOR
Gorilla in a Pink Mask CANIS MAJOR
Always Hope KEVIN FLEMEN
Pulp Fiction KEVIN FLEMEN
Anarchist Guard KEVIN FLEMEN
Happy Choppers SAM MARTIN

2003-2004
Grim Reaper CANIS MAJOR
Flower Thrower MICHAEL ROSE
This is not a Photo Opportunity SAM MARTIN
Thug For Life Bunny KEVIN FLEMEN
Dynamite Ice Cream MIRCO BRUNNER
Kissing Coppers KEVIN FLEMEN
Drunk Angel KEVIN FLEMEN
Because I'm Worthless KEVIN FLEMEN
Tourist Information KEVIN FLEMEN
What are you looking At? SAM MARTIN

2005-2006
Up Periscope KEVIN FLEMEN
Guantanamo KEVIN FLEMEN
Photographer Rat KEVIN FLEMEN
Thug for Life KEVIN FLEMEN
Snorting Copper SAM MARTIN
Balloon Debate SIPA PRESS/ REX/ SHUTTERSTOCK
Boy at the Beach MARCO DI LAURO/ GETTY IMAGES
Well Hung Lover PHILIP CERVI
Sweeping it Under the Carpet SAM MARTIN
Graffiti Removal Hotline KEVIN FLEMEN
No More Heroes LORD JIM
I'm Out of Bed What More Do You Want? LORD JIM

2007-2008
Police Sniper CANIS MAJOR
Angel In a Bullet-proof Vest KEVIN FLEMEN
Vandalism is Art SAM MARTIN
ATM KEVIN FLEMEN
Yellow Lines Flower Painter SAM MARTIN
You Looked Better on My Space LORD JIM
Girl Searching Soldier MICHAEL ROSE
Dove of Peace ROSS HOLDSWORTH
Very Little Helps KEVIN FLEMEN
Bubble Slide Girl KEVIN FLEMEN
Caveman LORD JIM
Aerial Flower Girl LORD JIM
One Nation Under CCTV SAM MARTIN
Let Them Eat Crack ALLAN MOLHO
Flower Girl LORD JIM
Whitewashing Lascaux SAM MARTIN
Nola Girl with Umbrella MARGARET COBLE
Abe Lincoln MARGARET COBLE
Looting National Guards MARGARET COBLE

2009-2010
Last Graffiti Before Motorway SAM MARTIN
Boombox SAM MARTIN
No Fishing SAM MARTIN
Exit Through The Gift Shop EVERETT/REX/SHUTTERSTOCK
Will Work for Idiots ALLAN MOLHO
Wheat Paster ALLAN MOLHO
Guard On Duty LORD JIM
Park LORD JIM
Liberty ALLAN MOLHO
Tesco Sand Castles SAM MARTIN
Roller Head Heron SAM MARTIN
I Remember When All This Was Trees BRIAN DAY
Call an Airstrke FLICKR.COM/THE STIG2009
I Love NY ALLAN MOLHO

2011-2012
Firestarter LORD JIM
Crayola Shooter LORD JIM
Drunk Mickey LORD JIM
Shop Till You Drop SAM MARTIN
Slave Labour SAM MARTIN
The Lifestyle You Ordered ROSS HOLDSWORTH
Sperm Alarm ROSS HOLDSWORTH

2013 THE NEW YORK RESIDENCY
The Street is in Play ALLAN MOLHO
You Complete Me ALLAN MOLHO
Boy With Hammer ALLAN MOLHO
Ghetto 4 Life ALLAN MOLHO
Waiting in Vain ALLAN MOLHO
The Banality of the Banality of Evil ALLAN MOLHO
Japanese Scene ALLAN MOLHO
Crazy Horses ALLAN MOLHO
Shoe Shine Boy ALLAN MOLHO
Silence of the Lambs ALLAN MOLHO
Twin Towers ALLAN MOLHO
What We Do in Life Echoes in Eternity ALLAN MOLHO
Os Gemeos Collaboration ALLAN MOLHO

RECENT WORKS
Girl With a Pierced Ear Drum CANIS MAJOR
Eavesdropping PHILIP CERVI
Dismaland LUCAS ROSS
Son of a Syrian Refugee RICK FINDLER//REX/SHUTTERSTOCK
Kitten NURPHOTO/REX/SHUTTERSTOCK
Bridge Farm Primary School REX/SHUTTERSTOCK
The Walled-Off Hotel LEVINE/SIPA/REX/SHUTTERSTOCK
Brexit SAM MILLEN
Basquiat PAUL MENDOZA
Love is in the Bin ALAMY
Venice in Oil ALAMY
Migrant Child With Pink Flare ALAMY
Devolved Parliament ALAMY
God Bless Birmingham GETTY IMAGES
Valentine's Day GETTY IMAGES
Hula Hoop Girl ALAMY
Aachoo!! ALAMY
Create Escape ALAMY
We are all in the same boat ALAMY
Seagull and Chips ALAMY
High Street Sandcastle ALAMY
Luxury Rentals Only ALAMY